# Routing and Switching Essentials v6
## Companion Guide

**Cisco Networking Academy**

**Cisco Press**

800 East 96th Street

Indianapolis, Indiana 46240 USA

# Routing and Switching Essentials v6 Companion Guide

Cisco Networking Academy

Copyright © 2017 Cisco Systems, Inc.

Published by:
Cisco Press
800 East 96th Street
Indianapolis, IN 46240 USA

Printed in the United States of America

2   17

Library of Congress Control Number: 2016956756

ISBN-13: 978-1-58713-428-9

ISBN-10: 1-58713-428-4

## Warning and Disclaimer

This book is designed to provide information about the Cisco Networking Academy Routing and Switching Essentials course. Every effort has been made to make this book as complete and as accurate as possible, but no warranty or fitness is implied.

The information is provided on an "as is" basis. The authors, Cisco Press, and Cisco Systems, Inc. shall have neither liability nor responsibility to any person or entity with respect to any loss or damages arising from the information contained in this book or from the use of the discs or programs that may accompany it.

The opinions expressed in this book belong to the author and are not necessarily those of Cisco Systems, Inc.

**Editor-in-Chief**
Mark Taub

**Alliances Manager, Cisco Press**
Ron Fligge

**Product Line Manager**
Brett Bartow

**Executive Editor**
Mary Beth Ray

**Managing Editor**
Sandra Schroeder

**Development Editor**
Ellie C. Bru

**Senior Project Editor**
Tonya Simpson

**Copy Editor**
Gill Editorial Services

**Technical Editor**
Rick McDonald

**Editorial Assistant**
Vanessa Evans

**Cover Designer**
Ockomon Haus

**Composition**
codeMantra

**Indexer**
Erika Millen

**Proofreader**
Sam Sunder

## Trademark Acknowledgments

All terms mentioned in this book that are known to be trademarks or service marks have been appropriately capitalized. Cisco Press or Cisco Systems, Inc., cannot attest to the accuracy of this information. Use of a term in this book should not be regarded as affecting the validity of any trademark or service mark.

## Special Sales

For government sales inquiries, please contact governmentsales@pearsoned.com.

For questions about sales outside the U.S., please contact intlcs@pearson.com.

## Feedback Information

At Cisco Press, our goal is to create in-depth technical books of the highest quality and value. Each book is crafted with care and precision, undergoing rigorous development that involves the unique expertise of members from the professional technical community.

Readers' feedback is a natural continuation of this process. If you have any comments regarding how we could improve the quality of this book, or otherwise alter it to better suit your needs, you can contact us through email at feedback@ciscopress.com. Please make sure to include the book title and ISBN in your message.

We greatly appreciate your assistance.

| Americas Headquarters | Asia Pacific Headquarters | Europe Headquarters |
| --- | --- | --- |
| Cisco Systems, Inc. | Cisco Systems, Inc. | Cisco Systems International BV |
| 170 West Tasman Drive | 168 Robinson Road | Haarlerbergpark |
| San Jose, CA 95134-1706 | #28-01 Capital Tower | Haarlerbergweg 13-19 |
| USA | Singapore 068912 | 1101 CH Amsterdam |
| www.cisco.com | www.cisco.com | The Netherlands |
| Tel: 408 526-4000 | Tel: +65 6317 7777 | www-europe.cisco.com |
| 800 553-NETS (6387) | Fax: +65 6317 7799 | Tel: +31 0 800 020 0791 |
| Fax: 408 527-0883 | | Fax: +31 0 20 357 1100 |

Cisco has more than 200 offices worldwide. Addresses, phone numbers, and fax numbers are listed on the Cisco Website at **www.cisco.com/go/offices.**

©2007 Cisco Systems, Inc. All rights reserved. CCVP, the Cisco logo, and the Cisco Square Bridge logo are trademarks of Cisco Systems, Inc.; Changing the Way We Work, Live, Play, and Learn is a service mark of Cisco Systems, Inc.; and Access Registrar, Aironet, BPX, Catalyst, CCDA, CCDP, CCIE, CCIP, CCNA, CCNP, CCSP, Cisco, the Cisco Certified Internetwork Expert logo, Cisco IOS, Cisco Press, Cisco Systems, Cisco Systems Capital, the Cisco Systems logo, Cisco Unity, Enterprise/Solver, EtherChannel, EtherFast, EtherSwitch, Fast Step, Follow Me Browsing, FormShare, GigaDrive, GigaStack, HomeLink, Internet Quotient, IOS, IP/TV, iQ Expertise, the iQ logo, iQ Net Readiness Scorecard, iQuick Study, LightStream, Linksys, MeetingPlace, MGX, Networking Academy, Network Registrar, Packet, PIX, ProConnect, RateMUX, ScriptShare, SlideCast, SMARTnet, StackWise, The Fastest Way to Increase Your Internet Quotient, and TransPath are registered trademarks of Cisco Systems, Inc. and/or its affiliates in the United States and certain other countries.

All other trademarks mentioned in this document or Website are the property of their respective owners. The use of the word partner does not imply a partnership relationship between Cisco and any other company. (0609R)

# About the Contributing Authors

**Bob Vachon** is a professor in the Computer Systems Technology program at Cambrian College in Sudbury, Ontario, Canada, where he teaches networking infrastructure courses. He has worked and taught in the computer networking and information technology field since 1984. He has collaborated on various CCNA, CCNA Security, CCNP, and IoT projects for the Cisco Networking Academy as team lead, lead author, and subject matter expert. He enjoys playing guitar and being outdoors.

**Allan Johnson** entered the academic world in 1999 after 10 years as a business owner/operator to dedicate his efforts to his passion for teaching. He holds both an MBA and an M.Ed in training and development. He taught CCNA courses at the high school level for seven years and has taught both CCNA and CCNP courses at Del Mar College in Corpus Christi, Texas. In 2003, Allan began to commit much of his time and energy to the CCNA Instructional Support Team providing services to Networking Academy instructors worldwide and creating training materials. He now works full time for Cisco Networking Academy as Curriculum Lead.

# Contents at a Glance

# Contents

# Icons Used in This Book

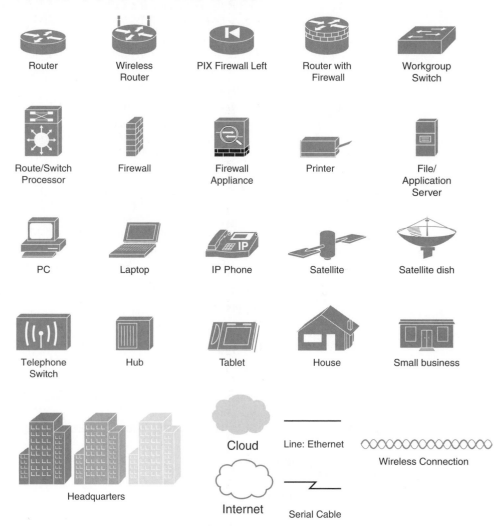

Router

Wireless Router

PIX Firewall Left

Router with Firewall

Workgroup Switch

Route/Switch Processor

Firewall

Firewall Appliance

Printer

File/ Application Server

PC

Laptop

IP Phone

Satellite

Satellite dish

Telephone Switch

Hub

Tablet

House

Small business

Headquarters

Cloud

Internet

Line: Ethernet

Serial Cable

Wireless Connection

# Command Syntax Conventions

The conventions used to present command syntax in this book are the same conventions used in the IOS Command Reference. The Command Reference describes these conventions as follows:

- **Boldface** indicates commands and keywords that are entered literally as shown. In actual configuration examples and output (not general command syntax), boldface indicates commands that are manually input by the user (such as a **show** command).

- *Italic* indicates arguments for which you supply actual values.

- Vertical bars (|) separate alternative, mutually exclusive elements.

- Square brackets ([ ]) indicate an optional element.

- Braces ({ }) indicate a required choice.

- Braces within brackets ([{ }]) indicate a required choice within an optional element.

# Introduction

*Routing and Switching Essentials v6 Companion Guide* is the official supplemental textbook for the Cisco Network Academy CCNA Routing and Switching Essentials course. Cisco Networking Academy is a comprehensive program that delivers information technology skills to students around the world. The curriculum emphasizes real-world practical application, while providing opportunities for you to gain the skills and hands-on experience needed to design, install, operate, and maintain networks in small- to medium-sized businesses, as well as enterprise and service provider environments.

As a textbook, this book provides a ready reference to explain the same networking concepts, technologies, protocols, and devices as the online curriculum. This book emphasizes key topics, terms, and activities and provides some alternate explanations and examples as compared with the course. You can use the online curriculum as directed by your instructor and then use this Companion Guide's study tools to help solidify your understanding of all the topics.

# Who Should Read This Book

The book, as well as the course, is designed as an introduction to data network technology for those pursuing careers as network professionals as well as those who need only an introduction to network technology for professional growth. Topics are presented concisely, starting with the most fundamental concepts and progressing to a comprehensive understanding of network communication. The content of this text provides the foundation for additional Cisco Networking Academy courses and preparation for the CCENT and CCNA Routing and Switching certifications.

# Book Features

The educational features of this book focus on supporting topic coverage, readability, and practice of the course material to facilitate your full understanding of the course material.

## Topic Coverage

The following features give you a thorough overview of the topics covered in each chapter so that you can make constructive use of your study time:

- **Objectives**—Listed at the beginning of each chapter, the objectives reference the core concepts covered in the chapter. The objectives match the objectives stated in the corresponding chapters of the online curriculum; however, the question format in the Companion Guide encourages you to think about finding the answers as you read the chapter.

- **Notes**—These are short sidebars that point out interesting facts, timesaving methods, and important safety issues.

- **Chapter summaries**—At the end of each chapter is a summary of the chapter's key concepts that provides a synopsis of the chapter and serves as a study aid.

- **Practice**—At the end of chapters is a full list of all the labs, class activities, and Packet Tracer activities to refer back to for study time.

## Readability

The following features have been updated to assist your understanding of the networking vocabulary:

- **Key terms**—Each chapter begins with a list of key terms, along with a page-number reference from inside the chapter. The terms are listed in the order in which they are explained in the chapter. This handy reference allows you to find a term, flip to the page where the term appears, and see the term used in context. The Glossary defines all the key terms.

- **Glossary**—This book contains an all-new Glossary with more than 200 terms.

## Practice

Practice makes perfect. This new Companion Guide offers you ample opportunities to put what you learn into practice. You will find the following features valuable and effective in reinforcing the instruction that you receive:

- **Check Your Understanding questions and answer key**—Review questions are presented at the end of each chapter as a self-assessment tool. These questions match the style of questions that you see in the online course. Appendix A, "Answers to the 'Check Your Understanding' Questions," provides an answer key to all the questions and includes an explanation of each answer.

- **Labs and activities**—Throughout each chapter, you will be directed back to the online course to take advantage of the activities created to reinforce concepts. In addition, at the end of each chapter, there is a practice section that collects a list of all the labs and activities to provide practice with the topics introduced in this chapter. The Labs, class activities, and Packet Tracer instructions are available in the companion *Routing and Switching Essentials v6 Labs & Study Guide* (ISBN 9781587134265). The Packet Tracer PKA files are found in the online course.

- **Page references to online course**—After headings, you will see, for example, (1.1.2.3). This number refers to the page number in the online course so that you can easily jump to that spot online to view a video, practice an activity, perform a lab, or review a topic.

## Lab Study Guide

The supplementary book *Routing and Switching Essentials v6 Labs & Study Guide*, by Allan Johnson (ISBN 9781587134265) includes a Study Guide section and a Lab section for each chapter. The Study Guide section offers exercises that help you learn the concepts, configurations, and troubleshooting skill crucial to your success as a CCNA exam candidate. Some chapters include unique Packet Tracer activities available for download from the book's companion website. The Labs and Activities section contains all the labs, class activities, and Packet Tracer instructions from the course.

## About Packet Tracer Software and Activities

Interspersed throughout the chapters you'll find many activities to work with the Cisco Packet Tracer tool. Packet Tracer allows you to create networks, visualize how packets flow in the network, and use basic testing tools to determine whether the network would work. When you see this icon, you can use Packet Tracer with the listed file to perform a task suggested in this book. The activity files are available in the course. Packet Tracer software is available through the Cisco Networking Academy website. Ask your instructor for access to Packet Tracer.

## Companion Website

Register this book to get for any updates or errata that might become available for this book. Be sure to check the box that you would like to hear from us to receive news of updates and exclusive discounts on related products.

To access this companion website, follow these steps:

1.  Go to www.ciscopress.com/register and log in or create a new account.

2.  Enter the ISBN: 9781587134289.

3.  Answer the challenge question as proof of purchase.

4.  Click the "Access Bonus Content" link in the Registered Products section of your account page, to be taken to the page where your downloadable content is available.

Please note that many of our companion content files can be very large, especially image and video files. If you are unable to locate the files for this title by following the steps, please visit www.ciscopress.com/contact and select Site Problems/Comments under the Select a Topic drop-down.

## How This Book Is Organized

This book corresponds closely to the Cisco Academy Routing and Switching Essentials course and is divided into 10 chapters, one appendix, and a glossary of key terms:

- **Chapter 1, "Routing Concepts":** Introduces basic routing concepts including how to complete an initial router configuration and how routers make decisions. Routers use the routing table to determine the next hop for a packet. This chapter explores how the routing table is built with connected, statically learned, and dynamically learned routes.

- **Chapter 2, "Static Routing":** Focuses on the configuration, verification, and troubleshooting of static routes for IPv4 and IPv6, including default routes, floating static routes, and static host routes.

- **Chapter 3, "Dynamic Routing":** Introduces all the important IPv4 and IPv6 dynamic routing protocols. RIPv2 is used to demonstrate basic routing protocol configuration. The chapter concludes with an in-depth analysis of the IPv4 and IPv6 routing tables and the route lookup process.

- **Chapter 4, "Switched Networks":** Introduces the concepts of a converged network, hierarchical network design, and the role of switches in the network. Switching operation, including frame forwarding, broadcast domains, and collision domains, is discussed.

- **Chapter 5, "Switch Configuration":** Focuses on the implementation of a basic switch configuration, verifying the configuration, and troubleshooting the configuration. Switch security is then discussed, including configuring secure remote access with SSH and securing switch ports.

- **Chapter 6, "VLANs":** Introduces the concepts of VLANs, including how VLANs segment broadcast domains. VLAN implementation, including configuration, verification, and troubleshooting, is then covered. The chapter concludes with configuring router-on-a-stick inter-VLAN routing.

- **Chapter 7, "Access Control Lists":** Introduces the concept of using ACLs to filter traffic. Configuration, verification, and troubleshooting of standard IPv4 ACLs are covered. Securing remote access with an ACL is also discussed.

- **Chapter 8, "DHCP":** Dynamically assigning IP addressing to hosts is introduced. The operation of DHCPv4 and DHCPv6 is discussed. Configuration, verification, and troubleshooting of DHCPv4 and DHCPv6 implementations are covered.

- **Chapter 9, "NAT for IPv4":** Translating private IPv4 addresses to another IPv4 address using NAT for IPv4 is introduced. Configuration, verification, and troubleshooting of NAT for IPv4 are covered.

- **Chapter 10, "Device Discovery, Management, and Maintenance":** Introduces the concept of device discovery using CDP and LLDP. Device management topics include NTP and Syslog. The chapter concludes with a discussion of how to manage IOS and configuration files as well as IOS licenses.

- **Appendix A, "Answers to the 'Check Your Understanding' Questions":** This appendix lists the answers to the "Check Your Understanding" review questions that are included at the end of each chapter.

- **Glossary:** The glossary provides definitions for all the key terms identified in each chapter.

# CHAPTER 1

# Routing Concepts

## Objectives

Upon completion of this chapter, you will be able to answer the following questions:

- What are the primary functions and features of a router?

- How do you connect devices for a small, routed network?

- How do you configure basic settings on a router to route between two directly connected networks, using CLI?

- How do you verify connectivity between two networks that are directly connected to a router?

- What is the encapsulation and de-encapsulation process used by routers when switching packets between interfaces?

- What is the path determination function of a router?

- What are the routing table entries for directly connected networks?

- How does a router build a routing table of directly connected networks?

- How does a router build a routing table using static routes?

- How does a router build a routing table using a dynamic routing protocol?

## Key Terms

This chapter uses the following key terms. You can find the definitions in the Glossary.

# Introduction (1.0.1.1)

Networks allow people to communicate, collaborate, and interact in many ways. Networks are used to access web pages, talk using IP telephones, participate in video conferences, compete in interactive gaming, shop using the Internet, complete online coursework, and more.

Ethernet switches function at the data link layer, Layer 2, and are used to forward Ethernet frames between devices within the same network. However, when the source IP and destination IP addresses are on different networks, the Ethernet frame must be sent to a router.

A router connects one network to another network. The router is responsible for the delivery of packets across different networks. The destination of the IP packet might be a web server in another country or an email server on the LAN.

The router uses its routing table to determine the best path to use to forward a packet. It is the responsibility of the routers to deliver those packets in a timely manner. The effectiveness of internetwork communications depends, to a large degree, on the ability of routers to forward packets in the most efficient way possible.

When a host sends a packet to a device on a different IP network, the packet is forwarded to the default gateway because a host device cannot communicate directly with devices outside of the local network. The default gateway is the intermediary device that routes traffic from the local network to devices on remote networks. It is often used to connect a local network to the Internet.

This chapter will answer the question, "What does a router do with a packet received from one network and destined for another network?" Details of the routing table will be examined, including connected, static, and dynamic routes.

Because the router can route packets between networks, devices on different networks can communicate. This chapter introduces the router, its role in networks, its main hardware and software components, and the routing process. Exercises that demonstrate how to access the router, configure basic router settings, and verify settings are provided.

### Activity 1.0.1.2: Do We Really Need a Map?

This modeling activity asks you to research travel directions from source to destination. Its purpose is to compare those types of directions to network routing directions.

### Scenario

Using the Internet and Google Maps, located at http://maps.google.com, find a route between the capital city of your country and some other distant town or between two places within your own city. Pay close attention to the driving or walking directions that Google Maps suggests.

Notice that in many cases, Google Maps suggests more than one route between the two locations you chose. It also allows you to put additional constraints on the route, such as avoiding highways or tolls.

Copy at least two route instructions supplied by Google Maps for this activity. Place your copies into a word processing document and save it for use with the next step.

Open the .pdf accompanying this modeling activity and complete it with a fellow student. Discuss the reflection questions listed on the .pdf and record your answers.

Be prepared to present your answers to the class.

# Router Initial Configuration (1.1)

A router must be configured with specific settings before it can be deployed. New routers are not configured. They must be initially configured using the console port.

In this section, you learn how to configure basic settings on a router.

## Router Functions (1.1.1)

Modern routers are capable of providing many network connectivity functions. The focus of this topic is to examine how routers route packets to their destinations.

### Characteristics of a Network (1.1.1.1)

Networks have had a significant impact on our lives. They have changed the way we live, work, and play. They allow us to communicate, collaborate, and interact in ways we never did before. We use the network in a variety of ways, including web applications, IP telephony, video conferencing, interactive gaming, electronic commerce, education, and more.

As shown in Figure 1-1, there are many key structures and performance-related characteristics referred to when discussing networks:

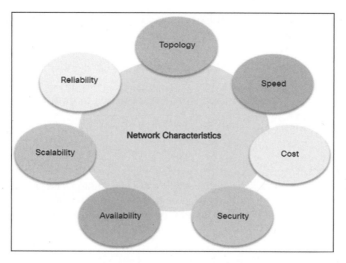

**Figure 1-1**    Network Characteristics

- *Topology*—There are physical and logical topologies. The *physical topology* is the arrangement of the cables, network devices, and end systems. It describes how the network devices are actually interconnected with wires and cables. The *logical topology* is the path over which the data is transferred in a network. It describes how the network devices appear connected to network users.

- *Speed*—Speed is a measure of the data rate in bits per second (b/s) of a given link in the network.

- **Cost**—Cost indicates the general expense for purchasing of network components, and installation and maintenance of the network.

- **Security**—Security indicates how protected the network is, including the information that is transmitted over the network. The subject of security is important, and techniques and practices are constantly evolving. Consider security whenever actions are taken that affect the network.

- *Availability*—Availability is the likelihood that the network is available for use when it is required.

- *Scalability*—Scalability indicates how easily the network can accommodate more users and data transmission requirements. If a network design is optimized to only meet current requirements, it can be very difficult and expensive to meet new needs when the network grows.

■ *Reliability*—Reliability indicates the dependability of the components that make up the network, such as the routers, switches, PCs, and servers. Reliability is often measured as a probability of failure or as the *mean time between failures (MTBF)*.

These characteristics and attributes provide a means to compare different networking solutions.

**Note**

Although the term "speed" is commonly used when referring to the network bandwidth, it is not technically accurate. The actual speed that the bits are transmitted does not vary over the same medium. The difference in bandwidth is due to the number of bits transmitted per second, not how fast they travel over wire or wireless medium.

## Why Routing? (1.1.1.2)

How does clicking a link in a web browser return the desired information in mere seconds? Although there are many devices and technologies collaboratively working together to enable this, the primary device is the router. Stated simply, a router connects one network to another network.

Communication between networks would not be possible without a router determining the best path to the destination and forwarding traffic to the next router along that path. The router is responsible for the routing of traffic between networks.

In the topology in Figure 1-2, the routers interconnect the networks at the different sites.

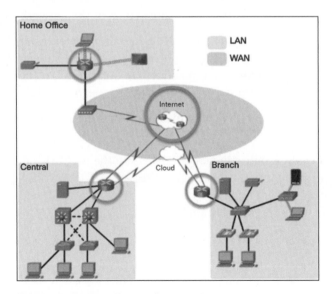

**Figure 1-2**  The Router Connection

When a packet arrives on a router interface, the router uses its *routing table* to determine how to reach the destination network. The destination of the IP packet might be a web server in another country or an email server on the LAN. It is the responsibility of routers to deliver those packets efficiently. The effectiveness of internetwork communications depends, to a large degree, on the ability of routers to forward packets in the most efficient way possible.

## Routers Are Computers (1.1.1.3)

Most network-capable devices (such as computers, tablets, and smartphones) require the following components to operate, as shown in Figure 1-3:

- *CPU*
- Operating system (OS)
- Memory and storage (RAM, ROM, NVRAM, Flash, hard drive)

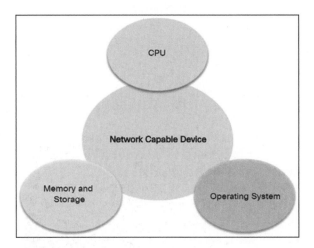

**Figure 1-3**   The Router Connection

A router is essentially a specialized computer. It requires a CPU and memory to temporarily and permanently store data to execute operating system instructions, such as system initialization, routing functions, and switching functions.

Cisco devices also require an OS; Cisco devices commonly use the Cisco *IOS* as its system software.

Router memory is classified as *volatile* or *nonvolatile*. Volatile memory loses its content when the power is turned off, whereas nonvolatile memory does not lose its content when the power is turned off.

Table 1-1 summarizes the types of router memory, the volatility, and examples of what is stored in each.

**Table 1-1**   Router Memory

| Memory | Description |
|---|---|
| *RAM* | Volatile memory that provides temporary storage for various applications and processes including the following:<br>■ Running IOS<br>■ Running configuration file<br>■ IP routing and ARP tables<br>■ Packet buffer |
| *ROM* | Nonvolatile memory that provides permanent storage for the following:<br>■ Bootup instructions<br>■ Basic diagnostic software<br>■ Limited IOS in case the router cannot load the full-featured IOS |
| *NVRAM* | Nonvolatile memory that provides permanent storage for the following:<br>■ Startup configuration file (startup-config) |
| *Flash* | Nonvolatile memory that provides permanent storage for the following:<br>■ IOS<br>■ Other system-related files |

Unlike a computer, a router does not have video adapters or sound card adapters. Instead, routers have specialized ports and network interface cards to interconnect devices to other networks. Figure 1-4 identifies some of these ports and interfaces found on a Cisco 1941 Integrated Service Router (ISR).

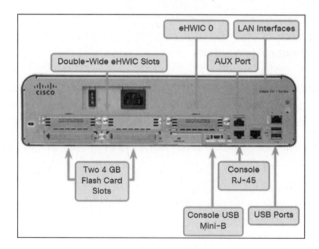

**Figure 1-4**   Back Panel of a Router

## Routers Interconnect Networks (1.1.1.4)

Most users are unaware of the presence of numerous routers on their own network or on the Internet. Users expect to be able to access web pages, send emails, and download music, regardless of whether the server accessed is on their own network or on another network. Networking professionals know that it is the router that is responsible for forwarding packets from network to network, from the original source to the final destination.

A router connects multiple networks, which means that it has multiple interfaces that each belong to a different IP network. When a router receives an IP packet on one interface, it determines which interface to use to forward the packet to the destination. The interface that the router uses to forward the packet may be the final destination, or it may be a network connected to another router that is used to reach the destination network.

In Figure 1-5, routers R1 and R2 are responsible for receiving the packet on one network and forwarding the packet out another network toward the destination network.

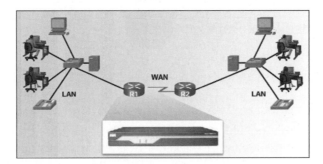

**Figure 1-5**   Routers Connect

Each network that a router connects to typically requires a separate interface. These interfaces are used to connect a combination of both LANs and WANs. LANs are commonly Ethernet networks that contain devices, such as PCs, printers, and servers. WANs are used to connect networks over a large geographical area. For example, a WAN connection is commonly used to connect a LAN to the Internet service provider (ISP) network.

Notice that each site in Figure 1-6 requires the use of a router to interconnect to other sites. Even the Home Office requires a router. In this topology, the router located at the Home Office is a specialized device that performs multiple services for the home network.

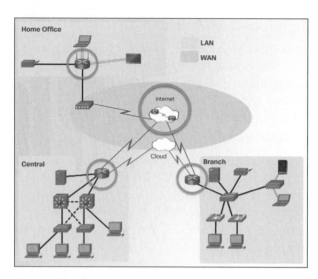

**Figure 1-6**   The Router Connection

## Routers Choose Best Paths (1.1.1.5)

Following are the primary functions of a router:

- Determine the best path to send packets

- Forward packets toward their destination

The router uses its routing table to determine the best path to use to forward a packet. When the router receives a packet, it examines the destination address of the packet and uses the routing table to search for the best path to that network. The routing table also includes the interface to be used to forward packets for each known network. When a match is found, the router encapsulates the packet into the data link frame of the outgoing or exit interface, and the packet is forwarded toward its destination.

It is possible for a router to receive a packet that is encapsulated in one type of data link frame and to forward the packet out of an interface that uses a different type of data link frame. For example, a router may receive a packet on an Ethernet interface, but it must forward the packet out of an interface configured with the *Point-to-Point Protocol (PPP)*. The data link encapsulation depends on the type of interface on the router and the type of medium to which it connects. The different data link technologies that a router can connect to include Ethernet, PPP, Frame Relay, DSL, cable, and wireless (802.11, Bluetooth, and so on).

In Figure 1-7, notice that it is the responsibility of the router to find the destination network in its routing table and forward the packet toward its destination.

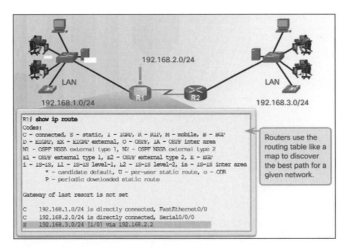

**Figure 1-7**   How the Router Works

In this example, router R1 receives the packet encapsulated in an Ethernet frame. After de-encapsulating the packet, R1 uses the destination IP address of the packet to search its routing table for a matching network address. After a destination network address is found in the routing table, R1 encapsulates the packet inside a PPP frame and forwards the packet to R2. R2 performs a similar process.

**Note**

Routers use *static routes* and *dynamic routing protocols* to learn about remote networks and build their routing tables.

## Packet-Forwarding Mechanisms (1.1.1.6)

Routers support three packet-forwarding mechanisms:

- *Process switching*—Shown in Figure 1-8, this is an older packet-forwarding mechanism still available for Cisco routers. When a packet arrives on an interface, it is forwarded to the control plane where the CPU matches the destination address with an entry in its routing table, and then it determines the exit interface and forwards the packet. It is important to understand that the router does this for every packet, even if the destination is the same for a stream of packets. This process-switching mechanism is slow and rarely implemented in modern networks.

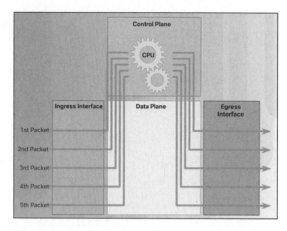

**Figure 1-8**   Process Switching

- *Fast switching*—Shown in Figure 1-9, this is a common packet-forwarding mechanism that uses a fast-switching cache to store next-hop information. When a packet arrives on an interface, it is forwarded to the control plane, where the CPU searches for a match in the fast-switching cache. If it is not there, it is process-switched and forwarded to the exit interface. The flow information for the packet is also stored in the *fast-switching cache*. If another packet going to the same destination arrives on an interface, the next-hop information in the cache is reused without CPU intervention.

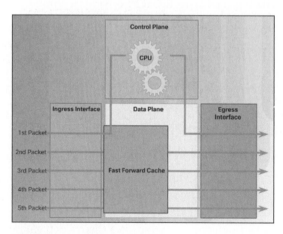

**Figure 1-9**   Fast Switching

- *Cisco Express Forwarding (CEF)*—Shown in Figure 1-10, CEF is the most recent and preferred Cisco IOS packet-forwarding mechanism. Like fast switching, CEF builds a *Forwarding Information Base (FIB)*, and an *adjacency table*.

However, the table entries are not packet-triggered like fast switching but change-triggered, such as when something changes in the network topology. Therefore, when a network has converged, the FIB and adjacency tables contain all the information a router would have to consider when forwarding a packet. The FIB contains precomputed reverse lookups, next-hop information for routes including the interface, and Layer 2 information. CEF is the fastest forwarding mechanism and the preferred choice on Cisco routers.

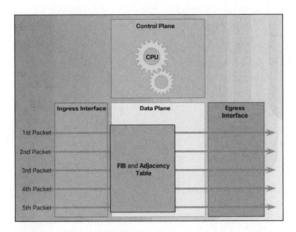

**Figure 1-10**   Cisco Express Forwarding

Assume that all five packets in a traffic flow are going to the same destination. As shown in Figure 1-8, with process switching, each packet must be processed by the CPU individually. Contrast this with fast switching, shown in Figure 1-9. With fast switching, notice how only the first packet of a flow is process-switched and added to the fast-switching cache. The next four packets are quickly processed based on the information in the fast-switching cache. Finally, in Figure 1-10, CEF builds the FIB and adjacency tables, after the network has converged. All five packets are quickly processed in the data plane.

A common analogy used to describe the three packet-forwarding mechanisms is as follows:

■ Process switching solves a problem by doing math long hand, even if it is the identical problem.

■ Fast switching solves a problem by doing math long hand one time and remembering the answer for subsequent identical problems.

■ CEF solves every possible problem ahead of time in a spreadsheet.

**Activity 1.1.1.7: Identify Router Components**

Refer to the online course to complete this activity.

**Packet Tracer 1.1.1.8: Using Traceroute to Discover the Network**

The company you work for has acquired a new branch location. You asked for a topology map of the new location, but apparently one does not exist. However, you have username and password information for the new branch's networking devices, and you know the web address for the new branch's server. Therefore, you will verify connectivity and use the **tracert** command to determine the path to the location. You will connect to the edge router of the new location to determine the devices and networks attached. As a part of this process, you will use various **show** commands to gather the necessary information to finish documenting the IP addressing scheme and create a diagram of the topology.

**Lab 1.1.1.9: Mapping the Internet**

In this lab, you will complete the following objectives:

- Part 1: Determine Network Connectivity to a Destination Host
- Part 2: Trace a Route to a Remote Server Using Tracert

# Connect Devices (1.1.2)

LAN hosts typically connect to a router using Layer 3 IP addresses. The focus of this topic is to examine how devices connect to a small, routed network.

## Connect to a Network (1.1.2.1)

Network devices and end users typically connect to a network using a wired Ethernet or wireless connection. Refer to Figure 1-11 as a sample reference topology. The LANs in the figure serve as an example of how users and network devices can connect to networks.

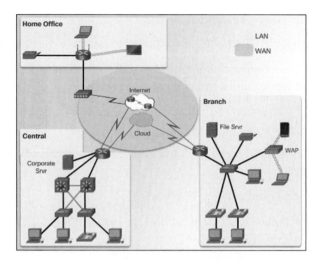

**Figure 1-11**    Sample LAN and WAN Connections

Home Office devices can connect as follows:

- Laptops and tablets connect wirelessly to a home router.

- A network printer connects using an Ethernet cable to the switch port on the home router.

- The home router connects to the service provider cable modem using an Ethernet cable.

- The cable modem connects to the ISP network.

The Branch site devices connect as follows:

- Corporate resources (that is, file servers and printers) connect to Layer 2 switches using Ethernet cables.

- Desktop PCs and *VoIP phones* connect to Layer 2 switches using Ethernet cables.

- Laptops and smartphones connect wirelessly to *wireless access points (WAP)*.

- The WAPs connect to switches using Ethernet cables.

- Layer 2 switches connect to an Ethernet interface on the edge router using Ethernet cables. An edge router is a device that sits at the edge or boundary of a network and routes between that network and another, such as between a LAN and a WAN.

- The edge router connects to a WAN service provider (SP).

- The edge router also connects to an ISP for backup purposes.

The Central site devices connect as follows:

- Desktop PCs and VoIP phones connect to Layer 2 switches using Ethernet cables.
- Layer 2 switches connect redundantly to multilayer Layer 3 switches using Ethernet fiber-optic cables (orange connections).
- Layer 3 multilayer switches connect to an Ethernet interface on the edge router using Ethernet cables.
- The corporate website server is connected using an Ethernet cable to the edge router interface.
- The edge router connects to a WAN SP.
- The edge router also connects to an ISP for backup purposes.

In the Branch and Central LANs, hosts are connected either directly or indirectly (via WAPs) to the network infrastructure using a Layer 2 switch.

## Default Gateways (1.1.2.2)

To enable network access, devices must be configured with IP address information to identify the appropriate

- **IP address**—Identifies a unique host on a local network.
- **Subnet mask**—Identifies with which network subnet the host can communicate.
- **Default gateway**—Identifies the IP address of the router to send a packet to when the destination is not on the same local network subnet.

When a host sends a packet to a device that is on the same IP network, the packet is simply forwarded out of the host interface to the destination device.

When a host sends a packet to a device on a different IP network, the packet is forwarded to the default gateway because a host device cannot communicate directly with devices outside of the local network. The default gateway is the destination that routes traffic from the local network to devices on remote networks. It is often used to connect a local network to the Internet.

The default gateway is usually the address of the interface on the router connected to the local network. The router maintains routing table entries of all connected networks as well as entries of remote networks, and it determines the best path to reach those destinations.

For example, if PC1 sends a packet to the Web Server located at 176.16.1.99, it would discover that the Web Server is not on the local network. It would therefore send the packet to the MAC address of its default gateway. The packet protocol data unit (PDU) at the top in Figure 1-12 identifies the source and destination IP and MAC addresses.

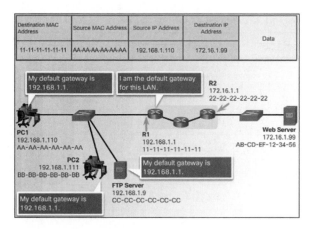

**Figure 1-12**   Getting the Pieces to the Correct Network

## Document Network Addressing (1.1.2.3)

When designing a new network or mapping an existing network, document the network. At a minimum, the documentation should identify the following:

- Device names

- Interfaces used in the design

- IP addresses and subnet masks

- Default gateway addresses

This information is captured by creating two useful network documents:

- **Topology diagram**—As shown in Figure 1-13, the topology diagram provides a visual reference that indicates the physical connectivity and logical Layer 3 addressing. Often created using diagramming software, such as Microsoft Visio.

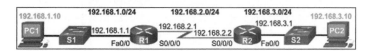

**Figure 1-13**   Topology Diagram

- **An addressing table**—A table, such as Table 1-2, is used to capture device names, interfaces, IPv4 addresses, subnet masks, and default gateway addresses.

**Table 1-2**    Addressing Table

| Device | Interface | IP Address | Subnet Mask | Default Gateway |
|--------|-----------|------------|-------------|-----------------|
| R1 | Fa0/0 | 192.168.1.1 | 255.255.255.0 | N/A |
|    | S0/0/0 | 192.168.2.1 | 255.255.255.0 | N/A |
| R2 | Fa0/0 | 192.168.3.1 | 255.255.255.0 | N/A |
|    | S0/0/0 | 192.168.2.2 | 255.255.255.0 | N/A |
| PC1 | N/A | 192.168.1.10 | 255.255.255.0 | 192.168.1.1 |
| PC2 | N/A | 192.168.3.10 | 255.255.255.0 | 192.168.3.1 |

## Enable IP on a Host (1.1.2.4)

A host can be assigned IP address information in one of two ways:

- **Statically**—The host is manually assigned a unique IP address, subnet mask, and default gateway. The DNS server IP address can also be configured.

- **Dynamically**—The host receives its IP address information automatically from a DHCP server. The DHCP server offers the host a valid IP address, subnet mask, and default gateway information. The DHCP server may provide other information.

Figure 1-14 provides a static IPv4 configuration example.

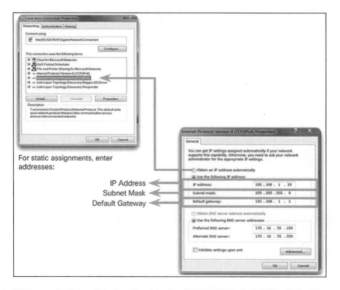

**Figure 1-14**    Statically Assigning an IPv4 Address

Figure 1-15 provides a dynamic IPv4 address configuration examples.

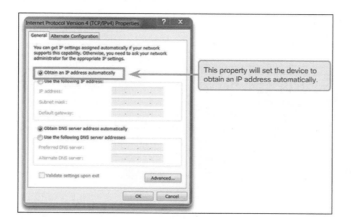

**Figure 1-15**   Dynamically Assigning an IPv4 Address

Statically assigned addresses are commonly used to identify specific network resources, such as network servers and printers. They can also be used in smaller networks with few hosts. However, most host devices acquire their IPv4 address information by accessing a DHCPv4 server. In large enterprises, dedicated DHCPv4 servers providing services to many LANs are implemented. In a smaller branch or small office setting, DHCPv4 services can be provided by a Cisco Catalyst switch or a Cisco ISR.

## Device LEDs (1.1.2.5)

Host computers connect to a wired network using a network interface and RJ-45 Ethernet cable. Most network interfaces have one or two LED link indicators next to the interface. The significance and meaning of the LED colors vary between manufacturers. However, a green LED typically means a good connection, whereas a blinking green LED indicates network activity.

If the link light is not on, there may be a problem with either the network cable or the network itself. The switch port where the connection terminates would also have an LED indicator lit. If one or both ends are not lit, try a different network cable.

**Note**

The actual function of the LEDs varies between computer manufacturers.

Similarly, network infrastructure devices commonly use multiple LED indicators to provide a quick status view. For example, a Cisco Catalyst 2960 switch has several status LEDs to help monitor system activity and performance. These LEDs are generally lit green when the switch is functioning normally and lit amber when there is a malfunction.

Cisco ISRs use various LED indicators to provide status information. A Cisco 1941 router is shown in Figure 1-16.

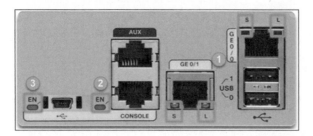

**Figure 1-16**   Cisco 1941 LEDs

Table 1-3 lists the LED descriptions for the Cisco 1941 router.

**Table 1-3**   Cisco 1941 LED Descriptions

| # | Port | LED | Color | Description |
|---|------|-----|-------|-------------|
| 1 | GE0/0 and GE0/1 | S (Speed) | 1 blink + pause | Port operating at 10 Mb/s |
|   |      |     | 2 blink + pause | Port operating at 100 Mb/s |
|   |      |     | 3 blink + pause | Port operating at 1000 Mb/s |
|   |      | L (Link) | Green | Link is active |
|   |      |     | Off | Link is inactive |
| 2 | Console | EN | Green | Port is active |
|   |      |     | Off | Port is inactive |
| 3 | USB | EN | Green | Port is active |
|   |      |     | Off | Port is inactive |

The LEDs on the router can help a network administrator quickly conduct some basic troubleshooting. Each device has a unique set of LEDs, and it is advisable that you become familiar with the significance of these LEDs. Consult the device-specific documentation for an accurate description of the LEDs.

## Console Access (1.1.2.6)

In a working network environment, infrastructure devices are commonly accessed remotely using Secure Shell (SSH) or Hypertext Transfer Protocol Secure (HTTPS). Console access is really only required when initially configuring a device, or if remote access fails.

Console access requires the following:

- **Console cable**—RJ-45-to-DB-9 serial cable or a USB serial cable

- **Terminal emulation software**—Tera Term, PuTTY

The cable is connected between the serial port of the host and the console port on the device. Most computers and notebooks no longer include built-in serial ports; therefore, a USB port can establish a console connection. However, a special *USB-to-RS-232 compatible serial port adapter* is required when using the USB port.

The Cisco ISR G2 supports a USB serial console connection. To establish connectivity, a *USB Type-A to USB Type-B (mini-B USB)* is required, as well as an operating system device driver. This device driver is available from www.cisco.com. Although these routers have two console ports, only one console port can be active at a time. When a cable is plugged into the USB console port, the RJ-45 port becomes inactive. When the USB cable is removed from the USB port, the RJ-45 port becomes active.

The table in Figure 1-17 summarizes the console connection requirements.

| Port on Computer | Cable Required | Port on ISR | Terminal Emulation |
|---|---|---|---|
| Serial Port | RJ-45-to-DB-9 Console Cable | RJ-45 Console Port |  Tera Term |
| USB Type-A Port | • USB-to-RS-232 compatible serial port adapter<br>• Adapter may require a software driver<br>• RJ-45-to-DB-9 console cable | |  |
| | • USB Type-A to USB Type-B (Mini-B USB)<br>• A device driver is required and available from cisco.com. | USB Type-B (Mini-B USB) | PuTTY |

**Figure 1-17**   Console Connection Requirements

Figure 1-18 displays the various ports and cables required.

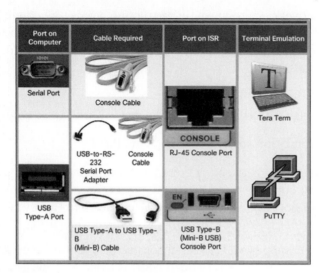

**Figure 1-18**   Ports and Cables

## Enable IP on a Switch (1.1.2.7)

Network infrastructure devices require IP addresses to enable remote management. Using the device IP address, the network administrator can remotely connect to the device using Telnet, SSH, HTTP, or HTTPS.

A switch does not have a dedicated interface to which an IP address can be assigned. Instead, the IP address information is configured on a virtual interface called a *switched virtual interface (SVI)*.

For example, in Figure 1-19, the SVI on the Layer 2 switch S1 is assigned the IP address 192.168.10.2/24 and a default gateway of 192.168.10.1.

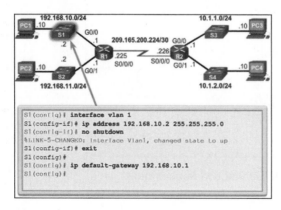

**Figure 1-19**   Configure the Switch Management Interface

**Activity 1.1.2.8: Document an Addressing Scheme**

Refer to the online course to complete this activity.

Packet Tracer
☐ Activity

**Packet Tracer 1.1.2.9: Documenting the Network**

Background/Scenario

Your job is to document the addressing scheme and connections used in the Central portion of the network. You need to use a variety of commands to gather the required information.

# Router Basic Settings (1.1.3)

Every network has unique settings that must be configured on a router. This topic introduces basic IOS commands that are required to configure a router.

## Configure Basic Router Settings (1.1.3.1)

Cisco routers and Cisco switches are a lot alike. They support a similar modal operating system, similar command structures, and many of the same commands. In addition, both devices have similar initial configuration steps.

For instance, the following configuration tasks should always be performed:

- **Name the device**—Distinguishes it from other routers.

- **Secure management access**—Secures privileged EXEC, user EXEC, and remote access.

- **Configure a banner**—Provides legal notification of unauthorized access.

Always save the changes on a router and verify the basic configuration and router operations.

Figure 1-20 shows the topology used for example configurations.

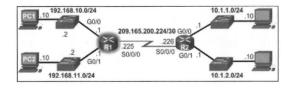

**Figure 1-20**   IPv4 Configuration Topology

Example 1-1 shows the basic router settings configured for R1.

**Example 1-1** Basic Router Settings

```
Router# configure terminal
Enter configuration commands, one per line.  End with CNTL/Z.
Router(config)# hostname R1
R1(config)# enable secret class
R1(config)# line console 0
R1(config-line)# password cisco
R1(config-line)# login
R1(config-line)# exit
R1(config)# line vty 0 4
R1(config-line)# password cisco
R1(config-line)# login
R1(config-line)# exit
R1(config)# service password-encryption
R1(config)# banner motd $ Authorized Access Only! $
R1(config)# end
R1# copy running-config startup-config
Destination filename [startup-config]?
Building configuration...
[OK]
R1#
```

## Configure an IPv4 Router Interface (1.1.3.2)

One distinguishing feature between switches and routers is the type of interfaces supported by each. For example, Layer 2 switches support LANs and, therefore, have multiple FastEthernet or Gigabit Ethernet ports.

Routers support LANs and WANs and can interconnect different types of networks; therefore, they support many types of interfaces. For example, G2 ISRs have one or two integrated Gigabit Ethernet interfaces and *High-Speed WAN Interface Card (HWIC) slots* to accommodate other types of network interfaces, including serial, DSL, and cable interfaces.

To be available, an interface must be both of the following:

- **Configured with an IP address and a subnet mask**—Use the **ip address** *ip-address subnet-mask* interface configuration command.

- **Activated**—By default, LAN and WAN interfaces are not activated (**shutdown**). To enable an interface, it must be activated using the **no shutdown** command.

(This is similar to powering on the interface.) The interface must also be connected to another device such as a switch or another router for the physical layer to be active.

Optionally, the interface could also be configured with a short description of up to 240 characters using the **description** command. It is good practice to configure a description on each interface. On production networks, the benefits of interface descriptions are quickly realized because they are helpful in troubleshooting and identifying a third-party connection and contact information.

Depending on the type of interface, additional parameters may be required. For example, in our lab environment, the serial interface connecting to the serial cable end labeled DCE must be configured with the **clock rate** command.

**Note**

The service provider router would typically provide the clock rate to the customer router. However, in a lab environment, the **clock rate** command is required on the DCE end when interconnecting two serial interfaces.

**Note**

Accidentally using the **clock rate** command on a DTE interface generates the following informational message:

```
%Error: This command applies only to DCE interface
```

Example 1-2 shows the router interfaces configuration for R1. Notice that the state of Serial0/0/0 is "down". The status will change to "up" when the Serial0/0/0 interface on R2 is configured and activated.

**Example 1-2**  Router Interface Configurations for IPv4

```
R1(config)# interface gigabitethernet 0/0
R1(config-if)# description Link to LAN 1
R1(config-if)# ip address 192.168.10.1 255.255.255.0
R1(config-if)# no shutdown
R1(config-if)# exit
*Jan 30 22:04:47.551: %LINK-3-UPDOWN: Interface GigabitEthernet0/0, changed state
  to down
*Jan 30 22:04:50.899: %LINK-3-UPDOWN: Interface GigabitEthernet0/0, changed state
  to up
*Jan 30 22:04:51.899: %LINEPROTO-5-UPDOWN: Line protocol on Interface GigabitEther-
  net0/0, changed state to up
R1(config)# interface gigabitethernet 0/1
R1(config-if)# description Link to LAN 2
```

```
R1(config-if)# ip address 192.168.11.1 255.255.255.0
R1(config-if)# no shutdown
R1(config-if)# exit
*Jan 30 22:06:02.543: %LINK-3-UPDOWN: Interface GigabitEthernet0/1, changed state
  to down
*Jan 30 22:06:05.899: %LINK-3-UPDOWN: Interface GigabitEthernet0/1, changed state
  to up
*Jan 30 22:06:06.899: %LINEPROTO-5-UPDOWN: Line protocol on Interface Gigabit
  Ethernet0/1, changed state to up
R1(config)# interface serial 0/0/0
R1(config-if)# description Link to R2
R1(config-if)# ip address 209.165.200.225 255.255.255.252
R1(config-if)# clockrate 128000
R1(config-if)# no shutdown
R1(config-if)# exit
*Jan 30 23:01:17.323: %LINK-3-UPDOWN: Interface Serial0/0/0, changed state to down
R1(config)#
```

## Configure an IPv6 Router Interface (1.1.3.3)

Configuring an IPv6 interface is similar to configuring an interface for IPv4. Most IPv6 configuration and verification commands in the Cisco IOS are similar to their IPv4 counterparts. In many cases, the only difference is the use of **ipv6** in place of **ip** in commands.

An IPv6 interface must be

- **Configured with IPv6 address and subnet mask**—Use the **ipv6 address** *ipv6-address/prefix-length* [**link-local** | **eui-64**] interface configuration command.

- **Activated**—The interface must be activated using the **no shutdown** command.

> **Note**
>
> An interface can generate its own IPv6 link-local address without having a global unicast address by using the **ipv6 enable** interface configuration command.

Unlike IPv4, IPv6 interfaces will typically have more than one IPv6 address. At a minimum, an IPv6 device must have an *IPv6 link-local address* but will most likely also have an *IPv6 global unicast address*. IPv6 also supports the ability for an interface to have multiple IPv6 global unicast addresses from the same subnet.

The following commands can be used to statically create a global unicast or link-local IPv6 address:

- **ipv6 address** *ipv6-address/prefix-length*—Creates a global unicast IPv6 address as specified.

- **ipv6 address** *ipv6-address/prefix-length* **eui-64**—Configures a global unicast IPv6 address with an interface identifier (ID) in the low-order 64 bits of the IPv6 address using the *EUI-64* process.

- **ipv6 address** *ipv6-address/prefix-length* **link-local**—Configures a static link-local address on the interface that is used instead of the link-local address that is automatically configured when the global unicast IPv6 address is assigned to the interface or enabled using the **ipv6 enable** interface command. Recall that the **ipv6 enable** interface command is used to automatically create an IPv6 link-local address whether or not an IPv6 global unicast address has been assigned.

In the example topology shown in Figure 1-21, R1 must be configured to support the following IPv6 network addresses:

- 2001:0DB8:ACAD:0001:/64 or equivalently 2001:DB8:ACAD:1::/64

- 2001:0DB8:ACAD:0002:/64 or equivalently 2001:DB8:ACAD:2::/64

- 2001:0DB8:ACAD:0003:/64 or equivalently 2001:DB8:ACAD:3::/64

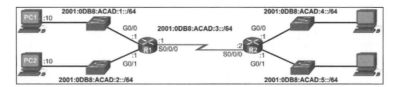

**Figure 1-21**   IPv6 Configuration Topology

When the router is configured using the **ipv6 unicast-routing** global configuration command, the router begins sending ICMPv6 Router Advertisement messages out the interface. This enables a PC connected to the interface to automatically configure an IPv6 address and to set a default gateway without needing the services of a DHCPv6 server. Alternatively, a PC connected to the IPv6 network can have an IPv6 address manually configured, as shown in Figure 1-22. Notice that the default gateway address configured for PC1 is the IPv6 global unicast address of the R1 GigabitEthernet 0/0 interface.

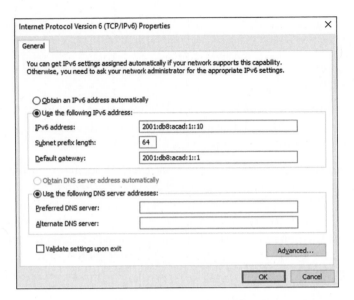

**Figure 1-22**   Statically Assign an IPv6 Address to PC1

The router interfaces in the Figure 1-21 must be configured and enabled, as shown in Example 1-3.

**Example 1-3** Router Interface Configurations for IPv6

```
R1(config)# interface gigabitethernet 0/0
R1(config-if)# description Link to LAN 1
R1(config-if)# ipv6 address 2001:db8:acad:1::1/64
R1(config-if)# no shutdown
R1(config-if)# exit
*Feb  3 21:38:37.279: %LINK-3-UPDOWN: Interface GigabitEthernet0/0, changed state
  to down
*Feb  3 21:38:40.967: %LINK-3-UPDOWN: Interface GigabitEthernet0/0, changed state
  to up
*Feb  3 21:38:41.967: %LINEPROTO-5-UPDOWN: Line protocol on Interface GigabitEther-
  net0/0, changed state to up
R1(config)# interface gigabitethernet 0/1
R1(config-if)# description Link to LAN 2
R1(config-if)# ipv6 address 2001:db8:acad:2::1/64
R1(config-if)# no shutdown
R1(config-if)# exit
*Feb  3 21:39:21.867: %LINK-3-UPDOWN: Interface GigabitEthernet0/1, changed state
  to down
*Feb  3 21:39:24.967: %LINK-3-UPDOWN: Interface GigabitEthernet0/1, changed state
  to up
*Feb  3 21:39:25.967: %LINEPROTO-5-UPDOWN: Line protocol on Interface GigabitEther-
  net0/1, changed state to up
```

```
R1(config)# interface serial 0/0/0
R1(config-if)# description Link to R2
R1(config-if)# ipv6 address 2001:db8:acad:3::1/64
R1(config-if)# clock rate 128000
R1(config-if)# no shutdown
*Feb  3 21:39:43.307: %LINK-3-UPDOWN: Interface Serial0/0/0, changed state to down
R1(config-if)#
```

## Configure an IPv4 Loopback Interface (1.1.3.4)

Another common configuration of Cisco IOS routers is enabling a *loopback interface*.

The loopback interface is a logical interface internal to the router. It is not assigned to a physical port and can therefore never be connected to any other device. It is considered a software interface that is automatically placed in an "up" state, as long as the router is functioning.

The loopback interface is useful in testing and managing a Cisco IOS device because it ensures that at least one interface will always be available. For example, it can be used for testing purposes, such as testing internal routing processes, by emulating networks behind the router.

Additionally, the IPv4 address assigned to the loopback interface can be significant to processes on the router that use an interface IPv4 address for identification purposes, such as the Open Shortest Path First (OSPF) routing process. By enabling a loopback interface, the router will use the always available loopback interface address for identification, rather than an IP address assigned to a physical port that may go down.

The task of enabling and assigning a loopback address is simple:

```
Router(config)# interface loopback number
Router(config-if)# ip address ip-address subnet-mask
Router(config-if)# exit
```

Example 1-4 shows the loopback configuration for R1.

**Example 1-4**  Configure a Loopback Interface

```
R1(config)# interface loopback 0
R1(config-if)# ip address 10.0.0.1 255.255.255.0
R1(config-if)# end
R1(config)#
*Jan 30 22:04:50.899: %LINK-3-UPDOWN: Interface loopback0, changed state to up
*Jan 30 22:04:51.899: %LINEPROTO-5-UPDOWN: Line protocol on Interface loopback0,
  changed state to up
```

Multiple loopback interfaces can be enabled on a router. The IPv4 address for each loopback interface must be unique and unused by any other interface.

**Packet Tracer 1.1.3.5: Configuring IPv4 and IPv6 Interfaces**

Background/Scenario

Routers R1 and R2 each have two LANs. Your task is to configure the appropriate addressing on each device and verify connectivity between the LANs.

## Verify Connectivity of Directly Connected Networks (1.1.4)

It is always important to know how to troubleshoot and verify whether a device is configured correctly. The focus of this topic is on how to verify connectivity between two networks that are directly connected to a router.

### Verify Interface Settings (1.1.4.1)

There are several privileged EXEC mode **show** commands that can be used to verify the operation and configuration of an interface. The following three commands are especially useful to quickly identify an interface status:

- **show ip interface brief**—Displays a summary for all interfaces, including the IPv4 address of the interface and current operational status.

- **show ip route**—Displays the contents of the IPv4 routing table stored in RAM. In Cisco IOS 15, active interfaces should appear in the routing table with two related entries identified by the code 'C' (Connected) or 'L' (Local). In previous IOS versions, only a single entry with the code 'C' will appear.

- **show running-config interface** *interface-id*—Displays the commands configured on the specified interface.

Example 1-5 displays the output of the **show ip interface brief** command. The output reveals that the LAN interfaces and the WAN link are activated and operational, as indicated by the Status of "up" and Protocol of "up." A different output would indicate a problem with either the configuration or the cabling.

**Example 1-5**  Verify the IPv4 Interface Status

```
R1# show ip interface brief
Interface                  IP-Address       OK? Method Status                 Protocol
Embedded-Service-Engine0/0 unassigned       YES unset  administratively down  down
GigabitEthernet0/0         192.168.10.1     YES manual up                     up
GigabitEthernet0/1         192.168.11.1     YES manual up                     up
Serial0/0/0                209.165.200.225  YES manual up                     up
Serial0/0/1                unassigned       YES unset  administratively down  down
R1#
```

**Note**

In Example 1-5, the Embedded-Service-Engine0/0 interface is displayed because Cisco ISRs G2 have dual core CPUs on the motherboard. The Embedded-Service-Engine0/0 interface is outside the scope of this course.

Example 1-6 displays the output of the **show ip route** command. Notice the three directly connected network entries and the three local host route interface entries. A local host route has an administrative distance of 0. It also has a /32 mask for IPv4, and a /128 mask for IPv6. The local host route is for routes on the router owning the IP address. It is used to allow the router to process packets destined to that IP.

**Example 1-6**  Verify the IPv4 Routing Table

```
R1# show ip route
Codes: L - local, C - connected, S - static, R - RIP, M - mobile, B - BGP

<output omitted.

Gateway of last resort is not set

      192.168.10.0/24 is variably subnetted, 2 subnets, 2 masks
C        192.168.10.0/24 is directly connected, GigabitEthernet0/0
L        192.168.10.1/32 is directly connected, GigabitEthernet0/0
      192.168.11.0/24 is variably subnetted, 2 subnets, 2 masks
C        192.168.11.0/24 is directly connected, GigabitEthernet0/1
L        192.168.11.1/32 is directly connected, GigabitEthernet0/1
      209.165.200.0/24 is variably subnetted, 2 subnets, 2 masks
C        209.165.200.224/30 is directly connected, Serial0/0/0
L        209.165.200.225/32 is directly connected, Serial0/0/0
R1#
```

Example 1-7 displays the output of the **show running-config interface** command. The output displays the current commands configured on the specified interface.

**Example 1-7** Verify the IPv4 Interface Configuration

```
R1# show running-config interface gigabitEthernet 0/0
Building configuration...

Current configuration : 128 bytes
!
interface GigabitEthernet0/0
 description Link to LAN 1
 ip address 192.168.10.1 255.255.255.0
 duplex auto
 speed auto
end

R1#
```

The following two commands are used to gather more detailed interface information:

- **show interfaces**—Displays interface information and packet flow count for all interfaces on the device.

- **show ip interface**—Displays the IPv4-related information for all interfaces on a router.

## Verify IPv6 Interface Settings (1.1.4.2)

The commands to verify the IPv6 interface configuration are similar to the commands used for IPv4.

The **show ipv6 interface brief** command in Example 1-8 displays a summary for each of the interfaces for the R1 router in Figure 1-21. The "up/up" output on the same line as the interface name indicates the Layer 1/Layer 2 interface state. This is the same as the Status and Protocol columns in the equivalent IPv4 command.

**Example 1-8** Verify the IPv6 Interface Status

```
R1# show ipv6 interface brief
GigabitEthernet0/0      [up/up]
    FE80::FE99:47FF:FE75:C3E0
    2001:DB8:ACAD:1::1
GigabitEthernet0/1      [up/up]
    FE80::FE99:47FF:FE75:C3E1
    2001:DB8:ACAD:2::1
```

```
Serial0/0/0                [up/up]
    FE80::FE99:47FF:FE75:C3E0
    2001:DB8:ACAD:3::1
Serial0/0/1                [administratively down/down]
    unassigned
R1#
```

The output displays two configured IPv6 addresses per interface. One address is the IPv6 global unicast address that was manually entered. The other address, which begins with FE80, is the link-local unicast address for the interface. A link-local address is automatically added to an interface whenever a global unicast address is assigned. An IPv6 network interface is required to have a link-local address, but not necessarily a global unicast address.

The **show ipv6 interface gigabitethernet 0/0** command output shown in Example 1-9 displays the interface status and all the IPv6 addresses belonging to the interface. Along with the link-local address and global unicast address, the output includes the multicast addresses assigned to the interface, beginning with prefix FF02.

**Example 1-9** Verify the IPv6 Interface Configuration

```
R1# show ipv6 interface gigabitEthernet 0/0
GigabitEthernet0/0 is up, line protocol is up
  IPv6 is enabled, link-local address is FE80::32F7:DFF:FEA3:DA0
  No Virtual link-local address(es):
  Global unicast address(es):
    2001:DB8:ACAD:1::1, subnet is 2001:DB8:ACAD:1::/64
  Joined group address(es):
    FF02::1
    FF02::1:FF00:1
    FF02::1:FFA3:DA0
  MTU is 1500 bytes
  ICMP error messages limited to one every 100 milliseconds
  ICMP redirects are enabled
  ICMP unreachables are sent
  ND DAD is enabled, number of DAD attempts: 1
  ND reachable time is 30000 milliseconds (using 30000)
  ND NS retransmit interval is 1000 milliseconds
R1#
```

The **show ipv6 route** command shown in Example 1-10 can be used to verify that IPv6 networks and specific IPv6 interface addresses have been installed in the IPv6 routing table. The **show ipv6 route** command will only display IPv6 networks, not IPv4 networks.

**Example 1-10** Verify the IPv6 Routing Table

```
R1# show ipv6 route
IPv6 Routing Table - default - 7 entries
Codes: C - Connected, L - Local, S - Static, U - Per-user Static

<output omitted>

C    2001:DB8:ACAD:1::/64 [0/0]
      via GigabitEthernet0/0, directly connected
L    2001:DB8:ACAD:1::1/128 [0/0]
      via GigabitEthernet0/0, receive
C    2001:DB8:ACAD:2::/64 [0/0]
      via GigabitEthernet0/1, directly connected
L    2001:DB8:ACAD:2::1/128 [0/0]
      via GigabitEthernet0/1, receive
C    2001:DB8:ACAD:3::/64 [0/0]
      via Serial0/0/0, directly connected
L    2001:DB8:ACAD:3::1/128 [0/0]
      via Serial0/0/0, receive
L    FF00::/8 [0/0]
      via Null0, receive
R1#
```

Within the routing table, a 'C' next to a route indicates that this is a directly connected network. When the router interface is configured with a global unicast address and is in the "up/up" state, the IPv6 prefix and prefix length is added to the IPv6 routing table as a connected route.

The IPv6 global unicast address configured on the interface is also installed in the routing table as a local route. The local route has a /128 prefix. Local routes are used by the routing table to efficiently process packets with the interface address of the router as the destination.

The **ping** command for IPv6 is identical to the command used with IPv4 except that an IPv6 address is used. As shown in Example 1-11, the **ping** command is used to verify Layer 3 connectivity between R1 and PC1.

**Example 1-11** Verify R1 Connectivity to PC1

```
R1# ping 2001:db8:acad:1::10
Type escape sequence to abort.
Sending 5, 100-byte ICMP Echos to 2001:DB8:ACAD:1::10, timeout is 2 seconds:
!!!!!
Success rate is 100 percent (5/5)
R1#
```

## Filter Show Command Output (1.1.4.3)

Commands that generate multiple screens of output are, by default, paused after 24 lines. At the end of the paused output, the --More-- text displays. Pressing Enter displays the next line, and pressing the Spacebar displays the next set of lines. Use the **terminal length** command to specify the number of lines to be displayed. A value of 0 (zero) prevents the router from pausing between screens of output.

Another useful feature that improves the user experience in the command-line interface (CLI) is the filtering of **show** output. Filtering commands can be used to display specific sections of output. To enable the filtering command, enter a pipe (l) character after the **show** command and then enter a filtering parameter and a filtering expression.

The filtering parameters that can be configured after the pipe include these:

- **section**—Shows entire section that starts with the filtering expression
- **include**—Includes all output lines that match the filtering expression
- **exclude**—Excludes all output lines that match the filtering expression
- **begin**—Shows all the output lines from a certain point, starting with the line that matches the filtering expression

**Note**

Output filters can be used in combination with any **show** command.

Example 1-12 shows the usage of these various output filters.

**Example 1-12** Filtering **show** Commands

```
R1# show running-config | section line vty
line vty 0 4
 password 7 030752180500
 login
 transport input all
R1# show ip interface brief | include up
GigabitEthernet0/0        192.168.10.1     YES manual up              up
GigabitEthernet0/1        192.168.11.1     YES manual up              up
Serial0/0/0               209.165.200.225 YES manual up              up
R1# show ip interface brief | exclude unassigned
Interface                 IP-Address       OK? Method Status          Protocol
GigabitEthernet0/0        192.168.10.1     YES manual up              up
GigabitEthernet0/1        192.168.11.1     YES manual up              up
Serial0/0/0               209.165.200.225 YES manual up              up
```

```
R1# show ip route | begin Gateway
Gateway of last resort is not set


      192.168.10.0/24 is variably subnetted, 2 subnets, 2 masks
C        192.168.10.0/24 is directly connected, GigabitEthernet0/0
L        192.168.10.1/32 is directly connected, GigabitEthernet0/0
      192.168.11.0/24 is variably subnetted, 2 subnets, 2 masks
C        192.168.11.0/24 is directly connected, GigabitEthernet0/1
L        192.168.11.1/32 is directly connected, GigabitEthernet0/1
      209.165.200.0/24 is variably subnetted, 2 subnets, 2 masks
C        209.165.200.224/30 is directly connected, Serial0/0/0
L        209.165.200.225/32 is directly connected, Serial0/0/0
R1#
```

## Command History Feature (1.1.4.4)

The command history feature is useful because it temporarily stores the list of executed commands to be recalled.

To recall commands in the history buffer, press Ctrl+P or the Up Arrow key. The command output begins with the most recent command. Repeat the key sequence to recall successively older commands. To return to more recent commands in the history buffer, press Ctrl+N or the Down Arrow key. Repeat the key sequence to recall successively more recent commands.

By default, command history is enabled and the system captures the last 10 command lines in its history buffer. Use the **show history** privileged EXEC command to display the contents of the buffer.

It is also practical to increase the number of command lines that the history buffer records during the current terminal session only. Use the **terminal history size** user EXEC command to increase or decrease the size of the buffer.

Example 1-13 displays a sample of the **terminal history size** and **show history** commands.

**Example 1-13** Command History Feature

```
R1# terminal history size 200
R1# show history
  show ip interface brief
  show interface g0/0
  show ip interface g0/1
  show ip route
  show ip route 209.165.200.224
  show running-config interface s0/0/0
  terminal history size 200
  show history
R1#
```

**Packet Tracer 1.1.4.5: Configuring and Verifying a Small Network**

Background/Scenario

In this activity, you will configure a router with basic settings including IP addressing. You will also configure a switch for remote management and configure the PCs. After you have successfully verified connectivity, you will use **show** commands to gather information about the network.

**Lab 1.1.4.6: Configuring Basic Router Settings with IOS CLI**

In this lab, you will complete the following objectives:

- Part 1: Set Up the Topology and Initialize Devices
- Part 2: Configure Devices and Verify Connectivity
- Part 3: Display Router Information
- Part 4: Configure IPv6 and Verify Connectivity

# Routing Decisions (1.2)

This section explains how routers use information in data packets to make forwarding decisions in a small to medium-sized business network.

## Switching Packets Between Networks (1.2.1)

This topic explains the encapsulation and de-encapsulation process that routers use when switching packets between interfaces.

## Router Switching Function (1.2.1.1)

A primary function of a router is to forward packets toward their destination. This is accomplished by using a switching function, which is the process used by a router to accept a packet on one interface and forward it out another interface. A key responsibility of the switching function is to encapsulate packets in the appropriate data link frame type for the outgoing data link.

**Note**

In this context, the term "switching" literally means moving packets from source to destination and should not be confused with the function of a Layer 2 switch.

After the router has determined the exit interface using the path determination function, the router must encapsulate the packet into the data link frame of the outgoing interface.

What does a router do with a packet received from one network and destined for another network? Refer to Figure 1-23.

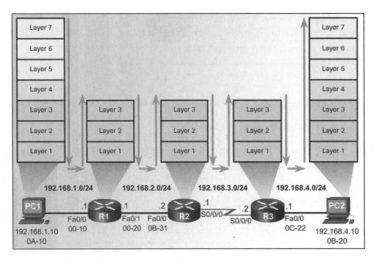

**Figure 1-23**   Encapsulating and De-Encapsulating Packets

The router performs the following three major steps:

**Step 1.**   De-encapsulates the Layer 2 frame header and trailer to expose the Layer 3 packet.

**Step 2.**   Examines the destination IP address of the IP packet to find the best path in the routing table.

**Step 3.**   If the router finds a path to the destination, it encapsulates the Layer 3 packet into a new Layer 2 frame and forwards the frame out the exit interface.

As shown in Figure 1-23, devices have Layer 3 IPv4 addresses, and Ethernet interfaces have Layer 2 data link addresses. For example, PC1 is configured with IPv4 address 192.168.1.10 and an example MAC address of 0A-10. As a packet travels from the source device to the final destination device, the Layer 3 IP addresses do not change. However, the Layer 2 data link addresses change at every hop as the packet is de-encapsulated and re-encapsulated in a new Layer 2 frame by each router.

It is common for packets to require encapsulation into a different type of Layer 2 frame than the one in which it was received. For example, a router might receive an Ethernet encapsulated frame on a FastEthernet interface and then process that frame to be forwarded out of a serial interface.

Notice in Figure 1-23 that the ports between R2 and R3 do not have associated MAC addresses. This is because it is a serial link. MAC addresses are only required on Ethernet multiaccess networks. A serial link is a point-to-point connection and uses a different Layer 2 frame that does not require the use of a MAC address. In this example, when Ethernet frames are received on R2 from the Fa0/0 interface, destined for PC2, they are de-encapsulated and then re-encapsulated for the serial interface, such as a *PPP* encapsulated frame. When R3 receives the PPP frame, it is de-encapsulated again and then re-encapsulated into an Ethernet frame with a destination MAC address of 0B-20, prior to being forwarded out the Fa0/0 interface.

## Send a Packet (1.2.1.2)

In Figure 1-24, PC1 is sending a packet to PC2. PC1 must determine if the destination IPv4 address is on the same network. PC1 determines its own subnet by doing an **AND** operation on its own IPv4 address and subnet mask. This produces the network address that PC1 belongs to. Next, PC1 does this same **AND** operation using the packet destination IPv4 address and the PC1 subnet mask.

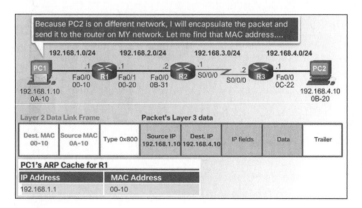

**Figure 1-24**   PC1 Sends a Packet to PC2

If the destination network address is the same network as PC1, then PC1 does not use the default gateway. Instead, PC1 refers to its Address Resolution Protocol (ARP) cache for the MAC address of the device with that destination IPv4 address. If the MAC address is not in the cache, then PC1 generates an ARP request to acquire the address to complete the packet and send it to the destination. If the destination network address is on a different network, then PC1 forwards the packet to its default gateway.

To determine the MAC address of the default gateway, PC1 checks its ARP table for the IPv4 address of the default gateway and its associated MAC address.

If an ARP entry does not exist in the ARP table for the default gateway, PC1 sends an ARP request. Router R1 sends back an ARP reply. PC1 can then forward the packet to the MAC address of the default gateway, the Fa0/0 interface of router R1.

A similar process is used for IPv6 packets. However, instead of the ARP process, IPv6 address resolution uses *ICMPv6 Neighbor Solicitation and Neighbor Advertisement messages*. IPv6-to-MAC address mappings are kept in a table similar to the ARP cache, called the *neighbor cache*.

### Forward to the Next Hop (1.2.1.3)

Figure 1-25 shows the processes that take place when R1 receives the Ethernet frame from PC1.

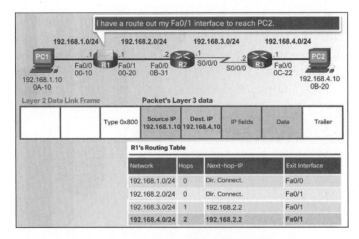

**Figure 1-25**   R1 Looks Up Route to Destination

1. R1 examines the destination MAC address, which matches the MAC address of the receiving interface on R1, FastEthernet 0/0. R1, therefore, copies the frame into its buffer.

2. R1 identifies the Ethernet Type field as $0 \times 800$, which means that the Ethernet frame contains an IPv4 packet in the data portion of the frame.

3. R1 de-encapsulates the Ethernet frame to examine the Layer 3 information.

4. Because the destination IPv4 address of the packet does not match any of the directly connected networks of R1, R1 consults its routing table to route this packet. R1 searches the routing table for a network address that would include the destination IPv4 address of the packet as a host address within that network. In this example, the routing table has a route for the 192.168.4.0/24 network. The destination IPv4 address of the packet is 192.168.4.10, which is a host IPv4 address on that network.

The route that R1 finds to the 192.168.4.0/24 network has a next-hop IPv4 address of 192.168.2.2 and an exit interface of FastEthernet 0/1. This means that the IPv4 packet is encapsulated in a new Ethernet frame with the destination MAC address of the IPv4 address of the next-hop router.

Figure 1-26 show the processes that take place when R1 forwards the packet to R2.

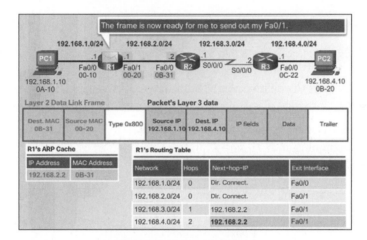

**Figure 1-26**   R1 Forwards Packet to R2

Because the exit interface is on an Ethernet network, R1 must resolve the next-hop IPv4 address with a destination MAC address using ARP:

1. R1 looks up the next-hop IPv4 address of 192.168.2.2 in its ARP cache. If the entry is not in the ARP cache, R1 would send an ARP request out of its FastEthernet 0/1 interface and R2 would return an ARP reply. R1 would then update its ARP cache with an entry for 192.168.2.2 and the associated MAC address.

2. The IPv4 packet is now encapsulated into a new Ethernet frame and forwarded out the FastEthernet 0/1 interface of R1.

## Packet Routing (1.2.1.4)

Figure 1-27 shows the processes that take place when R2 receives the frame on its Fa0/0 interface.

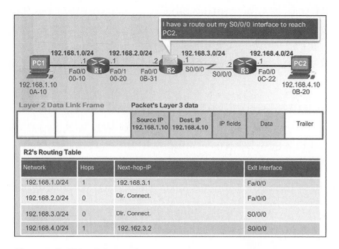

**Figure 1-27**   R2 Looks Up Route to Destination

1. R2 examines the destination MAC address, which matches the MAC address of the receiving interface, FastEthernet 0/0. R2, therefore, copies the frame into its buffer.

2. R2 identifies the Ethernet Type field as 0×800, which means that the Ethernet frame contains an IPv4 packet in the data portion of the frame.

3. R2 de-encapsulates the Ethernet frame.

Figure 1-28 shows the processes that take place when R2 forwards the packet to R3.

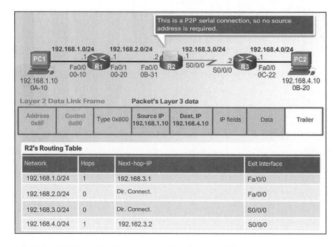

**Figure 1-28**   R2 Forwards Packet to R3

1. Because the destination IPv4 address of the packet does not match any of the interface addresses of R2, R2 consults its routing table to route this packet. R2 searches the routing table for the destination IPv4 address of the packet using the same process R1 used.

   The routing table of R2 has a route to the 192.168.4.0/24 network, with a next-hop IPv4 address of 192.168.3.2 and an exit interface of Serial 0/0/0. Because the exit interface is not an Ethernet network, R2 does not have to resolve the next-hop IPv4 address with a destination MAC address.

2. The IPv4 packet is now encapsulated into a new data link frame and sent out the Serial 0/0/0 exit interface.

When the interface is a point-to-point (P2P) serial connection, the router encapsulates the IPv4 packet into the proper data link frame format used by the exit interface (HDLC, PPP, and so on). Because there are no MAC addresses on serial interfaces, R2 sets the data link destination address to an equivalent of a broadcast.

## Reach the Destination (1.2.1.5)

The following processes take place when the frame arrives at R3:

1. R3 copies the data link PPP frame into its buffer.

2. R3 de-encapsulates the data link PPP frame.

3. R3 searches the routing table for the destination IPv4 address of the packet. The routing table has a route to a directly connected network on R3. This means that the packet can be sent directly to the destination device and does not need to be sent to another router.

Figure 1-29 shows the processes that take place when R3 forwards the packet to PC2.

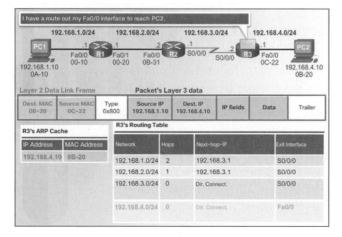

**Figure 1-29**   R3 Forwards Packet to PC2

Because the exit interface is a directly connected Ethernet network, R3 must resolve the destination IPv4 address of the packet with a destination MAC address:

1. R3 searches for the destination IPv4 address of the packet in its ARP cache. If the entry is not in the ARP cache, R3 sends an ARP request out of its FastEthernet 0/0 interface. PC2 sends back an ARP reply with its MAC address. R3 then updates its ARP cache with an entry for 192.168.4.10 and the MAC address that is returned in the ARP reply.

2. The IPv4 packet is encapsulated into a new Ethernet data link frame and sent out the FastEthernet 0/0 interface of R3.

3. When PC2 receives the frame, it examines the destination MAC address, which matches the MAC address of the receiving interface, its Ethernet network interface card (NIC). PC2, therefore, copies the rest of the frame into its buffer.

4. PC2 identifies the Ethernet Type field as $0\times800$, which means that the Ethernet frame contains an IPv4 packet in the data portion of the frame.

5. PC2 de-encapsulates the Ethernet frame and passes the IPv4 packet to the IPv4 process of its operating system.

**Interactive Graphic**

**Activity 1.2.1.6: Match Layer 2 and Layer 3 Addressing**

Refer to the online course to complete this activity.

# Path Determination (1.2.2)

A router refers to its routing table when making best path decisions. In this topic, we will examine the path determination function of a router.

## Routing Decisions (1.2.2.1)

A primary function of a router is to determine the best path to use to send packets. To determine the best path, the router searches its routing table for a network address that matches the destination IP address of the packet.

The routing table search results in one of three path determinations:

- **Directly connected network**—If the destination IP address of the packet belongs to a device on a network that is directly connected to one of the interfaces of the router, that packet is forwarded directly to the destination device. This means that the destination IP address of the packet is a host address on the same network as the interface of the router.

- **Remote network**—If the destination IP address of the packet belongs to a remote network, then the packet is forwarded to another router. Remote networks can only be reached by forwarding packets to another router.

- **No route determined**—If the destination IP address of the packet does not belong to either a connected or a remote network, the router determines if there is a Gateway of Last Resort available. A Gateway of Last Resort is set when a default route is configured or learned on a router. If there is a default route, the packet is forwarded to the Gateway of Last Resort. If the router does not have a default route, then the packet is discarded.

The logic flowchart in Figure 1-30 illustrates the router packet-forwarding decision process.

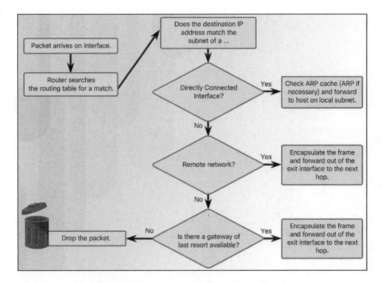

**Figure 1-30**   Packet-Forwarding Decision Process

## Best Path (1.2.2.2)

Determining the best path involves the evaluation of multiple paths to the same destination network and selecting the optimum or shortest path to reach that network. Whenever multiple paths to the same network exist, each path uses a different exit interface on the router to reach that network.

The best path is selected by a routing protocol based on the value or *metric* it uses to determine the distance to reach a network. A metric is the quantitative value used to measure the distance to a given network. The best path to a network is the path with the lowest metric.

Dynamic routing protocols typically use their own rules and metrics to build and update routing tables. The routing algorithm generates a value, or a metric, for each path through the network. Metrics can be based on either a single characteristic or several characteristics of a path. Some routing protocols can base route selection on multiple metrics, combining them into a single metric.

The following lists some dynamic protocols and the metrics they use:

- **Routing Information Protocol (RIP)**—Hop count

- **Open Shortest Path First (OSPF)**—Cisco's cost based on cumulative bandwidth from source to destination

- **Enhanced Interior Gateway Routing Protocol (EIGRP)**—Bandwidth, delay, load, reliability

Figure 1-31 highlights how the path may be different depending on the metric being used.

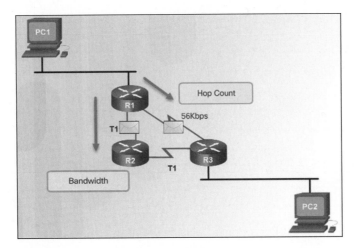

**Figure 1-31**   Hop Count Versus Bandwidth as a Metric

## Load Balancing (1.2.2.3)

What happens if a routing table has two or more paths with identical metrics to the same destination network?

When a router has two or more paths to a destination with equal cost metrics, then the router forwards the packets using both paths equally. This is called *equal cost load balancing*. The routing table contains the single destination network but has multiple exit interfaces, one for each equal cost path. The router forwards packets using the multiple exit interfaces listed in the routing table.

If configured correctly, load balancing can increase the effectiveness and performance of the network. Equal cost load balancing can be configured to use both dynamic routing protocols and static routes.

**Note**

Only EIGRP supports *unequal cost load balancing*.

Figure 1-32 provides an example of equal cost load balancing.

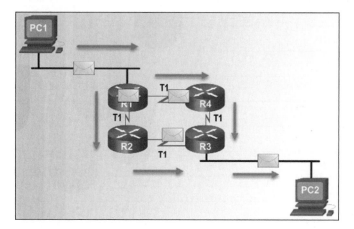

**Figure 1-32**   Equal Cost Load Balancing

## Administrative Distance (1.2.2.4)

It is possible for a router to be configured with multiple routing protocols and static routes. If this occurs, the routing table may have more than one route source for the same destination network. For example, if both RIP and EIGRP are configured on a router, both routing protocols may learn of the same destination network. However, each routing protocol may decide on a different path to reach the destination based on the metrics of that routing protocol. RIP chooses a path based on hop count, whereas EIGRP chooses a path based on its composite metric. How does the router know which route to use?

Cisco IOS uses what is known as the *administrative distance (AD)* to determine the route to install into the IP routing table. The AD represents the "trustworthiness" of the route; the lower the AD, the more trustworthy the route source. For example, a static route has an AD of 1, whereas an EIGRP-discovered route has an AD of 90. Given two separate routes to the same destination, the router chooses the route with the lowest AD. When a router has the choice of a static route and an EIGRP route, the static route takes precedence. Similarly, a directly connected route with an AD of 0 takes precedence over a static route with an AD of 1.

Table 1-4 lists various routing protocols and their associated ADs.

**Table 1-4** Default Administrative Distances

| Route Source | Administrative Distance |
|---|:---:|
| Connected | 0 |
| Static | 1 |
| EIGRP summary route | 5 |
| External BGP | 20 |
| Internal EIGRP | 90 |
| IGRP | 100 |
| OSPF | 110 |
| IS-IS | 115 |
| RIP | 120 |
| External EIGRP | 170 |
| Internal BGP | 200 |

**Interactive Graphic**

**Activity 1.2.2.5: Order the Steps in the Packet-Forwarding Process**

Refer to the online course to complete this activity.

**Interactive Graphic**

**Activity 1.2.2.6: Match the Administrative Distance to the Route Source**

Refer to the online course to complete this activity.

# Router Operation (1.3)

To make routing decisions, a router exchanges information with other routers. Alternatively, the router can also be manually configured on how to reach a specific network.

In this section you will explain how a router learns about remote networks when operating in a small to medium-sized business network.

# Analyze the Routing Table (1.3.1)

The routing table is at the heart of making routing decisions. It is important that you understand the information presented in a routing table. In this topic, you will learn about routing table entries for directly connected networks.

## The Routing Table (1.3.1.1)

The routing table of a router stores information about the following:

- *Directly connected routes*—These routes come from the active router interfaces. Routers add a directly connected route when an interface is configured with an IP address and is activated.

- *Remote routes*—These are remote networks connected to other routers. Routes to these networks can be either statically configured or dynamically learned through dynamic routing protocols.

Specifically, a routing table is a data file in RAM that stores route information about directly connected and remote networks. The routing table contains network or next-hop associations. These associations tell a router that a particular destination can be optimally reached by sending the packet to a specific router that represents the next hop on the way to the final destination. The next-hop association can also be the outgoing or exit interface to the next destination.

Figure 1-33 identifies the directly connected networks and remote networks of router R1.

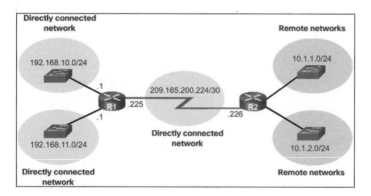

**Figure 1-33**   Directly Connected and Remote Network Routes

## Routing Table Sources (1.3.1.2)

On a Cisco router, the **show ip route** command is used to display the IPv4 routing table of a router. A router provides additional route information, including how the route was learned, how long the route has been in the table, and which specific interface to use to get to a predefined destination.

Entries in the routing table can be added as follows:

- *Local route interfaces*—Added when an interface is configured and active. This entry is only displayed in IOS 15 or newer for IPv4 routes and all IOS releases for IPv6 routes.

- *Directly connected interfaces*—Added to the routing table when an interface is configured and active.

- **Static routes**—Added when a route is manually configured and the exit interface is active.

- **Dynamic routing protocol**—Added when routing protocols that dynamically learn about the network, such as EIGRP and OSPF, are implemented and networks are identified.

The sources of the routing table entries are identified by a code. The code identifies how the route was learned. For instance, common codes include the following:

- **L**—Identifies the address assigned to a router's interface. This allows the router to efficiently determine when it receives a packet for the interface instead of being forwarded.

- **C**—Identifies a directly connected network.

- **S**—Identifies a static route created to reach a specific network.

- **D**—Identifies a dynamically learned network from another router using EIGRP.

- **O**—Identifies a dynamically learned network from another router using the OSPF routing protocol.

Example 1-14 shows the routing table for the R1 router in Figure 1-20.

**Example 1-14**  Routing Table for R1

```
R1# show ip route
Codes: L - local, C - connected, S - static, R - RIP, M - mobile, B - BGP
       D - EIGRP, EX - EIGRP external, O - OSPF, IA - OSPF inter area
       N1 - OSPF NSSA external type 1, N2 - OSPF NSSA external type 2
       E1 - OSPF external type 1, E2 - OSPF external type 2, E - EGP
       i - IS-IS, L1 - IS-IS level-1, L2 - IS-IS level-2, ia - IS-IS inter area
     * - candidate default, U - per-user static route, o - ODR
       P - periodic downloaded static route

Gateway of last resort is not set
```

```
        10.0.0.0/24 is subnetted, 2 subnets
D          10.1.1.0/24 [90/2170112] via 209.165.200.226, 00:01:30, Serial0/0/0
D          10.1.2.0/24 [90/2170112] via 209.165.200.226, 00:01:30, Serial0/0/0
        192.168.10.0/24 is variably subnetted, 2 subnets, 2 masks
C          192.168.10.0/24 is directly connected, GigabitEthernet0/0
L          192.168.10.1/32 is directly connected, GigabitEthernet0/0
        192.168.11.0/24 is variably subnetted, 2 subnets, 2 masks
C          192.168.11.0/24 is directly connected, GigabitEthernet0/1
L          192.168.11.1/32 is directly connected, GigabitEthernet0/1
        209.165.200.0/24 is variably subnetted, 2 subnets, 2 masks
C          209.165.200.224/30 is directly connected, Serial0/0/0
L          209.165.200.225/32 is directly connected, Serial0/0/0
R1#
```

## Remote Network Routing Entries (1.3.1.3)

As a network administrator, it is imperative to know how to interpret the content of IPv4 and IPv6 routing tables. Figure 1-34 displays an IPv4 routing table entry on R1 for the route to remote network 10.1.1.0.

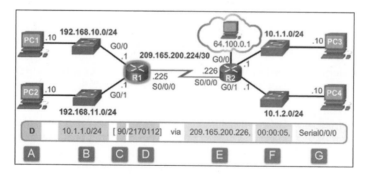

**Figure 1-34**   Remote Network Entry Identifiers

Table 1-5 describes the parts of the routing table entry shown in Figure 1-34.

**Table 1-5**   Parts of a Remote Network Entry

| Legend | Name | Description |
|--------|------|-------------|
| A | Route Source | Identifies how the route was learned. |
| B | Destination Network | Identifies the IPv4 address of the remote network. |
| C | Administrative Distance | Identifies the trustworthiness of the route source. Lower values indicate preferred route source. |

| Legend | Name | Description |
|--------|------|-------------|
| D | Metric | Identifies the value assigned to reach the remote network. Lower values indicate preferred routes. |
| E | Next Hop | Identifies the IPv4 address of the next router to forward the packet to. |
| F | Route Timestamp | Identifies how much time has passed since the route was learned. |
| G | Outgoing Interface | Identifies the exit interface to use to forward a packet toward the final destination. |

**Interactive Graphic**

**Activity 1.3.1.4: Interpret the Content of a Routing Table Entry**

Refer to the online course to complete this activity.

## Directly Connected Routes (1.3.2)

In this topic you will learn how a router builds a routing table of directly connected networks.

### Directly Connected Interfaces (1.3.2.1)

A newly deployed router, without configured interfaces, has an empty routing table, as shown in Example 1-15.

**Example 1-15** Empty Routing Table

```
R1# show ip route
Codes: L - local, C - connected, S - static, R - RIP, M - mobile, B - BGP
       D - EIGRP, EX - EIGRP external, O - OSPF, IA - OSPF inter area
       N1 - OSPF NSSA external type 1, N2 - OSPF NSSA external type 2
       E1 - OSPF external type 1, E2 - OSPF external type 2, E - EGP
       i - IS-IS, L1 - IS-IS level-1, L2 - IS-IS level-2, ia - IS-IS inter area
       * - candidate default, U - per-user static route, o - ODR
       P - periodic downloaded static route

Gateway of last resort is not set

R1#
```

Before the interface state is considered up/up and added to the IPv4 routing table, the interface must

- Be assigned a valid IPv4 or IPv6 address

- Be activated with the **no shutdown** command

- Receive a carrier signal from another device (router, switch, host, and so on)

When the interface is up, the network of that interface is added to the routing table as a directly connected network.

## Directly Connected Routing Table Entries (1.3.2.2)

An active, properly configured, directly connected interface actually creates two routing table entries. Figure 1-35 displays the IPv4 routing table entries on R1 for the directly connected network 192.168.10.0.

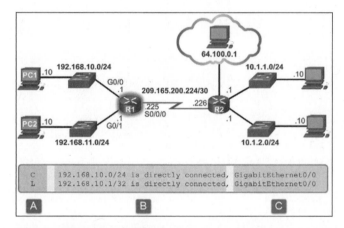

**Figure 1-35**    Directly Connected Network Entry Identifiers

The routing table entry for directly connected interfaces is simpler than the entries for remote networks. Table 1-6 describes the parts of the routing table entry shown in Figure 1-35.

**Table 1-6**    Parts of a Directly Connected Network Entry

| Legend | Name | Description |
|---|---|---|
| A | Route Source | Identifies how the network was learned by the router. Directly connected interfaces have two route source codes. 'C' identifies a directly connected network. 'L' identifies the IPv4 address assigned to the router's interface. |
| B | Destination Network | Identifies the destination network and how it is connected. |
| C | Outgoing Interface | Identifies the exit interface to use when forwarding packets to the destination network. |

**Note**

Prior to IOS 15, local route routing table entries (L) were not displayed in the IPv4 routing table. Local route (L) entries have always been part of the IPv6 routing table.

## Directly Connected Examples (1.3.2.3)

Example 1-16 shows the steps to configure and activate the interfaces attached to R1 in Figure 1-20. Notice the Layer 1 and 2 informational messages generated as each interface is activated.

**Example 1-16**  Configuring the Directly Connected IPv4 Interfaces

```
R1(config)# interface gigabitethernet 0/0
R1(config-if)# description Link to LAN 1
R1(config-if)# ip address 192.168.10.1 255.255.255.0
R1(config-if)# no shutdown
R1(config-if)# exit
*Feb  1 13:37:35.035: %LINK-3-UPDOWN: Interface GigabitEthernet0/0, changed state
  to down
*Feb  1 13:37:38.211: %LINK-3-UPDOWN: Interface GigabitEthernet0/0, changed state
  to up
*Feb  1 13:37:39.211: %LINEPROTO-5-UPDOWN: Line protocol on Interface Gigabit
  Ethernet0/0, changed state to up
R1(config)# interface gigabitethernet 0/1
R1(config-if)# description Link to LAN 2
R1(config-if)# ip address 192.168.11.1 255.255.255.0
R1(config-if)# no shutdown
R1(config-if)# exit
*Feb  1 13:38:01.471: %LINK-3-UPDOWN: Interface GigabitEthernet0/1, changed state
  to down
*Feb  1 13:38:04.211: %LINK-3-UPDOWN: Interface GigabitEthernet0/1, changed state
  to up
*Feb  1 13:38:05.211: %LINEPROTO-5-UPDOWN: Line protocol on Interface Gigabit
  Ethernet0/1, changed state to up
R1(config)# interface serial 0/0/0
R1(config-if)# description Link to R1
R1(config-if)# ip address 209.165.200.225 255.255.255.252
R1(config-if)# clock rate 128000
R1(config-if)# no shutdown
R1(config-if)# end
*Feb  1 13:38:22.723: %LINK-3-UPDOWN: Interface Serial0/0/0, changed state to up
*Feb  1 13:38:23.723: %LINEPROTO-5-UPDOWN: Line protocol on Interface Serial0/0/0,
  changed state to up
R1#
```

As each interface is added, the routing table automatically adds the connected ('C') and local ('L') entries. Example 1-17 provides an example of the routing table with the directly connected interfaces of R1 configured and activated.

**Example 1-17** Verifying the Directly Connected Routing Table Entries

```
R1# show ip route | begin Gateway
Gateway of last resort is not set


      192.168.10.0/24 is variably subnetted, 2 subnets, 2 masks
C        192.168.10.0/24 is directly connected, GigabitEthernet0/0
L        192.168.10.1/32 is directly connected, GigabitEthernet0/0
      192.168.11.0/24 is variably subnetted, 2 subnets, 2 masks
C        192.168.11.0/24 is directly connected, GigabitEthernet0/1
L        192.168.11.1/32 is directly connected, GigabitEthernet0/1
      209.165.200.0/24 is variably subnetted, 2 subnets, 2 masks
C        209.165.200.224/30 is directly connected, Serial0/0/0
L        209.165.200.225/32 is directly connected, Serial0/0/0
R1#
```

## Directly Connected IPv6 Example (1.3.2.4)

Example 1-18 shows the configuration steps for the directly connected interfaces of R1 in Figure 1-21 with the indicated IPv6 addresses. Notice the Layer 1 and Layer 2 informational messages generated as each interface is configured and activated.

**Example 1-18** Configuring the Directly Connected IPv6 Interfaces

```
R1(config)# interface gigabitethernet 0/0
R1(config-if)# description Link to LAN 1
R1(config-if)# ipv6 address 2001:db8:acad:1::1/64
R1(config-if)# no shutdown
R1(config-if)# exit
*Feb  3 21:38:37.279: %LINK-3-UPDOWN: Interface GigabitEthernet0/0, changed state
  to down
*Feb  3 21:38:40.967: %LINK-3-UPDOWN: Interface GigabitEthernet0/0, changed state
  to up
*Feb  3 21:38:41.967: %LINEPROTO-5-UPDOWN: Line protocol on Interface GigabitEther-
  net0/0, changed state to up
R1(config)# interface gigabitethernet 0/1
R1(config-if)# description Link to LAN 2
R1(config-if)# ipv6 address 2001:db8:acad:2::1/64
R1(config-if)# no shutdown
R1(config-if)# exit
```

```
*Feb  3 21:39:21.867: %LINK-3-UPDOWN: Interface GigabitEthernet0/1, changed state
  to down
*Feb  3 21:39:24.967: %LINK-3-UPDOWN: Interface GigabitEthernet0/1, changed state
  to up
*Feb  3 21:39:25.967: %LINEPROTO-5-UPDOWN: Line protocol on Interface Gigabit
  Ethernet0/1, changed state to up
R1(config)# interface serial 0/0/0
R1(config-if)# description Link to R2
R1(config-if)# ipv6 address 2001:db8:acad:3::1/64
R1(config-if)# clock rate 128000
R1(config-if)# no shutdown
*Feb  3 21:39:43.307: %LINK-3-UPDOWN: Interface Serial0/0/0, changed state to down
R1(config-if)# end
R1#
```

The **show ipv6 route** command shown in Example 1-19 is used to verify that
IPv6 networks and specific IPv6 interface addresses have been installed in the
IPv6 routing table. Like IPv4, a 'C' next to a route indicates that this is a directly
connected network. An 'L' indicates the local route. In an IPv6 network, the local
route has a /128 prefix. Local routes are used by the routing table to efficiently
process packets with a destination address of the interface of the router.

**Example 1-19**  Verifying IPv6 Routing Table

```
R1# show ipv6 route
IPv6 Routing Table - default - 5 entries
Codes: C - Connected, L - Local, S - Static, U - Per-user Static route
       B - BGP, R - RIP, H - NHRP, I1 - ISIS L1
       I2 - ISIS L2, IA - ISIS interarea, IS - ISIS summary, D - EIGRP
       EX - EIGRP external, ND - ND Default, NDp - ND Prefix, DCE - Destination
       NDr - Redirect, O - OSPF Intra, OI - OSPF Inter, OE1 - OSPF ext 1
       OE2 - OSPF ext 2, ON1 - OSPF NSSA ext 1, ON2 - OSPF NSSA ext 2
C    2001:DB8:ACAD:1::/64 [0/0]
      via GigabitEthernet0/0, directly connected
L    2001:DB8:ACAD:1::1/128 [0/0]
      via GigabitEthernet0/0, receive
C    2001:DB8:ACAD:2::/64 [0/0]
      via GigabitEthernet0/1, directly connected
L    2001:DB8:ACAD:2::1/128 [0/0]
      via GigabitEthernet0/1, receive
L    FF00::/8 [0/0]
      via Null0, receive
R1#
```

Notice that there is also a route installed to the FF00::/8 network. This route is required for multicast routing.

Example 1-20 displays how the **show ipv6 route** command can be combined with a specific network destination to display the details of how the router learned that route.

**Example 1-20** Verifying a Single IPv6 Route Entry

```
R1# show ipv6 route 2001:db8:acad:1::/64
Routing entry for 2001:DB8:ACAD:1::/64
  Known via "connected", distance 0, metric 0, type connected
  Route count is 1/1, share count 0
  Routing paths:
    directly connected via GigabitEthernet0/0
      Last updated 03:14:56 ago

R1#
```

Example 1-21 displays how connectivity to R2 can be verified using the **ping** command. Notice what happens when the G0/0 LAN interface of R2 is the target of the **ping** command. The pings are unsuccessful. This is because R1 does not have an entry in the routing table to reach the 2001:DB8:ACAD:4::/64 network.

**Example 1-21** Testing Connectivity to R2

```
R1# ping 2001:db8:acad:3::2
Type escape sequence to abort.
Sending 5, 100-byte ICMP Echos to 2001:DB8:ACAD:3::2, timeout is 2 seconds:
!!!!!
Success rate is 100 percent (5/5), round-trip min/avg/max = 12/13/16 ms
R1# ping 2001:db8:acad:4::1
Type escape sequence to abort.
Sending 5, 100-byte ICMP Echos to 2001:DB8:ACAD:4::1, timeout is 2 seconds:

% No valid route for destination
Success rate is 0 percent (0/1)
R1#
```

R1 requires additional information to reach a remote network. Remote network route entries can be added to the routing table using either of the following:

- Static routing
- Dynamic routing protocols

**Packet Tracer 1.3.2.5: Investigating Directly Connected Routes**

Background

The network in the activity is already configured. You will log in to the routers and use **show** commands to discover and answer the questions below about the directly connected routes.

# Statically Learned Routes (1.3.3)

In this topic you will learn how a router builds a routing table using static routes.

## Static Routes (1.3.3.1)

After directly connected interfaces are configured and added to the routing table, static or dynamic routing can be implemented.

Static routes are manually configured. They define an explicit path between two networking devices. Unlike a dynamic routing protocol, static routes are not automatically updated and must be manually reconfigured if the network topology changes. The benefits of using static routes include improved security and resource efficiency. Static routes use less bandwidth than dynamic routing protocols, and no CPU cycles are used to calculate and communicate routes. The main disadvantage to using static routes is the lack of automatic reconfiguration if the network topology changes.

There are two common types of static routes in the routing table:

- Static route to a specific network
- Default static route

A static route can be configured to reach a specific remote network. IPv4 static routes are configured using the following command:

```
Router(config)# ip route network mask { next-hop-ip | exit-intf }
```

A static route is identified in the routing table with the code 'S.'

A *default static route* is similar to a default gateway on a host. The default static route specifies the exit point to use when the routing table does not contain a path for the destination network. A default static route is useful when a router has only one exit point to another router, such as when the router connects to a central router or service provider.

To configure an IPv4 default static route, use the following command:

```
Router(config)# ip route 0.0.0.0 0.0.0.0 { exit-intf | next-hop-ip }
```

Figure 1-36 provides a simple scenario of how default and static routes can be applied.

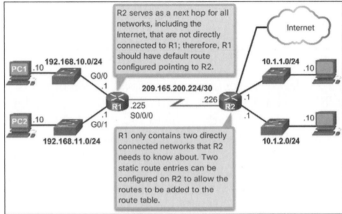

**Figure 1-36** Static and Default Route Scenario

## Static Route Examples (1.3.3.2)

Example 1-22 shows the configuration and verification of an IPv4 default static route on R1 from Figure 1-20. The static route is using Serial 0/0/0 as the exit interface. Notice that the configuration of the route generated an 'S*' entry in the routing table. The 'S' signifies that the route source is a static route, whereas the asterisk (*) identifies this route as a possible candidate to be the default route. In fact, it has been chosen as the default route as evidenced by the line that reads, "Gateway of Last Resort is 0.0.0.0 to network 0.0.0.0."

**Example 1-22** Configuring and Verifying a Default Static IPv4 Route

```
R1(config)# ip route 0.0.0.0 0.0.0.0 Serial0/0/0
R1(config)# exit
R1#
*Feb  1 10:19:34.483: %SYS-5-CONFIG_I: Configured from console by console
R1# show ip route | begin Gateway
Gateway of last resort is 0.0.0.0 to network 0.0.0.0

S*      0.0.0.0/0 is directly connected, Serial0/0/0
        192.168.10.0/24 is variably subnetted, 2 subnets, 2 masks
C          192.168.10.0/24 is directly connected, GigabitEthernet0/0
L          192.168.10.1/32 is directly connected, GigabitEthernet0/0
        192.168.11.0/24 is variably subnetted, 2 subnets, 2 masks
```

```
C           192.168.11.0/24 is directly connected, GigabitEthernet0/1
L           192.168.11.1/32 is directly connected, GigabitEthernet0/1
         209.165.200.0/24 is variably subnetted, 2 subnets, 2 masks
C           209.165.200.224/30 is directly connected, Serial0/0/0
L           209.165.200.225/32 is directly connected, Serial0/0/0
R1#
```

Example 1-23 shows the configuration and verification of two static routes from R2 to reach the two LANs on R1. The route to 192.168.10.0/24 has been configured using the exit interface while the route to 192.168.11.0/24 has been configured using the next-hop IPv4 address. Although both are acceptable, there are some differences in how they operate. For instance, notice how different they look in the routing table. Also notice that because these static routes were to specific networks, the output indicates that the Gateway of Last Resort is not set.

**Example 1-23** Configuring and Verifying Static IPv4 Routes

```
R2(config)# ip route 192.168.10.0 255.255.255.0 s0/0/0
R2(config)# ip route 192.168.11.0 255.255.255.0 209.165.200.225
R2(config)# exit
R2#
R2# show ip route | begin Gateway
Gateway of last resort is not set

         10.0.0.0/8 is variably subnetted, 4 subnets, 2 masks
C           10.1.1.0/24 is directly connected, GigabitEthernet0/0
L           10.1.1.1/32 is directly connected, GigabitEthernet0/0
C           10.1.2.0/24 is directly connected, GigabitEthernet0/1
L           10.1.2.1/32 is directly connected, GigabitEthernet0/1
S           192.168.10.0/24 is directly connected, Serial0/0/0
S           192.168.11.0/24 [1/0] via 209.165.200.225
         209.165.200.0/24 is variably subnetted, 2 subnets, 2 masks
C           209.165.200.224/30 is directly connected, Serial0/0/0
L           209.165.200.226/32 is directly connected, Serial0/0/0
R2#
```

**Note**

Static and default static routes are discussed in detail in the next chapter.

## Static IPv6 Route Examples (1.3.3.3)

Like IPv4, IPv6 supports static and default static routes. They are used and configured like IPv4 static routes.

To configure a default static IPv6 route, use the **ipv6 route ::/0** {*ipv6-address* | *interface-type interface-number*} global configuration command.

Example 1-24 shows the configuration and verification of a default static route on R1 from Figure 1-21. The static route is using Serial 0/0/0 as the exit interface.

**Example 1-24** Configuring and Verifying a Default Static IPv6 Route

```
R1(config)# ipv6 route ::/0 s0/0/0
R1(config)# exit
R1# show ipv6 route
IPv6 Routing Table - default - 8 entries
Codes: C - Connected, L - Local, S - Static, U - Per-user Static route
       B - BGP, R - RIP, H - NHRP, I1 - ISIS L1
       I2 - ISIS L2, IA - ISIS interarea, IS - ISIS summary, D - EIGRP
       EX - EIGRP external, ND - ND Default, NDp - ND Prefix, DCE - Destination
       NDr - Redirect, O - OSPF Intra, OI - OSPF Inter, OE1 - OSPF ext 1
       OE2 - OSPF ext 2, ON1 - OSPF NSSA ext 1, ON2 - OSPF NSSA ext 2
S    ::/0 [1/0]
     via Serial0/0/0, directly connected
<output omitted>
```

Notice in the output that the default static route configuration generated an 'S' entry in the routing table. The 'S' signifies that the route source is a static route. Unlike the IPv4 static route, there is no asterisk (*) or Gateway of Last Resort explicitly identified.

Like IPv4, static routes are routes explicitly configured to reach a specific remote network. Static IPv6 routes are configured using the **ipv6 route** *ipv6-prefix/ prefix-length* {*ipv6-address*|*interface-type interface-number*} global configuration command.

Example 1-25 shows the configuration and verification of two static routes from R2 to reach the two LANs on R1. The route to the 2001:0DB8:ACAD:2::/64 LAN is configured with an exit interface, whereas the route to the 2001:0DB8:ACAD:1::/64 LAN is configured with the next-hop IPv6 address. The next-hop IPv6 address can be either an IPv6 global unicast or a link-local address.

**Example 1-25** Configuring and Verifying Static IPv6 Routes

```
R2(config)# ipv6 route 2001:DB8:ACAD:1::/64 2001:DB8:ACAD:3::1
R2(config)# ipv6 route 2001:DB8:ACAD:2::/64 s0/0/0
R2(config)# end
R2# show ipv6 route
IPv6 Routing Table - default - 9 entries
Codes:  C - Connected, L - Local, S - Static, U - Per-user Static route
        B - BGP, R - RIP, H - NHRP, I1 - ISIS L1
        I2 - ISIS L2, IA - ISIS interarea, IS - ISIS summary, D - EIGRP
        EX - EIGRP external, ND - ND Default, NDp - ND Prefix, DCE - Destination
        NDr - Redirect, O - OSPF Intra, OI - OSPF Inter, OE1 - OSPF ext 1
        OE2 - OSPF ext 2, ON1 - OSPF NSSA ext 1, ON2 - OSPF NSSA ext 2
S    2001:DB8:ACAD:1::/64 [1/0]
     via 2001:DB8:ACAD:3::1
S    2001:DB8:ACAD:2::/64 [1/0]
     via Serial0/0/0, directly connected
<output omitted>
```

Example 1-26 confirms remote network connectivity to the 2001:0DB8:ACAD:4::/64 LAN on R2 from R1.

**Example 1-26** Verify Connectivity to Remote Network

```
R1# ping 2001:db8:acad:4::1
Type escape sequence to abort.
Sending 5, 100-byte ICMP Echos to 2001:DB8:ACAD:4::1, timeout is 2 seconds:
!!!!!
Success rate is 100 percent (5/5), round-trip min/avg/max = 12/13/16 ms
R1#
```

# Dynamic Routing Protocols (1.3.4)

In this topic you will learn how a router builds a routing table using dynamic routes.

## Dynamic Routing (1.3.4.1)

Dynamic routing protocols are used by routers to share information about the reachability and status of remote networks. Dynamic routing protocols perform several activities, including network discovery and maintaining routing tables.

Network discovery is the ability of a routing protocol to share information about the networks that it knows about with other routers that are also using the same routing protocol. Instead of depending on manually configured static routes to remote networks on every router, a dynamic routing protocol allows the routers to automatically learn about these networks from other routers. These networks, and the best path to each, are added to the routing table of the router and identified as a network learned by a specific dynamic routing protocol.

During network discovery, routers exchange routes and update their routing tables. Routers have converged after they have finished exchanging and updating their routing tables. Routers then maintain the networks in their routing tables.

Figure 1-37 provides a simple scenario of how two neighboring routers would initially exchange routing information. In this simplified exchange, R1 introduces itself and the networks it can reach. R2 responds with its list of networks.

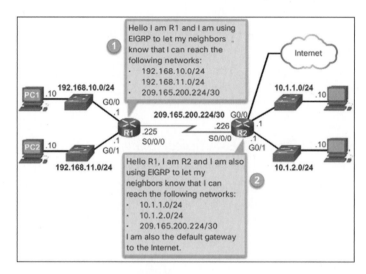

**Figure 1-37**   Dynamic Routing Scenario

## IPv4 Routing Protocols (1.3.4.2)

A router running a dynamic routing protocol does not only make a best path determination to a network; it also determines a new best path if the initial path becomes unusable (or if the topology changes). For these reasons, dynamic routing protocols have an advantage over static routes. Routers that use dynamic routing protocols automatically share routing information with other routers and compensate for any topology changes without involving the network administrator.

Cisco routers can support a variety of dynamic IPv4 routing protocols, including these:

- **EIGRP**—Enhanced Interior Gateway Routing Protocol
- **OSPF**—Open Shortest Path First
- **IS-IS**—Intermediate System-to-Intermediate System
- **RIP**—Routing Information Protocol

To determine which routing protocols the IOS supports, use the **router ?** command in global configuration mode, as shown in Example 1-27.

**Example 1-27** IPv4 Routing Protocols

```
R1(config)# router ?
  bgp        Border Gateway Protocol (BGP)
  eigrp      Enhanced Interior Gateway Routing Protocol (EIGRP)
  isis       ISO IS-IS
  iso-igrp   IGRP for OSI networks
  mobile     Mobile routes
  odr        On Demand stub Routes
  ospf       Open Shortest Path First (OSPF)
  ospfv3     OSPFv3
  rip        Routing Information Protocol (RIP)

R1(config)# router
```

## IPv4 Dynamic Routing Examples (1.3.4.3)

In this dynamic routing example, assume that R1 and R2 have been configured to support the dynamic routing protocol EIGRP. R2 now has a connection to the Internet, as shown in Figure 1-38. The routers also advertise directly connected networks. R2 advertises that it is the default gateway to other networks.

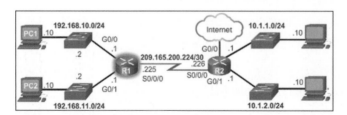

**Figure 1-38** IPv4 Topology with Connection to the Internet

The output in Example 1-28 displays the routing table of R1 after the routers have exchanged updates and converged.

**Example 1-28** Verify Dynamic IPv4 Routes

```
R1# show ip route | begin Gateway

Gateway of last resort is 209.165.200.226 to network 0.0.0.0

D*EX  0.0.0.0/0 [170/2297856] via 209.165.200.226, 00:07:29, Serial0/0/0
        10.0.0.0/24 is subnetted, 2 subnets
```

```
D          10.1.1.0 [90/2172416] via 209.165.200.226, 00:07:29, Serial0/0/0
D          10.1.2.0 [90/2172416] via 209.165.200.226, 00:07:29, Serial0/0/0
      192.168.10.0/24 is variably subnetted, 2 subnets, 2 masks
C        192.168.10.0/24 is directly connected, GigabitEthernet0/0
L        192.168.10.1/32 is directly connected, GigabitEthernet0/0
      192.168.11.0/24 is variably subnetted, 2 subnets, 2 masks
C        192.168.11.0/24 is directly connected, GigabitEthernet0/1
L        192.168.11.1/32 is directly connected, GigabitEthernet0/1
      209.165.200.0/24 is variably subnetted, 2 subnets, 2 masks
C        209.165.200.224/30 is directly connected, Serial0/0/0
L        209.165.200.225/32 is directly connected, Serial0/0/0
R1#
```

Along with the connected and link-local interfaces, there are three 'D' entries in the routing table.

■ The entry beginning with 'D*EX' identifies that the source of this entry was EIGRP ('D'). The route is a candidate to be a default route ("*"), and the route is an external route ("*EX") forwarded by EIGRP.

■ The other two 'D' entries are routes installed in the routing table based on the update from R2 advertising its LANs.

## IPv6 Routing Protocols (1.3.4.4)

ISR devices support the dynamic IPv6 routing protocols shown in Example 1-29.

**Example 1-29** IPv6 Routing Protocols

```
R1(config)# ipv6 router ?
  eigrp      Enhanced Interior Gateway Routing Protocol (EIGRP)
  ospf       Open Shortest Path First (OSPF)
  rip        IPv6 Routing Information Protocol (RIPv6)

R1(config)# ipv6 router
```

Support for dynamic IPv6 routing protocols is dependent on hardware and IOS version. Most of the modifications in the routing protocols are to support the longer IPv6 addresses and different header structures.

IPv6 routing is not enabled by default. Therefore, to enable IPv6 routers to forward traffic, you must configure the **ipv6 unicast-routing** global configuration command.

## IPv6 Dynamic Routing Examples (1.3.4.5)

Routers R1 and R2 in Figure 1-21 have been configured with the dynamic routing protocol EIGRP for IPv6. (This is the IPv6 equivalent of EIGRP for IPv4.)

To view the routing table on R1, enter the **show ipv6 route** command, as shown in Example 1-30.

**Example 1-30** Verify Dynamic IPv6 Routes

```
R1# show ipv6 route
IPv6 Routing Table - default - 9 entries
Codes:  C - Connected, L - Local, S - Static, U - Per-user Static route
        B - BGP, R - RIP, H - NHRP, I1 - ISIS L1
        I2 - ISIS L2, IA - ISIS interarea, IS - ISIS summary, D - EIGRP
        EX - EIGRP external, ND - ND Default, NDp - ND Prefix, DCE - Destination
        NDr - Redirect, O - OSPF Intra, OI - OSPF Inter, OE1 - OSPF ext 1
        OE2 - OSPF ext 2, ON1 - OSPF NSSA ext 1, ON2 - OSPF NSSA ext 2
C    2001:DB8:ACAD:1::/64 [0/0]
     via GigabitEthernet0/0, directly connected
L    2001:DB8:ACAD:1::1/128 [0/0]
     via GigabitEthernet0/0, receive
C    2001:DB8:ACAD:2::/64 [0/0]
     via GigabitEthernet0/1, directly connected
L    2001:DB8:ACAD:2::1/128 [0/0]
     via GigabitEthernet0/1, receive
C    2001:DB8:ACAD:3::/64 [0/0]
     via Serial0/0/0, directly connected
L    2001:DB8:ACAD:3::1/128 [0/0]
     via Serial0/0/0, receive
D    2001:DB8:ACAD:4::/64 [90/2172416]
     via FE80::D68C:B5FF:FECE:A120, Serial0/0/0
D    2001:DB8:ACAD:5::/64 [90/2172416]
     via FE80::D68C:B5FF:FECE:A120, Serial0/0/0
L    FF00::/8 [0/0]
     via Null0, receive
R1#
```

The output shows the routing table of R1 after the routers have exchanged updates and converged. Along with the connected and local routes, there are two 'D' entries (EIGRP routes) in the routing table.

# Summary (1.4)

**Class Activity 1.4.1.1: We Really Could Use a Map!**

Scenario

Use the Ashland and Richmond routing tables shown in the file provided with this activity.

With the help of a classmate, draw a network topology using the information from the tables.

To assist you with this activity, follow these guidelines:

- Start with the Ashland router; use its routing table to identify ports and IP addresses/networks.

- Add the Richmond router; use its routing table to identify ports and IP addresses/networks.

- Add any other intermediary and end devices as specified by the tables.

In addition, record answers from your group to the reflection questions provided with this activity.

Be prepared to share your work with another group or the class.

---

There are many key structures and performance-related characteristics referred to when discussing networks: topology, speed, cost, security, availability, scalability, and reliability.

Cisco routers and Cisco switches have many similarities. They support a similar modal operating system, similar command structures, and many of the same commands. One distinguishing feature between switches and routers is the type of interfaces supported by each. Once an interface is configured on both devices, the appropriate **show** commands need to be used to verify a working interface.

The main purpose of a router is to connect multiple networks and forward packets from one network to the next. This means that a router typically has multiple interfaces. Each interface is a member or host on a different IP network.

Cisco IOS uses what is known as the administrative distance (AD) to determine the route to install into the IP routing table. The routing table is a list of networks the router knows. The routing table includes network addresses for its own interfaces, which are the directly connected networks, as well as network addresses for remote networks. A remote network is a network that can only be reached by forwarding the packet to another router.

Remote networks are added to the routing table in two ways: either by the network administrator manually configuring static routes or by implementing a dynamic routing protocol. Static routes do not have as much overhead as dynamic routing protocols; however, static routes can require more maintenance if the topology is constantly changing or is unstable.

Dynamic routing protocols automatically adjust to changes without intervention from the network administrator. Dynamic routing protocols require more CPU processing and use a certain amount of link capacity for routing updates and messages. In many cases, a routing table will contain both static and dynamic routes.

Routers make their primary forwarding decision at Layer 3, the network layer. However, router interfaces participate in Layers 1, 2, and 3. Layer 3 IP packets are encapsulated into a Layer 2 data link frame and encoded into bits at Layer 1. Router interfaces participate in Layer 2 processes associated with their encapsulation. For example, an Ethernet interface on a router participates in the ARP process like other hosts on that LAN.

The Cisco IP routing table is not a flat database. The routing table is actually a hierarchical structure that is used to speed up the lookup process when locating routes and forwarding packets.

Components of the IPv6 routing table are similar to the IPv4 routing table. For instance, it is populated using directly connected interfaces, static routes, and dynamically learned routes.

## Practice

The following activities provide practice with the topics introduced in this chapter. The Labs and Class Activities are available in the companion *Routing and Switching Essentials v6 Labs and Study Guide* (ISBN 9781587134265). The Packet Tracer Activities PKA files are found in the online course.

**Class Activities**

Class Activity 1.0.1.2: Do We Really Need a Map Final

Class Activity 1.4.1.1: We Really Could Use A Map

**Labs**

Lab 1.1.1.9: Mapping the Internet

Lab 1.1.4.6: Configuring Basic Router Settings with IOS CLI

Packet Tracer
☐ Activity

**Packet Tracer Activities**

Packet Tracer 1.1.1.8: Using Traceroute to Discover the Network

Packet Tracer 1.1.2.9: Documenting the Network

Packet Tracer 1.1.3.5: Configuring IPv4 and IPv6 Interfaces

Packet Tracer 1.1.4.5: Configuring and Verifying a Small Network

Packet Tracer 1.3.2.5: Investigating Directly Connected Routes

# Check Your Understanding Questions

Complete all the review questions listed here to test your understanding of the topics and concepts in this chapter. The appendix, "Answers to the 'Check Your Understanding' Questions," lists the answers.

1. Which of the following correctly explains a network characteristic?

   A. Availability indicates how easily the network can accommodate more users and data transmission requirements.

   B. Reliability is often measured as a probability of failure or as the mean time between failures (MTBF).

   C. Scalability is the likelihood that the network is available for use when it is required.

   D. Usability is how effectively end users can use the network.

2. What are two functions of a router? (Choose two.)

   A. It connects multiple IP networks.

   B. It controls the flow of data via the use of Layer 2 addresses.

   C. It determines the best path to send packets.

   D. It increases the size of the broadcast domain.

   E. It manages the VLAN database.

3. Which two statements correctly describe the concepts of administrative distance and metric? (Choose two.)

   A. Administrative distance refers to the trustworthiness of a particular route.

   B. A router first installs routes with higher administrative distances.

   C. Routes with the smallest metric to a destination indicate the best path.

   D. The metric is always determined based on hop count.

E.  The metric varies depending which Layer 3 protocol is being routed, such as IP.

F.  The value of the administrative distance cannot be altered by the network administrator.

4.  For packets to be sent to a remote destination, what three pieces of information must be configured on a host? (Choose three.)

A.  Default gateway

B.  DHCP server address

C.  DNS server address

D.  Hostname

E.  IP address

F.  Subnet mask

5.  What is a characteristic of an IPv4 loopback interface on a Cisco IOS router?

A.  It is a logical interface internal to the router.

B.  It is assigned to a physical port and can be connected to other devices.

C.  Only one loopback interface can be enabled on a router.

D.  The **no shutdown** command is required to place this interface in an "up" state.

6.  What two pieces of information are displayed in the output of the **show ip interface brief** command? (Choose two.)

A.  Interface descriptions

B.  IP addresses

C.  Layer 1 statuses

D.  MAC addresses

E.  Next-hop addresses

F.  Speed and duplex settings

7.  A packet moves from a host on one network to a device on a remote network within the same company. In most cases, which two items remain unchanged during the transfer of the packet from source to destination? (Choose two.)

A.  Destination MAC address

B.  Destination IP address

C.  Layer 2 header

D.  Source ARP table

E.  Source MAC address

F.  Source IP address

8. Which two items are used by a host device when performing an ANDing operation to determine whether a destination address is on the same local network? (Choose two.)

   A. Destination MAC address

   B. Destination IP address

   C. Network number

   D. Source MAC address

   E. Subnet mask

9. Refer to Example 1-28. What will the router do with a packet that has a destination IP address of 192.168.12.227?

   A. Drop the packet.

   B. Send the packet out the GigabitEthernet0/0 interface.

   C. Send the packet out the GigabitEthernet0/1 interface.

   D. Send the packet out the Serial0/0/0 interface.

10. Which two parameters does EIGRP use as metrics to select the best path to reach a network? (Choose two.)

    A. Bandwidth

    B. Confidentiality

    C. Delay

    D. Hop count

    E. Jitter

    F. Resiliency

11. What route would have the lowest administrative distance?

    A. A directly connected network

    B. A route received through the EIGRP routing protocol

    C. A route received through the OSPF routing protocol

    D. A static route

12. Consider the following routing table entry for R1:

    ```
    D 10.1.1.0/24 [90/2170112] via 10.2.1.1, 00:00:05, Serial0/0/0
    ```

    What is the significance of the Serial0/0/0?

    A. It is the interface on R1 used to send data that is destined for 10.1.1.0/24.

    B. It is the interface on the final destination router that is directly connected to the 10.1.1.0/24 network.

C. It is the interface on the next-hop router when the destination IP address is on the 10.1.1.0/24 network.

D. It is the R1 interface through which the EIGRP update was learned.

13. Refer to Example 1-19. A network administrator issues the **show ipv6 route** command on R1. What two conclusions can be drawn from the routing table? (Choose two.)

A. Interface G0/1 is configured with IPv6 address 2001:DB8:ACAD:2::12.

B. Network FF00::/8 was learned from a static route.

C. Packets destined for the network 2001:DB8:ACAD:1::/64 will be forwarded through G0/1.

D. Packets destined for the network 2001:DB8:ACAD:2::/64 will be forwarded through G0/1.

E. R1 does not have any remote network routes.

14. A network administrator configures interface G0/0 on R1 with the **ip address 172.16.1.254 255.255.255.0** command. However, when the administrator issues the **show ip route** command, the routing table does not show the directly connected network. What is the possible cause of the problem?

A. Interface G0/0 has not been activated.

B. No packets with a destination network of 172.16.1.0 have been sent to R1.

C. The configuration needs to be saved first.

D. The subnet mask is incorrect for the IPv4 address.

15. A network administrator configures a router using the command **ip route 0.0.0.0 0.0.0.0 209.165.200.226**. What is the purpose of this command?

A. To add a dynamic route for the destination network 0.0.0.0 to the routing table

B. To forward all packets to the device with IP address 209.165.200.226

C. To forward packets destined for the network 0.0.0.0 to the device with IP address 209.165.200.226

D. To provide a route to forward packets for which there is no route in the routing table

16. What are two common types of static routes in routing tables? (Choose two.)

A. A built-in static route by IOS

B. A default static route

C. A static route converted from a route that is learned through a dynamic routing protocol

D.  A static route that is dynamically created between two neighboring routers

E.  A static route to a specific network

17.  What command will enable a router to begin sending messages that allow it to configure a link-local address without using an IPv6 DHCP server?

A.  A static route

B.  The **ip routing** command

C.  The **ipv6 route ::/0** command

D.  The **ipv6 unicast-routing** command

# CHAPTER 2

# Static Routing

## Objectives

Upon completion of this chapter, you will be able to answer the following questions:

- What are the advantages and disadvantages of static routing?

- What is the purpose of different types of static routes?

- How do you configure IPv4 static routes by specifying a next-hop address?

- How do you configure an IPv4 default route?

- How do you configure IPv6 static routes by specifying a next-hop address?

- How do you configure an IPv6 default route?

- How do you configure a floating static route to provide a backup connection?

- How do you configure IPv4 and IPv6 static host routes that direct traffic to a specific host?

- How does a router process packets when a static route is configured?

- How do you troubleshoot common static and default route configuration issues?

## Key Terms

This chapter uses the following key terms. You can find the definitions in the Glossary.

*stub network*   Page 79

*stub router*   Page 79

*standard static route*   Page 81

*summary static route*   Page 81

*floating static route*   Page 81

*exit interface*   Page 82

*next-hop IP address*   Page 82

*next-hop static route*   Page 87

*directly connected static route*   Page 87

*fully specified static route*   Page 87

*recursive lookup*   Page 88

*link-local address*   Page 102

*host route*   Page 111

*local host route*   Page 112

# Introduction (2.0.1.1)

Routing is at the core of every data network, moving information across an internetwork from source to destination. Routers are the devices responsible for the transfer of packets from one network to the next.

Routers learn about remote networks either dynamically, using routing protocols, or manually, or using static routes. In many cases, routers use a combination of both dynamic routing protocols and static routes. This chapter focuses on static routing.

Static routes are common and do not require the same amount of processing and overhead as dynamic routing protocols.

In this chapter, sample topologies will be used to configure IPv4 and IPv6 static routes and to present troubleshooting techniques. In the process, several important IOS commands and the resulting output will be examined. An introduction to the routing table using both directly connected networks and static routes will be included.

**Class Activity 2.0.1.2: Which Way Should We Go**

A huge sporting event is about to take place in your city. To attend the event, you make concise plans to arrive at the sports arena on time to see the entire game.

There are two routes you can take to drive to the event:

- **Highway route**—It is easy to follow, and fast driving speeds are allowed.

- **Alternate, direct route**—You found this route using a city map. Depending on conditions, such as the amount of traffic or congestion, this just may be the way to get to the arena on time.

With a partner, discuss these options. Choose a preferred route to arrive at the arena in time to see every second of the huge sporting event.

Compare your optional preferences to network traffic. Which route would you choose to deliver data communications for your small- to medium-sized business? Would it be the fastest, easiest route or the alternative, direct route? Justify your choice.

Complete the modeling activity .pdf and be prepared to justify your answers to the class or with another group.

# Implement Static Routes (2.1)

To reach remote networks, it is essential that routing be implemented. Routing can be accomplished dynamically using a routing protocol or manually using static routes. Very small organizations with a few remote networks would most likely use only static routes. However, larger networks typically use a combination of a dynamic routing protocol and static routes.

In this section, you will learn how static routes are implemented in a small-to medium-sized business network.

# Static Routing (2.1.1)

In this topic, you will learn about the advantages and disadvantages of static routing.

### Reach Remote Networks (2.1.1.1)

A router can learn about remote networks in one of two ways:

- **Manually**—Remote networks are manually entered into the route table using static routes.

- **Dynamically**—Remote routes are automatically learned using a dynamic routing protocol.

Figure 2-1 provides a sample scenario of static routing.

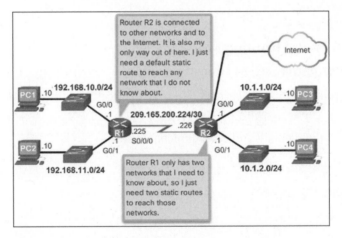

**Figure 2-1**    Static and Default Routing Scenario

Figure 2-2 provides a sample scenario of dynamic routing using Enhanced Interior Gateway Routing Protocol (EIGRP).

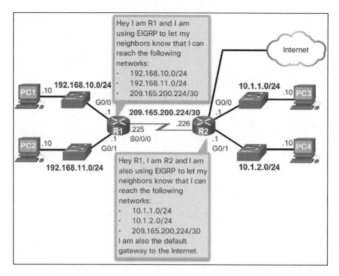

**Figure 2-2** Dynamic Routing Scenario

A network administrator can manually configure a static route to reach a specific network. Unlike a dynamic routing protocol, static routes are not automatically updated and must be manually reconfigured any time the network topology changes.

## Why Use Static Routing? (2.1.1.2)

Static routing provides some advantages over dynamic routing:

- Static routes are not advertised over the network, resulting in better security.
- Static routes use less bandwidth than dynamic routing protocols; no CPU cycles are used to calculate and communicate routes.
- The path a static route uses to send data is known.

Static routing has the following disadvantages:

- Initial configuration and maintenance is time consuming.
- Configuration is error-prone, especially in large networks.
- Administrator intervention is required to maintain changing route information.
- It does not scale well with growing networks; maintenance becomes cumbersome.
- It requires complete knowledge of the whole network for proper implementation.

Table 2-1 compares dynamic and static routing features. Notice that the advantages of one method are the disadvantages of the other.

**Table 2-1**   Dynamic Versus Static Routing

| Feature | Dynamic Routing | Static Routing |
|---|---|---|
| Configuration Complexity | Generally independent of the network size | Increases with network size |
| Topology Changes | Automatically adapts to topology changes | Administrator intervention required |
| Scaling | Suitable for simple and complex topologies | Suitable for simple topologies |
| Resource Usage | Uses CPU, memory, link bandwidth | No extra resources needed |
| Predictability | Route depends on the current topology | Route to destination is always the same |

Static routes are useful for smaller networks with only one path to an outside network. They also provide security in a larger network for certain types of traffic or links to other networks that need more control. It is important to understand that static and dynamic routing are not mutually exclusive. Rather, most networks use a combination of dynamic routing protocols and static routes. This may result in the router having multiple paths to a destination network via static routes and dynamically learned routes. However, recall that the administrative distance (AD) value is a measure of the preference of route sources. Route sources with low AD values are preferred over route sources with higher AD values. The AD value for a static route is 1. Therefore, a static route will take precedence over all dynamically learned routes, which will have higher AD values.

## When to Use Static Routes (2.1.1.3)

Static routing has three primary uses:

- Providing ease of routing table maintenance in smaller networks that are not expected to grow significantly.

- Routing to and from stub networks. A *stub network* is a network accessed by a single route, and the router has only one neighbor.

- Using a single default route to represent a path to any network that does not have a more specific match with another route in the routing table. Default routes are used to send traffic to any destination beyond the next upstream router.

Figure 2-3 shows an example of a stub network connection and a default route connection. Notice that any network attached to R1 would only have one way to reach other destinations, whether to networks attached to R2 or to destinations beyond R2. This means that network 172.16.3.0 is a stub network and R1 is a *stub router*.

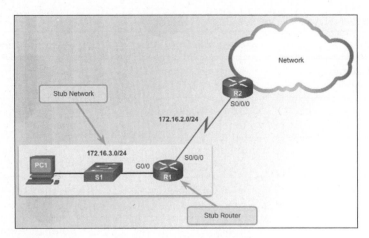

**Figure 2-3**  Stub Networks and Stub Routers

In the figure, a static route can be configured on R2 to reach the R1 LAN. Additionally, because R1 has only one way to send out nonlocal traffic, a default static route can be configured on R1 to point to R2 as the next hop for all other networks.

**Activity 2.1.1.4: Identify the Advantages and Disadvantages of Static Routing**

Refer to the online course to complete this activity.

## Types of Static Routes (2.1.2)

In this topic, you will learn about the different types of static routes.

### Static Route Applications (2.1.2.1)

Static routes are most often used for the following reasons:

- Connect to a specific network
- Connect a stub router
- Summarize routing table entries
- Create a backup route

They can also be used to do the following:

- Reduce the number of routes advertised by summarizing several contiguous networks as one static route
- Create a backup route in case a primary route link fails

The following types of IPv4 and IPv6 static routes will be discussed:

- *Standard static route*
- Default static route
- *Summary static route*
- *Floating static route*

## Standard Static Route (2.1.2.2)

Both IPv4 and IPv6 support the configuration of static routes. Static routes are useful when connecting to a specific remote network.

Figure 2-4 shows that R2 can be configured with a static route to reach the stub network 172.16.3.0/24.

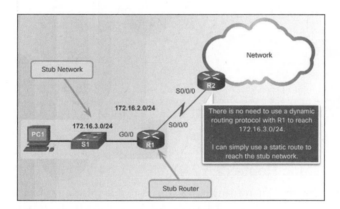

**Figure 2-4**   Connecting to a Stub Network

---

**Note**

The example is highlighting a stub network, but in fact, a static route can be used to connect to any network.

---

## Default Static Route (2.1.2.3)

A default route is one that matches all packets and is used by the router if a packet does not match any other, more specific route in the routing table. A default route can be dynamically learned or statically configured. A default static route is simply a static route with 0.0.0.0/0 as the destination IPv4 address. Configuring a default static route creates a Gateway of Last Resort.

Default static routes are used in two situations:

- When no other routes in the routing table match the packet destination IP address. In other words, when a more specific match does not exist. A common use is when connecting a company's edge router to the ISP network.

- When a router has only one other router to which it is connected. In this situation, the router is known as a stub router.

Refer to Figure 2-5 for a stub network default route scenario.

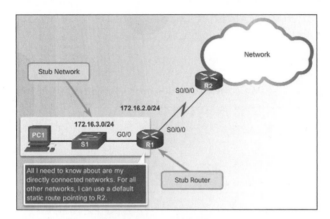

**Figure 2-5**   Connecting a Stub Router

## Summary Static Route (2.1.2.4)

To reduce the number of routing table entries, multiple static routes can be summarized into a single static route in the following circumstances:

- The destination networks are contiguous and can be summarized into a single network address.

- All the multiple static routes use the same *exit interface* or *next-hop IP address*.

In Figure 2-6, R1 would require four separate static routes to reach the 172.20.0.0/16 to 172.23.0.0/16 networks. However, instead of configuring four separate static routes, the networks could be summarized and configured using one summary static route only. R1 would still be able to reach those four networks using the one static route. Summarization helps reduce the size of the routing table, making it more efficient.

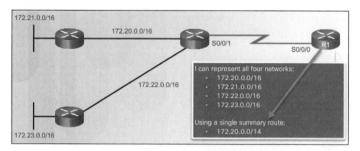

**Figure 2-6**   Using One Summary Static Route

## Floating Static Route (2.1.2.5)

Another type of static route is a floating static route. Floating static routes are static routes that are used to provide a backup path to a primary static or dynamic route, in the event of a link failure. The floating static route is only used when the primary route is not available.

To accomplish this, the floating static route is configured with a higher AD than the primary route. The AD represents the trustworthiness of a route. If multiple paths to the destination exist, the router will choose the path with the lowest AD.

For example, assume an administrator wants a backup route to an EIGRP-learned route. Recall that the AD for EIGRP is 90; therefore, the administrator would need to configure a floating static route with an AD higher than 90. The resulting configuration would populate the routing table with the EIGRP learned route. However, if that route was ever lost, the router would use the floating static route to reach the identified destination network. When the EIGRP route recovers, the router would reselect it as the preferred route.

In Figure 2-7, the Branch router typically forwards all traffic to the HQ router over the private WAN link.

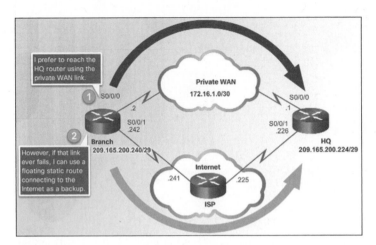

**Figure 2-7**    Configuring a Backup Route

In this example, the routers exchange route information using EIGRP. A floating static route, with an AD of 91 or higher, could be configured to serve as a backup route. If the private WAN link fails and the EIGRP route disappears from the routing table, the router selects the floating static route as the best path to reach the HQ LAN.

**Interactive Graphic**

### Activity 2.1.2.6: Identify the Type of Static Route

Refer to the online course to complete this activity.

## Configure Static and Default Routes (2.2)

Static routes are manually entered; therefore, careful consideration and attention must be given when configuring them.

In this section, you learn how to configure IPv4 and IPv6 static routes to enable remote network connectivity in a small-to medium-sized business network.

### Configure IPv4 Static Routes (2.2.1)

In this topic, you learn how to configure IPv4 static routes.

### The ip route Command (2.2.1.1)

Static routes are configured using the **ip route** global configuration command. The basic syntax for the command is as follows:

```
Router(config)# ip route network-address subnet-mask {ip-address | exit-intf}
   [distance]
```

The following parameters are required to configure static routing:

- *network-address*—Destination network address of the remote network to be added to the routing table; often this is referred to as the prefix.

- *subnet-mask*—Subnet mask, or just mask, of the remote network to be added to the routing table. The subnet mask can be modified to summarize a group of networks.

One or both of the following parameters must also be used:

- *ip-address*—The IP address of the connecting router to use to forward the packet to the remote destination network. Commonly referred to as the next hop.

- *exit-intf*—The outgoing interface to use to forward the packet to the next hop.

The *distance* parameter is used to create a floating static route by setting an AD that is higher than a dynamically learned route.

## Next-Hop Options (2.2.1.2)

Figure 2-8 displays the topology used for the static routing scenario.

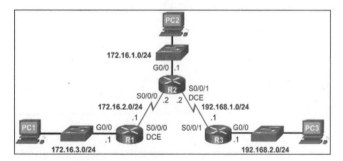

**Figure 2-8**   IPv4 Topology

Examples 2-1, 2-2, and 2-3 display the routing tables of R1, R2, and R3. Notice that each router has entries only for directly connected networks and their associated local addresses. None of the routers have knowledge of any networks beyond their directly connected interfaces.

**Example 2-1**  Verify the R1 IPv4 Routing Table

```
R1# show ip route | begin Gateway
Gateway of last resort is not set


     172.16.0.0/16 is variably subnetted, 4 subnets, 2 masks
C        172.16.2.0/24 is directly connected, Serial0/0/0
L        172.16.2.1/32 is directly connected, Serial0/0/0
C        172.16.3.0/24 is directly connected, GigabitEthernet0/0
L        172.16.3.1/32 is directly connected, GigabitEthernet0/0
R1#
```

**Example 2-2**  Verify the R2 IPv4 Routing Table

```
R2# show ip route | begin Gateway
Gateway of last resort is not set


     172.16.0.0/16 is variably subnetted, 4 subnets, 2 masks
C        172.16.1.0/24 is directly connected, GigabitEthernet0/0
L        172.16.1.1/32 is directly connected, GigabitEthernet0/0
C        172.16.2.0/24 is directly connected, Serial0/0/0
L        172.16.2.2/32 is directly connected, Serial0/0/0
     192.168.1.0/24 is variably subnetted, 2 subnets, 2 masks
C        192.168.1.0/24 is directly connected, Serial0/0/1
L        192.168.1.2/32 is directly connected, Serial0/0/1
R2#
```

**Example 2-3**  Verify the R3 IPv4 Routing Table

```
R3# show ip route | include C
Codes: L - local, C - connected, S - static, R - RIP, M - mobile, B - BGP
C        192.168.1.0/24 is directly connected, Serial0/0/1
C        192.168.2.0/24 is directly connected, GigabitEthernet0/0
R3#
```

For example, R1 has no knowledge of networks:

- **172.16.1.0/24**—LAN on R2
- **192.168.1.0/24**—Serial network between R2 and R3
- **192.168.2.0/24**—LAN on R3

Example 2-4 displays a successful ping from R1 to R2 and an unsuccessful ping to the R3 LAN. The second ping is unsuccessful because R1 does not have an entry in its routing table for the R3 LAN network.

**Example 2-4**  Verify Connectivity from R1 to R2 and R3

```
R1# ping 172.16.2.2
Type escape sequence to abort.
Sending 5, 100-byte ICMP Echos to 172.16.2.2, timeout is 2 seconds:
!!!!!
Success rate is 100 percent (5/5), round-trip min/avg/max = 12/13/16 ms
R1#
R1# ping 192.168.2.1
Type escape sequence to abort.
Sending 5, 100-byte ICMP Echos to 192.168.2.1, timeout is 2 seconds:
.....
Success rate is 0 percent (0/5)
R1#
```

The next hop can be identified by an IP address, exit interface, or both. The way the destination is specified creates one of the three following route types:

- *Next-hop static route*—Only the next-hop IP address is specified.

- *Directly connected static route*—Only the router exit interface is specified.

- *Fully specified static route*—The next-hop IP address and exit interface are specified.

## Configure a Next-Hop Static Route (2.2.1.3)

In a next-hop static route, only the next-hop IP address is specified. The exit interface is derived from the next hop. In Example 2-5, three next-hop static routes are configured on R1 using the IP address of the next hop, R2.

**Example 2-5**  Configure Next-Hop IPv4 Static Routes on R1

```
R1(config)# ip route 172.16.1.0 255.255.255.0 172.16.2.2
R1(config)# ip route 192.168.1.0 255.255.255.0 172.16.2.2
R1(config)# ip route 192.168.2.0 255.255.255.0 172.16.2.2
R1(config)#
```

Before a router forwards any packet, the routing table process must determine the exit interface to use to forward the packet. This is known as route resolvability.

Routes highlighted in Example 2-6 are used by R1 to forward packets destined for the 192.168.2.0/24 network:

**Example 2-6** Verify the R1 IPv4 Routing Table

```
R1# show ip route | begin Gateway
Gateway of last resort is not set

      172.16.0.0/16 is variably subnetted, 5 subnets, 2 masks
S         172.16.1.0/24 [1/0] via 172.16.2.2
C         172.16.2.0/24 is directly connected, Serial0/0/0
L         172.16.2.1/32 is directly connected, Serial0/0/0
C         172.16.3.0/24 is directly connected, GigabitEthernet0/0
L         172.16.3.1/32 is directly connected, GigabitEthernet0/0
S      192.168.1.0/24 [1/0] via 172.16.2.2
S      192.168.2.0/24 [1/0] via 172.16.2.2
R1#
```

R1 completes the following steps to find the exit interface for the packet:

1. It looks for a match in the routing table and finds that it has to forward the packets to the next-hop IPv4 address 172.16.2.2. Every route that references only a next-hop IPv4 address and does not reference an exit interface must have the next-hop IPv4 address resolved using another route in the routing table with an exit interface.

2. R1 must now determine how to reach 172.16.2.2; therefore, it searches a second time for a 172.16.2.2 match. In this case, the IPv4 address matches the route for the directly connected network 172.16.2.0/24 with the exit interface Serial 0/0/0, as indicated by the label 2. This lookup tells the routing table process that this packet is forwarded out of that interface.

It actually takes two routing table lookup processes to forward any packet to the 192.168.2.0/24 network. When the router performs multiple lookups in the routing table before forwarding a packet, it is performing a process known as a *recursive lookup*. Because recursive lookups consume router resources, they should be avoided when possible.

A recursive static route is valid (that is, it is a candidate for insertion in the routing table) only when the specified next hop resolves, either directly or indirectly, to a valid exit interface. If the exit interface is "down" or "administratively down," then the static route will not be installed in the routing table.

## Configure a Directly Connected Static Route (2.2.1.4)

When configuring a static route, another option is to use the exit interface to specify the next-hop address.

In Example 2-7, three directly connected static routes are configured on R1 using the exit interface.

**Example 2-7**  Configure Directly Connected IPv4 Static Routes on R1

```
R1(config)# ip route 172.16.1.0 255.255.255.0 s0/0/0
R1(config)# ip route 192.168.1.0 255.255.255.0 s0/0/0
R1(config)# ip route 192.168.2.0 255.255.255.0 s0/0/0
R1(config)#
```

The routing table for R1 in Example 2-8 shows that when a packet is destined for the 192.168.2.0/24 network, R1 looks for a match in the routing table and finds that it can forward the packet out of its Serial 0/0/0 interface. No other lookups are required.

**Example 2-8**  Verify the R1 IPv4 Routing Table

```
R1# show ip route | begin Gateway
Gateway of last resort is not set


      172.16.0.0/16 is variably subnetted, 5 subnets, 2 masks
S        172.16.1.0/24 is directly connected, Serial0/0/0
C        172.16.2.0/24 is directly connected, Serial0/0/0
L        172.16.2.1/32 is directly connected, Serial0/0/0
C        172.16.3.0/24 is directly connected, GigabitEthernet0/0
L        172.16.3.1/32 is directly connected, GigabitEthernet0/0
S     192.168.1.0/24 is directly connected, Serial0/0/0
S     192.168.2.0/24 is directly connected, Serial0/0/0
R1#
```

Notice how the routing table looks different for the route configured with an exit interface than for the route configured with a recursive entry.

Configuring a directly connected static route with an exit interface allows the routing table to resolve the exit interface in a single search, instead of two searches. Although the routing table entry indicates "directly connected," the AD of the static route is still 1. Only a directly connected interface can have an AD of 0.

**Note**

For point-to-point interfaces, you can use static routes that point to the exit interface or to the next-hop address. For multipoint/broadcast interfaces, it is more suitable to use static routes that point to a next-hop address.

**Note**

Cisco Express Forwarding (CEF) is the default behavior on most platforms running IOS 12.0 or later. CEF provides optimized lookup for efficient packet forwarding by using two main data structures stored in the data plane: a Forwarding Information Base (FIB), which is a copy of the routing table, and an adjacency table that includes Layer 2 addressing information. The information combined in both of these tables works together so there is no recursive lookup needed for next-hop IP address lookups. In other words, a static route using a next-hop IP requires only a single lookup when CEF is enabled on the router. Although static routes that use only an exit interface on point-to-point networks are common, the use of the default CEF forwarding mechanism makes this practice unnecessary. CEF is discussed in more detail later in the course.

## Configure a Fully Specified Static Route (2.2.1.5)

In a fully specified static route, both the exit interface and the next-hop IP address are specified. This is another type of static route that is used in older IOSs, prior to CEF. This form of static route is used when the exit interface is a multiaccess interface and it is necessary to explicitly identify the next hop. The next hop must be directly connected to the specified exit interface.

Suppose that the network link between R1 and R2 is an Ethernet link and that the GigabitEthernet 0/1 interface of R1 is connected to that network, as shown in Figure 2-9. CEF is not enabled.

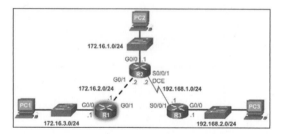

**Figure 2-9**   Modified IPv4 Topology

To eliminate the recursive lookup, a directly connected static route can be implemented using the **ip route 192.168.2.0 255.255.255.0 GigabitEthernet 0/1** global configuration command.

However, this may cause unexpected or inconsistent results. The difference between an Ethernet multiaccess network and a point-to-point serial network is that a point-to-point serial network has only one other device on that network: the router at the other end of the link. With Ethernet networks, there may be many different devices sharing the same multiaccess network, including hosts and even multiple routers. By only designating the Ethernet exit interface in the static route, the router will not have sufficient information to determine which device is the next-hop device.

R1 knows that the packet needs to be encapsulated in an Ethernet frame and sent out the GigabitEthernet 0/1 interface. However, R1 does not know the next-hop IPv4 address; therefore, it cannot determine the destination MAC address for the Ethernet frame.

Depending upon the topology and the configurations on other routers, this static route may or may not work. When the exit interface is an Ethernet network, it is recommended that a fully specified static route be used. This includes both the exit interface and the next-hop address, as shown in Example 2-9.

**Example 2-9**  Configure Fully Specified IPv4 Static Routes on R1

```
R1(config)# ip route 172.16.1.0 255.255.255.0 G0/1 172.16.2.2
R1(config)# ip route 192.168.1.0 255.255.255.0 G0/1 172.16.2.2
R1(config)# ip route 192.168.2.0 255.255.255.0 G0/1 172.16.2.2
R1(config)#
```

As shown in Example 2-10, when forwarding packets to R2, the exit interface is GigabitEthernet 0/1 and the next-hop IPv4 address is 172.16.2.2.

**Example 2-10**  Verify the R1 IPv4 Routing Table

```
R1# show ip route | begin Gateway
Gateway of last resort is not set


      172.16.0.0/16 is variably subnetted, 5 subnets, 2 masks
S         172.16.1.0/24 [1/0] via 172.16.2.2, GigabitEthernet0/1
C         172.16.2.0/24 is directly connected, GigabitEthernet0/1
L         172.16.2.1/32 is directly connected, GigabitEthernet0/1
C         172.16.3.0/24 is directly connected, GigabitEthernet0/0
L         172.16.3.1/32 is directly connected, GigabitEthernet0/0
S      192.168.1.0/24 [1/0] via 172.16.2.2, GigabitEthernet0/1
S      192.168.2.0/24 [1/0] via 172.16.2.2, GigabitEthernet0/1
R1#
```

**Note**

With the use of CEF, a fully specified static route is no longer necessary. A static route using a next-hop address should be used.

## Verify a Static Route (2.2.1.6)

Along with **ping** and **traceroute**, useful commands to verify static routes include these:

- **show ip route**
- **show ip route static**
- **show ip route** *network*

Example 2-11 displays sample output of the **show ip route static** command. In the example, the output is filtered using the pipe and **begin** parameter. The output reflects the use of static routes using the next-hop address.

**Example 2-11** Verify the R1 IPv4 Routing Table

```
R1# show ip route static | begin Gateway
Gateway of last resort is not set


      172.16.0.0/16 is variably subnetted, 5 subnets, 2 masks
S        172.16.1.0/24 [1/0] via 172.16.2.2
S     192.168.1.0/24 [1/0] via 172.16.2.2
S     192.168.2.0/24 [1/0] via 172.16.2.2
R1#
```

Example 2-12 displays sample output of the **show ip route 192.168.2.1** command.

**Example 2-12** Verify a Specific Entry in the IPv4 Routing Table

```
R1# show ip route 192.168.2.1
Routing entry for 192.168.2.0/24
  Known via "static", distance 1, metric 0
  Routing Descriptor Blocks:
  * 172.16.2.2
      Route metric is 0, traffic share count is 1
R1#
```

Example 2-13 verifies the **ip route** configuration in the running configuration.

**Example 2-13** Verify the IPv4 Static Route Configuration

```
R1# show running-config | section ip route
ip route 172.16.1.0 255.255.255.0 172.16.2.2
ip route 192.168.1.0 255.255.255.0 172.16.2.2
ip route 192.168.2.0 255.255.255.0 172.16.2.2
R1#
```

# Configure IPv4 Default Routes (2.2.2)

In this topic, you learn how to configure an IPv4 default static route.

## Default Static Route (2.2.2.1)

Routers commonly use default routes that are either configured locally or learned from another router, using a dynamic routing protocol. A default route does not require leftmost bits to match between the default route and the destination IPv4 address. A default route is used when no other routes in the routing table match the destination IP address of the packet. In other words, if a more specific match does not exist, then the default route is used as the Gateway of Last Resort.

Default static routes are commonly used when connecting the following:

- An edge router to a service provider network

- A stub router (a router with only one upstream neighbor router)

The command syntax for a default static route is similar to any other static route, except that the network address is **0.0.0.0** and the subnet mask is **0.0.0.0**.

```
Router(config)# ip route 0.0.0.0 0.0.0.0 {ip-address | exit-intf} [distance]
```

**Note**

An IPv4 default static route is commonly referred to as a quad-zero route.

## Configure a Default Static Route (2.2.2.2)

In Figure 2-8, R1 can be configured with three static routes to reach all the remote networks in the example topology. However, R1 is a stub router because it is only connected to R2. Therefore, it would be more efficient to configure a default static route.

Example 2-14 configures a default static route on R1. With the configuration shown in the example, any packets not matching more specific route entries are forwarded to 172.16.2.2.

**Example 2-14**  Configure an IPv4 Default Static Route on R1

```
R1(config)# ip route 0.0.0.0 0.0.0.0 172.16.2.2
R1(config)#
```

## Verify a Default Static Route (2.2.2.3)

In Example 2-15, the **show ip route static** command output displays the contents of the static routes in the routing table. Note the asterisk (*) next to the route with code 'S.' As displayed in the Codes legend, the asterisk indicates that this static route is a candidate default route, which is why it is selected as the Gateway of Last Resort.

**Example 2-15**  Verify an IPv4 Default Static Route on R1

```
R1# show ip route static
Codes: L - local, C - connected, S - static, R - RIP, M - mobile, B - BGP
       D - EIGRP, EX - EIGRP external, O - OSPF, IA - OSPF inter area
       N1 - OSPF NSSA external type 1, N2 - OSPF NSSA external type 2
       E1 - OSPF external type 1, E2 - OSPF external type 2
       i - IS-IS, su - IS-IS summary, L1 - IS-IS level-1, L2 - IS-IS level-2
       ia - IS-IS inter area, * - candidate default, U - per-user static route
       o - ODR, P - periodic downloaded static route, H - NHRP, l - LISP
       + - replicated route, % - next hop override

Gateway of last resort is 172.16.2.2 to network 0.0.0.0

S*      0.0.0.0/0 [1/0] via 172.16.2.2
R1#
```

The key to this configuration is the /0 mask. The subnet mask in a routing table determines how many bits must match between the destination IP address of the packet and the route in the routing table. A binary 1 indicates that the bits must match. A binary 0 indicates that the bits do not have to match. A /0 mask in this route entry indicates that none of the bits are required to match. The default static route matches all packets for which a more specific match does not exist.

Packet Tracer
☐ Activity

**Packet Tracer 2.2.2.4: Configuring IPv4 Static and Default Routes**

Background/Scenario

In this activity, you will configure static and default routes. A static route is a route that is entered manually by the network administrator to create a route that is reliable and safe. There are four different static routes that are used in this activity: a recursive static route, a directly connected static route, a fully specified static route, and a default route.

**Lab 2.2.2.5: Configuring IPv4 Static and Default Routes**

In this lab, you will complete the following objectives:

- Part 1: Set Up the Topology and Initialize Devices
- Part 2: Configure Basic Device Settings and Verify Connectivity
- Part 3: Configure Static Routes
- Part 4: Configure and Verify a Default Route

# Configure IPv6 Static Routes (2.2.3)

In this topic, you learn how to configure IPv6 static routes.

## The ipv6 route Command (2.2.3.1)

Static routes for IPv6 are configured using the **ipv6 route** global configuration command. The syntax is as follows:

```
Router(config)# ipv6 route ipv6-prefix/prefix-length {ipv6-address | exit-intf}
```

Table 2-2 describes the parameters for the **ipv6 route** command.

**Table 2-2**   Parameters for the IPv6 Static Route Command

| Parameter | Description |
|-----------|-------------|
| *ipv6-prefix* | Destination IPv6 network address of the remote network to be added to the routing table. |
| *prefix-length* | Prefix length of the remote network to be added to the routing table. |
| *ipv6-address* | Commonly referred to as the next-hop router's IPv6 address. |
| | Typically used when connecting to a broadcast media (that is, Ethernet). |
| | Commonly creates a recursive lookup. |
| *exit-intf* | Use the outgoing interface to forward packets to the destination network. |
| | Also referred to as a directly attached static route. |
| | Typically used when connecting in a point-to-point configuration. |

Most of the parameters are identical to the IPv4 version of the command. An IPv6 static route can also be implemented as one of these:

- Standard IPv6 static route
- Default IPv6 static route

- Summary IPv6 static route
- Floating IPv6 static route

As with IPv4, these routes can be configured as recursive, directly connected, or fully specified.

The **ipv6 unicast-routing** global configuration command must be configured to enable the router to forward IPv6 packets. Figure 2-10 shows the IPv6 topology

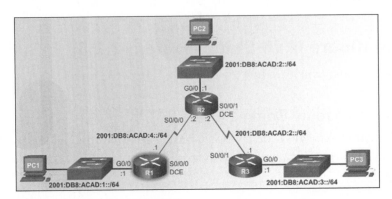

**Figure 2-10**   IPv6 Topology

Example 2-16 enables IPv6 unicast routing on R1.

**Example 2-16**  Enable IPv6 Routing

```
R1(config)# ipv6 unicast-routing
R1(config)#
```

## Next-Hop Options (2.2.3.2)

Examples 2-17, 2-18, and 2-19 display the routing tables of R1, R2, and R3. Each router has entries only for directly connected networks and their associated local addresses.

**Example 2-17**  Verify the R1 IPv6 Routing Table

```
R1# show ipv6 route

<output omitted>

C    2001:DB8:ACAD:1::/64 [0/0]
     via GigabitEthernet0/0, directly connected
L    2001:DB8:ACAD:1::1/128 [0/0]
     via GigabitEthernet0/0, receive
```

```
C    2001:DB8:ACAD:4::/64 [0/0]
       via Serial0/0/0, directly connected
L    2001:DB8:ACAD:4::1/128 [0/0]
       via Serial0/0/0, receive
L    FF00::/8 [0/0]
       via Null0, receive
R1#
```

**Example 2-18** Verify the R2 IPv6 Routing Table

```
R2# show ipv6 route

<output omitted>

C    2001:DB8:ACAD:2::/64 [0/0]
       via GigabitEthernet0/0, directly connected
L    2001:DB8:ACAD:2::1/128 [0/0]
       via GigabitEthernet0/0, receive
C    2001:DB8:ACAD:4::/64 [0/0]
       via Serial0/0/0, directly connected
L    2001:DB8:ACAD:4::2/128 [0/0]
       via Serial0/0/0, receive
C    2001:DB8:ACAD:5::/64 [0/0]
       via Serial0/0/1, directly connected
L    2001:DB8:ACAD:5::2/128 [0/0]
       via Serial0/0/1, receive
L    FF00::/8 [0/0]
       via Null0, receive
R2#
```

**Example 2-19** Verify the R3 IPv6 Routing Table

```
R3# show ipv6 route

<output omitted>

C    2001:DB8:ACAD:3::/64 [0/0]
      via GigabitEthernet0/0, directly connected
L    2001:DB8:ACAD:3::1/128 [0/0]
      via GigabitEthernet0/0, receive
```

```
C    2001:DB8:ACAD:5::/64 [0/0]
        via Serial0/0/1, directly connected
L    2001:DB8:ACAD:5::1/128 [0/0]
        via Serial0/0/1, receive
L    FF00::/8 [0/0]
        via Null0, receive
R3#
```

None of the routers have knowledge of networks beyond their directly connected interfaces.

For example, R1 has no knowledge of networks:

- **2001:DB8:ACAD:2::/64**—LAN on R2

- **2001:DB8:ACAD:5::/64**—Serial network between R2 and R3

- **2001:DB8:ACAD:3::/64**—LAN on R3

Example 2-20 displays a successful ping from R1 to R2 and an unsuccessful ping to the R3 LAN. The ping is unsuccessful because R1 does not have an entry in its routing table for that network.

**Example 2-20** Verify Connectivity from R1 to R2 and R3

```
R1# ping ipv6 2001:DB8:ACAD:4::2
Type escape sequence to abort.
Sending 5, 100-byte ICMP Echos to 2001:DB8:ACAD:4::2, timeout is 2 seconds:
!!!!!
Success rate is 100 percent (5/5), round-trip min/avg/max = 12/30/96 ms
R1#
R1# ping ipv6 2001:DB8:ACAD:3::1
Type escape sequence to abort.
Sending 5, 100-byte ICMP Echos to 2001:DB8:ACAD:3::1, timeout is 2 seconds:

% No valid route for destination
Success rate is 0 percent (0/1)
R1#
```

The next hop can be identified by an IPv6 address, exit interface, or both. The way the destination is specified creates one of three route types:

- **Next-hop static IPv6 route**—Only the next-hop IPv6 address is specified.

- **Directly connected static IPv6 route**—Only the router exit interface is specified.

- **Fully specified static IPv6 route**—The next-hop IPv6 address and exit interface are specified.

## Configure a Next-Hop Static IPv6 Route (2.2.3.3)

In a next-hop static route, only the next-hop IPv6 address is specified. The exit interface is derived from the next hop. For instance, in Example 2-21, three next-hop static routes are configured on R1.

**Example 2-21**  Configure Next-Hop IPv6 Static Routes on R1

```
R1(config)# ipv6 route 2001:DB8:ACAD:2::/64 2001:DB8:ACAD:4::2
R1(config)# ipv6 route 2001:DB8:ACAD:5::/64 2001:DB8:ACAD:4::2
R1(config)# ipv6 route 2001:DB8:ACAD:3::/64 2001:DB8:ACAD:4::2
R1(config)#
```

As with IPv4, before the router forwards a packet, the routing table process must resolve the route to determine the exit interface to use to forward the packet. The route resolvability process varies depending upon the type of forwarding mechanism the router is using. CEF is the default behavior on most platforms running IOS 12.0 or later.

When CEF is not in use, R1 uses routes highlighted in Example 2-22 to forward packets destined for the 2001:DB8:ACAD:3::/64 network.

**Example 2-22**  Verify the R1 IPv6 Routing Table

```
R1# show ipv6 route
IPv6 Routing Table - default - 8 entries
Codes: C - Connected, L - Local, S - Static, U - Per-user Static route
       B - BGP, R - RIP, H - NHRP, I1 - ISIS L1
       I2 - ISIS L2, IA - ISIS interarea, IS - ISIS summary, D - EIGRP
       EX - EIGRP external, ND - ND Default, NDp - ND Prefix, DCE - Destination
       NDr - Redirect, O - OSPF Intra, OI - OSPF Inter, OE1 - OSPF ext 1
       OE2 - OSPF ext 2, ON1 - OSPF NSSA ext 1, ON2 - OSPF NSSA ext 2
C    2001:DB8:ACAD:1::/64 [0/0]
     via GigabitEthernet0/0, directly connected
L    2001:DB8:ACAD:1::1/128 [0/0]
     via GigabitEthernet0/0, receive
S    2001:DB8:ACAD:2::/64 [1/0]
     via 2001:DB8:ACAD:4::2
S    2001:DB8:ACAD:3::/64 [1/0]
     via 2001:DB8:ACAD:4::2
```

```
C    2001:DB8:ACAD:4::/64 [0/0]
       via Serial0/0/0, directly connected
L    2001:DB8:ACAD:4::1/128 [0/0]
       via Serial0/0/0, receive
S    2001:DB8:ACAD:5::/64 [1/0]
       via 2001:DB8:ACAD:4::2
L    FF00::/8 [0/0]
       via Null0, receive
R1#
```

R1 completes the following steps to find the exit interface for the packet:

1. It looks for a match in the routing table and finds that it has to forward the packets to the next-hop IPv6 address 2001:DB8:ACAD:4::2. Every route that references only a next-hop IPv6 address and does not reference an exit interface must have the next-hop IPv6 address resolved using another route in the routing table with an exit interface.

2. R1 must now determine how to reach 2001:DB8:ACAD:4::2; therefore, it searches a second time looking for a match. In this case, the IPv6 address matches the route for the directly connected network 2001:DB8:ACAD:4::/64 with the exit interface Serial 0/0/0. This lookup tells the routing table process that this packet is forwarded out of that interface.

Therefore, it actually takes two routing table lookup processes to forward any packet to the 2001:DB8:ACAD:3::/64 network. When the router has to perform multiple lookups in the routing table before forwarding a packet, it is performing a recursive lookup.

A recursive static IPv6 route is valid (that is, it is a candidate for insertion in the routing table) only when the specified next hop resolves, either directly or indirectly, to a valid exit interface.

## Configure a Directly Connected Static IPv6 Route (2.2.3.4)

When configuring a static route on point-to-point networks, an alternative to using the next-hop IPv6 address is to specify the exit interface. This is an alternative used in older IOSs or whenever CEF is disabled, to avoid the recursive lookup problem.

For instance, in Example 2-23, three directly connected static routes are configured on R1 using the exit interface.

**Example 2-23** Configure Directly Connected IPv6 Static Routes on R1

```
R1(config)# ipv6 route 2001:DB8:ACAD:2::/64 s0/0/0
R1(config)# ipv6 route 2001:DB8:ACAD:5::/64 s0/0/0
R1(config)# ipv6 route 2001:DB8:ACAD:3::/64 s0/0/0
R1(config)#
```

The IPv6 routing table for R1 in Example 2-24 shows that when a packet is destined for the 2001:DB8:ACAD:3::/64 network, R1 looks for a match in the routing table and finds that it can forward the packet out of its Serial 0/0/0 interface. No other lookups are required.

**Example 2-24** Verify the R1 IPv6 Routing Table

```
R1# show ipv6 route
IPv6 Routing Table - default - 8 entries
Codes: C - Connected, L - Local, S - Static, U - Per-user Static route
       B - BGP, R - RIP, I1 - ISIS L1, I2 - ISIS L2
       IA - ISIS interarea, IS - ISIS summary, D - EIGRP, EX - EIGRP external
       ND - ND Default, NDp - ND Prefix, DCE - Destination, NDr - Redirect
       O - OSPF Intra, OI - OSPF Inter, OE1 - OSPF ext 1, OE2 - OSPF ext 2
       ON1 - OSPF NSSA ext 1, ON2 - OSPF NSSA ext 2
C   2001:DB8:ACAD:1::/64 [0/0]
     via GigabitEthernet0/0, directly connected
L   2001:DB8:ACAD:1::1/128 [0/0]
     via GigabitEthernet0/0, receive
S   2001:DB8:ACAD:2::/64 [1/0]
     via Serial0/0/0, directly connected
S   2001:DB8:ACAD:3::/64 [1/0]
     via Serial0/0/0, directly connected
C   2001:DB8:ACAD:4::/64 [0/0]
     via Serial0/0/0, directly connected
L   2001:DB8:ACAD:4::1/128 [0/0]
     via Serial0/0/0, receive
S   2001:DB8:ACAD:5::/64 [1/0]
     via Serial0/0/0, directly connected
L   FF00::/8 [0/0]
     via Null0, receive
R1#
```

Notice how the routing table looks different for the route configured with an exit interface than the route configured with a recursive entry.

Configuring a directly connected static route with an exit interface allows the routing table to resolve the exit interface in a single search instead of two searches. Recall that with the use of the CEF forwarding mechanism, static routes with an exit interface are considered unnecessary. A single lookup is performed using a combination of the FIB and adjacency table stored in the data plane.

## Configure a Fully Specified Static IPv6 Route (2.2.3.5)

In a fully specified static route, both the exit interface and the next-hop IPv6 address are specified. Similar to fully specified static routes used with IPv4, this would be used if CEF were not enabled on the router and the exit interface was on a multi-access network. With CEF, a static route using only a next-hop IPv6 address would be the preferred method even when the exit interface is a multiaccess network.

Unlike IPv4, there is a situation in IPv6 when a fully specified static route must be used. If the IPv6 static route uses an IPv6 *link-local address* as the next-hop address, a fully specified static route including the exit interface must be used. Figure 2-11 shows the link-local addresses for R1 and R2.

**Figure 2-11**    IPv6 Topology with Link-Local

The reason a fully specified static route must be used is because IPv6 link-local addresses are not contained in the IPv6 routing table. Link-local addresses are only unique on a given link or network. The next-hop link-local address may be a valid address on multiple networks connected to the router. Therefore, it is necessary that the exit interface be included.

In Example 2-25, a fully specified static route is configured using R2's link-local address as the next-hop address. Notice that IOS requires that an exit interface be specified.

**Example 2-25**    Configure Fully Specified IPv6 Static Route on R1

```
R1(config)# ipv6 route 2001:db8:acad:2::/64 fe80::2
% Interface has to be specified for a link-local nexthop
R1(config)# ipv6 route 2001:db8:acad:2::/64 s0/0/0 fe80::2
R1(config)#
```

Example 2-26 shows the IPv6 routing table entry for this route. Notice that both the next-hop link-local address and the exit interface are included.

**Example 2-26** Verify the R1 IPv6 Routing Table

```
R1# show ipv6 route static | begin 2001:DB8:ACAD:2::/64
S    2001:DB8:ACAD:2::/64 [1/0]
     via FE80::2, Serial0/0/0
```

## Verify IPv6 Static Routes (2.2.3.6)

Along with **ping** and **traceroute**, useful commands to verify static routes include these:

- **show ipv6 route**
- **show ipv6 route static**
- **show ipv6 route network**

Example 2-27 displays sample output of the **show ipv6 route static** command. The output reflects the use of static routes using next-hop global unicast addresses.

**Example 2-27** Verify the R1 IPv6 Routing Table

```
R1# show ipv6 route static
IPv6 Routing Table - default - 8 entries
Codes: C - Connected, L - Local, S - Static, U - Per-user Static route
       B - BGP, R - RIP, H - NHRP, I1 - ISIS L1
       I2 - ISIS L2, IA - ISIS interarea, IS - ISIS summary, D - EIGRP
       EX - EIGRP external, ND - ND Default, NDp - ND Prefix, DCE - Destination
       NDr - Redirect, O - OSPF Intra, OI - OSPF Inter, OE1 - OSPF ext 1
       OE2 - OSPF ext 2, ON1 - OSPF NSSA ext 1, ON2 - OSPF NSSA ext 2
S    2001:DB8:ACAD:2::/64 [1/0]
     via 2001:DB8:ACAD:4::2
S    2001:DB8:ACAD:3::/64 [1/0]
     via 2001:DB8:ACAD:4::2
S    2001:DB8:ACAD:5::/64 [1/0]
     via 2001:DB8:ACAD:4::2
R1#
```

Example 2-28 displays sample output from the **show ip route 2001:DB8:ACAD:3::** command.

**Example 2-28** Verify a Specific Entry in the IPv6 Routing Table

```
R1# show ipv6 route 2001:db8:acad:3::
Routing entry for 2001:DB8:ACAD:3::/64
  Known via "static", distance 1, metric 0
  Route count is 1/1, share count 0
  Routing paths:
    2001:DB8:ACAD:4::2
      Last updated 15:28:05 ago

R1#
```

Example 2-29 verifies the **ipv6 route** configuration in the running configuration.

**Example 2-29** Verify the IPv6 Static Route Configuration

```
R1# show running-config | section ipv6 route
ipv6 route 2001:DB8:ACAD:2::/64 2001:DB8:ACAD:4::2
ipv6 route 2001:DB8:ACAD:3::/64 2001:DB8:ACAD:4::2
ipv6 route 2001:DB8:ACAD:5::/64 2001:DB8:ACAD:4::2
R1#
```

# Configure IPv6 Default Routes (2.2.4)

In this topic, you learn how to configure an IPv6 default static route.

## Default Static IPv6 Route (2.2.4.1)

A default route is a static route that matches all packets. Instead of routers storing routes for all of the networks in the Internet, they can store a single default route to represent any network that is not in the routing table. A default route does not require leftmost bits to match between the default route and the destination IPv6 address.

Routers commonly use default routes that are either configured locally, or learned from another router using a dynamic routing protocol. They are used when no other routes match the packet's destination IP address in the routing table. In other words, if a more specific match does not exist, then use the default route as the Gateway of Last Resort.

Default static routes are commonly used when connecting the following:

- A company's edge router to a service provider network.

- A router with only an upstream neighbor router. The router has no other neighbors and is therefore referred to as a stub router.

The command syntax for a default static route is similar to any other static route, except that the ipv6-prefix/prefix-length is **::/0**, which matches all routes.

```
Router(config)# ipv6 route ::/0 {ipv6-address | exit-intf}
```

## Configure a Default Static IPv6 Route (2.2.4.2)

R1 in Figure 2-10 can be configured with three static routes to reach all of the remote networks in the topology. However, R1 is a stub router because it is only connected to R2. Therefore, it would be more efficient to configure a default static IPv6 route.

Example 2-30 displays a configuration for a default static IPv6 route on R1.

**Example 2-30**  Configure an IPv6 Default Static Route

```
R1(config)# ipv6 route ::/0 2001:DB8:ACAD:4::2
R1(config)#
```

## Verify a Default Static Route (2.2.4.3)

In Example 2-31, the **show ipv6 route static** command output displays the contents of the routing table.

**Example 2-31**  Verify the R1 IPv6 Routing Table

```
R1# show ipv6 route static
IPv6 Routing Table - default - 6 entries
Codes: C - Connected, L - Local, S - Static, U - Per-user Static route
       B - BGP, R - RIP, I1 - ISIS L1, I2 - ISIS L2
       IA - ISIS interarea, IS - ISIS summary, D - EIGRP, EX - EIGRP external
       ND - ND Default, NDp - ND Prefix, DCE - Destination, NDr - Redirect
       O - OSPF Intra, OI - OSPF Inter, OE1 - OSPF ext 1, OE2 - OSPF ext 2
       ON1 - OSPF NSSA ext 1, ON2 - OSPF NSSA ext 2
S    ::/0 [1/0]
     via 2001:DB8:ACAD:4::2
R1#
```

Unlike IPv4, IPv6 does not explicitly state that the default IPv6 is the Gateway of Last Resort.

The key to this configuration is the ::/0 mask. Remember that the IPv6 prefix-length in a routing table determines how many bits must match between the destination IP address of the packet and the route in the routing table. The ::/0 mask indicates that none of the bits are required to match. As long as a more specific match does not exist, the default static IPv6 route matches all packets.

Example 2-32 displays a successful ping to the R3 LAN interface.

**Example 2-32** Verify Connectivity to the R3 LAN

```
R1# ping 2001:0DB8:ACAD:3::1
Type escape sequence to abort.
Sending 5, 100-byte ICMP Echos to 2001:DB8:ACAD:3::1, timeout is 2 seconds:
!!!!!
Success rate is 100 percent (5/5), round-trip min/avg/max = 28/28/28 ms
R1#
```

### Packet Tracer 2.2.4.4: Configuring IPv6 Static and Default Routes

In this activity, you will configure IPv6 static and default routes. A static route is one that the network administrator enters manually to create a route that is reliable and safe. There are four different static routes used in this activity: a recursive static route; a directly connected static route; a fully specified static route; and a default route.

### Lab 2.2.4.5: Configuring IPv6 Static and Default Routes

In this lab, you will complete the following objectives:

- Part 1: Build the Network and Configure Basic Device Settings
- Part 2: Configure IPv6 Static and Default Routes

# Configure Floating Static Routes (2.2.5)

In this topic, you learn how to configure IPv4 and IPv6 floating static routes to provide a backup connection.

## Floating Static Routes (2.2.5.1)

Floating static routes are static routes that have an AD greater than that of another static route or dynamic routes. They are useful when providing a backup to a primary link, as shown in Figure 2-12.

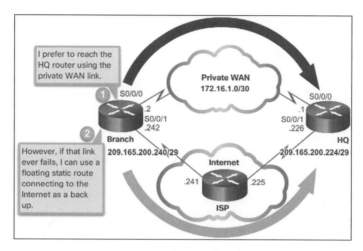

**Figure 2-12**   Why Configure a Floating Static Route?

By default, static routes have an AD of 1, making them preferable to routes learned from dynamic routing protocols. For example, following are the ADs of some common dynamic routing protocols:

- EIGRP = 90

- IGRP = 100

- OSPF = 110

- IS-IS = 115

- RIP = 120

The AD of a static route can be increased to make the route less desirable than that of another static route or a route learned through a dynamic routing protocol. In this way, the static route "floats" and is not used when the route with the better AD is active. However, if the preferred route is lost, the floating static route can take over, and traffic can be sent through this alternate route.

## Configure an IPv4 Floating Static Route (2.2.5.2)

IPv4 floating static routes are configured using the **ip route** global configuration command and specifying an AD. If no AD is configured, the default value (1) is used.

Refer to the topology in Figure 2-13. In this scenario, the preferred default route from R1 is to R2. The connection to R3 should be used for backup only.

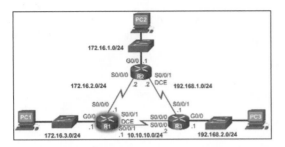

**Figure 2-13**   IPv4 Topology with Backup Route

In Example 2-33, R1 is configured with a default static route pointing to R2. Because no AD is configured, the default value (1) is used for this static route. R1 is also configured with a floating static default pointing to R3 with an AD of 5. This value is greater than the default value of 1; therefore, this route floats and is not present in the routing table unless the preferred route fails.

**Example 2-33**  Configuring an IPv4 Floating Static Route to R3

```
R1(config)# ip route 0.0.0.0 0.0.0.0 172.16.2.2
R1(config)# ip route 0.0.0.0 0.0.0.0 10.10.10.2 5
R1(config)#
```

Example 2-34 verifies that the default route to R2 is installed in the routing table. Note that the backup route to R3 is not present in the routing table.

**Example 2-34**  Verify the R1 IPv4 Routing Table

```
R1# show ip route static | begin Gateway

Gateway of last resort is 172.16.2.2 to network 0.0.0.0

S*    0.0.0.0/0 [1/0] via 172.16.2.2
R1#
```

## Test the IPv4 Floating Static Route (2.2.5.3)

Because the default static route on R1 to R2 has an AD of 1, traffic from R1 to R3 should go through R2. The output in Example 2-35 confirms that traffic between R1 and R3 flows through R2.

**Example 2-35**  Verify the Path to the R3 LAN

```
R1# traceroute 192.168.2.1
Type escape sequence to abort.
Tracing the route to 192.168.2.1
VRF info: (vrf in name/id, vrf out name/id)
  1 172.16.2.2 8 msec 4 msec 8 msec
  2 192.168.1.1 12 msec *  12 msec
R1#
```

What would happen if R2 failed? To simulate this failure, both serial interfaces of R2 are shut down, as shown in Example 2-36.

**Example 2-36**  Simulate an Interface Failure on R2

```
R2(config)# int s0/0/0
R2(config-if)# shut
*Feb 21 16:33:35.939: %LINK-5-CHANGED: Interface Serial0/0/0, changed state to
  administratively down
*Feb 21 16:33:36.939: %LINEPROTO-5-UPDOWN: Line protocol on Interface Serial0/0/0,
  changed state to down
R2(config-if)# int s0/0/1
R2(config-if)# shut
R2(config-if)#
*Feb 21 16:33:42.543: %LINK-5-CHANGED: Interface Serial0/0/1, changed state to
  administratively down
*Feb 21 16:33:43.543: %LINEPROTO-5-UPDOWN: Line protocol on Interface Serial0/0/1,
  changed state to down
```

Notice in Example 2-37 that R1 automatically generates messages indicating that the serial interface to R2 is down. A look at the routing table verifies that the default route is now pointing to R3 using the floating static default route configured with an AD value of 5 and a next-hop of 10.10.10.2.

**Example 2-37**  Verify the Backup Route is in the R1 IPv4 Routing Table

```
*Feb 21 16:35:58.435: %LINK-3-UPDOWN: Interface Serial0/0/0, changed state to
  down
*Feb 21 16:35:59.435: %LINEPROTO-5-UPDOWN: Line protocol on Interface Serial0/0/0,
  changed state to down
R1#
R1# show ip route static | begin Gateway
Gateway of last resort is 10.10.10.2 to network 0.0.0.0

S*     0.0.0.0/0 [5/0] via 10.10.10.2
R1#
```

The output in Example 2-38 confirms that traffic now flows directly between R1 and R3.

**Example 2-38**  Verify the New Path to the R3 LAN

```
R1# traceroute 192.168.2.1
Type escape sequence to abort.
Tracing the route to 192.168.2.1
VRF info: (vrf in name/id, vrf out name/id)
  1 10.10.10.2 4 msec 4 msec *
R1#
```

## Configure an IPv6 Floating Static Route (2.2.5.4)

IPv6 floating static routes are configured using the **ipv6 route** global configuration command and specifying an AD. If no AD is configured, the default value (1) is used.

Refer to the topology in Figure 2-14. In this scenario, the preferred default route from R1 is to R2. The connection to R3 should be used for backup only.

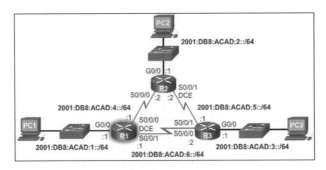

**Figure 2-14**   IPv6 Topology with Backup Route

In Example 2-39, R1 is configured with an IPv6 default static route pointing to R2. Because no AD is configured, the default value (1) is used for this static route. R1 is also configured with an IPv6 floating static default pointing to R3 with an AD of 5. This value is greater than the default value of 1; therefore, this route floats and is not present in the routing table unless the preferred route fails.

**Example 2-39**  Configuring an IPv6 Floating Static Route to R3

```
R3(config)# ipv6 route ::/0 2001:db8:acad:4::2
R3(config)# ipv6 route ::/0 2001:db8:acad:6::2 5
R3(config)#
```

Example 2-40 verifies that both IPv6 static default routes are in the running configuration.

**Example 2-40** Verifying IPv6 Static Routes on R1

```
R1# show run | include ipv6 route
ipv6 route ::/0 2001:DB8:ACAD:6::2 5
ipv6 route ::/0 2001:DB8:ACAD:4::2
R1#
```

Example 2-41 verifies that the IPv6 static default route to R2 is installed in the routing table. Note that the backup route to R3 is not present in the routing table.

**Example 2-41** Verify the Backup Route Is Not in the R1 IPv6 Routing Table

```
R1# show ipv6 route static | begin S   :
S    ::/0 [1/0]
     via 2001:DB8:ACAD:4::2
R1#
```

The process for testing the IPv6 floating static route is the same as for the IPv4 floating static route. Shut down the interfaces on R2 to simulate a failure. R1 will install the route to R3 in the route table and use it to send default traffic.

Packet Tracer
☐ Activity

**Packet Tracer 2.2.5.5: Configuring Floating Static Routes**

In this activity, you will configure IPv4 and IPv6 floating static routes. These routes are manually configured with an AD greater than that of the primary route; therefore, they would not be in the routing table until the primary route fails. You will test failover to the backup routes and then restore connectivity to the primary route.

# Configure Static Host Routes (2.2.6)

In this topic, you learn how to configure IPv4 and IPv6 static host routes that direct traffic to a specific host.

## Automatically Installed Host Routes (2.2.6.1)

A *host route* is an IPv4 address with a 32-bit mask or an IPv6 address with a 128-bit mask. There are three ways a host route can be added to the routing table:

- Automatically installed when an IP address is configured on the router

- Configured as a static host route

- Host route automatically obtained through other methods (discussed in later courses)

Cisco IOS automatically installs a host route, also known as a *local host route*, when an interface address is configured on the router. A host route allows for a more efficient process for packets that are directed to the router itself, rather than for packet forwarding. This is in addition to the connected route, designated with a C in the routing table for the network address of the interface.

The topology in Figure 2-15 is used to demonstrate host route entries.

**Figure 2-15**   Topology for Static Host Route Configurations

When an active interface on a router is configured with an IP address, a local host route is automatically added to the routing table. The local routes are marked with "L" in the output of the routing table. The IP addresses assigned to the Branch Serial0/0/0 interface are 198.51.100.1/30 for IPv4 and 2001:DB8:ACAD:1::1/64 for IPv6. The local routes for the interface are installed by the IOS in the routing table, as shown in the output in Example 2-42 for IPv4 and Example 2-43 for IPv6.

**Example 2-42** Branch IPv4 Routing Table

```
Branch# show ip route
Codes: L - local, C - connected, S - static, R - RIP, M - mobile, B - BGP
       D - EIGRP, EX - EIGRP external, O - OSPF, IA - OSPF inter area
       N1 - OSPF NSSA external type 1, N2 - OSPF NSSA external type 2
       E1 - OSPF external type 1, E2 - OSPF external type 2
        i - IS-IS, su - IS-IS summary, L1 - IS-IS level-1, L2 - IS-IS level-2
       ia - IS-IS inter area, * - candidate default, U - per-user static route
       o - ODR, P - periodic downloaded static route, H - NHRP, l - LISP
       a - application route
       + - replicated route, % - next hop override
Gateway of last resort is not set

      198.51.100.0/24 is variably subnetted, 2 subnets, 2 masks
C        198.51.100.0/30 is directly connected, Serial0/0/0
L        198.51.100.1/32 is directly connected, Serial0/0/0
Branch#
```

**Example 2-43** Branch IPv6 Routing Table

```
Branch# show ipv6 route
IPv6 Routing Table - default - 3 entries
Codes: C - Connected, L - Local, S - Static, U - Per-user Static route
       B - BGP, R - RIP, H - NHRP, I1 - ISIS L1
       I2 - ISIS L2, IA - ISIS interarea, IS - ISIS summary, D - EIGRP
       EX - EIGRP external, ND - ND Default, NDp - ND Prefix, DCE - Destination
       NDr - Redirect, O - OSPF Intra, OI - OSPF Inter, OE1 - OSPF ext 1
       OE2 - OSPF ext 2, ON1 - OSPF NSSA ext 1, ON2 - OSPF NSSA ext 2
       a - Application
C   2001:DB8:ACAD:1::/64 [0/0]
     via Serial0/0/0, directly connected
L   2001:DB8:ACAD:1::1/128 [0/0]
     via Serial0/0/0, receive
L   FF00::/8 [0/0]
     via Null0, receive
Branch#
```

**Note**

For IPv4, the local routes marked with "L" were introduced with IOS version 15.

## Configure IPv4 and IPv6 Static Host Routes (2.2.6.2)

A host route can be a manually configured static route to direct traffic to a specific destination device, such as an authentication server. The static route uses a destination IP address and a 255.255.255.255 (/32) mask for IPv4 host routes and a /128 prefix length for IPv6 host routes. Static routes are marked with "S" in the output of the routing table. An IPv4 and an IPv6 host route are configured on the BRANCH router to access the server in Example 2-44.

**Example 2-44** IPv4 and IPv6 Host Route Configuration and Verification

```
Branch(config)# ip route 209.165.200.238 255.255.255.255 198.51.100.2
Branch(config)# ipv6 route 2001:db8:acad:2::99/128 2001:db8:acad:1::2
Branch(config)# end
Branch#
Branch# show ip route | begin Gateway
Gateway of last resort is not set

      198.51.100.0/24 is variably subnetted, 2 subnets, 2 masks
C        198.51.100.0/30 is directly connected, Serial0/0/0
L        198.51.100.1/32 is directly connected, Serial0/0/0
```

```
         209.165.200.0/32 is subnetted, 1 subnets
S          209.165.200.38 [1/0] via 198.51.100.2
Branch#
Branch# show ipv6 route
<output omitted>
C    2001:DB8:ACAD:1::/64 [0/0]
     via Serial0/0/0, directly connected
L    2001:DB8:ACAD:1::1/128 [0/0]
     via Serial0/0/0, receive
S    2001:DB8:ACAD:2::99/128 [1/0]
     via 2001:DB8:ACAD:1::2
L    FF00::/8 [0/0]
     via Null0, receive
Branch#
```

For IPv6 static routes, the next-hop address can be the link-local address of the adjacent router. However, you must specify an interface type and an interface number when using a link-local address as the next hop, as shown in Example 2-45.

**Example 2-45** Fully Specified IPv6 Host Route with the Next-Hop Link-Local Address

```
Branch(config)# no ipv6 route 2001:db8:acad:2::99/128 2001:db8:acad:1::2
Branch(config)# ipv6 route 2001:db8:acad:2::99/128 serial 0/0/0 fe80::2
Branch(config)# end
Branch#
Branch# show ipv6 route
<output omitted>
S    ::/0 [1/0]
     via 2001:DB8:ACAD:1::2
C    2001:DB8:ACAD:1::/64 [0/0]
     via Serial0/0/0, directly connected
L    2001:DB8:ACAD:1::1/128 [0/0]
     via Serial0/0/0, receive
S    2001:DB8:ACAD:2::99/128 [1/0]
     via FE80::2, Serial0/0/0
L    FF00::/8 [0/0]
     via Null0, receive
Branch#
```

# Troubleshoot Static and Default Route (2.3)

Troubleshooting is a well sought-after skill that is acquired through practice and experience.

In this section, you practice troubleshooting skills to solve static and default route configuration problems.

## Packet Processing with Static Routes (2.3.1)

In this topic, you learn how a router processes packets when a static route is configured.

### Static Routes and Packet Forwarding (2.3.1.1)

The following example describes the packet-forwarding process with static routes shown in Figure 2-16.

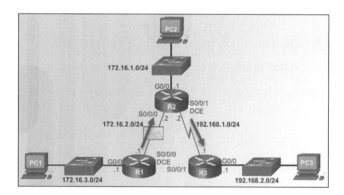

**Figure 2-16**   Static Routes and Packet Forwarding

In the figure, PC1 is sending a packet to PC3:

1. The packet arrives on the GigabitEthernet 0/0 interface of R1.

2. R1 does not have a specific route to the destination network, 192.168.2.0/24; therefore, R1 uses the default static route.

3. R1 encapsulates the packet in a new frame. Because the link to R2 is a point-to-point link, R1 adds an "all 1s" address for the Layer 2 destination address.

4. The frame is forwarded out of the Serial 0/0/0 interface. The packet arrives on the Serial 0/0/0 interface on R2.

5. R2 de-encapsulates the frame and looks for a route to the destination. R2 has a static route to 192.168.2.0/24 out of the Serial 0/0/1 interface.

6.  R2 encapsulates the packet in a new frame. Because the link to R3 is a point-to-point link, R2 adds an "all 1s" address for the Layer 2 destination address.

7.  The frame is forwarded out the Serial 0/0/1 interface. The packet arrives on the Serial 0/0/1 interface on R3.

8.  R3 de-encapsulates the frame and looks for a route to the destination. R3 has a connected route to 192.168.2.0/24 out of the GigabitEthernet 0/0 interface.

9.  R3 looks up the ARP table entry for 192.168.2.10 to find the Layer 2 MAC address for PC3. If no entry exists, R3 sends an Address Resolution Protocol (ARP) request out of the GigabitEthernet 0/0 interface, and PC3 responds with an ARP reply, which includes the PC3 MAC address.

10. R3 encapsulates the packet in a new frame with the MAC address of the GigabitEthernet 0/0 interface as the source Layer 2 address and the MAC address of PC3 as the destination MAC address.

11. The frame is forwarded out of the GigabitEthernet 0/0 interface. The packet arrives on the network interface card (NIC) interface of PC3.

## Troubleshoot IPv4 Static and Default Route Configuration (2.3.2)

In this topic, you gain troubleshooting skills by solving common static and default route configuration issues.

### Troubleshoot a Missing Route (2.3.2.1)

Networks are subject to forces that can cause their status to change quite often:

- An interface fails
- A service provider drops a connection
- Links become oversaturated
- An administrator enters a wrong configuration

When there is a change in the network, connectivity may be lost. Network administrators are responsible for pinpointing and solving the problem. To find and solve these issues, a network administrator must be familiar with tools to help isolate routing problems quickly.

Following are some common IOS troubleshooting commands:

- ping
- traceroute
- show ip route

- show ip interface brief

- show cdp neighbors detail

Example 2-46 displays the result of an extended ping from the source interface of R1 to the LAN interface of R3. An extended ping is an enhanced version of the ping utility. Extended ping enables you to specify the source IP address for the ping packets.

**Example 2-46** Extended Ping

```
R1# ping 192.168.2.1 source 172.16.3.1
Type escape sequence to abort.
Sending 5, 100-byte ICMP Echos to 192.168.2.1, timeout is 2 seconds:
Packet sent with a source address of 172.16.3.1
!!!!!
Success rate is 100 percent (5/5), round-trip min/avg/max = 28/28/28 ms
R1#
```

Example 2-47 displays the result of a traceroute from the R1 to the R3 LAN.

**Example 2-47** Traceroute from R1 to R3

```
R1# traceroute 192.168.2.1
Type escape sequence to abort.
Tracing the route to 192.168.2.1
VRF info: (vrf in name/id, vrf out name/id)
  1 172.16.2.2 4 msec 4 msec 8 msec
  2 192.168.1.1 12 msec 12 msec *
R1#
```

Example 2-48 displays the routing table of R1.

**Example 2-48** Verify the Routing Table of R1

```
R1# show ip route | begin Gateway
Gateway of last resort is not set

      172.16.0.0/16 is variably subnetted, 5 subnets, 2 masks
S        172.16.1.0/24 [1/0] via 172.16.2.2
C        172.16.2.0/24 is directly connected, Serial0/0/0
L        172.16.2.1/32 is directly connected, Serial0/0/0
C        172.16.3.0/24 is directly connected, GigabitEthernet0/0
L        172.16.3.1/32 is directly connected, GigabitEthernet0/0
S     192.168.1.0/24 [1/0] via 172.16.2.2
S     192.168.2.0/24 [1/0] via 172.16.2.2
R1#
```

Example 2-49 provides a quick status of all interfaces on the router.

**Example 2-49**  Verify Interface Status

```
R1# show ip interface brief
Interface                      IP-Address    OK? Method Status                 Protocol
Embedded-Service-Engine0/0 unassigned    YES unset  administratively down down
GigabitEthernet0/0             172.16.3.1    YES manual up                     up
GigabitEthernet0/1             unassigned    YES unset  administratively down down
Serial0/0/0                    172.16.2.1    YES manual up                     up
Serial0/0/1                    unassigned    YES unset  administratively down down
R1#
```

Example 2-50 provides a list of directly connected Cisco devices. This command validates Layer 2 (and therefore Layer 1) connectivity. For example, if a neighbor device is listed in the command output, but it cannot be pinged, then Layer 3 addressing should be investigated.

**Example 2-50**  Verify Directly Connected Cisco Devices

```
R1# show cdp neighbors
Capability Codes: R - Router, T - Trans Bridge, B - Source Route Bridge
                  S - Switch, H - Host, I - IGMP, r - Repeater, P - Phone,
                  D - Remote, C - CVTA, M - Two-port Mac Relay


Device ID        Local Intrfce     Holdtme    Capability  Platform  Port ID
netlab-cs5       Gig 0/0             156            S I    WS-C2960- Fas 0/1
R2               Ser 0/0/0           153          R S I    CISCO1941 Ser 0/0/0
R1#
```

## Solve a Connectivity Problem (2.3.2.2)

Finding a missing (or misconfigured) route is a relatively straightforward process, if the right tools are used in a methodical manner.

For instance, in this example, the user at PC1 reports that he cannot access resources on the R3 LAN. This can be confirmed by pinging the LAN interface of R3 using the LAN interface of R1 as the source (see Example 2-51). The results indicate that there is no connectivity between these LANs.

**Example 2-51**  Verify Connectivity to R3 LAN

```
R1# ping 192.168.2.1 source g0/0
Type escape sequence to abort.
Sending 5, 100-byte ICMP Echos to 192.168.2.1, timeout is 2 seconds:
Packet sent with a source address of 172.16.3.1
.....
Success rate is 0 percent (0/5)
R1#
```

A traceroute in Example 2-52 reveals that R2 is not responding as expected. For some reason, R2 forwards the traceroute back to R1. R1 returns it to R2. This loop would continue until the time to live (TTL) value decrements to zero, in which case, the router would then send an Internet Control Message Protocol (ICMP) destination unreachable message to R1.

**Example 2-52**  Traceroute from R1 to R3

```
R1# traceroute 192.168.2.1
Type escape sequence to abort.
Tracing the route to 192.168.2.1
VRF info: (vrf in name/id, vrf out name/id)
  1 172.16.2.2 4 msec 4 msec 8 msec
  2 172.16.2.1 12 msec 12 msec 12 msec
  3 172.16.2.2 12 msec 8 msec 8 msec
  4 172.16.2.1 20 msec 16 msec 20 msec
  5 172.16.2.2 16 msec 16 msec 16 msec
  6 172.16.2.1 20 msec 20 msec 24 msec
  7 172.16.2.2 20 msec
R1#
```

The next step is to investigate the routing table of R2 because it is the router displaying a strange forwarding pattern. The routing table in Example 2-53 reveals that the 192.168.2.0/24 network is configured incorrectly.

**Example 2-53**  Verify the Routing Table of R2

```
R2# show ip route | begin Gateway
Gateway of last resort is not set

      172.16.0.0/16 is variably subnetted, 5 subnets, 2 masks
C        172.16.1.0/24 is directly connected, GigabitEthernet0/0
L        172.16.1.1/32 is directly connected, GigabitEthernet0/0
C        172.16.2.0/24 is directly connected, Serial0/0/0
```

```
L          172.16.2.2/32 is directly connected, Serial0/0/0
S          172.16.3.0/24 [1/0] via 172.16.2.1
        192.168,1.0/24 is variably subnetted, 2 subnets, 2 masks
C          192.168.1.0/24 is directly connected, Serial0/0/1
L          192.168.1.2/32 is directly connected, Serial0/0/1
S        192.168.2.0/24 [1/0] via 172.16.2.1
R2#
```

A static route to the 192.168.2.0/24 network has been configured using the next-hop
address 172.16.2.1. Using the configured next-hop address, packets destined for the
192.168.2.0/24 network are sent back to R1. It is clear from the topology that the
192.168.2.0/24 network is connected to R3, not R1. Therefore, the static route to the
192.168.2.0/24 network on R2 must use next-hop 192.168.1.1, not 172.16.2.1.

Example 2-54 shows output from the running configuration that reveals the
incorrect **ip route** statement. The incorrect route is removed and the correct route is
then entered.

**Example 2-54** Identify and Solve the Problem

```
R2# show running-config | section ip route
ip route 172.16.3.0 255.255.255.0 172.16.2.1
ip route 192.168.2.0 255.255.255.0 172.16.2.1
R2#
R2# conf t
R2(config)# no ip route 192.168.2.0 255.255.255.0 172.16.2.1
R2(config)# ip route 192.168.2.0 255.255.255.0 192.168.1.1
R2(config)#
```

Example 2-55 verifies that R1 can now reach the LAN interface of R3. As a last step in
confirmation, the user on PC1 should also test connectivity to the 192.168.2.0/24 LAN.

**Example 2-55** Verify Connectivity to R3 LAN

```
R1# ping 192.168.2.1 source g0/0
Type escape sequence to abort.
Sending 5, 100-byte ICMP Echos to 192.168.2.1, timeout is 2 seconds:
Packet sent with a source address of 172.16.3.1
!!!!!
Success rate is 100 percent (5/5), round-trip min/avg/max = 28/28/28 ms
R1#
```

**Packet Tracer 2.3.2.3: Troubleshooting Static Routes**

In this activity, PC1 reports that it cannot access resources at the server. Locate the problem, decide on an appropriate solution, and resolve the issue.

**Lab 2.3.2.4: Troubleshooting Static Routes**

In this lab, you will complete the following objectives:

- Part 1: Build the Network and Configure Basic Device Settings
- Part 2: Troubleshoot Static Routes in an IPv4 Network
- Part 3: Troubleshoot Static Routes in an IPv6 Network

## Summary (2.4)

**Class Activity 2.4.1.1: Make It Static**

As the use of IPv6 addressing becomes more prevalent, it is important for network administrators to be able to direct network traffic between routers.

To prove that you are able to direct IPv6 traffic correctly and review the IPv6 default static route curriculum concepts, use the topology as shown in the .pdf file provided, specifically for this activity.

Work with a partner to write an IPv6 statement for each of the three scenarios. Try to write the route statements without the assistance of completed labs, Packet Tracer files, and so on.

**Scenario 1:** IPv6 default static route from R2 directing all data through your S0/0/0 interface to the next hop address on R1

**Scenario 2:** IPv6 default static route from R3 directing all data through your S0/0/1 interface to the next hop address on R2

**Scenario 3:** IPv6 default static route from R2 directing all data through your S0/0/1 interface to the next hop address on R3

When complete, get together with another group and compare your written answers. Discuss any differences found in your comparisons.

In this chapter, you learned how IPv4 and IPv6 static routes can be used to reach remote networks. Remote networks are networks that can only be reached by forwarding the packet to another router. Static routes are easily configured. However, in large networks, this manual operation can become quite cumbersome. Static routes are still used, even when a dynamic routing protocol is implemented.

Static routes can be configured with a next-hop IP address, which is commonly the IP address of the next-hop router. When a next-hop IP address is used, the routing table process must resolve this address to an exit interface. On point-to-point serial links, it is usually more efficient to configure the static route with an exit interface. On multiaccess networks, such as Ethernet, both a next-hop IP address and an exit interface can be configured on the static route.

Static routes have a default AD of 1. This AD also applies to static routes configured with a next-hop address, as well as an exit interface.

A static route is only entered in the routing table if the next-hop IP address can be resolved through an exit interface. Whether the static route is configured with a next-hop IP address or exit interface, if the exit interface that is used to forward that packet is not in the routing table, the static route is not included in the routing table.

A default route is configured with a 0.0.0.0 network address and a 0.0.0.0 subnet mask for IPv4, and the prefix/prefix-length ::/0 for IPv6. If there is not a more specific match in the routing table, the routing table uses the default route to forward the packet to another router.

A floating static route can be configured to back up a main link by manipulating its administrative value.

# Practice

The following activities provide practice with the topics introduced in this chapter. The Labs and Class Activities are available in the companion *Routing and Switching Essentials v6 Labs and Study Guide* (ISBN 9781587134265). The Packet Tracer Activities PKA files are found in the online course.

**Class Activities**

Class Activity 2.0.1.2: Which Way Should We Go

Class Activity 2.4.1.1: Make It Static

**Labs**

Lab 2.2.2.5: Configuring IPv4 Static and Default Routes

Lab 2.2.4.5: Configuring IPv6 Static and Default Routes

Lab 2.3.2.4: Troubleshooting IPv4 and IPv6 Static Routes

**Packet Tracer Activities**

Packet Tracer 2.2.2.4: Configuring IPv4 Static and Default Routes

Packet Tracer 2.2.4.4: Configuring IPv6 Static and Default Routes

Packet Tracer 2.2.5.5: Configuring Floating Static Routes

Packet Tracer 2.3.2.3: Troubleshooting Static Routes

# Check Your Understanding Questions

Complete all the review questions listed here to test your understanding of the topics and concepts in this chapter. The appendix "Answers to the 'Check Your Understanding' Questions" lists the answers.

1. What are two advantages of static routing over dynamic routing? (Choose two.)

   A. Static routing is more secure because it does not advertise over the network.

   B. Static routing is relatively easy to configure for large networks.

   C. Static routing requires little knowledge of the network for correct implementation.

   D. Static routing scales well with expanding networks.

   E. Static routing uses fewer router resources than dynamic routing.

2. What type of route allows a router to forward packets even though its routing table contains no specific route to the destination network?

   A. Default route

   B. Destination route

   C. Dynamic route

   D. Generic route

3. Why would a floating static route be configured with an AD that is higher than the AD of a dynamic routing protocol that is running on the same router?

   A. To act as a gateway of last resort

   B. To be the priority route in the routing table

   C. To be used as a backup route

   D. To load-balance the traffic

4. What is the correct syntax of a floating static route?

   A. **ip route 0.0.0.0 0.0.0.0 serial 0/0/0**

   B. **ip route 172.16.0.0 255.248.0.0 10.0.0.1**

   C. **ip route 209.165.200.228 255.255.255.248** serial 0/0/0

   D. **ip route 209.165.200.228 255.255.255.248 10.0.0.1 120**

5. Which type of static route that is configured on a router uses only the exit interface?

   A. Default static route

   B. Directly connected static route

   C. Fully specified static route

   D. Recursive static route

6. The network administrator configures the router with the **ip route 172.16.1.0 255.255.255.0 172.16.2.2** command. How will this route appear in the routing table?

    A. C 172.16.1.0 [1/0] via 172.16.2.2

    B. C 172.16.1.0 is directly connected, Serial0/0

    C. S 172.16.1.0 [1/0] via 172.16.2.2

    D. S 172.16.1.0 is directly connected, Serial0/0

7. What two pieces of information are needed in a fully specified static route to eliminate recursive lookups? (Choose two.)

    A. The AD for the destination network

    B. The interface ID exit interface

    C. The interface ID of the next-hop neighbor

    D. The IP address of the exit interface

    E. The IP address of the next-hop neighbor

8. Assume the administrator has entered the **ip route 192.168.10.0 255.255.255.0 10.10.10.2 5** command. How would an administrator test this configuration?

    A. Delete the default gateway route on the router.

    B. Manually shut down the router interface used as a primary route.

    C. Ping any valid address on the 192.168.10.0/24 network.

    D. Ping from the 192.168.10.0 network to the 10.10.10.2 address.

9. Which three IOS troubleshooting commands can help to isolate problems with a static route? (Choose three.)

    A. **ping**

    B. **show arp**

    C. **show ip interface brief**

    D. **show ip route**

    E. **show version**

    F. **tracert**

10. What happens to a static route entry in a routing table when the outgoing interface associated with that route goes into the down state?

    A. The router automatically redirects the static route to use another interface.

    B. The router polls neighbors for a replacement route.

    C. The static route is removed from the routing table.

    D. The static route remains in the table because it was defined as static.

# CHAPTER 3

# Dynamic Routing

## Objectives

Upon completion of this chapter, you will be able to answer the following questions:

- What is the purpose of dynamic routing protocols?

- How do you use dynamic routing and static routing?

- How do you configure the RIPv2 routing protocol?

- What are the components of an IPv4 routing table entry for a given route?

- What is the parent/child relationship in a dynamically built routing table?

- How does a router determine which route will be used to forward an IPv4 packet?

- How does a router determine which route will be used to forward an IPv6 packet?

## Key Terms

This chapter uses the following key terms. You can find the definitions in the Glossary.

# Introduction (3.0.1.1)

The data networks that we use in our everyday lives to learn, play, and work range from small, local networks to large, global internetworks. At home, a user may have a router and two or more devices such as computers, tablets, smartphones, and more. At work, an organization may have multiple routers and switches servicing the data communication needs of hundreds or even thousands of PCs.

Routers forward packets by using information in the routing table. Routes to remote networks can be learned by the router in two ways: static routes and dynamic routes.

In a large network with numerous networks and subnets, configuring and maintaining static routes between these networks requires a great deal of administrative and operational overhead. This operational overhead is especially cumbersome when changes to the network occur, such as a down link or implementing a new subnet. Implementing dynamic routing protocols can ease the burden of configuration and maintenance tasks and give the network scalability.

This chapter introduces dynamic routing protocols. It compares the use of static and dynamic routing. Then the implementation of dynamic routing using the Routing Information Protocol version 1 (RIPv1) and version 2 (RIPv2) is discussed. The chapter concludes with an in-depth look at the routing table.

**Class Activity 3.0.1.2: How Much Does This Cost?**

This modeling activity illustrates the network concept of routing cost.

You will be a member of a team of five students who travel routes to complete the activity scenarios. One digital camera or bring your own device (BYOD) with camera, a stopwatch, and the student file for this activity will be required per group. One person will function as the photographer and event recorder, as selected by each group. The remaining four team members will actively participate in the scenarios that follow.

A school or university classroom, hallway, outdoor track area, school parking lot, or any other location can serve as the venue for these activities.

### Activity 1

The tallest person in the group establishes a start and finish line by marking 15 steps from start to finish, indicating the distance of the team route. Each student will take 15 steps from the start line toward the finish line and then stop on the 15th step—no further steps are allowed.

**Note:** Not all of the students may reach the same distance from the start line due to their height and stride differences. The photographer will take a group picture of the entire team's final location after taking the 15 steps required.

### Activity 2

A new start and finish line will be established; however, this time, a longer distance for the route will be established than the distance specified in Activity 1. No maximum steps are to be used as a basis for creating this particular route. One at a time, students will "walk the new route from beginning to end twice."

Each team member will count the steps taken to complete the route. The recorder will time each student, and at the end of each team member's route, record the time that it took to complete the full route and how many steps were taken, as recounted by each team member and recorded on the team's student file.

After both activities have been completed, teams will use the digital picture taken for Activity 1 and their recorded data from Activity 2 file to answer the reflection questions.

Group answers can be discussed as a class, time permitting.

# Dynamic Routing Protocols (3.1)

To reach remote networks, it is imperative that routing be established. Routing is commonly implemented in organizations using dynamic routing protocols and static routing.

In this section, you learn about the function of dynamic routing protocols.

## Dynamic Routing Protocol Overview (3.1.1)

In this topic, you learn about the purpose of dynamic routing protocols.

### Dynamic Routing Protocol Evolution (3.1.1.1)

Dynamic routing protocols have been used in networks since the late 1980s. One of the first routing protocols was *Routing Information Protocol (RIP)*. *RIPv1* was released in 1988, but some of the basic algorithms within the protocol were used on the Advanced Research Projects Agency Network (ARPANET) as early as 1969.

As networks evolved and became more complex, new routing protocols emerged. RIP was updated to *RIPv2* to accommodate growth in the network environment. However, RIPv2 still does not scale to the larger network implementations of today. To address the needs of larger networks, two advanced routing protocols were developed: *Open Shortest Path First (OSPF)* and *Intermediate System-to-Intermediate System (IS-IS)*. Cisco developed the *Interior Gateway Routing Protocol (IGRP)* and *Enhanced IGRP (EIGRP)*, which also scales well in larger network implementations.

Additionally, there was the need to connect different internetworks and provide routing between them. The *Border Gateway Protocol (BGP)* is now used between Internet service providers (ISPs). BGP is also used between ISPs and their larger private clients to exchange routing information.

Table 3-1 provides a timeline of when the various protocols were introduced.

**Table 3-1**    Routing Protocol Evolution

| Year | IPv4 Routing Protocol | IPv6 Routing Protocol |
|------|----------------------|----------------------|
| 2005 | | EIGRP for IPv6 |
| 2000 | | IS-IS for IPv6 |
| | | OSPFv3 |
| | | BGP-MP |
| | | RIPng |
| 1995 | BGP-4 | |
| | RIPv2 | |
| | EIGRP for IPv4 | |
| | OSPFv2 | |
| 1990 | IS-IS | |
| | OSPFv1 | |
| | RIPv1 | |
| 1985 | IGRP | |
| | EGP | |

Table 3-2 classifies the protocols.

**Table 3-2**    Routing Protocol Classification

| | Interior Gateway Protocols | | | | Exterior Gateway Protocols |
|------|----------------|----------------|---------|----------------|-------------|
| | *Distance Vector* | | *Link-State* | | *Path Vector* |
| IPv4 | RIPv2 | EIGRP | OSPFv2 | IS-IS | BGP-4 |
| IPv6 | RIPng | EIGRP for IPv6 | OSPFv3 | IS-IS for IPv6 | BGP-MP |

With the advent of numerous consumer devices using IP, the *IPv4 addressing space* is nearly exhausted; thus, IPv6 has emerged. To support the communication based on

IPv6, newer versions of the IP routing protocols have been developed, as shown in the IPv6 row in Table 3-2.

## Dynamic Routing Protocol Components (3.1.1.2)

Routing protocols are used to facilitate the exchange of routing information between routers. A routing protocol is a set of processes, algorithms, and messages that are used to exchange routing information and populate the routing table with the routing protocol's choice of best paths. Dynamic routing protocols have several purposes:

- Discovery of remote networks

- Maintaining up-to-date routing information

- Choosing the best path to destination networks

- Finding a new best path if the current path is no longer available

The main components of dynamic routing protocols include the following:

- *Data structures*—Routing protocols typically use tables or databases for their operations. This information is kept in RAM.

- *Routing protocol messages*—Routing protocols use various types of messages to discover neighboring routers, exchange routing information, and perform other tasks to learn and maintain accurate information about the network.

- *Algorithm*—An algorithm is a finite list of steps used to accomplish a task. Routing protocols use algorithms for facilitating routing information and for best path determination.

As shown in Figure 3-1, routing protocols allow routers to dynamically share information about remote networks and automatically offer this information to their own routing tables.

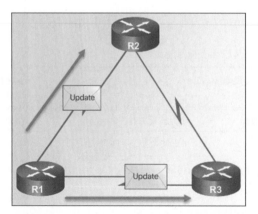

**Figure 3-1**   Routers Dynamically Share Updates

Routing protocols determine the best path, or route, to each network. That route is then offered to the routing table. The route will be installed in the routing table if there is not another routing source with a lower administrative distance (AD). For example, a static route with an AD of 1 will have precedence over the same network learned by a dynamic routing protocol.

A primary benefit of dynamic routing protocols is that routers exchange routing information when there is a topology change. This exchange allows routers to automatically learn about new networks and to find alternate paths when there is a link failure to a current network.

# Dynamic Versus Static Routing (3.1.2)

In this topic, you learn about the differences and use of dynamic routing and static routing.

### Static Routing Uses (3.1.2.1)

Before identifying the benefits of dynamic routing protocols, consider the reasons why network professionals use static routing.

Static routing has several primary uses, including these:

- Providing ease of routing table maintenance in smaller networks that are not expected to grow significantly.

- Routing to and from a stub network, which is a network with only one default route out and no knowledge of remote networks.

- Accessing a single default route (which is used to represent a path to any network that does not have a more specific match with another route in the routing table).

Figure 3-2 provides a sample scenario of static routing.

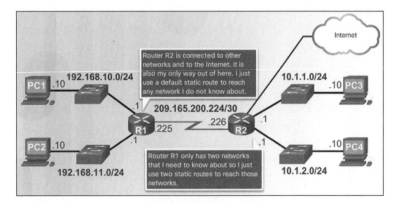

**Figure 3-2**    Static Routing Scenario

## Static Routing Advantages and Disadvantages (3.1.2.2)

Table 3-3 highlights the advantages and disadvantages of static routing.

**Table 3-3**   Static Routing Advantages and Disadvantages

| Advantages | Disadvantages |
|---|---|
| Easy to implement in a small network. | Static routes are not easy to implement in a large network. Configuration complexity increases dramatically as a network grows. Therefore, static routes are suitable only for simple topologies or for special purposes such as a default static route. |
| Very secure. No advertisements are sent, as compared to dynamic routing protocols. | Configuration complexity increases dramatically as a network grows. Therefore, managing the static configurations can become time consuming. |
| Route to destination is always the same, which makes them fairly easy to troubleshoot. | If a link fails, a static route cannot reroute traffic. Therefore, manual intervention is required to reroute traffic. |
| No routing algorithm or update mechanism required; therefore, extra resources (CPU or RAM) are not used. | |

## Dynamic Routing Protocols Uses (3.1.2.3)

Dynamic routing protocols help the network administrator manage the time consuming and exacting process of configuring and maintaining static routes.

Imagine maintaining the static routing configurations for the seven routers. What if the company grew and now had four regions and 28 routers to manage, as shown in Figure 3-3? What happens when a link goes down? How do you ensure that redundant paths are available? Dynamic routing is the best choice for large networks like the one shown.

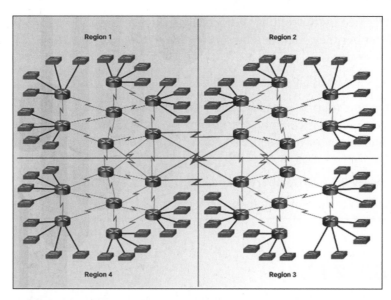

**Figure 3-3**  Dynamic Routing Scenario

## Dynamic Routing Advantages and Disadvantages (3.1.2.4)

Table 3-4 highlights the advantages and disadvantages of dynamic routing. Dynamic routing protocols work well in any type of network consisting of several routers. They are scalable and automatically determine better routes if there is a change in the topology. Although there is more to the configuration of dynamic routing protocols, they are simpler to configure than static routing in a large network.

**Table 3-4**  Dynamic Routing Advantages and Disadvantages

| Advantages | Disadvantages |
| --- | --- |
| Suitable in all topologies where multiple routers are required. | Can be more complex to implement. |
| Generally independent of the network size. | Less secure. Additional configuration settings are required to secure. |
| Automatically adapts topology to reroute traffic if possible. | Route depends on the current topology. |
|  | Requires additional CPU, RAM, and link bandwidth. |

There are disadvantages to dynamic routing. Dynamic routing requires knowledge of additional commands. It is also less secure than static routing because the interfaces identified by the routing protocol send out routing updates. Routes taken may differ between packets. The *routing algorithm* uses additional CPU, RAM, and link bandwidth.

Notice how dynamic routing addresses the disadvantages of static routing.

Dynamic routing certainly has several advantages over static routing. However, static routing is commonly used in networks today. Most networks typically use a combination of both static and dynamic routing.

Interactive Graphic

**Activity 3.1.2.5: Compare Static and Dynamic Routing**

Refer to the online course to complete this activity.

# RIPv2 (3.2)

There are only a few routing protocols to choose from. Each has its advantages and disadvantages. However, the easiest to configure and understand is Routing Information Protocol (RIP).

In this section, you will configure and verify basic RIPv2 settings.

## Configuring the RIP Protocol (3.2.1)

In this topic, you will configure the RIPv2 routing protocol.

### Router RIP Configuration Mode (3.2.1.1)

Although RIP is rarely used in modern networks, it is useful as a foundation for understanding basic network routing.

To help explain how to configure the RIPv2 routing protocol, refer to the reference topology in Figure 3-4 and the addressing table in Table 3-5.

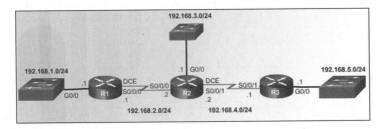

**Figure 3-4** RIPv2 Topology

**Table 3-5**   Addressing Table

| Device | Interface | IPv4 Address | Subnet Mask |
|--------|-----------|--------------|-------------|
| R1     | G0/0      | 192.168.1.1  | 255.255.255.0 |
|        | S0/0/0    | 192.168.2.1  | 255.255.255.0 |
| R2     | G0/0      | 192.168.3.1  | 255.255.255.0 |
|        | S0/0/0    | 192.168.2.2  | 255.255.255.0 |
|        | S0/0/1    | 192.168.4.2  | 255.255.255.0 |
| R3     | G0/0      | 192.168.5.1  | 255.255.255.0 |
|        | S0/01     | 192.168.4.1  | 255.255.255.0 |

In this scenario, all routers have been configured with basic management features, and all interfaces identified in the reference topology are configured and enabled. There are no static routes configured and no routing protocols enabled; therefore, remote network access is currently impossible. RIPv1 is used as the dynamic routing protocol. To enable RIP, use the **router rip** command, as shown in Example 3-1.

**Example 3-1** Enable RIP Routing

```
R1# conf t
Enter configuration commands, one per line.  End with CNTL/Z.
R1(config)# router rip
R1(config-router)#
```

This command does not directly start the RIP process. Instead, it provides access to the router configuration mode where the RIP routing settings are configured. When enabling RIP, the default version is RIPv1.

Example 3-2 displays the various RIP commands that can be configured. The highlighted keywords are covered in this section.

**Example 3-2** RIP Configuration Options

```
R1(config-router)# ?
Router configuration commands:
  address-family        Enter Address Family command mode
  auto-summary          Enable automatic network number summarization
  default               Set a command to its defaults
  default-information    Control distribution of default information
  default-metric        Set metric of redistributed routes
  distance              Define an administrative distance
```

```
distribute-list          Filter networks in routing updates
exit                     Exit from routing protocol configuration mode
flash-update-threshold   Specify flash update threshold in second
help                     Description of the interactive help system
input-queue              Specify input queue depth
maximum-paths            Forward packets over multiple paths
neighbor                 Specify a neighbor router
network                  Enable routing on an IP network
no                       Negate a command or set its defaults
offset-list              Add or subtract offset from RIP metrics
output-delay             Interpacket delay for RIP updates
passive-interface        Suppress routing updates on an interface
redistribute             Redistribute information from another routing
                         protocol
timers                   Adjust routing timers
traffic-share            How to compute traffic share over alternate paths
validate-update-source   Perform sanity checks against source address of
                         routing updates
version                  Set routing protocol version

R1(config-router)#
```

To disable and eliminate RIP, use the **no router rip** global configuration command. This command stops the RIP process and erases all existing RIP configurations.

## Advertise Networks (3.2.1.2)

By entering the RIP router configuration mode, the router is instructed to run RIPv1. But the router still needs to know which local interfaces it should use for communication with other routers, as well as which locally connected networks it should advertise to those routers.

To enable RIP routing for a network, use the **network** *network-address* router configuration mode command. Enter the classful network address for each directly connected network. This command does the following:

- Activates RIP on all interfaces that belong to a specific network. Associated interfaces now both send and receive RIP updates.

- Advertises the specified network in RIP routing updates sent to other routers every 30 seconds.

**Note**

RIPv1 is a *classful routing protocol* for IPv4. Therefore, if a subnet address is entered, the IOS automatically converts it to the classful network address. For example, entering the **network 192.168.1.32** command would automatically be converted to **network 192.168.1.0** in the running configuration file. The IOS does not give an error message but instead corrects the input and enters the classful network address.

Example 3-3, the **network** command is used to advertise the R1 directly connected networks.

**Example 3-3** Advertise RIP Networks

```
R1(config)# router rip
R1(config-router)# network 192.168.1.0
R1(config-router)# network 192.168.2.0
R1(config-router)#
```

## Verify RIP Routing (3.2.1.3)

The **show ip protocols** command displays the IPv4 routing protocol settings currently configured on the router. Refer to the output in Example 3-4.

**Example 3-4** Verify RIP Settings

```
R1# show ip protocols
*** IP Routing is NSF aware ***

Routing Protocol is "rip"
  Outgoing update filter list for all interfaces is not set
  Incoming update filter list for all interfaces is not set
  Sending updates every 30 seconds, next due in 16 seconds
  Invalid after 180 seconds, hold down 180, flushed after 240
  Redistributing: rip
  Default version control: send version 1, receive any version
    Interface          Send  Recv  Triggered RIP  Key-chain
    GigabitEthernet0/0  1     1 2
    Serial0/0/0         1     1 2
  Automatic network summarization is in effect
  Maximum path: 4
  Routing for Networks:
    192.168.1.0
    192.168.2.0
  Routing Information Sources:
    Gateway          Distance      Last Update
    192.168.2.2        120         00:00:15
  Distance: (default is 120)

R1#
```

This output confirms most RIP parameters, including the following:

- RIP routing is configured and running on router R1.
- The values of various timers; for example, the next routing update will be sent by R1 in 16 seconds.
- The version of RIP configured is currently RIPv1.
- R1 is currently summarizing at the classful network boundary.
- The classful networks are advertised by R1. These are the networks that R1 includes in its RIP updates.
- The RIP neighbors are listed, including their next-hop IP address, the associated advertised distance that R2 uses for updates sent by this neighbor, and when the last update was received from this neighbor.

> **Note**
>
> This command is also useful when verifying the operations of other routing protocols (that is, EIGRP and OSPF).

The **show ip route** command displays the RIP routes installed in the routing table. In Example 3-5, R1 has learned about the highlighted remote networks from RIP.

**Example 3-5** Verify RIP Routes

```
R1# show ip route | begin Gateway
Gateway of last resort is not set

      192.168.1.0/24 is variably subnetted, 2 subnets, 2 masks
C        192.168.1.0/24 is directly connected, GigabitEthernet0/0
L        192.168.1.1/32 is directly connected, GigabitEthernet0/0
      192.168.2.0/24 is variably subnetted, 2 subnets, 2 masks
C        192.168.2.0/24 is directly connected, Serial0/0/0
L        192.168.2.1/32 is directly connected, Serial0/0/0
R     192.168.3.0/24 [120/1] via 192.168.2.2, 00:00:24, Serial0/0/0
R     192.168.4.0/24 [120/1] via 192.168.2.2, 00:00:24, Serial0/0/0
R     192.168.5.0/24 [120/2] via 192.168.2.2, 00:00:24, Serial0/0/0
R1#
```

## Enable and Verify RIPv2 (3.2.1.4)

By default, when a RIP process is configured on a Cisco router, it is running RIPv1, as shown in Example 3-6. However, even though the router only sends RIPv1 messages, it can interpret both RIPv1 and RIPv2 messages. A RIPv1 router ignores the RIPv2 fields in the route entry.

**Example 3-6** Verify Default RIP Version

```
R1# show ip protocols
*** IP Routing is NSF aware ***

Routing Protocol is "rip"
  Outgoing update filter list for all interfaces is not set
  Incoming update filter list for all interfaces is not set
  Sending updates every 30 seconds, next due in 16 seconds
  Invalid after 180 seconds, hold down 180, flushed after 240
  Redistributing: rip
  Default version control: send version 1, receive any version
    Interface             Send  Recv  Triggered RIP  Key-chain
    GigabitEthernet0/0    1     1 2
    Serial0/0/0           1     1 2
  Automatic network summarization is in effect
  Maximum path: 4
  Routing for Networks:
    192.168.1.0
    192.168.2.0
  Routing Information Sources:
    Gateway         Distance      Last Update
    192.168.2.2        120        00:00:15
  Distance: (default is 120)

R1#
```

Use the **version 2** router configuration mode command to enable RIPv2, as shown in Example 3-7. Notice how the **show ip protocols** command verifies that R2 is now configured to send and receive version 2 messages only. The RIP process now includes the subnet mask in all updates, making RIPv2 a *classless routing protocol*.

**Example 3-7** Enable and Verify RIPv2 on R1

```
R1(config)# router rip
R1(config-router)# version 2
R1(config-router)# end
R1#
R1# show ip protocols | section Default
  Default version control: send version 2, receive version 2
    Interface             Send  Recv  Triggered RIP  Key-chain
    GigabitEthernet0/0    2     2
    Serial0/0/0           2     2
R1#
```

**Note**

Configuring **version 1** enables RIPv1 only, whereas configuring **no version** returns the router to the default setting of sending version 1 updates but listening for version 1 and version 2 updates.

Example 3-8 verifies the routing table of R1.

**Example 3-8** Verify the Routing Table

```
R1# show ip route | begin Gateway
Gateway of last resort is not set

      192.168.1.0/24 is variably subnetted, 2 subnets, 2 masks
C        192.168.1.0/24 is directly connected, GigabitEthernet0/0
L        192.168.1.1/32 is directly connected, GigabitEthernet0/0
      192.168.2.0/24 is variably subnetted, 2 subnets, 2 masks
C        192.168.2.0/24 is directly connected, Serial0/0/0
L        192.168.2.1/32 is directly connected, Serial0/0/0
R1#
```

Notice how the RIP routes are no longer in the routing table. This is because R1 is now only listening for RIPv2 updates. R2 and R3 are still sending RIPv1 updates. Therefore, the **version 2** command must be configured on all routers in the routing domain.

## Disable Auto Summarization (3.2.1.5)

Just like RIPv1, RIPv2 automatically summarizes networks at major network boundaries by default. This is confirmed in Example 3-9.

**Example 3-9** Automatic Summarization with RIPv2

```
R1# show ip protocols
*** IP Routing is NSF aware ***

Routing Protocol is "rip"
  Outgoing update filter list for all interfaces is not set
  Incoming update filter list for all interfaces is not set
  Sending updates every 30 seconds, next due in 16 seconds
  Invalid after 180 seconds, hold down 180, flushed after 240
  Redistributing: rip
  Default version control: send version 1, receive any version
    Interface           Send  Recv  Triggered RIP  Key-chain
    GigabitEthernet0/0  1     1 2
    Serial0/0/0         1     1 2
```

```
 Automatic network summarization is in effect
 Maximum path: 4
 Routing for Networks:
    192.168.1.0
    192.168.2.0
 Routing Information Sources:
    Gateway          Distance      Last Update
    192.168.2.2           120      00:00:15
 Distance: (default is 120)

R1#
```

To modify the default RIPv2 behavior of *automatic summarization*, use the **no auto-summary** router configuration mode command, as shown in Example 3-10.

**Example 3-10**  Disable Automatic Summarization on R1

```
R1(config)# router rip
R1(config-router)# no auto-summary
R1(config-router)# end
R1#
*Mar 10 14:11:49.659: %SYS-5-CONFIG_I: Configured from console by console
R1# show ip protocols | section Automatic
  Automatic network summarization is not in effect
R1#
```

The **show ip protocols** command now states that "Automatic network summarization is not in effect." When automatic summarization is disabled, RIPv2 no longer summarizes networks to their classful address at boundary routers. RIPv2 now includes all subnets and their appropriate masks in its routing updates.

It should be noted that the **no auto-summary** command has no effect in RIPv1. It only affects the behavior of RIPv2. Therefore, RIPv2 must be enabled before automatic summarization can be disabled.

## Configure Passive Interfaces (3.2.1.6)

By default, RIP updates are forwarded out all RIP-activated interfaces. However, RIP updates really only need to be sent out interfaces that are connected to other RIP enabled routers.

For instance, refer to the topology in Figure 3-4. RIP sends updates out of its G0/0 interface even though no RIP device exists on that LAN. R1 has no way of knowing this and, as a result, sends an update every 30 seconds. Sending out unneeded updates on a LAN impacts the network in three ways:

- **Wasted Bandwidth**—Bandwidth is used to transport unnecessary updates. Because RIP updates are either broadcasted or multicasted, switches also forward the updates out all ports.

- **Wasted Resources**—All devices on the LAN must process the update up to the transport layers, at which point the devices will discard the update.

- **Security Risk**—Advertising updates on a broadcast network is a security risk. RIP updates can be intercepted with packet sniffing software. Routing updates can be modified and sent back to the router, corrupting the routing table with false metrics that misdirect traffic.

Use the **passive-interface** router configuration command to prevent the transmission of routing updates through a router interface, but still allow that network to be advertised to other routers. The command stops routing updates out the specified interface. However, the network that the specified interface belongs to is still advertised in routing updates that are sent out other interfaces.

There is no need for R1, R2, and R3 to forward RIP updates out of their LAN interfaces. The configuration in Example 3-11 identifies the R1 G0/0 interface as passive. The **show ip protocols** command is then used to verify that the Gigabit Ethernet interface was passive.

**Example 3-11**  Configure and Verify a Passive Interface on R1

```
R1(config)# router rip
R1(config-router)# passive-interface g0/0
R1(config-router)# end
R1#
R1# show ip protocols | begin Default
  Default version control: send version 2, receive version 2
    Interface            Send  Recv  Triggered RIP  Key-chain
    Serial0/0/0          2     2
  Automatic network summarization is not in effect
  Maximum path: 4
  Routing for Networks:
    192.168.1.0
    192.168.2.0
  Passive Interface(s):
    GigabitEthernet0/0
```

```
   Routing Information Sources:
      Gateway          Distance      Last Update
      192.168.2.2           120      00:00:06
   Distance: (default is 120)


R1#
```

Notice that the G0/0 interface is no longer listed as sending or receiving version 2 updates; instead, it is now listed under the Passive Interface(s) section. Also notice that the network 192.168.1.0 is still listed under Routing for Networks, which means that this network is still included as a route entry in RIP updates that are sent to R2.

**Note**

All routing protocols support the **passive-interface** command.

As an alternative, all interfaces can be made passive using the **passive-interface default** command. Interfaces that should not be passive can be re-enabled using the **no passive-interface** command.

## Propagate a Default Route (3.2.1.7)

In Figure 3-5, R1 is the *edge router*, *single-homed* to a service provider. Therefore, all that is required for R1 to reach the Internet is a default static route going out of the Serial 0/0/1 interface.

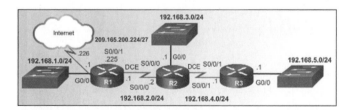

**Figure 3-5**   Modified RIPv2 Topology

Similar default static routes could be configured on R2 and R3, but it is much more scalable to enter it one time on the edge router R1 and then have R1 propagate it to all other routers using RIP. To provide Internet connectivity to all other networks in the RIP routing domain, the default static route needs to be advertised to all other routers that use the dynamic routing protocol.

To *propagate a default route* in RIP, the edge router must be configured with two things:

- A default static route using the **ip route 0.0.0.0 0.0.0.0** command.

- The **default-information originate** router configuration command. This instructs R1 to originate default information by propagating the static default route in RIP updates.

The example in Example 3-12 configures a fully specified default static route to the service provider, and then the route is propagated by RIP. Notice that R1 now has a Gateway of Last Resort and default route installed in its routing table.

**Example 3-12** Propagating a Default Route in RIP on R1

```
R1(config)# ip route 0.0.0.0 0.0.0.0 S0/0/1 209.165.200.226
R1(config)#
R1(config)# router rip
R1(config-router)# default-information originate
R1(config-router)# end
R1#
*Mar 10 23:33:51.801: %SYS-5-CONFIG_I: Configured from console by console
R1# show ip route | begin Gateway
Gateway of last resort is 209.165.200.226 to network 0.0.0.0

S*      0.0.0.0/0 [1/0] via 209.165.200.226, Serial0/0/1
        192.168.1.0/24 is variably subnetted, 2 subnets, 2 masks
C          192.168.1.0/24 is directly connected, GigabitEthernet0/0
L          192.168.1.1/32 is directly connected, GigabitEthernet0/0
        192.168.2.0/24 is variably subnetted, 2 subnets, 2 masks
C          192.168.2.0/24 is directly connected, Serial0/0/0
L          192.168.2.1/32 is directly connected, Serial0/0/0
R       192.168.3.0/24 [120/1] via 192.168.2.2, 00:00:08, Serial0/0/0
R       192.168.4.0/24 [120/1] via 192.168.2.2, 00:00:08, Serial0/0/0
R       192.168.5.0/24 [120/2] via 192.168.2.2, 00:00:08, Serial0/0/0
        209.165.200.0/24 is variably subnetted, 2 subnets, 2 masks
C          209.165.200.0/24 is directly connected, Serial0/0/1
L          209.165.200.225/27 is directly connected, Serial0/0/1
R1#
```

The output in Example 3-13 verifies that the default route has propagated to R3.

**Example 3-13**  Verify the Routing Table on R3

```
R3# show ip route | begin Gateway
Gateway of last resort is 192.168.4.2 to network 0.0.0.0
R*      0.0.0.0/0 [120/2] via 192.168.4.2, 00:00:00, Serial0/0/1
R       192.168.1.0/24 [120/2] via 192.168.4.2, 00:00:00, Serial0/0/1
R       192.168.2.0/24 [120/1] via 192.168.4.2, 00:00:00, Serial0/0/1
R       192.168.3.0/24 [120/1] via 192.168.4.2, 00:00:00, Serial0/0/1
        192.168.4.0/24 is variably subnetted, 2 subnets, 2 masks
C          192.168.4.0/24 is directly connected, Serial0/0/1
L          192.168.4.1/32 is directly connected, Serial0/0/1
        192.168.5.0/24 is variably subnetted, 2 subnets, 2 masks
C          192.168.5.0/24 is directly connected, GigabitEthernet0/0
L          192.168.5.1/32 is directly connected, GigabitEthernet0/0
R3#
```

Packet Tracer
☐ **Activity**

**Packet Tracer 3.2.1.8: Configuring RIPv2**

Although RIP is rarely used in modern networks, it is helpful as a foundation for understanding basic network routing. In this activity, you configure a default route, RIPv2 with appropriate network statements and passive interfaces, and verify full connectivity.

**Lab 3.2.1.9: Configuring Basic RIPv2**

In this lab you complete the following objectives:

- Part 1: Build the Network and Configure Basic Device Settings
- Part 2: Configure and Verify RIPv2 Routing

# The Routing Table (3.3)

The primary function of a router is to route packets to their destination. Therefore, the routing table is core to the operation of the router. It contains key routing information; for this reason, it is important that you understand routing table output.

In this section, you learn how to determine the route source, AD, and metric for a given route.

## Parts of an IPv4 Route Entry (3.3.1)

In this topic, you learn about the components of an IPv4 routing table entry for a given route.

## Routing Table Entries (3.3.1.1)

The topology displayed in Figure 3-6 is used as the reference topology for this section.

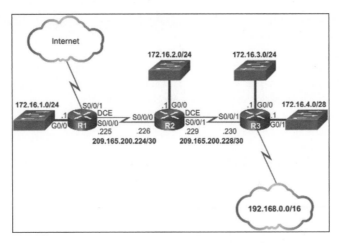

**Figure 3-6**    Reference Topology for IPv4 Routing Table Examples

Notice that in the topology, the following is true:

- R1 is the edge router that connects to the Internet; therefore, it is propagating a default static route to R2 and R3.

- R1, R2, and R3 contain *discontiguous networks* separated by another classful network.

- R3 is also introducing a 192.168.0.0/16 *supernet* route.

Example 3-14 displays the IPv4 routing table of R1 with directly connected, static, and dynamic routes.

**Example 3-14** IPv4 Routing Table for R1

```
R1# show ip route | begin Gateway
Gateway of last resort is 209.165.200.234 to network 0.0.0.0
S*      0.0.0.0/0 [1/0] via 209.165.200.234, Serial0/0/1
                  is directly connected, Serial0/0/1
        172.16.0.0/16 is variably subnetted, 5 subnets, 3 masks
C           172.16.1.0/24 is directly connected, GigabitEthernet0/0
L           172.16.1.1/32 is directly connected, GigabitEthernet0/0
R           172.16.2.0/24 [120/1] via 209.165.200.226, 00:00:12, Serial0/0/0
R           172.16.3.0/24 [120/2] via 209.165.200.226, 00:00:12, Serial0/0/0
R           172.16.4.0/28 [120/2] via 209.165.200.226, 00:00:12, Serial0/0/0
```

```
R       192.168.0.0/16 [120/2] via 209.165.200.226, 00:00:03, Serial0/0/0
        209.165.200.0/24 is variably subnetted, 5 subnets, 2 masks
C          209.165.200.224/30 is directly connected, Serial0/0/0
L          209.165.200.225/32 is directly connected, Serial0/0/0
R          209.165.200.228/30 [120/1] via 209.165.200.226, 00:00:12, Serial0/0/0
C          209.165.200.232/30 is directly connected, Serial0/0/1
L          209.165.200.233/30 is directly connected, Serial0/0/1
R1#
```

**Note**

The routing table hierarchy in Cisco IOS was originally implemented with the classful routing scheme. Although the routing table incorporates both classful and classless addressing, the overall structure is still built around this classful scheme.

## Directly Connected Entries (3.3.1.2)

As highlighted Example 3-14, the routing table of R1 contains three directly connected networks. Notice that two routing table entries are automatically created when an active router interface is configured with an IP address and subnet mask.

Figure 3-7 displays one of the routing table entries on R1 for the directly connected network 172.16.1.0.

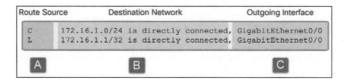

**Figure 3-7**    Parts of a Directly Connected IPv4 Route Entry

These entries were automatically added to the routing table when the GigabitEthernet 0/0 interface was configured and activated. The entries contain the information shown in Table 3-6.

**Table 3-6**   Parts of a Directly Connected Network Entry

| Legend | Part | Description |
|--------|------|-------------|
| A | Route source | Identifies how the route was learned. Directly connected interfaces have two route source codes. C identifies a directly connected network. Directly connected networks are automatically created whenever an interface is configured with an IP address and activated. L identifies that this is a local route. Local routes are automatically created whenever an interface is configured with an IP address and activated. |
| B | Destination network | The address of the remote network and how that network is connected. |
| C | Outgoing interface | Identifies the exit interface to use when forwarding packets to the destination network. |

A router typically has multiple interfaces configured. The routing table stores information about both directly connected and remote routes. As with directly connected networks, the route source identifies how the route was learned. For instance, common codes for remote networks include the following:

- S—Identifies that an administrator created the route to reach a specific network. This is known as a static route.

- D—Identifies that the route was learned dynamically from another router using the EIGRP routing protocol.

- O—Identifies that the route was learned dynamically from another router using the OSPF routing protocol.

- R—Identifies that the route was learned dynamically from another router using the RIP routing protocol.

### Remote Network Entries (3.3.1.3)

Figure 3-8 displays an IPv4 routing table entry on R1 for the route to remote network 172.16.4.0 on R3.

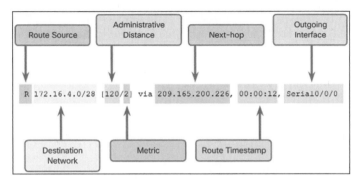

**Figure 3-8**    Parts of a Remote Network IPv4 Route Entry

The entry identifies the following information:

- **Route source**—Identifies how the route was learned.

- **Destination network**—Identifies the address of the remote network.

- **Administrative distance (AD)**—Identifies the trustworthiness of the route source. The AD for static routes is 1, and the AD for connected routes is 0. Dynamic routing protocols have an AD higher than 1 depending upon the protocol.

- **Metric**—Identifies the value assigned to reach the remote network. Lower values indicate preferred routes. The metric for static and connected routes is 0.

- **Next hop**—Identifies the IPv4 address of the next router to forward the packet to.

- **Route timestamp**—Identifies from when the route was last heard.

- **Outgoing interface**—Identifies the exit interface to use to forward a packet toward the final destination.

**Interactive Graphic**

**Activity 3.3.1.4: Identify Parts of an IPv4 Routing Table Entry**

Refer to the online course to complete this activity.

# Dynamically Learned IPv4 Routes (3.3.2)

In this topic, you learn about the parent/child relationship in a dynamically built routing table.

## Routing Table Terms (3.3.2.1)

A dynamically built routing table provides a great deal of information. Therefore, it is crucial to understand the output the routing table generates. Special terms are applied when discussing the contents of a routing table.

The Cisco IP routing table is not a flat database. The routing table is actually a hierarchical structure that is used to speed up the lookup process when locating routes and forwarding packets. Within this structure, the hierarchy includes several levels.

Routes are discussed in terms of the following:

- Ultimate route
- Level 1 route
- Level 1 parent route
- Level 2 child routes

## Ultimate Route (3.3.2.2)

An *ultimate route* is a routing table entry that contains either a next-hop IPv4 address or an exit interface. Directly connected, dynamically learned, and local routes are ultimate routes.

In Example 3-15, the highlighted areas are examples of ultimate routes. Notice that all of these routes specify either a next-hop IPv4 address or an exit interface.

**Example 3-15** Ultimate Routes on R1

```
R1# show ip route | begin Gateway
Gateway of last resort is 209.165.200.234 to network 0.0.0.0

S*      0.0.0.0/0 [1/0] via 209.165.200.234, Serial0/0/1
                 is directly connected, Serial0/0/1
        172.16.0.0/16 is variably subnetted, 5 subnets, 3 masks
C          172.16.1.0/24 is directly connected, GigabitEthernet0/0
L          172.16.1.1/32 is directly connected, GigabitEthernet0/0
R          172.16.2.0/24 [120/1] via 209.165.200.226, 00:00:12, Serial0/0/0
R          172.16.3.0/24 [120/2] via 209.165.200.226, 00:00:12, Serial0/0/0
R          172.16.4.0/28 [120/2] via 209.165.200.226, 00:00:12, Serial0/0/0
R      192.168.0.0/16 [120/2] via 209.165.200.226, 00:00:03, Serial0/0/0
        209.165.200.0/24 is variably subnetted, 5 subnets, 2 masks
C          209.165.200.224/30 is directly connected, Serial0/0/0
L          209.165.200.225/32 is directly connected, Serial0/0/0
R          209.165.200.228/30 [120/1] via 209.165.200.226, 00:00:12, Serial0/0/0
C          209.165.200.232/30 is directly connected, Serial0/0/1
L          209.165.200.233/30 is directly connected, Serial0/0/1
R1#
```

## Level 1 Route (3.3.2.3)

A *level 1 route* is a route with a subnet mask equal to or less than the classful mask of the network address. Therefore, a level 1 route can be one of the following:

- *Network route*—A network route that has a subnet mask equal to that of the classful mask.

- *Supernet route*—A supernet route is a network address with a mask less than the classful mask, such as a summary address.

- **Default route**—A default route is a static route with the address 0.0.0.0/0.

The source of the level 1 route can be a directly connected network, a static route, or a dynamic routing protocol.

Figure 3-9 highlights how level 1 routes are also ultimate routes.

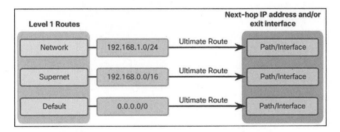

**Figure 3-9**    Sources of Level 1 Routes

Example 3-16 highlights level 1 routes.

**Example 3-16** Level 1 Routes on R1

```
R1# show ip route | begin Gateway
Gateway of last resort is 209.165.200.234 to network 0.0.0.0

S*       0.0.0.0/0 [1/0] via 209.165.200.234, Serial0/0/1
                  is directly connected, Serial0/0/1
         172.16.0.0/16 is variably subnetted, 5 subnets, 3 masks
C           172.16.1.0/24 is directly connected, GigabitEthernet0/0
L           172.16.1.1/32 is directly connected, GigabitEthernet0/0
R           172.16.2.0/24 [120/1] via 209.165.200.226, 00:00:12, Serial0/0/0
R           172.16.3.0/24 [120/2] via 209.165.200.226, 00:00:12, Serial0/0/0
R           172.16.4.0/28 [120/2] via 209.165.200.226, 00:00:12, Serial0/0/0
R         192.168.0.0/16 [120/2] via 209.165.200.226, 00:00:03, Serial0/0/0
          209.165.200.0/24 is variably subnetted, 5 subnets, 2 masks
```

```
C        209.165.200.224/30 is directly connected, Serial0/0/0
L        209.165.200.225/32 is directly connected, Serial0/0/0
R        209.165.200.228/30 [120/1] via 209.165.200.226, 00:00:12, Serial0/0/0
C        209.165.200.232/30 is directly connected, Serial0/0/1
L        209.165.200.233/30 is directly connected, Serial0/0/1
R1#
```

## Level 1 Parent Route (3.3.2.4)

As illustrated in Figure 3-10, the 172.16.0.0 and 209.165.200.0 routes are *level 1 parent routes*. A parent route is a level 1 network route that is subnetted. A parent route can never be an ultimate route.

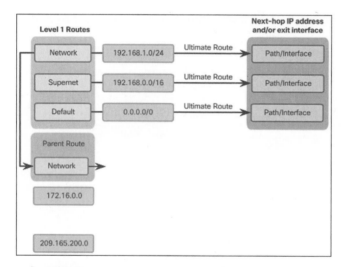

**Figure 3-10**   Level 1 Parent Routes

Example 3-17 highlights the level 1 parent routes in the routing table of R1.

**Example 3-17** Level 1 Parent Routes on R1

```
R1# show ip route | begin Gateway
Gateway of last resort is 209.165.200.234 to network 0.0.0.0

S*     0.0.0.0/0 [1/0] via 209.165.200.234, Serial0/0/1
                  is directly connected, Serial0/0/1
       172.16.0.0/16 is variably subnetted, 5 subnets, 3 masks
C         172.16.1.0/24 is directly connected, GigabitEthernet0/0
L         172.16.1.1/32 is directly connected, GigabitEthernet0/0
R         172.16.2.0/24 [120/1] via 209.165.200.226, 00:00:12, Serial0/0/0
R         172.16.3.0/24 [120/2] via 209.165.200.226, 00:00:12, Serial0/0/0
```

```
R         172.16.4.0/28 [120/2] via 209.165.200.226, 00:00:12, Serial0/0/0
R      192.168.0.0/16 [120/2] via 209.165.200.226, 00:00:03, Serial0/0/0
       209.165.200.0/24 is variably subnetted, 5 subnets, 2 masks
C         209.165.200.224/30 is directly connected, Serial0/0/0
L         209.165.200.225/32 is directly connected, Serial0/0/0
R         209.165.200.228/30 [120/1] via 209.165.200.226, 00:00:12, Serial0/0/0
C         209.165.200.232/30 is directly connected, Serial0/0/1
L         209.165.200.233/30 is directly connected, Serial0/0/1
R1#
```

In the routing table, the level 1 parent route basically provides a heading for the specific subnets it contains. Each entry displays the classful network address, the number of subnets, and the number of different subnet masks into which the classful address has been subdivided.

## Level 2 Child Route (3.3.2.5)

A *level 2 child route* is a route that is a subnet of a classful network address. A level 1 parent route is a level 1 network route that is subnetted. Level 1 parent routes contain level 2 child routes, as shown in Figure 3-11.

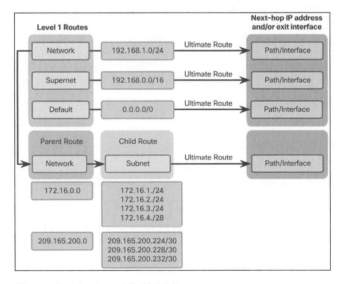

**Figure 3-11**   Level 2 Child Routes

Like a level 1 route, the source of a level 2 route can be a directly connected network, a static route, or a dynamically learned route. Level 2 child routes are also ultimate routes.

**Note**

The routing table hierarchy in Cisco IOS has a classful routing scheme. A level 1 parent route is the classful network address of the subnet route. This is the case even if a classless routing protocol is the source of the subnet route.

Example 3-18 highlights the child routes in the routing table of R1.

**Example 3-18** Level 2 Child Routes on R1

```
R1# show ip route | begin Gateway
Gateway of last resort is 209.165.200.234 to network 0.0.0.0

S*     0.0.0.0/0 [1/0] via 209.165.200.234, Serial0/0/1
              is directly connected, Serial0/0/1
       172.16.0.0/16 is variably subnetted, 5 subnets, 3 masks
C         172.16.1.0/24 is directly connected, GigabitEthernet0/0
L         172.16.1.1/32 is directly connected, GigabitEthernet0/0
R         172.16.2.0/24 [120/1] via 209.165.200.226, 00:00:12, Serial0/0/0
R         172.16.3.0/24 [120/2] via 209.165.200.226, 00:00:12, Serial0/0/0
R         172.16.4.0/28 [120/2] via 209.165.200.226, 00:00:12, Serial0/0/0
R      192.168.0.0/16 [120/2] via 209.165.200.226, 00:00:03, Serial0/0/0
       209.165.200.0/24 is variably subnetted, 5 subnets, 2 masks
C         209.165.200.224/30 is directly connected, Serial0/0/0
L         209.165.200.225/32 is directly connected, Serial0/0/0
R         209.165.200.228/30 [120/1] via 209.165.200.226, 00:00:12, Serial0/0/0
C         209.165.200.232/30 is directly connected, Serial0/0/1
L         209.165.200.233/30 is directly connected, Serial0/0/1
R1#
```

**Interactive Graphic**

**Activity 3.3.2.6: Identify Parent and Child IPv4 Routes**

Refer to the online course to complete this activity.

# The IPv4 Route Lookup Process (3.3.3)

In this topic, you learn how a router determines which route to use when forwarding an IPv4 packet.

## Route Lookup Process (3.3.3.1)

When a packet arrives on a router interface, the router examines the IPv4 header, identifies the destination IPv4 address, and proceeds through the *route lookup process*.

In Figure 3-12, the router examines level 1 network routes for the best match with the destination address of the IPv4 packet.

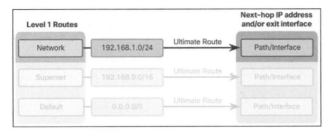

**Figure 3-12**   Match Level 1 Routes

1. If the best match is a level 1 ultimate route, then this route is used to forward the packet.

2. If the best match is a level 1 parent route, proceed to the next step.

   In Figure 3-13, the router examines child routes (the subnet routes) of the parent route for a best match.

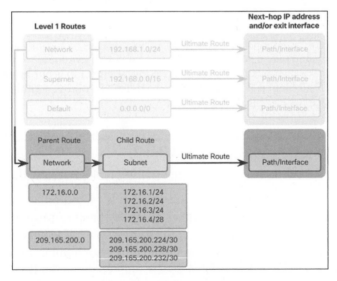

**Figure 3-13**   Match Level 2 Child Routes

3. If there is a match with a level 2 child route, that subnet is used to forward the packet.

4. If there is not a match with any of the level 2 child routes, proceed to the next step.

In Figure 3-14, the router continues searching level 1 supernet routes in the routing table for a match, including the default route, if there is one.

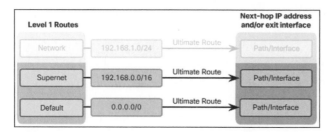

**Figure 3-14** Match Supernet and then Default Route

5. If there is now a lesser match with a level 1 supernet or default routes, the router uses that route to forward the packet.

6. If there is not a match with any route in the routing table, the router drops the packet.

**Note**

A route referencing only a next-hop IP address and not an exit interface must be resolved to a route with an exit interface if Cisco Express Forwarding (CEF) is not being used. Without CEF, a recursive lookup is performed on the next-hop IP address until the route is resolved to an exit interface. CEF is enabled by default.

## Best Route = Longest Match (3.3.3.2)

A router must find the best match in the routing table. But how does it do that?

For there to be a match between the destination IPv4 address of a packet and a route in the routing table, a minimum number of far-left bits must match between the IPv4 address of the packet and the route in the routing table. The subnet mask of the route in the routing table is used to determine the minimum number of far-left bits that must match. Remember that an IPv4 packet only contains the IPv4 address and not the subnet mask.

The best match is equal to the longest match in the routing table. This means that the best match is the route in the routing table that has the most far-left matching bits with the destination IPv4 address of the packet. The route with the greatest number of equivalent far-left bits, or the longest match, is always the preferred route.

In Figure 3-15, a packet is destined for 172.16.0.10.

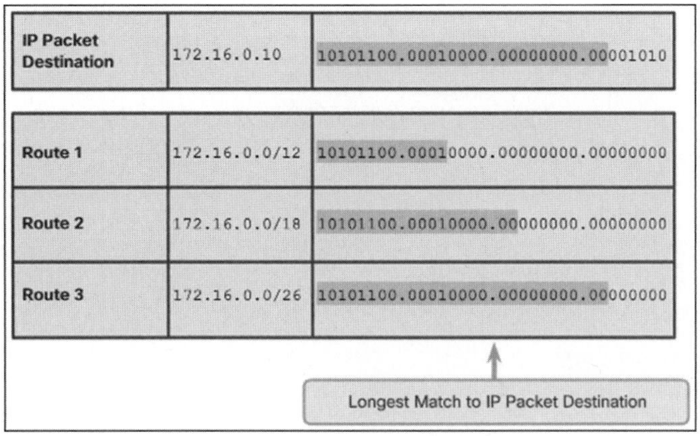

| IP Packet Destination | 172.16.0.10 | 10101100.00010000.00000000.00001010 |
|---|---|---|
| Route 1 | 172.16.0.0/12 | 10101100.00010000.00000000.00000000 |
| Route 2 | 172.16.0.0/18 | 10101100.00010000.00000000.00000000 |
| Route 3 | 172.16.0.0/26 | 10101100.00010000.00000000.00000000 |

Longest Match to IP Packet Destination

**Figure 3-15**    Match for Packets Destined to 172.16.0.10

The router has three possible routes that match this packet: 172.16.0.0/12, 172.16.0.0/18, and 172.16.0.0/26. Of the three routes, 172.16.0.0/26 has the longest match and is chosen to forward the packet. Remember, for any of these routes to be considered a match, there must be at least the number of matching bits indicated by the subnet mask of the route.

**Interactive Graphic**

**Activity 3.3.3.3: Determine the Longest Match Route**

Refer to the online course to complete this activity.

# Analyze an IPv6 Routing Table (3.3.4)

In this topic, you learn about the components of an IPv6 routing table entry for a given route.

## IPv6 Routing Table Entries (3.3.4.1)

Components of the IPv6 routing table are similar to the IPv4 routing table. For instance, IPv6 is populated using directly connected interfaces, static routes, and dynamically learned routes.

Because IPv6 is classless by design, all routes are effectively level 1 ultimate routes. There is no level 1 parent of level 2 child routes.

The topology in Figure 3-16 is used as the reference topology for this section.

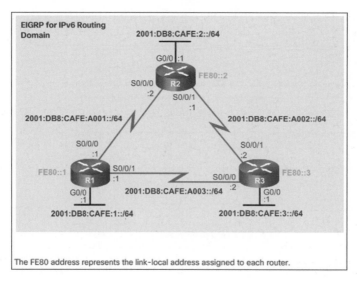

**Figure 3-16**   Reference Topology for IPv6 Routing Table Examples

Notice that in the topology, the following is true:

- R1, R2, and R3 are configured in a full mesh topology. All routers have redundant paths to various networks.

- R2 is the edge router and connects to the ISP; however, a default static route is not being advertised.

- EIGRP for IPv6 has been configured on all three routers.

**Note**

Although EIGRP for IPv6 is used to populate the routing tables, the operation and configuration of EIGRP is beyond the scope of this course.

## Directly Connected Entries (3.3.4.2)

The routing table of R1 is displayed in Example 3-19 using the **show ipv6 route** command. Although the command output is displayed slightly differently than in the IPv4 version, it still contains the relevant route information.

**Example 3-19**  Directly Connected IPv6 Routes on R1

```
R1# show ipv6 route
<Output omitted>

C    2001:DB8:CAFE:1::/64 [0/0]
     via GigabitEthernet0/0, directly connected
```

```
L    2001:DB8:CAFE:1::1/128 [0/0]
        via GigabitEthernet0/0, receive
D    2001:DB8:CAFE:2::/64 [90/3524096]
        via FE80::3, Serial0/0/1
D    2001:DB8:CAFE:3::/64 [90/2170112]
        via FE80::3, Serial0/0/1
C    2001:DB8:CAFE:A001::/64 [0/0]
        via Serial0/0/0, directly connected
L    2001:DB8:CAFE:A001::1/128 [0/0]
        via Serial0/0/0, receive
D    2001:DB8:CAFE:A002::/64 [90/3523840]
        via FE80::3, Serial0/0/1
C    2001:DB8:CAFE:A003::/64 [0/0]
        via Serial0/0/1, directly connected
L    2001:DB8:CAFE:A003::1/128 [0/0]
        via Serial0/0/1, receive
L    FF00::/8 [0/0]
        via Null0, receive
R1#
```

The connected network and local routing table entries of the directly connected interfaces are highlighted. The three entries were added when the interfaces were configured and activated.

As shown in Figure 3-17, directly connected route entries display the following information:

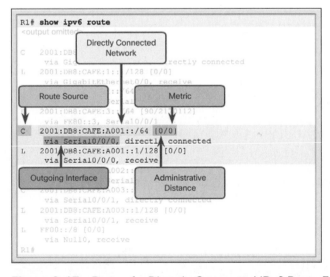

**Figure 3-17**   Parts of a Directly Connected IPv6 Route Entry

- **Route source**—Identifies how the route was learned. Directly connected interfaces have two route source codes (C identifies a directly connected network, whereas L identifies that this is a local route.)

- **Directly connected network**—The IPv6 address of the directly connected network.

- **Administrative distance**—Identifies the trustworthiness of the route source. IPv6 uses the same distances as IPv4. A value of 0 indicates the best, most trustworthy source.

- **Metric**—Identifies the value assigned to reach the remote network. Lower values indicate preferred routes.

- **Outgoing interface**—Identifies the exit interface to use when forwarding packets to the destination network.

---

**Note**

The serial links have reference bandwidths configured to observe how EIGRP metrics select the best route. The reference bandwidth is not a realistic representation of modern networks. It is used only to provide a visual depiction of link speed.

---

## Remote IPv6 Network Entries (3.3.4.3)

Example 3-20 highlights the routing table entries for the three remote networks (that is, R2 LAN, R3 LAN, and the link between R2 and R3). The three entries were added by the EIGRP.

**Example 3-20**  Remote Network IPv6 Routes on R1

```
R1# show ipv6 route
<Output omitted>

C    2001:DB8:CAFE:1::/64 [0/0]
     via GigabitEthernet0/0, directly connected
L    2001:DB8:CAFE:1::1/128 [0/0]
     via GigabitEthernet0/0, receive
D    2001:DB8:CAFE:2::/64 [90/3524096]
     via FE80::3, Serial0/0/1
D    2001:DB8:CAFE:3::/64 [90/2170112]
     via FE80::3, Serial0/0/1
C    2001:DB8:CAFE:A001::/64 [0/0]
     via Serial0/0/0, directly connected
L    2001:DB8:CAFE:A001::1/128 [0/0]
     via Serial0/0/0, receive
D    2001:DB8:CAFE:A002::/64 [90/3523840]
     via FE80::3, Serial0/0/1
```

```
C    2001:DB8:CAFE:A003::/64 [0/0]
       via Serial0/0/1, directly connected
L    2001:DB8:CAFE:A003::1/128 [0/0]
       via Serial0/0/1, receive
L    FF00::/8 [0/0]
       via Null0, receive
R1#
```

Figure 3-18 displays a routing table entry on R1 for the route to remote network 2001:DB8:CAFE:3::/64 on R3.

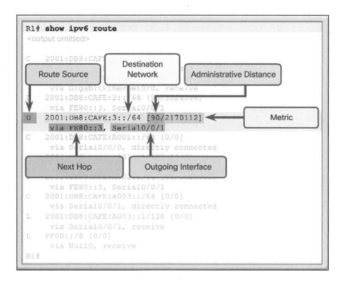

**Figure 3-18**    Parts of a Remote Network IPv6 Route Entry

The entry identifies the following information:

- **Route source**—Identifies how the route was learned. Common codes include O (OSPF), D (EIGRP), R (RIP), and S (Static route).

- **Destination network**—Identifies the address of the remote IPv6 network.

- **Administrative distance**—Identifies the trustworthiness of the route source. IPv6 uses the same distances as IPv4.

- **Metric**—Identifies the value assigned to reach the remote network. Lower values indicate preferred routes.

- **Next hop**—Identifies the IPv6 address of the next router to forward the packet to.

- **Outgoing interface**—Identifies the exit interface to use to forward a packet toward the final destination.

When an IPv6 packet arrives on a router interface, the router examines the IPv6 header and identifies the destination IPv6 address. The router then proceeds through the following router lookup process.

The router examines level 1 network routes for the best match with the destination address of the IPv6 packet. Just like IPv4, the longest match is the best match. For example, if there are multiple matches in the routing table, the router chooses the route with the longest match. A match is made by matching the far-left bits of the packet's destination IPv6 address with the IPv6 prefix and prefix-length in the IPv6 routing table.

**Interactive Graphic**

**Activity 3.3.4.4: Identify Parts of an IPv6 Routing Table Entry**

Refer to the online course to complete this activity.

# Summary (3.4)

### Class Activity 3.4.1.1: IPv6—Details, Details...

After studying the concepts presented in this chapter concerning IPv6, you should be able to read a routing table easily and interpret the IPv6 routing information listed within it.

With a partner, use the IPv6 routing table diagram and the .pdf provided with this activity.

Record your answers to the Reflection questions.

Then compare your answers with at least one other group from the class.

Routers use dynamic routing protocols to facilitate the exchange of routing information between routers. The purpose of dynamic routing protocols includes discovering remote networks, maintaining up-to-date routing information, choosing the best path to destination networks, and finding a new best path if the current path is no longer available. Although dynamic routing protocols require less administrative overhead than static routing, they do require dedicating part of a router's resources for protocol operation, including CPU time and network link bandwidth.

Networks typically use a combination of both static and dynamic routing. Dynamic routing is the best choice for large networks, and static routing is better for stub networks.

Routing protocols are responsible for discovering remote networks, as well as maintaining accurate network information. When there is a change in the topology, routing protocols propagate that information throughout the routing domain. The process of bringing all routing tables to a state of consistency, where all of the routers in the same routing domain, or area, have complete and accurate information about the network, is called convergence. Some routing protocols converge faster than others.

Routers sometimes learn about multiple routes to the same network from both static routes and dynamic routing protocols. When a router learns about a destination network from more than one routing source, Cisco routers use the AD value to determine which source to use. Each dynamic routing protocol has a unique administrative value, along with static routes and directly connected networks. The lower the administrative value, the more preferred the route source. A directly connected network is always the preferred source, followed by static routes and then various dynamic routing protocols.

Routing table entries contain a route source, a destination network, and an outgoing interface. Route sources can be connected, local, static, or from a dynamic routing protocol.

IPv4 routing tables can contain four types of routes: ultimate routes, level 1 routes, level 1 parent routes, and level 2 child routes. Because IPv6 is classless by design, all routes are effectively level 1 ultimate routes. There is no level 1 parent of level 2 child routes.

## Practice

The following activities provide practice with the topics introduced in this chapter. The labs and class activities are available in the companion Routing and Switching Essentials v6 Labs and Study Guide (ISBN 9781587134265). The packet tracer activities PKA files are found in the online course.

**Class Activities**

Class Activity 3.0.1.2: How Much Does This Cost?

Class Activity 3.4.1.1: IPv6—Details, Details...

**Labs**

Lab 3.2.1.9: Configuring Basic RIPv2.doc

Packet Tracer
☐ Activity

**Packet Tracer Activities**

Packet Tracer 3.2.1.8: Configuring RIPv2

## Check Your Understanding Questions

Complete all the review questions listed here to test your understanding of the topics and concepts in this chapter. The appendix "Answers to 'Check Your Understanding' Questions" lists the answers.

1. What two tasks do dynamic routing protocols perform? (Choose two.)

    A. Assign IP addressing

    B. Discover hosts

    C. Discover networks

    D. Propagate host default gateways

    E. Update and maintain routing tables

2. What is a disadvantage of using dynamic routing protocols?

   A. Their configuration complexity increases as the size of the network grows.

   B. They are only suitable for simple topologies.

   C. They require administrator intervention when the pathway of traffic changes.

   D. They send messages about network status insecurely across networks by default.

3. Which dynamic routing protocol was developed as an exterior gateway protocol to interconnect different Internet providers?

   A. BGP

   B. EIGRP

   C. IGRP

   D. OSPF

   E. RIP

4. Which two statements are true regarding classless routing protocols? (Choose two.)

   A. They allow use of both 192.168.1.0/30 and 192.168.1.16/28 subnets in the same topology.

   B. They are supported by RIP version 1.

   C. They reduce the amount of address space available in an organization.

   D. They send complete routing table updates to all neighbors.

   E. They send subnet mask information in routing updates.

5. What is the purpose of the **passive-interface** command?

   A. It allows a router to receive routing updates on an interface but not send updates via that interface

   B. It allows a router to send routing updates on an interface but not receive updates via that interface

   C. It allows a routing protocol to forward updates out an interface that is missing its IP address

   D. It allows an interface to remain up without receiving keepalives

   E. It allows interfaces to share IP addresses

6. Having configured RIPv2 on an enterprise network, an engineer enters the command **network 192.168.10.0** into router configuration mode. What is the result of entering this command?

   A. The interface of the 192.168.10.0 network is receiving version 1 and version 2 updates.

   B. The interface of the 192.168.10.0 network is sending only version 2 updates.

C. The interface of the 192.168.10.0 network is sending RIP hello messages.

D. The interface of the 192.168.10.0 network is sending version 1 and version 2 updates.

7. A destination route in the routing table is indicated with a code D. Which kind of route entry is this?

A. A network directly connected to a router interface

B. A route dynamically learned through the EIGRP routing protocol

C. A route used as the default gateway

D. A static route

8. Which two requirements are used to determine if a route can be considered an ultimate route in a router's routing table? (Choose two.)

A. Be a classful network entry

B. Be a default route

C. Contain a next-hop IP address

D. Contain an exit interface

E. Contain subnets

9. Which route is the best match for a packet entering a router with a destination address of 10.16.0.2?

A. S 10.0.0.0/8 [1/0] via 192.168.0.2

B. S 10.16.0.0/24 [1/0] via 192.168.0.9

C. S 10.16.0.0/16 is directly connected, Ethernet 0/1

D. S 10.0.0.0/16 is directly connected, Ethernet 0/0

10. Which type of route requires a router to perform a recursive lookup?

A. A level 1 network route that is using a next-hop IP address on a router that is using CEF

B. A level 2 child route that is using an exit interface on a router that is not using CEF

C. A parent route on a router that is using CEF

D. An ultimate route that is using a next-hop IP address on a router that is not using CEF

11. What is different between IPv6 routing table entries compared to IPv4 routing table entries?

   A. By design, IPv6 is classless, so all routes are effectively level 1 ultimate routes.

   B. IPv6 does not use static routes to populate the routing table as used in IPv4.

   C. IPv6 routing tables include local route entries, and IPv4 routing tables do not.

   D. The selection of IPv6 routes is based on the shortest matching prefix, unlike IPv4 route selection, which is based on the longest matching prefix.

# CHAPTER 4

# Switched Networks

## Objectives

Upon completion of this chapter, you will be able to answer the following questions:

- How do data, voice, and video converge in a switched network?

- How does a switched network operate in a small-to medium-sized business?

- How are frames forwarded in a switched network?

- What is the difference between a collision domain and a broadcast domain?

## Key Terms

This chapter uses the following key terms. You can find the definitions in the Glossary.

# Introduction (4.0.1.1)

Modern networks continue to evolve to keep pace with the changing way organizations carry out their daily business. Users now expect instant access to company resources from anywhere and at any time. These resources not only include traditional data, but also video and voice. There is also an increasing need for collaboration technologies. These technologies allow real-time sharing of resources between multiple remote individuals, as though they were at the same physical location.

Different devices must seamlessly work together to provide a fast, secure, and reliable connection between hosts. LAN switches provide the connection point for end users into the enterprise network and are primarily responsible for the control of information within the LAN environment. Routers facilitate the movement of information between LANs and are generally unaware of individual hosts. All advanced services depend on the availability of a robust routing and switching infrastructure on which they can build. This infrastructure must be carefully designed, deployed, and managed to provide a stable platform.

This chapter begins an examination of the flow of traffic in a modern network. It examines some of the current network design models and the way LAN switches build forwarding tables and use the MAC address information to efficiently switch data between hosts.

### Class Activity 4.0.1.2—Sent or Received Instructions

Individually, or in groups (per the instructor's decision), discuss various ways hosts send and receive data, voice, and streaming video.

Develop a matrix (table) listing network data types that can be sent and received. Provide five examples.

**Note:** For an example of the matrix, see the document prepared for this modeling activity.

Save your work in either hard- or soft-copy format. Be prepared to discuss your matrix and statements in a class discussion.

# LAN Design (4.1)

The requirements of the network affect LAN design. Enterprise networks are now converged and must support data, voice, and video. It is important that networks be designed properly to support the features requested.

In this section, you learn how enterprise networks support data, voice, and video.

# Converged Networks (4.1.1)

In this topic, you learn how data, voice, and video are converged in a switched network.

## Growing Complexity of Networks (4.1.1.1)

The digital world is changing. The ability to access the Internet and the corporate network is no longer confined to physical offices, geographical locations, or time zones. In today's globalized workplace, employees can access resources from anywhere in the world, and information must be available at any time and on any device. These requirements drive the need to build next-generation networks that are secure, reliable, and highly available.

These next-generation networks must not only support current expectations and equipment, but be able to integrate legacy platforms. Figure 4-1 shows some common legacy devices that must often be incorporated into network design.

**Figure 4-1**   Legacy Components

Figure 4-2 illustrates some of the newer platforms (*converged networks*) that help to provide access to the network anytime, anywhere, and on any device.

**Figure 4-2**    Converged Network Components

## Elements of a Converged Network (4.1.1.2)

To support collaboration, business networks employ converged solutions using voice systems, IP phones, voice gateways, video support, and video conferencing, as shown in Figure 4-3.

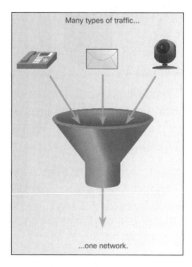

**Figure 4-3**    Converging Traffic Types

Including data services, a converged network with collaboration support may include the following features:

- *Call control*—Includes telephone call processing, caller ID, call transfer, hold, and conference, and more.

- **Voice messaging**—Includes voicemail features.

- **Mobility**—Receive important calls wherever you are.

- *Automated attendant*—Serves customers faster by enabling callers to locate people in the organization without talking to a receptionist.

One of the primary benefits of transitioning to the converged network is that there is just one physical network to install and manage. This results in substantial savings over the installation and management of separate voice, video, and data networks. Such a converged network solution integrates IT management so that any moves, additions, and changes are completed with an intuitive management interface. A converged network solution also provides *PC softphone* application support, as well as point-to-point video, so that users can enjoy personal communications with the same ease of administration and use as a voice call.

The convergence of services onto the network has resulted in an evolution in networks from a traditional data transport role to a superhighway for data, voice, and video communication. This one physical network must be properly designed and implemented to allow the reliable handling of the various types of information that it must carry. A structured design is required to allow management of this complex environment.

## Cisco Borderless Networks (4.1.1.3)

With the increasing demands of the converged network, the network must be developed with an architectural approach that embeds intelligence, simplifies operations, and is scalable to meet future demands. One of the more recent developments in network design is the *Cisco Borderless Network*.

The Cisco Borderless Network is a network architecture that combines innovation and design. It allows organizations to support a borderless network that can connect anyone, anywhere, anytime, on any device, securely, reliably, and seamlessly. This architecture is designed to address IT and business challenges, such as supporting the converged network and changing work patterns.

The Cisco Borderless Network provides the framework to unify wired and wireless access, including policy, access control, and performance management across many different device types. Using this architecture, the borderless network is built on a hierarchical infrastructure of hardware that is scalable and resilient, as shown in Figure 4-4.

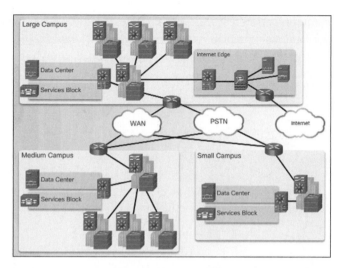

**Figure 4-4**   Cisco Borderless Network

By combining this hardware infrastructure with policy-based software solutions, the Cisco Borderless Network provides two primary sets of services: network services, and user and endpoint services that are all managed by an integrated management solution. It enables different network elements to work together and allows users to access resources from any place, at any time, while providing optimization, scalability, and security.

## Hierarchy in the Borderless Switched Network (4.1.1.4)

Creating a borderless switched network requires that sound network design principles are used to ensure maximum availability, flexibility, security, and manageability. The borderless switched network must deliver on current requirements and future required services and technologies. Borderless switched network design guidelines are built upon the following principles:

- **Hierarchical**—Facilitates understanding the role of each device at every tier, simplifies deployment, operation, and management, and reduces fault domains at every tier

- **Modularity**—Allows seamless network expansion and integrated service enablement on an on-demand basis

- **Resiliency**—Satisfies user expectations for keeping the network always on

- **Flexibility**—Allows intelligent traffic load sharing by using all network resources

These are not independent principles. Understanding how each principle fits in the context of the others is critical. Designing a borderless switched network in a hierarchical fashion creates a foundation that allows network designers to overlay security, mobility, and unified communication features. Two time-tested and proven hierarchical design frameworks for campus networks are the *three-layer hierarchical model*, shown in Figure 4-5, and the two-tier *collapsed core layer model*, shown in Figure 4-6.

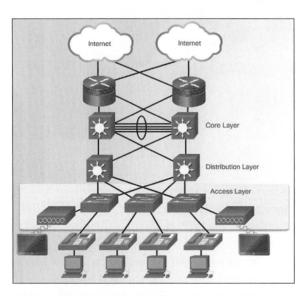

**Figure 4-5**    Three Layer Hierarchical Model

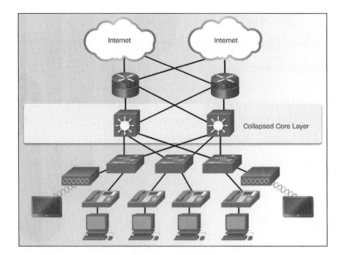

**Figure 4-6**    Collapsed Core Model

The three critical layers within these tiered designs are the access, distribution, and core layers. Each layer can be seen as a well-defined, structured module with specific roles and functions in the campus network. Introducing modularity into the campus hierarchical design further ensures that the campus network remains resilient and flexible enough to provide critical network services. Modularity also helps to allow for growth and changes that occur over time.

### Access, Distribution, and Core Layers (4.1.1.5)

The access, distribution, and core layers of the three-layer hierarchical model provide a well-defined structure with specific roles and functions in the campus network. The following describes the function of each layer.

## Access Layer

The *access layer* represents the network edge, where traffic enters or exits the campus network. Traditionally, the primary function of an access layer switch is to provide network access to the user. Access layer switches connect to distribution layer switches, which implement network foundation technologies such as routing, quality of service, and security.

To meet network application and end-user demand, the next-generation switching platforms now provide more converged, integrated, and intelligent services to various types of endpoints at the network edge. Building intelligence into access layer switches allows applications to operate on the network more efficiently and securely.

## Distribution Layer

The *distribution layer* interfaces between the access layer and the core layer to provide many important functions, including these:

- Aggregating large-scale wiring closet networks
- Aggregating Layer 2 broadcast domains and Layer 3 routing boundaries
- Providing intelligent switching, routing, and network access policy functions to access the rest of the network
- Providing high availability through redundant distribution layer switches to the end-user and equal cost paths to the core
- Providing differentiated services to various classes of service applications at the edge of the network

## Core Layer

The *core layer* is the network backbone. It connects several layers of the campus network. The core layer serves as the aggregator for all of the other campus blocks and ties the campus with the rest of the network. The primary purpose of the core layer is to provide fault isolation and high-speed backbone connectivity.

Figure 4-7 shows a three-tier campus network design for organizations where the access, distribution, and core are each separate layers. To build a simplified, scalable, cost-effective, and efficient physical cable layout design, the recommendation is to build an extended-star physical network topology from a centralized building location to all other buildings on the same campus.

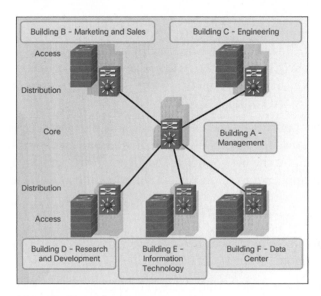

**Figure 4-7**   Three Layer Example

In some cases where extensive physical or network scalability does not exist, maintaining separate distribution and core layers is not required. In smaller campus locations where there are fewer users accessing the network or in campus sites consisting of a single building, separate core and distribution layers may not be needed. In this scenario, the recommendation is the alternate two-tier campus network design, also known as the collapsed core network design.

Figure 4-8 shows a two-tier campus network design example for an enterprise campus where the distribution and core layers are collapsed into a single layer.

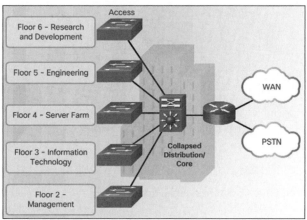

**Figure 4-8**   Collapsed Core Example

**Interactive Graphic**

**Activity 4.1.1.6: Identify Switched Network Terminology**

Refer to the online course to complete this activity.

# Switched Networks (4.1.2)

In this topic, you learn about the types of switches used in a small-to medium-sized business.

## Role of Switched Networks (4.1.2.1)

The role of switched networks has evolved dramatically in the past two decades. It was not long ago that flat Layer 2 switched networks were the norm. Flat Layer 2 switched networks relied on the Ethernet and the widespread use of hub repeaters to propagate LAN traffic throughout an organization. As shown in Figure 4-9, networks have fundamentally changed to switched LANs in a hierarchical network.

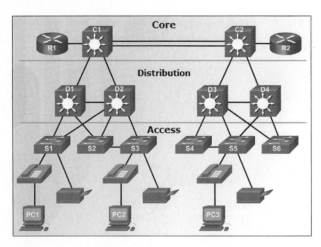

**Figure 4-9**   Three Layer Switched Network

A switched LAN allows more flexibility, traffic management, and additional features:

- Quality of service
- Additional security
- Support for wireless networking and connectivity
- Support for new technologies, such as IP telephony and mobility services

Figure 4-10 illustrates the hierarchical design used in the borderless switched network. The three interconnecting routers between the Large, Medium, and Small campuses represent the core layer. The switches interconnecting with the core routers represent the distribution layer, and the end switches connecting to the distribution layer represent the access layer.

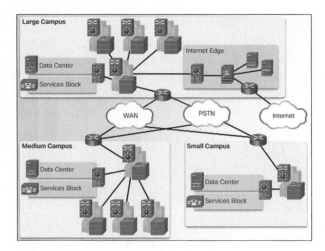

**Figure 4-10**   Borderless Switched Network

## Form Factors (4.1.2.2)

There are various types of switches used in business networks. It is important to deploy the appropriate types of switches based on network requirements. Common business considerations when selecting equipment include the following:

- **Cost**—The cost of a switch depends on the number and speed of the interfaces, supported features, and expansion capability.

- *Port density*—Network switches must support the appropriate number of devices on the network.

- **Power**—It is now common to power access points, IP phones, and even compact switches using Power over Ethernet (PoE). In addition to PoE considerations, some chassis-based switches support redundant power supplies.

- **Reliability**—The switch should provide continuous access to the network.

- **Port Speed**—The speed of the network connection is of primary concern to end users.

- *Frame buffers*—The ability of the switch to store frames is important in a network where there may be congested ports to servers or other areas of the network.

- *Scalability*—The number of users on a network typically grows over time; therefore, the switch should provide the opportunity for growth.

When selecting the type of switch, the network designer must choose between a fixed configuration or a modular configuration, and stackable or nonstackable. Another consideration is the thickness of the switch, which is expressed in number of *rack units*. This is important for switches that are mounted in a rack. For example, all the fixed configuration switches shown in Figure 4-11 are 1 rack unit (1U). These options are sometimes referred to as switch *form factors*.

Features and options are limited to those that originally come with the switch.

**Figure 4-11**    Fixed Configuration Switches

## Fixed Configuration Switches

*Fixed configuration switches* do not support features or options beyond those that originally came with the switch (Figure 4-11). The particular model determines the features and options available. For example, a 24-port gigabit fixed switch cannot support additional ports. There are typically different configuration choices that vary in how many and what types of ports are included with a fixed configuration switch.

## Modular Configuration Switches

*Modular configuration switches* offer more flexibility in their configuration. Modular configuration switches typically come with different sized chassis that allow for the installation of different numbers of modular line cards, as shown in Figure 4-12.

The chassis accepts line cards that contain the ports.

**Figure 4-12**  Modular Configuration Switches

The *line cards* actually contain the ports. The line card fits into the switch chassis the way that expansion cards fit into a PC. The larger the chassis, the more modules it can support. There are many different chassis sizes. A modular switch with a single 24-port line card could have an additional 24-port line card installed to bring the total number of ports up to 48.

## Stackable Configuration Switches

*Stackable configuration switches* can be interconnected using a special cable that provides high-bandwidth throughput between the switches, as shown in Figure 4-13.

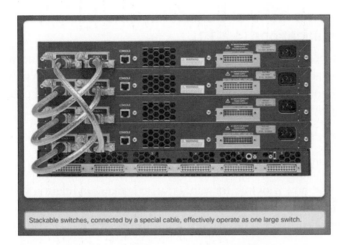

Stackable switches, connected by a special cable, effectively operate as one large switch.

**Figure 4-13**   Stackable Configuration Switches

*Cisco StackWise* technology allows the interconnection of up to nine switches. Switches can be stacked one on top of the other with cables connecting the switches in a daisy chain fashion. The stacked switches effectively operate as a single larger switch. Stackable switches are desirable where fault tolerance and bandwidth availability are critical and a modular switch is too costly to implement. By cross-connecting these stacked switches, the network can recover quickly if a single switch fails. Stackable switches use a special port for interconnections. Many Cisco stackable switches also support *Cisco StackPower* technology, which enables power sharing among stack members.

**Interactive Graphic**

**Activity 4.1.2.3: Identify Switch Hardware**

Refer to the online course to complete this activity.

# The Switched Environment (4.2)

Layer 2 switches forward frames between devices connected to them. Specifically, they maintain a MAC address table and forward frames based on a defined frame switching method.

In this section, you learn how Layer 2 switches forward data in a small-to medium-sized LAN.

# Frame Forwarding (4.2.1)

In this topic, you learn how frames are forwarded in a switched network.

## Switching as a General Concept in Networking and Telecommunications (4.2.1.1)

The concept of switching and forwarding frames is universal in networking and telecommunications. Various types of switches are used in LANs, WANs, and the *public switched telephone network (PSTN)*. The fundamental concept of switching refers to a device making a decision based on two criteria:

- *Ingress port*
- Destination address

The decision on how a switch forwards traffic is made in relation to the flow of that traffic. The term *ingress* is used to describe where a frame enters the device on a port. The term *egress* is used to describe frames leaving the device from a particular port.

A LAN switch maintains a table that it uses to determine how to forward traffic through the switch. Using the example shown in Figure 4-14, a message enters switch port 1 and has a destination address of EA. The switch looks up the outgoing port for EA and forwards the traffic out port 4.

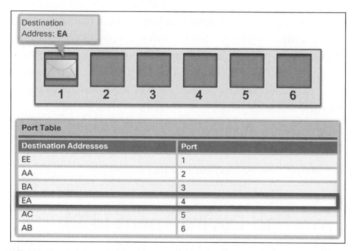

**Figure 4-14**    LAN Switching Example 1

Continuing the example in Figure 4-15, a message enters switch port 5 and has a destination address of EE. The switch looks up the outgoing port for EE and forwards the traffic out port 1.

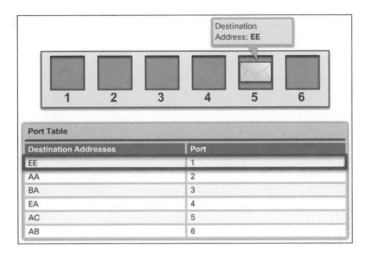

**Figure 4-15**  LAN Switching Example 2

In the final example in Figure 4-16, a message enters switch port 3 and has a destination address of AB. The switch looks up the outgoing port for AB and forwards the traffic out port 6.

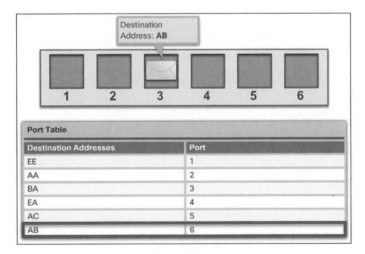

**Figure 4-16**  LAN Switching Example 3

The only intelligence of the LAN switch is its ability to use its table to forward traffic based on the ingress port and the destination address of a message. With a LAN switch, there is only one master switching table that describes a strict association between addresses and ports; therefore, a message with a given destination address always exits the same egress port, regardless of the ingress port it enters.

Layer 2 Ethernet switches forward Ethernet frames based on the destination MAC address of the frames.

## Dynamically Populating a Switch MAC Address Table (4.2.1.2)

Switches use MAC addresses to direct network communications through the switch, to the appropriate port, toward the destination. A switch is made up of integrated circuits and the accompanying software that controls the data paths through the switch. For a switch to know which port to use to transmit a frame, it must first learn which devices exist on each port. As the switch learns the relationship of ports to devices, it builds the *MAC address table* in the *content addressable memory (CAM)*. CAM is a special type of memory used in high-speed searching applications.

> **Note**
>
> The MAC address table is also commonly called the CAM table.

LAN switches determine how to handle incoming data frames by maintaining the MAC address table. A switch builds its MAC address table by recording the MAC address of each device connected to each of its ports. The switch uses the information in the MAC address table to send frames destined for a specific device out the port that has been assigned to that device.

The following two-step process is performed on every Ethernet frame that enters a switch.

### Step 1. Learn—Examining the Source MAC Address

Every frame that enters a switch is checked for new information to learn. It does this by examining the frame's source MAC address and port number where the frame entered the switch:

- If the source MAC address does not exist, it is added to the table along with the incoming port number.

- If the source MAC address does exist, the switch updates the refresh timer for that entry. By default, most Ethernet switches keep an entry in the table for five minutes.

---

**Note**

If the source MAC address does exist in the table but on a different port, the switch treats this as a new entry. The entry is replaced using the same MAC address, but with the more current port number.

---

### Step 2. Forward—Examining the Destination MAC Address

If the destination MAC address is a unicast address, the switch will look for a match between the destination MAC address of the frame and an entry in its MAC address table:

- If the destination MAC address is in the table, it forwards the frame out the specified port.

- If the destination MAC address is not in the table, the switch forwards the frame out all ports except the incoming port. This is called an unknown unicast.

---

**Note**

If the destination MAC address is a broadcast or a multicast, the frame is also flooded out all ports except the incoming port.

---

**Interactive Graphic**

**Video Demonstration: MAC Address Tables on Connected Switches**

Refer to the online course to view this video.

---

### Switch Forwarding Methods (4.2.1.3)

As networks grew and enterprises began to experience slower network performance, Ethernet bridges (an early version of a switch) were added to increase reliability. In the 1990s, advancements in integrated circuit technologies allowed for Ethernet LAN switches to replace *Ethernet bridges*. These switches were able to move the Layer 2 forwarding decisions from software to *application-specific-integrated circuits (ASIC)*. ASICs reduce the packet-handling time within the device and allow the device to handle an increased number of ports without degrading performance. This method of forwarding data frames at Layer 2 was referred to as *store-and-forward switching*. This term distinguished it from *cut-through switching*.

As shown in Figure 4-17, the store-and-forward method makes a forwarding decision on a frame after it has received the entire frame and checked the frame for errors using a mathematical error-checking mechanism known as a *cyclic redundancy check (CRC)*.

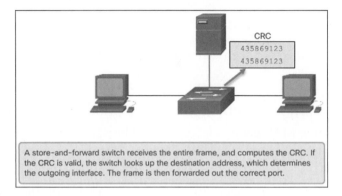

A store-and-forward switch receives the entire frame, and computes the CRC. If the CRC is valid, the switch looks up the destination address, which determines the outgoing interface. The frame is then forwarded out the correct port.

**Figure 4-17**    Store-and-Forward Switching

By contrast, the cut-through method, as shown in Figure 4-18, begins the forwarding process after the destination MAC address of an incoming frame and the *egress port* has been determined.

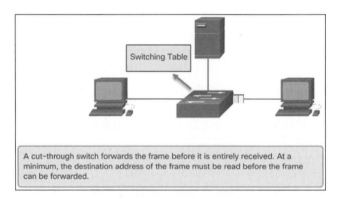

A cut-through switch forwards the frame before it is entirely received. At a minimum, the destination address of the frame must be read before the frame can be forwarded.

**Figure 4-18**    Cut-Through Switching

## Store-and-Forward Switching (4.2.1.4)

Store-and-forward switching has two primary characteristics that distinguish it from cut-through: error checking and automatic buffering.

### Error Checking

A switch using store-and-forward switching performs an error check on an incoming frame. After receiving the entire frame on the ingress port, as shown in Figure 4-19, the switch compares the *frame-check-sequence (FCS)* value in the last field of the datagram against its own FCS calculations.

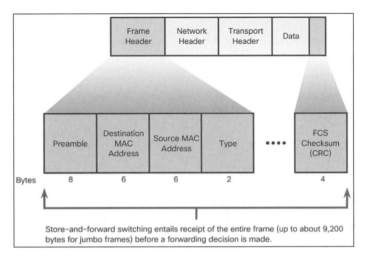

**Figure 4-19**    Store-and-Forward Stores Entire Frame Before Forwarding

The FCS is an error-checking process that helps to ensure that the frame is free of physical and data-link errors. If the frame is error-free, the switch forwards the frame. Otherwise, the frame is dropped.

### Automatic Buffering

The ingress port buffering process that store-and-forward switches use provides the flexibility to support any mix of Ethernet speeds. For example, handling an incoming frame traveling into a 100 Mb/s Ethernet port that must be sent out a 1 Gb/s interface would require using the store-and-forward method. With any mismatch in speeds between the ingress and egress ports, the switch stores the entire frame in a *buffer*, computes the FCS check, forwards it to the egress port buffer, and then sends it.

Store-and-forward switching is Cisco's primary LAN switching method.

A store-and-forward switch drops frames that do not pass the FCS check; therefore, it does not forward invalid frames. By contrast, a cut-through switch may forward invalid frames because no FCS check is performed.

### Cut-Through Switching (4.2.1.5)

An advantage to cut-through switching is the ability of the switch to start forwarding a frame earlier than store-and-forward switching. There are two primary characteristics of cut-through switching: *rapid frame forwarding* and *fragment free*.

## Rapid Frame Forwarding

As indicated in Figure 4-20, a switch using the cut-through method can make a forwarding decision as soon as it has looked up the destination MAC address of the frame in its MAC address table. The switch does not have to wait for the rest of the frame to enter the ingress port before making its forwarding decision.

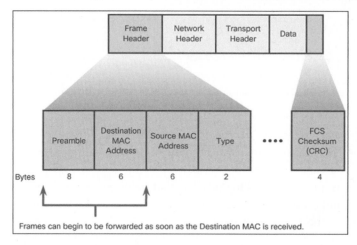

**Figure 4-20**  Cut-Through Forwards the Frame After the Destination MAC is Read

With today's MAC controllers and ASICs, a switch using the cut-through method can quickly decide whether it needs to examine a larger portion of a frame's headers for additional filtering purposes. For example, the switch can analyze past the first 14 bytes (the source MAC address, destination MAC, and the EtherType fields) and examine an additional 40 bytes to perform more sophisticated functions relative to IPv4 Layers 3 and 4.

The cut-through switching method does not drop most invalid frames. Frames with errors are forwarded to other segments of the network. If there is a high error rate (invalid frames) in the network, cut-through switching can have a negative impact on bandwidth, thus clogging up bandwidth with damaged and invalid frames.

## Fragment Free

*Fragment-free switching* is a modified form of cut-through switching in which the switch waits for the collision window (64 bytes) to pass before forwarding the frame. This means each frame is checked into the data field to make sure no fragmentation has occurred. Fragment-free switching provides better error checking than cut-through, with practically no increase in latency.

The lower latency speed of cut-through switching makes it more appropriate for extremely demanding, high-performance computing (HPC) applications that require process-to-process latencies of 10 microseconds or less.

**Interactive Graphic**

**Activity 4.2.1.6: Frame Forwarding Methods**

Refer to the online course to complete this activity.

**Interactive Graphic**

**Activity 4.2.1.7: Switch It!**

Refer to the online course to complete this activity.

## Switching Domains (4.2.2)

In this topic, you learn about *collision domains* and *broadcast domains*.

### Collision Domains (4.2.2.1)

In hub-based Ethernet segments, network devices compete for the medium because devices must take turns when transmitting. The network segments that share the same bandwidth between devices are known as collision domains. When two or more devices within that same collision domain try to communicate at the same time, a collision occurs.

A switch eliminates collisions on an Ethernet network. A switch provides microsegmentation so that no other device competes for the same Ethernet network bandwidth. Ethernet switch ports operating in *full duplex* eliminate collisions.

By default, Ethernet switch ports *autonegotiate* full duplex when the adjacent device can also operate in full duplex. If the switch port is connected to a device operating in *half duplex*, such as a legacy hub, then the switch port operates in half duplex and the switch port is part of a collision domain.

As illustrated in Figure 4-21, autonegotiation chooses full duplex if both devices have the capability along with their highest common bandwidth.

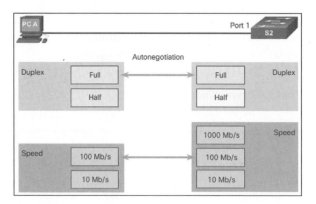

**Figure 4-21**    Duplex and Speed Settings

## Broadcast Domains (4.2.2.2)

A collection of interconnected switches forms a single broadcast domain. Only a network layer device, such as a router, can divide a Layer 2 broadcast domain. Routers are used to segment broadcast domains, but they also segment a collision domain.

When a device sends a Layer 2 broadcast, the destination MAC address in the frame is set to all binary ones.

The Layer 2 broadcast domain is referred to as the MAC broadcast domain. The MAC broadcast domain consists of all devices on the LAN that receive broadcast frames from a host. When two switches are connected, the broadcast domain is increased.

When a switch receives a broadcast frame, it forwards the frame out each of its ports, except the ingress port where the broadcast frame was received. Each device connected to the switch receives a copy of the broadcast frame and processes it.

For example, in Figure 4-22, the server sends a broadcast frame to S1.

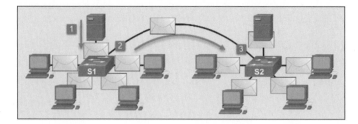

**Figure 4-22**    Broadcast Domain Example

S1 forwards the broadcast to all connected devices and to S2. S2 in turn sends the broadcast frame to all connected devices. All connected devices in the topology receive the broadcast frames from the server.

Broadcasts are sometimes necessary for initially locating other devices and network services, but they also reduce network efficiency. Network bandwidth is used to propagate the broadcast traffic. Too many broadcasts and a heavy traffic load on a network can result in congestion, which slows down network performance.

## Alleviating Network Congestion (4.2.2.3)

LAN switches have special characteristics that make them effective at alleviating network congestion. By default, interconnected switch ports attempt to establish a link in full duplex, thereby eliminating collision domains. Each full duplex port of the switch provides the full bandwidth to the device or devices that are connected to that port. A full-duplex connection can carry transmitted and received signals at the same time. Full-duplex connections have dramatically increased LAN network performance and are required for 1 Gb/s Ethernet speeds and higher.

Switches interconnect LAN segments, use a table of MAC addresses to determine the segment to which the frame is to be sent, and can lessen or eliminate collisions entirely. The following are some important characteristics of switches that contribute to alleviating network congestion:

- *High-port density*—Switches have high-port densities: 24- and 48-port switches are often just a single rack unit and operate at speeds of 100 Mb/s, 1 Gb/s, and 10 Gb/s. Large enterprise switches may support many hundreds of ports.

- **Large frame buffers**—The ability to store more received frames before having to start dropping them is useful, particularly when there may be congested ports to servers or other parts of the network.

- **Port speed**—Depending on the cost of a switch, it may be possible to support a mixture of speeds. Ports of 100 Mb/s and 1 or 10 Gb/s are common (100 Gb/s is also possible).

- **Fast internal switching**—Having fast internal forwarding capabilities allows high performance. The method that is used may be a fast internal bus or shared memory, which affects the overall performance of the switch.

- **Low per-port cost**—Switches provide high-port density at a lower cost.

Figure 4-23 provides examples of different types of Cisco switches.

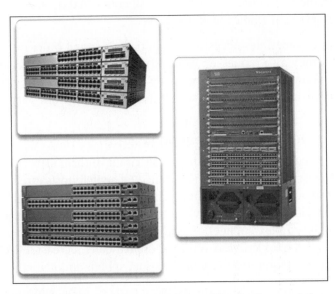

**Figure 4-23**   Examples of Access, Distribution, and Core Switches

**Activity 4.2.2.4: Circle the Domain (4.2.2.4)**

Refer to the online course to complete this activity.

# Summary (4.3)

### Class Activity 4.3.1.1: It's Network Access Time

Use Packet Tracer for this activity. Internet connectivity is not required. Work with a classmate to create two network designs to accommodate the following scenarios:

### Scenario 1—Classroom Design (LAN)

- 15 student end devices represented by 1 or 2 PCs
- 1 instructor end device preferably represented by a server
- Stream video presentations over LAN connection

### Scenario 2—Administrative Design (WAN)

- All requirements as listed in Scenario 1
- Access to and from a remote administrative server for video presentations and pushed updates for network application software

Both the LAN and WAN designs should fit on one Packet Tracer file screen. All intermediary devices should be labeled with the switch model (or name) and the router model (or name).

Save your work and be ready to justify your device decisions and layout to your instructor and to the class.

---

**Interactive Graphic**

### Activity 4.3.1.2: Basic Switch Configurations

Refer to the online course to complete this activity.

---

The trend in networks is toward convergence using a single set of wires and devices to handle voice, video, and data transmission. In addition, there has been a dramatic shift in the way businesses operate. No longer are employees constrained to physical offices or by geographic boundaries. Resources must now be seamlessly available anytime and anywhere. The Cisco Borderless Network architecture enables different elements, from access switches to wireless access points, to work together and allow users to access resources from any place at any time.

The traditional three-layer hierarchical design model divides the network into core, distribution, and access layers and allows each portion of the network to be optimized for specific functionality. It provides modularity, resiliency, and flexibility, which creates a foundation that allows network designers to overlay security, mobility, and unified communication features. In some networks, having a separate core and distribution layer is not required. In these networks, the functionality of the core layer and the distribution layer are often collapsed together.

Cisco LAN switches use ASICs to forward frames based on the destination MAC address. Before this can be accomplished, it must first use the source MAC address of incoming frames to build up a MAC address table in content-addressable memory (CAM). If the destination MAC address is contained in this table, the frame is forwarded only to the specific destination port. When the destination MAC address is not found in the MAC address table, the frames are flooded out all ports, except the one on which the frame was received.

Switches use either store-and-forward or cut-through switching. Store-and-forward reads the entire frame into a buffer and checks the CRC before forwarding the frame. Cut-through switching only reads the first portion of the frame and starts forwarding it as soon as the destination address is read. Although this is extremely fast, no error checking is done on the frame before forwarding.

Switches attempt to autonegotiate full duplex communication by default. Switch ports do not block broadcasts, and connecting switches can extend the size of the broadcast domain, often resulting in degraded network performance.

# Practice

The following activities provide practice with the topics introduced in this chapter. Instructions for the lab, packet tracer, and class activities are available in the companion *Routing and Switching Labs and Study Guide* (ISBN 9781587134265). The Packet Tracer Activities PKA files are found in the online course.

**Note**

For this chapter, there are no labs or packet tracer activities.

**Class Activities**

Class Activity 4.0.1.2: Sent or Received

Class Activity 4.3.1.1: It's Network Access Time

# Check Your Understanding Questions

Complete all the review questions listed here to test your understanding of the topics and concepts in this chapter. The appendix "Answers to 'Check Your Understanding' Questions" lists the answers.

1.  What is a basic function of the Cisco Borderless Architecture distribution layer?

    A.  Acting as a backbone

    B.  Aggregating all the campus blocks

    C.  Aggregating Layer 2 and Layer 3 routing boundaries

    D.  Providing access to end-user devices

2.  A network designer must provide a rationale to a customer for a design that will move an enterprise from a flat network topology to a hierarchical network topology. Which two features of the hierarchical design make it the better choice? (Choose two.)

    A.  Easier to provide redundant links to ensure higher availability

    B.  Less required equipment to provide the same performance levels

    C.  Lower bandwidth requirements

    D.  Reduced cost for equipment and user training

    E.  Simpler deployment for additional switch equipment

3.  What is a collapsed core in a network design?

    A.  A combination of the functionality of the access and core layers

    B.  A combination of the functionality of the access and distribution layers

    C.  A combination of the functionality of the access, distribution, and core layers

    D.  A combination of the functionality of the distribution and core layers

4.  Which two previously independent technologies should a network administrator attempt to combine after choosing to upgrade to a converged network infrastructure? (Choose two.)

    A.  User data traffic

    B.  VoIP phone traffic

    C.  Scanners and printers

    D.  Mobile cell phone traffic

    E.  Electrical system

5. What is a definition of a two-tier LAN network design?

   A. Access, distribution, and core layers collapsed into one tier, with a separate backbone layer

   B. Access and core layers collapsed into one tier, and the distribution layer on a separate tier

   C. Access and distribution layers collapsed into one tier, and the core layer on a separate tier

   D. Distribution and core layers collapsed into one tier, and the access layer on a separate tier

6. A local law firm is redesigning the company network so that all 20 employees can be connected to a LAN and to the Internet. The law firm would prefer a low-cost and easy solution for the project. What type of switch should be selected?

   A. Fixed configuration

   B. Modular configuration

   C. Stackable configuration

   D. StackPower

   E. StackWise

7. What are two advantages of modular switches over fixed-configuration switches? (Choose two.)

   A. Increased scalability

   B. Lower cost per switch

   C. Lower forwarding rates

   D. Need for fewer power outlets

8. What is one function of a Layer 2 switch?

   A. Determines which interface is used to forward a frame based on the destination MAC address

   B. Duplicates the electrical signal of each frame to every port

   C. Forwards data based on logical addressing

   D. Learns the port assigned to a host by examining the destination MAC address

9. What criteria are used by a Cisco LAN switch to decide how to forward Ethernet frames?

   A. Destination IP address

   B. Destination MAC address

C.  Egress port

D.  Path cost

10. Which network device can be used to eliminate collisions on an Ethernet network?

A.  Firewall

B.  Hub

C.  Router

D.  Switch

11. Which type of address does a switch use to build the MAC address table?

A.  Destination IP address

B.  Destination MAC address

C.  Source IP address

D.  Source MAC address

12. What are two reasons a network administrator would segment a network with a Layer 2 switch? (Choose two.)

A.  To create fewer collision domains

B.  To create more broadcast domains

C.  To eliminate virtual circuits

D.  To enhance user bandwidth

E.  To isolate ARP request messages from the rest of the network

F.  To isolate traffic between segments

13. Which statement describes the microsegmentation feature of a LAN switch?

A.  All ports inside the switch form one collision domain.

B.  Each port forms a collision domain.

C.  Frame collisions are forwarded.

D.  The switch will not forward broadcast frames.

14. A _____ network is one that uses the same infrastructure to carry voice, data, and video signals.

# CHAPTER 5

# Switch Configuration

## Objectives

Upon completion of this chapter, you will be able to answer the following questions:

- How do you configure initial settings on a Cisco switch?

- How do you configure switch ports to meet network requirements?

- How do you configure the management virtual interface on a switch?

- How do you configure the port-security feature to restrict network access?

## Key Terms

This chapter uses the following key terms. You can find the definitions in the Glossary.

# Introduction (5.0.1.1)

Switches are used to connect multiple devices on the same network. In a properly designed network, LAN switches are responsible for directing and controlling the data flow at the access layer to networked resources.

Cisco switches are self-configuring, and no additional configurations are necessary for them to function out of the box. However, Cisco switches run Cisco IOS and can be manually configured to better meet the needs of the network. This includes adjusting port speed, bandwidth, and security requirements.

Additionally, Cisco switches can be managed both locally and remotely. To remotely manage a switch, it needs to have an IP address and default gateway configured. These are just two of the configurations discussed in this chapter.

Switches operate at the access layer where client network devices connect directly to the network and IT departments want uncomplicated network access for the users. It is one of the most vulnerable areas of the network because it is so exposed to the user. Switches need to be configured to be resilient to attacks of all types while they are protecting user data and allowing for high-speed connections. Port security is one of the security features that Cisco managed switches provide.

This chapter examines some of the basic switch configuration settings required to maintain a secure, available, and switched LAN environment.

**Class Activity 5.0.1.2: Stand By Me**

When you arrived to class today, you were given a number by your instructor to use for this introductory class activity.

When class begins, your instructor will ask certain students with specific numbers to stand. Your job is to record the standing students' numbers for each scenario.

### Scenario 1

Students with numbers starting with the number 5 should stand. Record the numbers of the standing students.

### Scenario 2

Students with numbers ending in B should stand. Record the numbers of the standing students.

### Scenario 3

Students with the number 505C should stand. Record the number of the standing student.

At the end of this activity, divide into small groups and record answers to the Reflection questions on the .pdf file for this activity.

Save your work, and be prepared to share it with another student or the entire class.

# Basic Switch Configuration (5.1)

Switches interconnect devices. Unlike a router, which must be initially configured to be operational in a network, switches can be deployed *out of the box* without initially being configured. However, for management and security reasons, switches should always be manually configured to better meet the needs of the network.

In this section, you learn how to configure basic switch settings to meet network requirements.

## Configure a Switch with Initial Settings (5.1.1)

In this topic, you learn how to configure initial settings on a Cisco switch.

### Switch Boot Sequence (5.1.1.1)

After a Cisco switch is powered on, it goes through the following boot sequence:

1. First, the switch loads a *power-on self-test (POST)* program stored in ROM. POST checks the *CPU subsystem*. It tests the CPU, the DRAM, and the portion of the flash device that makes up the flash file system.

2. Next, the switch loads the *boot loader software*. The boot loader is a small program stored in ROM that is run immediately after POST successfully completes.

3. The boot loader performs low-level CPU initialization. It initializes the CPU registers, which control the mapping location of physical memory, the quantity of memory, and its speed.

4. The boot loader initializes the flash file system on the system board.

5. Finally, the boot loader locates and loads a default IOS image into memory and gives control of the switch to the IOS.

The boot loader software finds the Cisco IOS image on the switch as follows:

- The switch attempts to automatically boot by using information in the *BOOT environment variables*, which are boot methods the administrator selects.

- If this variable is not set, the switch attempts to load and execute the first executable file it finds. It does a recursive search of each subdirectory encountered before finally searching the root directory. For this reason, on a Cisco 2960 switch, the IOS image file is normally contained in a directory that has the same name root name as the image file.

The IOS operating system then initializes the interfaces using the Cisco IOS commands found in the startup-config file, which is stored in NVRAM.

In Example 5-1, the BOOT environment variable is set using the **boot system** global configuration mode command.

**Example 5-1**  The **boot system** Command

```
S1(config)# boot system flash:/c2960-lanbasek9-mz.150-2.SE/c2960-lanbasek9-
  mz.150-2.SE.bin
S1(config)#
```

Table 5-1 describes the parameters of the **boot system** command used in Example 5-1.

**Table 5-1**   The **boot system** Command Parameters

| Parameter | Description |
| --- | --- |
| Command | boot system |
| Storage | flash: |
| Path to location in file system | c2960-lanbasek9-mz.150-2.SE |
| Filename of IOS | c2960-lanbasek9-mz.150-2.SE.bin |

Notice that the IOS is located in a distinct folder and the folder path is specified. Use the command **show boot** to see content of the BOOT environment variable and what the current IOS boot file is set to.

## Recovering from a System Crash (5.1.1.2)

The boot loader provides access into the switch if the operating system cannot be used because of missing or damaged system files. The *boot loader command line* provides access to the files stored in flash memory.

The boot loader command line can be accessed through a console connection following these steps:

**Step 1.**   Connect a PC by console cable to the switch console port. Configure terminal emulation software to connect to the switch.

**Step 2.**   Power off the switch by unplugging the switch power cord.

**Step 3.**   Reconnect the power cord to the switch and, within 15 seconds, press and hold down the Mode button while the System LED is still flashing green.

**Step 4.**   Continue pressing the Mode button until the System LED turns briefly amber and then solid green; then release the Mode button.

**Step 5.**   The boot loader command line prompt **switch:** should appear in the terminal emulation software on the PC.

The boot loader command line supports commands to format the flash file system, reinstall the operating system software, and recover a lost or forgotten password. For example, the **dir** command can be used to view a list of files within a specified directory, as shown Example 5-2.

**Example 5-2**  Directory Listing in Boot Loader

```
switch: dir flash:
Directory of flash:/
 3 -rwx 1839 Mar 01 2002 00:48:15 config.text
11 -rwx 1140 Mar 01 2002 04:18:48 vlan.dat
21 -rwx 26 Mar 01 2002 00:01:39 env_vars
 9 drwx 768 Mar 01 2002 23:11:42 html
16 -rwx 1037 Mar 01 2002 00:01:11 config.text
14 -rwx 1099 Mar 01 2002 01:14:05 homepage.htm
22 -rwx 96 Mar 01 2002 00:01:39 system_env_vars
17 drwx 192 Mar 06 2002 23:22:03 c2960-lanbase-mz.122-25.FX

15998976 bytes total (6397440 bytes free)

switch#
```

**Note**

Notice that in this example, the IOS is located in the root of the flash folder.

## Switch LED Indicators (5.1.1.3)

When working in a wiring closet with equipment, it may be necessary to quickly diagnose the status of a switch. Cisco Catalyst switches have several status LED indicator lights. You can use the switch LEDs to quickly monitor switch activity and performance. Switches of different models and feature sets will have different LEDs and their placement on the front panel of the switch may also vary. Always take time to become familiar with the significance of the LEDs on a device.

Figure 5-1 shows the switch LEDs and the *Mode button* for a Cisco Catalyst 2960 switch.

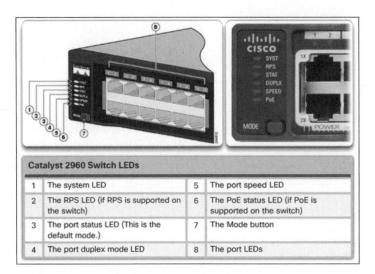

**Catalyst 2960 Switch LEDs**

| | | | |
|---|---|---|---|
| 1 | The system LED | 5 | The port speed LED |
| 2 | The RPS LED (if RPS is supported on the switch) | 6 | The PoE status LED (if PoE is supported on the switch) |
| 3 | The port status LED (This is the default mode.) | 7 | The Mode button |
| 4 | The port duplex mode LED | 8 | The port LEDs |

**Figure 5-1**   Switch LEDs

The Mode button is used to toggle through port status, port duplex, port speed, and PoE (if supported) status of the port LEDs. The following describes the purpose of the LED indicators and the meaning of their colors:

- *System LED*—Shows whether the system is receiving power and is functioning properly. If the LED is off, it means the system is not powered on. If the LED is green, the system is operating normally. If the LED is amber, the system is receiving power but is not functioning properly.

- *Redundant Power System (RPS)* **LED**—Shows the RPS status. If the LED is off, the RPS is off, or it is not properly connected. If the LED is green, the RPS is connected and ready to provide backup power. If the LED is blinking green, the RPS is connected but is unavailable because it is providing power to another device. If the LED is amber, the RPS is in standby mode or in a fault condition. If the LED is blinking amber, the internal power supply in the switch has failed, and the RPS is providing power.

- **Port Status LED**—Indicates that the port status mode is selected when the LED is green. This is the default mode. When selected, the port LEDs display colors with different meanings. If the LED is off, there is no link, or the port was administratively shut down. If the LED is green, a link is present. If the LED is blinking green, there is activity and the port is sending or receiving data. If the LED is alternating green-amber, there is a link fault. If the LED is amber, the port is blocked to ensure that a loop does not exist in the forwarding domain and is not forwarding data. (Typically, ports remain in this state for the first 30 seconds after being activated.) If the LED is blinking amber, the port is blocked to prevent a possible loop in the forwarding domain.

- **Port Duplex LED**—Indicates the port duplex mode is selected when the LED is green. When selected, port LEDs that are off are in half-duplex mode. If the port LED is green, the port is in full-duplex mode.

- **Port Speed LED**—Indicates the port speed mode is selected. When selected, the port LEDs display colors with different meanings. If the LED is off, the port is operating at 10 Mb/s. If the LED is green, the port is operating at 100 Mb/s. If the LED is blinking green, the port is operating at 1000 Mb/s.

- *Power over Ethernet (PoE)* **Mode LED**—If PoE is supported, a PoE mode LED is present. If the LED is off, it indicates the PoE mode is not selected and that none of the ports have been denied power or placed in a fault condition. If the LED is blinking amber, the PoE mode is not selected but at least one of the ports has been denied power or has a PoE fault. If the LED is green, it indicates the PoE mode is selected and the port LEDs will display colors with different meanings. If the port LED is off, the PoE is off. If the port LED is green, the PoE is on. If the port LED is alternating green-amber, PoE is denied because providing power to the powered device exceeds the switch power capacity. If the LED is blinking amber, PoE is off due to a fault. If the LED is amber, PoE for the port has been disabled.

## Preparing for Basic Switch Management (5.1.1.4)

A console connection as shown in Figure 5-2 is required to initially configure a switch.

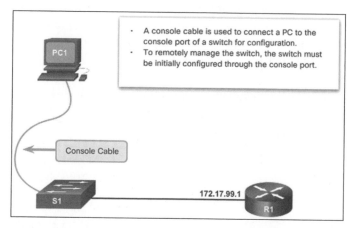

**Figure 5-2**   Preparing for Remote Management

To prepare a switch for remote management, it must be configured with an IP configuration. For example, the switch virtual interface (SVI) on S1 must be configured with an IP address, a subnet mask, and a default gateway. This is similar to configuring the IP address information on host devices.

Note that these IP settings are only for remote management access to the switch. The IP settings do not allow the switch to route Layer 3 packets.

## Configuring Basic Switch Management Access with IPv4 (5.1.1.5)

The topology to be used to configure basic switch management is shown in Figure 5-3.

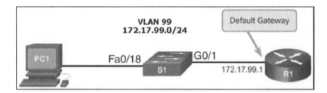

**Figure 5-3**    Switch IPv4 Configuration Topology

The management interface must be configured. The management interface is not a physical port on the switch; it is the SVI. An SVI is a *VLAN* related concept.

VLANs are numbered logical groups to which physical ports can be assigned. Configurations and settings applied to a VLAN are also applied to all the ports assigned to that VLAN. By default, all ports on a switch are assigned to VLAN 1. Therefore, the default SVI is on VLAN 1. However, for security reasons, it is best practice to use a VLAN other than VLAN 1 for the management VLAN.

Configuring the management interface with an IP configuration is similar to configuring a host with an IP configuration. In Example 5-3, S1 is assigned a management IP address and subnet mask, and it is enabled. It is also configured with a default gateway, which in this topology is 172.17.99.1.

**Example 5-3** Configuring a Management Interface

```
S1(config)# interface vlan 99
S1(config-if)# ip address 172.17.99.11 255.255.255.0
S1(config-if)# no shutdown
S1(config-if)# exit
S1(config)#
S1(config)# ip default-gateway 172.17.99.1
S1(config)# end
S1#
```

The default gateway would not be required if the switch were only managed on the local network. However, switches are commonly managed from remote networks; therefore, the default gateway is required.

To verify the status of the management interface, use **show ip interface brief**, as shown in Example 5-4.

**Example 5-4**  Verifying the Management Interface

```
S1# show ip interface brief
Interface          IP-Address     OK? Method Status                Protocol

<output omitted>


FastEthernet0/18   unassigned     YES manual up                    up


<output omitted>


GigabitEthernet0/1 unassigned     YES manual up                    up
GigabitEthernet0/2 unassigned     YES manual down                  down
Vlan1              unassigned     YES manual administratively down down
Vlan99             172.17.99.11 YES manual down                    down
S1#
```

Notice how the Fa0/18 and G0/1 are the only interfaces with a status of "up/up." That is because these are the interfaces connecting to R1 and to PC1.

The VLAN 99 SVI will not appear as "up/up" until VLAN 99 is created and there is a device connected to a switch port associated with VLAN 99. In Example 5-5, the management VLAN is created and named, and the interface connecting to the administrator computer (PC1) is assigned the management VLAN.

**Example 5-5** Enable the Management VLAN

```
S1(config)# vlan 99
S1(config-vlan)#
%LINK-5-CHANGED: Interface Vlan99, changed state to up

S1(config-vlan)# name MANAGEMENT-VLAN
S1(config-vlan)# exit
S1(config)#
S1(config)# interface fa0/18
S1(config-if)# switchport mode access
S1(config-if)# switchport access vlan 99
S1(config-if)#
%LINEPROTO-5-UPDOWN: Line protocol on Interface Vlan99, changed state to up

S1(config-if)# end
S1#
S1# show ip interface brief
Interface          IP-Address    OK? Method Status          Protocol

<Output omitted>

Vlan99             172.17.99.11 YES manual up                up
S1#
```

Remember to use the **copy running-config startup-config** command to back up your configuration.

**Lab 5.1.1.6: Basic Switch Configuration**

In this lab, you will complete the following objectives:

- Part 1: Cable the Network and Verify the Default Switch Configuration
- Part 2: Configure Basic Network Device Settings
- Part 3: Verify and Test Network Connectivity
- Part 4: Manage the MAC Address Table

## Configure Switch Ports (5.1.2)

In this topic, you learn how to configure switch ports to meet network requirements.

### Duplex Communication (5.1.2.1)

Full-duplex communication improves the performance of a switched LAN. Full-duplex communication increases effective bandwidth by allowing both ends of a connection to transmit and receive data simultaneously. This is also known as bidirectional communication. This method of optimizing network performance requires microsegmentation. A microsegmented LAN is created when a switch port has only one device connected and is operating in full-duplex mode. When a switch port is operating in full-duplex mode, there is no collision domain associated with the port.

Unlike full-duplex communication, half-duplex communication is unidirectional. Sending and receiving data does not occur at the same time. Half-duplex communication creates performance issues because data can flow in only one direction at a time, often resulting in collisions. Half-duplex connections are typically seen in older hardware, such as hubs. Full-duplex communication has replaced half-duplex in most hardware.

Figure 5-4 illustrates full-duplex and half-duplex communication.

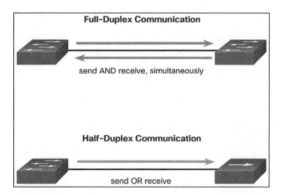

**Figure 5-4**   Full-Duplex and Half-Duplex Communication

Gigabit Ethernet and 10 Gb network interface cards (NIC) require full-duplex connections to operate. In full-duplex mode, the collision detection circuit on the NIC is disabled. Frames that are sent by the two connected devices cannot collide because the devices use two separate circuits in the network cable. Full-duplex connections require a switch that supports full-duplex configuration, or a direct connection using an Ethernet cable between two devices.

Standard, shared hub-based Ethernet configuration efficiency is typically rated at 50 to 60 percent of the stated bandwidth. Full-duplex offers 100 percent efficiency in both directions (transmitting and receiving). This results in a 200 percent potential use of the stated bandwidth.

## Configure Switch Ports at the Physical Layer (5.1.2.2)

Switch ports can autonegotiate duplex and speed settings. This is helpful when the type of device that will be connecting to the port is unknown. However, when the device connecting to the port is known and never changes, then duplex and speed settings can be manually configured. For example, the switch ports for S1 and S2 in Figure 5-5 can be manually configured with specific duplex and speed settings.

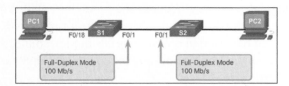

**Figure 5-5**   Duplex and Speed Topology

Use the **duplex** interface configuration mode command to manually specify the duplex mode for a switch port. Use the **speed** interface configuration mode command to manually specify the speed for a switch port.

In Example 5-6, the FastEthernet interface on S1 is manually set to full duplex and 100 Mb/s.

**Example 5-6** Manually Configuring the Duplex and Speed Interface Setting

```
S1(config)# interface fa 0/1
S1(config-if)# duplex full
S1(config-if)# speed 100
S1(config-if)# end
S1#
S1# show interface fa0/1 | include duplex
  Full-duplex, 100Mb/s
S1#
```

Notice how the **show interface** command can be used to verify if the interface accepted the settings.

The default setting for both duplex and speed for switch ports on Cisco Catalyst 2960 and 3560 switches is **auto**. The 10/100/1000 ports operate in either half- or full-duplex mode when they are set to 10 or 100 Mb/s, but when they are set to 1000 Mb/s (1 Gb/s), they operate only in full-duplex mode.

Auto-negotiation is useful when the speed and duplex settings of the device connecting to the port are unknown or may change. When connecting to known devices, such as servers, dedicated workstations, or network devices, best practice is to manually set the speed and duplex settings.

When troubleshooting switch port issues, check the duplex and speed settings.

**Note**

Mismatched settings for the duplex mode and speed of switch ports can cause connectivity issues. Auto-negotiation failure creates mismatched settings.

All fiber-optic ports, such as 1000BASE-SX ports, operate only at a preset speed and are always full-duplex.

## Auto-MDIX (5.1.2.3)

Until recently, certain cable types (straight-through or crossover) were required when connecting devices. Switch-to-switch or switch-to-router connections required using different Ethernet cables. Using the *automatic medium-dependent interface crossover (auto-MDIX)* feature on an interface eliminates this problem. When auto-MDIX is enabled, the interface automatically detects the required cable connection type (straight-through or crossover) and configures the connection appropriately. When connecting to switches without the auto-MDIX feature, straight-through cables must be used to connect to devices such as servers, workstations, or routers. Crossover cables must be used to connect to other switches or repeaters.

With auto-MDIX enabled, either type of cable can be used to connect to other devices, and the interface automatically adjusts to communicate successfully.

Before enabling auto-MDIX on an interface, ensure that the interface speed and duplex settings are set to **auto** so that the feature operates correctly. To enable auto-MDIX, use the **mdix auto** interface configuration mode command.

In Example 5-7, interface FastEthernet 0/2 is being configured to use auto-MDIX.

**Example 5-7** Manually Configuring the Duplex and Speed Interface Setting

```
S1(config)# interface fastethernet 0/2
S1(config-if)# duplex auto
S1(config-if)# speed auto
S1(config-if)# mdix auto
S1(config-if)# end
S1#
```

To examine the auto-MDIX setting for a specific interface, use the **show controllers ethernet-controller** command with the **phy** keyword. The **phy** keyword displays the status of the internal registers on the switch physical layer device (PHY) and includes the operational state of the auto-MDIX feature on an interface. To limit the output to lines referencing auto-MDIX, use the **include Auto-MDIX** filter. As shown in Example 5-8, the output indicates that the feature is active.

**Example 5-8** Verify Auto-MDIX

```
S1# show controllers ethernet-controller fa 0/2 phy | include Auto-MDIX
 Auto-MDIX            :   On   [AdminState=1   Flags=0x00056248]
S1#
```

**Note**

The auto-MDIX feature is enabled by default on Catalyst 2960 and Catalyst 3560 switches but is not available on the older Catalyst 2950 and Catalyst 3550 switches.

## Verifying Switch Port Configuration (5.1.2.4)

Table 5-2 describes some of the options for the **show** command that are helpful in verifying common configurable switch features.

**Table 5-2** Switch Verification Commands

| Description | Command |
|---|---|
| Display interface status and configuration. | show interfaces [*interface-id*] |
| Display current startup configuration. | show startup-config |
| Display current operating config. | show running-config |
| Display information about flash file system. | show flash |
| Display system hardware and software status. | show version |

| Description | Command |
|---|---|
| Display history of commands entered. | show history |
| Display IP information about an interface. | show ip [*interface-id*] |
| Display the MAC address table. | show mac-address-table OR show mac address-table |

Example 5-9 displays a sample abbreviated output of the **show running-config** command.

**Example 5-9**  Verify the Running Configuration

```
S1# show running-config
Building configuration…

Current configuration : 1664 bytes
!
<output omitted>
!
interface FastEthernet0/18
 switchport access vlan 99
 switchport mode access
!
<output omitted>
!
interface Vlan99
 ip address 172.17.99.11  255.255.0.0
!
<output omitted>
!
ip default-gateway 172.17.99.1
!
<output omitted>
```

Use this command to verify that the switch has been correctly configured. As displayed in the output for S1, some important information is shown:

- Fast Ethernet 0/18 interface configured with the management VLAN 99

- VLAN 99 configured with an IPv4 address of 172.17.99.11 255.255.255.0

- Default gateway set to 172.17.99.1

The **show interfaces** command is another commonly used command that displays status and statistics information on the network interfaces of the switch. The **show**

**interfaces** command is frequently used when configuring and monitoring network devices.

Example 5-10 shows the output from the **show interfaces FastEthernet 0/18** command.

**Example 5-10**  Verify Interface Status

```
S1# show interfaces FastEthernet 0/18
FastEthernet0/18 is up, line protocol is up (connected)
  Hardware is Fast Ethernet, address is 0cd9.96e8.8a01 (bia 0cd9.96e8.8a01)
  MTU 1500 bytes, BW 100000 Kbit/sec, DLY 100 usec,
      reliability 255/255, txload 1/255, rxload 1/255
  Encapsulation ARPA, loopback not set
  Keepalive set (10 sec)
  Full-duplex, 100Mb/s, media type is 10/100BaseTX
  input flow-control is off, output flow-control is unsupported
  ARP type: ARPA, ARP Timeout 04:00:00
  Last input 00:00:01, output 00:00:06, output hang never
  Last clearing of "show interface" counters never
  Input queue: 0/75/0/0 (size/max/drops/flushes); Total output drops: 0
  Queueing strategy: fifo
  Output queue: 0/40 (size/max)
  5 minute input rate 0 bits/sec, 0 packets/sec
  5 minute output rate 0 bits/sec, 0 packets/sec
     25994 packets input, 2013962 bytes, 0 no buffer
     Received 22213 broadcasts (21934 multicasts)
     0 runts, 0 giants, 0 throttles
     0 input errors, 0 CRC, 0 frame, 0 overrun, 0 ignored
     0 watchdog, 21934 multicast, 0 pause input
     0 input packets with dribble condition detected
     7203 packets output, 771291 bytes, 0 underruns
<output omitted>
```

The first line indicates that the FastEthernet 0/18 interface is up/up, meaning that it is operational. Further down, the output shows that the duplex is full and the speed is 100 Mb/s.

## Network Access Layer Issues (5.1.2.5)

The output from the **show interfaces** command can be used to detect common media issues. One of the most important parts of this output is the display of the line and data link protocol status. Example 5-11 indicates the summary line to check the status of an interface.

**Example 5-11**  The **show interface** Command Details

```
S1# show interfaces FastEthernet 0/1
FastEthernet0/1 is up, line protocol is up (connected)
  Hardware is Lance, address is 0022.91c4.0e01 (bia 0022.91c4.0e01)
  MTU 1500 bytes, BW 100000 Kbit/sec, DLY 100 usec,
<output omitted>
     2295197 packets input, 305539992 bytes, 0 no buffer
     Received 1925500 broadcasts (120 multicasts)
     0 runts, 0 giants, 0 throttles
     3 input errors, 3 CRC, 0 frame, 0 overrun, 0 ignored
     0 watchdog, 120 multicast, 0 pause input
     0 input packets with dribble condition detected
     3594664 packets output, 436549843 bytes, 0 underruns
     8 output errors, 1790 collisions, 10 interface resets
     0 unknown protocol drops
     0 babbles, 235 late collision, 0 deferred
     0 lost carrier, 0 no carrier, 0 pause output
     0 output buffer failures, 0 output buffers swapped out
S1#
```

The first parameter (FastEthernet0/1 is up) refers to the hardware layer and indicates whether the interface is receiving a carrier detect signal. The second parameter (line protocol is up) refers to the data link layer and indicates whether the data link layer protocol keepalives are being received.

Based on the output of the **show interfaces** command, possible problems can be fixed as follows:

- If the interface is up and the line protocol is down, a problem exists. There could be an encapsulation type mismatch, the interface on the other end could be error-disabled, or there could be a hardware problem.

- If the line protocol and the interface are both down, a cable is not attached or some other interface problem exists. For example, in a back-to-back connection, the other end of the connection may be administratively down.

- If the interface is administratively down, it has been manually disabled (the **shutdown** command has been issued) in the active configuration.

Also highlighted in Example 5-11 are the counters and statistics for the FastEthernet0/1 interface.

Some media errors are not severe enough to cause the circuit to fail, but they do cause network performance issues. Table 5-3 explains some of these common errors that can be detected using the **show interfaces** command.

**Table 5-3**    Network Access Layer Issues

| Error Type | Description |
| --- | --- |
| Input errors | Total number of errors. It includes runts, giants, no buffer, CRC, frame, overrun, and ignored counts. |
| Runts | Packets that are discarded because they are smaller than the minimum packet size for the medium. For instance, any Ethernet packet that is less than 64 bytes is considered a runt. |
| Giants | Packets that are discarded because they exceed the maximum packet size for the medium. For example, any Ethernet packet that is greater than 1,518 bytes is considered a giant. |
| CRC | CRC errors are generated when the calculated checksum is not the same as the checksum received. |
| Output errors | Sum of all errors that prevented the final transmission of datagrams out of the interface that is being examined. |
| Collisions | Number of messages retransmitted because of an Ethernet collision. |
| Late collisions | A collision that occurs after 512 bits of the frame have been transmitted. |

"*Input errors*" is the sum of all errors in datagrams that were received on the interface being examined. This includes runts, giants, CRC, no buffer, frame, overrun, and ignored counts. The reported input errors from the **show interfaces** command include the following:

- *Runt frames*—Ethernet frames that are shorter than the 64-byte minimum allowed length are called runts. Malfunctioning NICs are the usual cause of excessive runt frames, but they can also be caused by collisions.

- *Giants*—Ethernet frames that are larger than the maximum allowed size are called giants.

- *CRC errors*—On Ethernet and serial interfaces, CRC errors usually indicate a media or cable error. Common causes include electrical interference, loose or damaged connections, and incorrect cabling. If you see many CRC errors, there is too much noise on the link and you should inspect the cable. You should also search for and eliminate noise sources.

"*Output errors*" is the sum of all errors that prevented the final transmission of datagrams out the interface that is being examined. The reported output errors from the **show interfaces** command include the following:

- **Collisions**—Collisions in half-duplex operations are normal. However, you should never see collisions on an interface configured for full-duplex communication.

- *Late collisions*—A late collision refers to a collision that occurs after 512 bits of the frame have been transmitted. Excessive cable lengths are the most common cause of late collisions. Another common cause is duplex misconfiguration. For example, you could have one end of a connection configured for full-duplex and the other for half-duplex. You would see late collisions on the interface that is configured for half-duplex. In that case, you must configure the same duplex setting on both ends. A properly designed and configured network should never have late collisions.

## Troubleshooting Network Access Layer Issues (5.1.2.6)

Most issues that affect a switched network are encountered during the original implementation. Theoretically, after it is installed, a network continues to operate without problems. However, cabling gets damaged, configurations change, and new devices are connected to the switch that require switch configuration changes. Ongoing maintenance and troubleshooting of the network infrastructure are required.

Figure 5-6 shows a flowchart that can be used to troubleshoot scenarios involving no connection, or a bad connection, between a switch and another device.

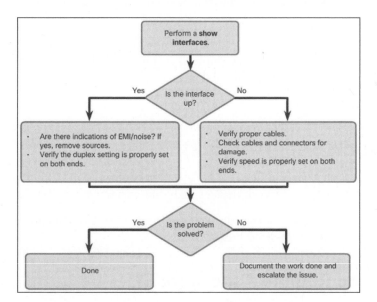

**Figure 5-6**   Troubleshooting Switch Media Issues

Use the **show interfaces** command to check the interface status.

If the interface is down, take these two actions:

- Check to make sure that the proper cables are being used. Additionally, check the cable and connectors for damage. If a bad or incorrect cable is suspected, replace the cable.

- If the interface is still down, the problem may be due to a mismatch in speed setting. The speed of an interface is typically auto-negotiated; therefore, even if it is manually configured on one interface, the connecting interface should auto-negotiate accordingly. If a speed mismatch does occur through misconfiguration, or a hardware or software issue, then that may result in the interface going down. Manually set the same speed on both connection ends if a problem is suspected.

If the interface is up, but issues with connectivity are still present, do the following:

- Using the **show interfaces** command, check for indications of excessive noise. Indications may include an increase in the counters for runts, giants, and CRC errors. If there is excessive noise, first find and remove the source of the noise, if possible. Also, verify that the cable does not exceed the maximum cable length and check the type of cable that is used.

- If noise is not an issue, check for excessive collisions. If there are collisions or late collisions, verify the duplex settings on both ends of the connection. Much like the speed setting, the duplex setting is usually autonegotiated. If there does appear to be a *duplex mismatch*, manually set the duplex to full on both ends of the connection.

# Switch Security (5.2)

Networks are always under attack. Although routers protect internal networks from outside threats, all network devices including switches must be secured.

In this section, you will learn how to configure a switch using security best practices in a small-to medium-sized business network.

## Secure Remote Access (5.2.1)

In this topic, you will learn how to configure the management virtual interface on a switch.

### SSH Operation (5.2.1.1)

Secure Shell (SSH) is a protocol that provides a secure (encrypted) management connection to a remote device. SSH should replace Telnet for management connections. Telnet is an older protocol that uses unsecure plaintext transmission of both the login authentication (username and password) and the data transmitted between the communicating devices. SSH provides security for remote connections by providing strong encryption when a device is authenticated (username and password) and for the transmitted data between the communicating devices. SSH is assigned to TCP port 22. Telnet is assigned to TCP port 23.

In Figure 5-7, an attacker can monitor packets using Wireshark. A Telnet stream can be targeted to capture the username and password.

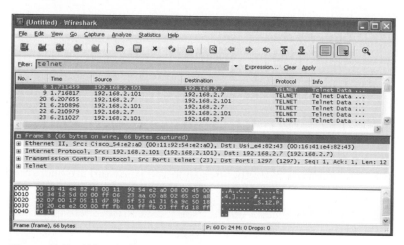

**Figure 5-7**   Wireshark Telnet Capture

In Figure 5-8, the attacker can capture the username and password of the administrator from the plaintext Telnet session.

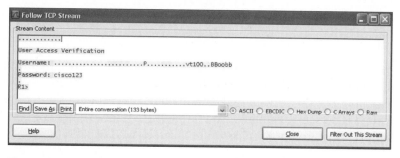

**Figure 5-8**   Plaintext Username and Password Captured

Figure 5-9 shows the Wireshark view of an SSH session. The attacker can track the session using the IP address of the administrator device.

**Figure 5-9**   Wireshark SSH Capture

However, in Figure 5-10, the username and password are encrypted.

**Figure 5-10**   Username and Password Encrypted

To enable SSH on a Catalyst 2960 switch, the switch must be using a version of the IOS software including cryptographic (encrypted) features and capabilities. In Example 5-12, use the **show version** command on the switch to see which IOS the switch is currently running. An IOS filename that includes the combination "k9" supports cryptographic (encrypted) features and capabilities.

**Example 5-12**  Verify Switch IOS Supports SSH

```
S1> show version
Cisco IOS Software, C2960 Software (C2960-LANBASEK9-M), Version 15.0(2)SE, RELEASE
  SOFTWARE (fc1)
<output omitted>
```

## Configuring SSH (5.2.1.2)

Before configuring SSH, the switch must be minimally configured with a unique hostname and the correct network connectivity settings. S1 in Figure 5-11 is configured with a hostname and network connectivity.

**Figure 5-11**    Topology for SSH Configuration

**Step 1.    Verify SSH support.**

Begin by verifying that the switch supports SSH. Use the **show ip ssh** command to verify SSH support. If the command is unrecognized, then the switch is not running an IOS that supports cryptographic features.

**Step 2.    Configure the IP domain.**

Configure the IP domain name of the network using the **ip domain-name** *domain-name* global configuration mode command.

**Step 3.    Enable SSH version 2.**

If you issue the command **show ip ssh**, the output would reveal that the switch is running version 1.99. This means the switch supports both SSHv1 and SSHv2. However, SSHv1 has known security flaws; therefore, it is recommended that only SSHv2 be enabled. To enable only SSHv2, use the **ip ssh version 2** global configuration mode command.

**Step 4.    Generate RSA key pairs.**

Generating an RSA key pair automatically enables SSH. Use the **crypto key generate rsa** global configuration mode command to enable the SSH server on the switch and generate an RSA key pair. When generating RSA keys, the administrator is prompted to enter a modulus length. Always use a longer modulus such as 1024 or 2048 bits instead of the default value of 512. A longer modulus length is more secure, but it takes longer to generate and to use.

**Note**

To delete the RSA key pair, use the **crypto key zeroize rsa** global configuration mode command. After the RSA key pair is deleted, the SSH server is automatically disabled.

**Step 5.**    **Configure user authentication.**

The SSH server can authenticate users locally or using an authentication server. To use the local authentication method, create a username and password pair using the **username** *username* **secret** *password* global configuration mode command.

**Step 6.**    **Configure the vty lines.**

Enable the SSH protocol on the vty lines using the **transport input ssh** line configuration mode command. The Catalyst 2960 has vty lines ranging from 0 to 15. This configuration prevents non-SSH (such as Telnet) connections and limits the switch to accept only SSH connections. Use the **line vty** global configuration mode command and then the **login local** line configuration mode command to require local authentication for SSH connections from the local username database.

In Example 5-13, SSHv2 is enabled using the domain name **cisco.com** and a modulus of 1024 bits, and an admin user account is created. SSH is then enabled on the VTY lines using the local database to authenticate the user.

**Example 5-13** SSH Configuration Example

```
S1# configure terminal
S1(config)# ip domain-name cisco.com
S1(config)#
S1(config)# ip ssh version 2
S1(config)#
S1(config)# crypto key generate rsa
The name for the keys will be: S1.cisco.com
...
How many bits in the modulus [512]: 1024
...
S1(config)#
S1(config)# username admin secret ccna
S1(config)#
S1(config)# line vty 0 15
S1(config-line)# transport input ssh
S1(config-line)# login local
S1(config-line)# end
S1#
```

## Verifying SSH (5.2.1.3)

On a PC, an SSH client such as PuTTY is used to connect to an SSH server. The switch and PC in Figure 5-11 have been configured with the following:

- SSH enabled on switch S1

- Interface VLAN 99 (SVI) with IPv4 address 172.17.99.11 on switch S1

- PC1 with IPv4 address 172.17.99.21

In Figure 5-12, the PC initiates an SSH connection to the SVI VLAN IPv4 address of S1.

**Figure 5-12**   Configure PuTTY SSH Client Connection Parameters

In Figure 5-13, the user has been prompted for a username and password. Using the configuration from the previous example, the username **admin** and password **ccna** are entered. After entering the correct combination, the user is connected via SSH to the CLI on the Catalyst 2960 switch.

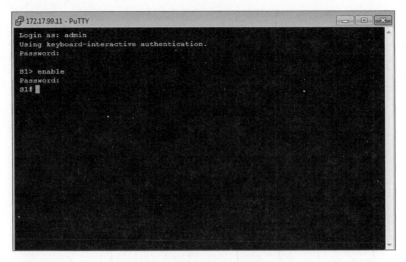

**Figure 5-13**   Verify Remote Management Access

To display the version and configuration data for SSH on the device that you config-ured as an SSH server, use the **show ip ssh** command. To check the SSH connections to the device, use the **show ssh** command.

Example 5-14 verifies the SSH version and which connections are currently established.

**Example 5-14**  Verify SSH Status and Settings

```
S1# show ip ssh
SSH Enabled - version 2.0
Authentication timeout: 90 secs; Authentication retries: 2
Minimum expected Diffie Hellman key size : 1024 bits
IOS Keys in SECSH format(ssh-rsa, base64 encoded):
ssh-rsa AAAAB3NzaC1yc2EAAAADAQABAAAAgQCdLksVz2QlREsoZt2f2scJHbW3aMDM8/8jg/srGFNLi+
    f+qJWwxt26BWmy694+6ZIQ/j7wUfIVNlQhI8GUOVIuKNqVMOMtLg8Ud4qAiLbGJfAaP3fyrKm
    ViPpOeOZof6tnKgKKvJz18Mz22XAf2u/7Jq2JnEFXycGMO88OUJQL3Q==

S1#
S1# show ssh
Connection Version Mode Encryption  Hmac      State            Username
0          2.0     IN   aes256-cbc  hmac-sha1  Session started   admin
0          2.0     OUT  aes256-cbc  hmac-sha1  Session started   admin
%No SSHv1 server connections running.
S1#
```

In the example, SSH version 2 is enabled, and the admin user is currently connected to the switch. Notice how it also confirms that SSHv1 is not activated.

**Packet Tracer 5.2.1.4: Configuring SSH**

SSH should replace Telnet for management connections. Telnet uses insecure plain-text communications. SSH provides security for remote connections by providing strong encryption of all transmitted data between devices. In this activity, you will secure a remote switch with password encryption and SSH.

# Switch Port Security (5.2.2)

In this topic, you learn how to configure the port-security feature to restrict network access.

## Secure Unused Ports (5.2.2.1)

A simple method that many administrators use to help secure the network from unauthorized access is to disable all unused ports on a switch. For example, if a Catalyst 2960 switch has 24 ports and there are three Fast Ethernet connections in use, it is good practice to disable the 21 unused ports. Navigate to each unused port and issue the Cisco IOS **shutdown** command. If, later on, a port must be reactivated, it can be enabled with the **no shutdown** command. Example 5-15 shows partial output for this configuration.

**Example 5-15** Disable Unused Ports

```
S1# show run
Building configuration...

<output omitted>

version 15.0
hostname S1

<output omitted>

interface FastEthernet0/4
 shutdown
!
```

```
interface FastEthernet0/5
 shutdown
!
interface FastEthernet0/6
description web server
!
interface FastEthernet0/7
 shutdown
!
<output omitted>
```

It is simple to make configuration changes to multiple ports on a switch. If a range of ports must be configured, use the **interface range** command.

```
Switch(config)# interface range type module/first-number - last-number
```

The process of enabling and disabling ports can be time-consuming, but it enhances security on the network and is well worth the effort.

## Port Security: Operation (5.2.2.2)

All switch ports (interfaces) should be secured before the switch is deployed for production use. One way to secure ports is by implementing a feature called *port security*. Port-security limits the number of valid MAC addresses allowed on a port. The MAC addresses of legitimate devices are allowed access, whereas other MAC addresses are denied.

Port security can be configured to allow one or more MAC addresses. If the number of MAC addresses allowed on the port is limited to one, then only the device with that specific MAC address can successfully connect to the port.

If a port is configured as a secure port and the maximum number of MAC addresses is reached, any additional attempts to connect by unknown MAC addresses generate a security violation.

Implement security on all switch ports to do the following:

- Specify a single MAC address or a group of valid MAC addresses allowed on a port.

- Specify that a port automatically shuts down if unauthorized MAC addresses are detected.

## Secure MAC Address Types

There are a number of ways to configure port security. The type of secure address is based on the configuration and includes the following:

- *Static secure MAC addresses*—MAC addresses that are manually configured on a port by using the **switchport port-security mac-address** *mac-address* interface configuration mode command. MAC addresses configured in this way are stored in the address table and are added to the running configuration on the switch.

- *Dynamic secure MAC addresses*—MAC addresses that are dynamically learned and stored only in the address table. MAC addresses configured in this way are removed when the switch restarts.

- *Sticky secure MAC addresses*—MAC addresses that can be dynamically learned or manually configured, and then stored in the address table and added to the running configuration.

## Sticky Secure MAC Addresses

To configure an interface to convert dynamically learned MAC addresses to sticky secure MAC addresses and add them to the running configuration, you must enable sticky learning.

To enable sticky learning on an interface, use the **switchport port-security mac-address sticky** interface configuration mode command. When this command is entered, the switch converts all dynamically learned MAC addresses, including those that were dynamically learned before sticky learning was enabled, into sticky secure MAC addresses. All sticky secure MAC addresses are added to the address table and to the running configuration.

Sticky secure MAC addresses can also be manually defined. When sticky secure MAC addresses are configured by using the **switchport port-security mac-address sticky** *mac-address* interface configuration mode command, all specified addresses are added to the address table and the running configuration.

If the sticky secure MAC addresses are saved to the startup configuration file, then when the switch restarts or the interface shuts down, the interface does not need to relearn the addresses. If the sticky secure addresses are not saved, they will be lost.

If sticky learning is disabled by using the **no switchport port-security mac-address sticky** interface configuration mode command, the sticky secure MAC addresses remain part of the address table but are removed from the running configuration.

Sticky secure addresses have the following characteristics:

- They are learned dynamically; they are converted to sticky secure MAC addresses stored in the running-config.

- They are removed from the running-config if port security is disabled.

- They are lost when the switch reboots (power cycled).

- They become permanent when they're saved in the startup-config, and the switch retains them after a reboot.

- They convert to dynamic secure addresses when they are disabled; this also removes them from the running-config.

## Port Security: Violation Modes (5.2.2.3)

An interface can be configured for one of three violation modes, specifying the action to be taken if a violation occurs. Table 5-4 presents which kinds of data traffic are forwarded when one of the following security violation modes are configured on a port.

**Table 5-4**   Security Violation Modes

| Violation Mode | Forwards Traffic | Sends Syslog Message | Displays Error Message | Increases Violation Counter | Shuts Down Port |
|---|---|---|---|---|---|
| Protected | No | No | No | No | No |
| Restricted | No | Yes | No | Yes | No |
| Shutdown | No | No | No | Yes | Yes |

- **Protect**—When the number of secure MAC addresses reaches the limit allowed on the port, packets with unknown source addresses are dropped until a sufficient number of secure MAC addresses are removed, or the number of maximum allowable addresses is increased. There is no notification that a security violation has occurred.

- **Restrict**—When the number of secure MAC addresses reaches the limit allowed on the port, packets with unknown source addresses are dropped until a sufficient number of secure MAC addresses are removed, or the number of maximum allowable addresses is increased. In this mode, there is a notification that a security violation has occurred.

- **Shutdown**—In this (default) mode, a port-security violation causes the interface to immediately become error-disabled and turns off the port LED. It increments the violation counter. When a secure port is in the error-disabled state, it can be brought out of this state by entering the **shutdown** interface configuration mode command followed by the **no shutdown** command.

To change the violation mode on a switch port, use the **switchport port-security violation** {**protect** | **restrict** | **shutdown**} interface configuration mode command.

## Port Security: Configuring (5.2.2.4)

Table 5-5 summarizes the default port-security settings on a Cisco Catalyst switch.

**Table 5-5**   Port-Security Default Settings

| Feature | Default Setting |
|---|---|
| Port security | Disabled on port |
| Maximum number of secure MAC addresses | 1 |
| Violation mode | Shutdown. The port shuts down when the maximum number of secure MAC addresses is exceeded. |
| Sticky address learning | Disabled |

Figure 5-14 displays a topology with two PCs connected to a switch.

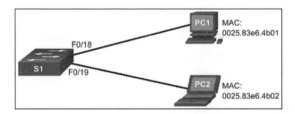

**Figure 5-14**   Port-Security Configuration Topology

In Example 5-16, port security is configured on the Fast Ethernet F0/18 port on the S1 switch. Entering this command enables port security with the default settings of 1 MAC address allowed and the violation set to shutdown.

**Example 5-16**  Enabling Port Security with Default Settings on Fa0/18

```
S1(config)# interface fastethernet 0/18
S1(config-if)# switchport mode access
S1(config-if)# switchport port-security
S1(config-if)#
```

**Note**

The port-security feature will not work until port security is enabled on the interface using the **switchport port-security** command.

In Example 5-17, the sticky secure MAC addresses learning is enabled on Fast Ethernet port 0/19 of S1. Also, the maximum number of MAC addresses is set to 10 and the violation mode is left to the default of shutdown.

**Example 5-17**  Enabling Port Security with Sticky Learning on Fa0/19

```
S1(config)# interface fastethernet 0/19
S1(config-if)# switchport mode access
S1(config-if)# switchport port-security
S1(config-if)# switchport port-security maximum 10
S1(config-if)# switchport port-security mac-address sticky
S1(config-if)#
```

## Port Security: Verifying (5.2.2.5)

After configuring port security on a switch, check each interface to verify that the port security is set correctly, and check to ensure that the static MAC addresses have been configured correctly.

## Verify Port-Security Settings

To display port-security settings for the switch, or for the specified interface, use the **show port-security interface** [*interface-id*] command. Example 5-18 displays the settings for FastEthernet 0/18.

**Example 5-18**  Verify MAC Address—Dynamic

```
S1# show port-security interface fastethernet 0/18
Port Security              : Enabled
Port Status               : Secure-up
Violation Mode            : Shutdown
Aging Time                : 0 mins
Aging Type                : Absolute
SecureStatic Address Aging : Disabled
Maximum MAC Addresses     : 1
Total MAC Addresses       : 1
Configured MAC Addresses  : 0
Sticky MAC Addresses      : 0
Last Source Address:Vlan  : 0025.83e6.4b01:1
Security Violation Count  : 0
```

No other port-security settings for Fa0/18 were altered in the configuration; therefore, the output displays the default settings for the port.

Example 5-19 displays the settings for FastEthernet 0/19, which was configured as sticky with a maximum of 10 MAC addresses permitted on the port.

**Example 5-19** Verify MAC Address—Sticky

```
S1# show port-security interface fastethernet 0/19
Port Security              : Enabled
Port Status                : Secure-up
Violation Mode             : Shutdown
Aging Time                 : 0 mins
Aging Type                 : Absolute
SecureStatic Address Aging : Disabled
Maximum MAC Addresses      : 10
Total MAC Addresses        : 1
Configured MAC Addresses   : 0
Sticky MAC Addresses       : 1
Last Source Address:Vlan   : 0025.83e6.4b02:1
Security Violation Count   : 0
```

**Note**

The MAC address is identified as a sticky MAC.

Sticky MAC addresses are added to the MAC address table and to the running configuration. As shown in Example 5-20, the sticky MAC for PC2 has been added to the running configuration for S1.

**Example 5-20** Verify Stick MAC Address Is in Running Config

```
S1# show run | begin FastEthernet 0/19
interface FastEthernet0/19
 switchport mode access
 switchport port-security maximum 10
 switchport port-security
 switchport port-security mac-address sticky
 switchport port-security mac-address sticky 0025.83e6.4b02
```

## Verify Secure MAC Addresses

To display all secure MAC addresses configured on all switch interfaces, or on a specified interface with aging information for each, use the **show port-security**

**address** command. As shown in Example 5-21, the secure MAC addresses are listed along with the types.

**Example 5-21** Verify Secure MAC Addresses

```
S1# show port-security address
Secure Mac Address Table
--------------------------------------------------------------------
Vlan    Mac Address       Type            Ports     Remaining Age
                                                    (mins)

----    -----------       ----            -----     ------------
1       0025.83e6.4b01    SecureDynamic   Fa0/18    -
1       0025.83e6.4b02    SecureSticky    Fa0/19    -

--------------------------------------------------------------------
Total Addresses in System (excluding one mac per port) : 0
Max Addresses limit in System (excluding one mac per port
```

## Ports in Error-Disabled State (5.2.2.6)

When a port is configured with port security, a violation can cause the port to become error disabled. When a port is error disabled, it is effectively shut down, and no traffic is sent or received on that port. A series of port security–related messages display on the console, as shown in Example 5-22.

**Example 5-22** Port-Security Violation Messages

```
Sep 20 06:44:54.966: %PM-4-ERR_DISABLE: psecure-violation error detected on
  Fa0/18, putting Fa0/18 in err-disable state
Sep 20 06:44:54.966: %PORT_SECURITY-2-PSECURE_VIOLATION: Security violation
  occurred, caused by MAC address 000c.292b.4c75 on port FastEthernet0/18.
Sep 20 06:44:55.973: %LINEPROTO-5-PPDOWN: Line protocol on Interface
FastEthernet0/18, changed state to down
Sep 20 06:44:56.971: %LINK-3-UPDOWN: Interface FastEthernet0/18, changed state to
  down
```

**Note**

The port protocol and link status is changed to down.

The port LED will turn off. The **show interfaces** command identifies the port status as **err-disabled**, as shown in Example 5-23. The output of the **show port-security interface** command now shows the port status as **secure-shutdown**. Because the port security violation mode is set to shutdown, the port with the security violation goes to the error-disabled state.

**Example 5-23** Verify Port Status

```
S1# show interface fa0/18 status
Port     Name  Status       Vlan  Duplex  Speed   Type
Fa0/18         err-disabled 1     auto    auto    10/100BaseTX


S1#
S1# show port-security interface fastethernet 0/18
Port Security              : Enabled
Port Status                : Secure-shutdown
Violation Mode             : Shutdown
Aging Time                 : 0 mins
Aging Type                 : Absolute
SecureStatic Address Aging : Disabled
Maximum MAC Addresses      : 1
Total MAC Addresses        : 0
Configured MAC Addresses   : 0
Sticky MAC Addresses       : 0
Last Source Address:Vlan   : 000c.292b.4c75:1
Security Violation Count   : 1
```

The administrator should determine what caused the security violation before re-enabling the port. If an unauthorized device is connected to a secure port, the port should not be re-enabled until the security threat is eliminated. To re-enable the port, use the **shutdown** interface configuration mode command, as shown in Example 5-24. Then use the **no shutdown** interface configuration command to make the port operational.

**Example 5-24** Re-Enabling an ERR_DISABLE Port

```
S1(config)# interface FastEthernet 0/18
S1(config-if)# shutdown
Sep 20 06:57:28.532: %LINK-5-CHANGED: Interface FastEthernet0/18, changed state to
  administratively down
S1(config-if)#
S1(config-if)# no shutdown
Sep 20 06:57:48.186: %LINK-3-UPDOWN: Interface FastEthernet0/18, changed state to
  up
Sep 20 06:57:49.193: %LINEPROTO-5-UPDOWN: Line protocol on Interface
FastEthernet0/18, changed state to up
```

### Packet Tracer 5.2.2.7: Configuring Switch Port Security

In this activity, you configure and verify port security on a switch. Port security allows you to restrict a port's ingress traffic by limiting the MAC addresses that are allowed to send traffic into the port.

### Packet Tracer 5.2.2.8: Troubleshooting Switch Port Security

The employee who normally uses PC1 brought his laptop from home, disconnected PC1, and connected the laptop to the telecommunication outlet. After reminding him of the security policy that does not allow personal devices on the network, you now must reconnect PC1 and re-enable the port.

### Lab 5.2.2.9: Configuring Switch Security Features

In this lab, you will complete the following objectives:

- Part 1: Set Up the Topology and Initialize Devices
- Part 2: Configure Basic Device Settings and Verify Connectivity
- Part 3: Configure and Verify SSH Access on S1
- Part 4: Configure and Verify Security Features on S1

# Summary (5.3)

**Class Activity 5.3.1.1: Switch Trio**

Scenario

You are the network administrator for a small- to medium-sized business. Corporate headquarters for your business has mandated that on all switches in all offices, security must be implemented. The memorandum delivered to you this morning states:

*"By Monday, April 18, 20xx, the first three ports of all configurable switches located in all offices must be secured with MAC addresses—one address will be reserved for the printer, one address will be reserved for the laptop in the office, and one address will be reserved for the office server.*

*If a port's security is breached, we ask you to shut it down until the reason for the breach can be certified.*

*Please implement this policy no later than the date stated in this memorandum. For questions, call 1.800.555.1212. Thank you. The Network Management Team"*

Work with a partner in the class and create a Packet Tracer example to test this new security policy. After you have created your file, test it with at least one device to ensure it is operational or validated.

Save your work, and be prepared to share it with the entire class.

**Packet Tracer 5.3.1.2: Skills Integration Challenge**

The network administrator asked you to configure a new switch. In this activity, you will use a list of requirements to configure the new switch with initial settings, SSH, and port security.

When a Cisco LAN switch is first powered on, it goes through the following boot sequence:

1. The switch loads a power-on self-test (POST) program stored in ROM. POST checks the CPU subsystem. It tests the CPU, the DRAM, and the portion of the flash device that makes up the flash file system.

2. The switch loads the boot loader software. The boot loader is a small program stored in ROM and is run immediately after POST successfully completes.

3. The boot loader performs low-level CPU initialization. It initializes the CPU registers, which control the mapping location of physical memory, the quantity of memory, and its speed.

4. The boot loader initializes the flash file system on the system board.

5. The boot loader locates and loads a default IOS operating system software image into memory and gives control of the switch to the IOS.

The specific Cisco IOS file that is loaded is specified by the BOOT environmental variable. After the Cisco IOS is loaded, it uses the commands found in the startup-config file to initialize and configure the interfaces. If the Cisco IOS files are missing or damaged, the boot loader program can be used to reload or recover from the problem.

The operational status of the switch is displayed by a series of LEDs on the front panel. These LEDs display such things as port status, duplex, and speed.

An IP address is configured on the SVI of the management VLAN to allow for remote configuration of the device. A default gateway belonging to the management VLAN must be configured on the switch using the **ip default-gateway** command. If the default gateway is not properly configured, remote management is not possible. It is recommended that Secure Shell (SSH) be used to provide a secure (encrypted) management connection to a remote device to prevent the sniffing of unencrypted user names and passwords, which is possible when using protocols such as Telnet.

One of the advantages of a switch is that it allows full-duplex communication between devices, effectively doubling the communication rate. Although it is possible to specify the speed and duplex settings of a switch interface, it is recommended that the switch be allowed to set these parameters automatically to avoid errors.

Switch port security is a requirement to help prevent Layer 2 attacks. Switch ports should be configured to allow only frames with specific source MAC addresses to enter. Frames from unknown source MAC addresses should be denied and cause the port to shut down to prevent further attacks.

## Practice

The following activities provide practice with the topics introduced in this chapter. The Labs and Class Activities are available in the companion *Routing and Switching Essentials v6 Labs & Study Guide* (ISBN 9781587134265). The Packet Tracer Activities PKA files are found in the online course.

**Class Activities**

Class Activity 5.0.1.2: Stand By Me

Class Activity 5.3.1.1: Switch Trio

**Labs**

Lab 5.1.1.6: Configuring Basic Switch Settings

Lab 5.2.2.9: Configuring Switch Security Features

**Packet Tracer Activities**

Packet Tracer 5.2.1.4: Configuring SSH Instruction

Packet Tracer 5.2.2.7: Configuring Switch Port Security

Packet Tracer 5.2.2.8: Troubleshooting Switch Port Security

Packet Tracer 5.3.1.2: Skills Integration Challenge

# Check Your Understanding Questions

Complete all the review questions listed here to test your understanding of the topics and concepts in this chapter. The appendix "Answers to the 'Check Your Understanding' Questions" lists the answers.

1. Which interface is the default location that would contain the IP address used to manage a 24-port Ethernet switch?

   A. Fa0/0

   B. Fa0/1

   C. Interface connected to the default gateway

   D. VLAN 1

   E. VLAN 99

2. A production switch is reloaded and finishes with a **Switch>** prompt. What two facts can be determined? (Choose two.)

   A. A full version of the Cisco IOS was located and loaded.

   B. POST occurred normally.

   C. The boot process was interrupted.

   D. There is not enough RAM or flash on this router.

   E. The switch did not locate the Cisco IOS in flash, so it defaulted to ROM.

3. Which two statements are true about using full-duplex Fast Ethernet? (Choose two.)

   A. Full-duplex Fast Ethernet offers 100 percent efficiency in both directions.

   B. Latency is reduced because the NIC processes frames faster.

   C. Nodes operate in full-duplex with unidirectional data flow.

   D. Performance is improved because the NIC is able to detect collisions.

   E. Performance is improved with bidirectional data flow.

4. Which statement describes the port speed LED on the Cisco Catalyst 2960 switch?

   A. If the LED is amber, the port is operating at 1000 Mb/s.

   B. If the LED is blinking green, the port is operating at 10 Mb/s.

   C. If the LED is green, the port is operating at 100 Mb/s.

   D. If the LED is off, the port is not operating.

5. What is a function of the switch boot loader?

   A. To control how much RAM is available to the switch during the boot process

   B. To provide an environment to operate in when the switch operating system cannot be found

   C. To provide security for the vulnerable state when the switch is booting

   D. To speed up the boot process

6. In which situation would a technician use the **show interfaces** command?

   A. To determine whether remote access is enabled

   B. To determine the MAC address of a directly attached network device on a particular interface

   C. When packets are being dropped from a particular directly attached host

   D. When an end device can reach local devices, but not remote devices

7. What is one difference between using Telnet or SSH to connect to a network device for management purposes?

   A. Telnet does not provide authentication, whereas SSH does.

   B. Telnet sends a username and password in plain text, whereas SSH encrypts the username and password.

   C. Telnet supports a host GUI, whereas SSH only supports a host CLI.

   D. Telnet uses UDP as the transport protocol, whereas SSH uses TCP.

8. Which action will bring an error-disabled switch port back to an operational state?

    A. Clear the MAC address table on the switch.

    B. Issue the **shutdown** and then **no shutdown** interface commands.

    C. Issue the **switchport mode access** command on the interface.

    D. Remove and reconfigure port security on the interface.

9. Which two statements are true regarding switch port security? (Choose two.)

    A. After entering the **sticky** parameter, only MAC addresses subsequently learned are converted to secure MAC addresses.

    B. Dynamically learned secure MAC addresses are lost when the switch reboots.

    C. If fewer than the maximum number of MAC addresses for a port are configured statically, dynamically learned addresses are added to CAM until the maximum number is reached.

    D. The three configurable violation modes all log violations via SNMP.

    E. The three configurable violation modes all require user intervention to re-enable ports.

10. A network administrator configures the port-security feature on a switch. The security policy specifies that each access port should allow up to two MAC addresses. When the maximum number of MAC addresses is reached, a frame with the unknown source MAC address is dropped and a notification is sent to the syslog server. Which security violation mode should be configured for each access port?

    A. Protect

    B. Restrict

    C. Shutdown

    D. Warning

# CHAPTER 6

# VLANs

## Objectives

Upon completion of this chapter, you will be able to answer the following questions:

- What is the purpose of VLANs in a switched network?

- How does a switch forward frames based on VLAN configuration in a multiswitch environment?

- How do you configure a switch port to be assigned to a VLAN based on requirements?

- How do you configure a trunk port on a LAN switch?

- How do you troubleshoot VLAN and trunk configurations in a switched network?

- Can you describe the two options configuring for inter-VLAN routing?

- How do you configure legacy inter-VLAN routing?

- How do you configure router-on-a-stick inter-VLAN routing?

## Key Terms

This chapter uses the following key terms. You can find the definitions in the Glossary.

# Introduction (6.0.1.1)

Network performance is an important factor in the productivity of an organization. One of the technologies used to improve network performance is the separation of large broadcast domains into smaller ones. By design, routers block broadcast traffic at an interface. However, routers normally have a limited number of LAN interfaces. A router's primary role is to move information between networks, not to provide network access to end devices.

The role of providing access into a LAN is normally reserved for an access layer switch. A VLAN can be created on a Layer 2 switch to reduce the size of broadcast domains, similar to a Layer 3 device. VLANs are commonly incorporated into network design, making it easier for a network to support the goals of an organization. Although VLANs are primarily used within switched LANs, modern implementations of VLANs allow them to span MANs and WANs.

Because VLANs segment the network, a Layer 3 process is required to allow traffic to move from one network segment to another.

This Layer 3 routing process can be implemented using either a router or a Layer 3 switch interface. The use of a Layer 3 device provides a method for controlling the flow of traffic between network segments, including network segments that VLANs create.

The first part of this chapter covers how to configure, manage, and troubleshoot VLANs and VLAN trunks. The second part of this chapter focuses on implementing inter-VLAN routing using a router. Inter-VLAN routing on a Layer 3 switch is covered in a later course.

**Class Activity 6.0.1.2: Vacation Station**

You have purchased a three-floor vacation home at the beach for rental purposes. The floor plan is identical on each floor. Each floor offers one digital television for renters to use.

According to the local Internet service provider (ISP), only three stations may be offered within a television package. It is your job to decide which television packages you offer your guests.

- Divide the class into groups of three students per group.

- Choose three different stations to make one subscription package for each floor of your rental home.

- Complete the PDF for this activity.

- Share your completed group-reflection answers with the class.

# VLAN Segmentation (6.1)

VLANs use logical connections to group devices within a LAN. Logically grouping devices into a VLAN enables better security, enhances network performance, reduces costs, and helps IT staff manage network users more efficiently.

In this section, you learn how VLANs segment broadcast domains in a small-to medium-sized business network.

## Overview of VLANs (6.1.1)

In this topic, you learn about the purpose of VLANs in a switched network.

### VLAN Definitions (6.1.1.1)

In a switched internetwork, VLANs provide segmentation and organizational flexibility. VLANs provide a way to group devices within a LAN. A group of devices within a VLAN communicate as if they were attached to the same cable. VLANs are based on logical connections instead of physical connections, as shown in Figure 6-1.

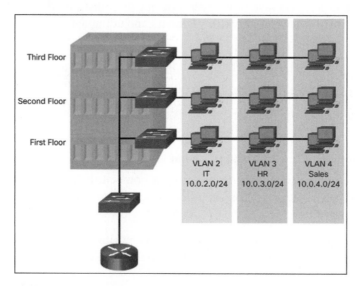

**Figure 6-1**   Defining VLAN Groups

VLANs allow an administrator to segment networks based on factors such as function, project team, or application, without regard for the physical location of the user or device. Devices within a VLAN act as if they are in their own independent network, even if they share a common infrastructure with other VLANs. Any switch port can belong to a VLAN, and unicast, broadcast, and multicast packets are forwarded and flooded only to end stations within the VLAN where the packets are sourced. Each VLAN is considered a separate logical network. Packets destined for stations that do not belong to the VLAN must be forwarded through a device that supports routing.

Multiple IP subnets can exist on a switched network, without the use of multiple VLANs. However, the devices will be in the same Layer 2 broadcast domain. This means that any Layer 2 broadcasts, such as an Address Resolution Protocol (ARP) request, are received by all devices on the switched network, even by those not intended to receive the broadcast.

A VLAN creates a logical broadcast domain that can span multiple physical LAN segments. VLANs improve network performance by separating large broadcast domains into smaller ones. If a device in one VLAN sends a broadcast Ethernet frame, all devices in the VLAN receive the frame, but devices in other VLANs do not.

VLANs enable the implementation of access and security policies according to specific groupings of users. Each switch port can be assigned to only one VLAN (with the exception of a port connected to an IP phone or to another switch).

## Benefits of VLANs (6.1.1.2)

User productivity and network adaptability are important for business growth and success. VLANs make it easier to design a network to support the goals of an organization. Each VLAN in a switched network corresponds to an IP network, as shown in Figure 6-2. Therefore, VLAN design must consider the implementation of a hierarchical network-addressing scheme.

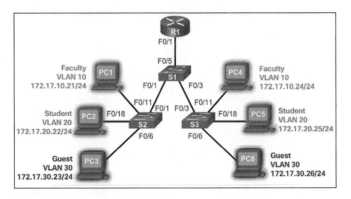

**Figure 6-2**   VLAN Topology

*Hierarchical network addressing* means that IP network numbers are applied to network segments or VLANs in an orderly fashion that considers the network as a whole. Blocks of contiguous network addresses are reserved for and configured on devices in a specific area of the network.

The primary benefits of using VLANs are as follows:

- **Security**—Groups that have sensitive data are separated from the rest of the network, decreasing the chances of confidential information breaches. In Figure 6-2, faculty computers are on VLAN 10 and completely separated from student and guest data traffic.

- **Cost reduction**—Cost savings result from a reduced need for expensive network upgrades and more efficient use of existing bandwidth and uplinks.

- **Better performance**—Dividing flat Layer 2 networks into multiple logical workgroups (broadcast domains) reduces unnecessary traffic on the network and boosts performance.

- **Smaller broadcast domains**—Dividing a network into VLANs reduces the number of devices in the broadcast domain. In Figure 6-2, there are six computers on this network, but there are three broadcast domains: Faculty, Student, and Guest.

- **Improved IT staff efficiency**—VLANs make it easier to manage the network because users with similar network requirements share the same VLAN. When a new switch is provisioned, all the policies and procedures already configured for the particular VLAN are implemented when the ports are assigned. It is also easy for the IT staff to identify the function of a VLAN by giving it an appropriate name. In Figure 6-2, for easy identification, VLAN 10 has been named "Faculty," VLAN 20 is named "Student," and VLAN 30 is named "Guest."

- **Simpler project and application management**—VLANs aggregate users and network devices to support business or geographic requirements. Having separate functions makes managing a project or working with a specialized application easier; an example of such an application is an e-learning development platform for faculty.

## Types of VLANs (6.1.1.3)

There are a number of distinct types of VLANs used in modern networks. Some VLAN types are defined by traffic classes. Other types of VLANs are defined by the specific function that they serve.

## Default VLAN

All switch ports become a part of the *default VLAN* after the initial bootup of a switch loading the default configuration. Switch ports that participate in the default VLAN are part of the same broadcast domain. This allows any device connected to any switch port to communicate with other devices on other switch ports. The default VLAN for Cisco switches is VLAN 1. In Example 6-1, the **show vlan brief** command was issued on a switch running the default configuration. Notice that all ports are assigned to VLAN 1 by default.

**Example 6-1**  VLAN 1 Default Port Assignments

```
Switch# show vlan brief

VLAN Name                            Status    Ports
---- -------------------------------- --------- -------------------------------
1    default                         active    Fa0/1,   Fa0/2,   Fa0/3,   Fa0/4
                                               Fa0/5,   Fa0/6,   Fa0/7,   Fa0/8
                                               Fa0/9,   Fa0/10,  Fa0/11,  Fa0/12
                                               Fa0/13,  Fa0/14,  Fa0/15,  Fa0/16
                                               Fa0/17,  Fa0/18,  Fa0/19,  Fa0/20
                                               Fa0/21,  Fa0/22,  Fa0/23,  Fa0/24
                                               Gi0/1,   Gi0/2
1002 fddi-default                    act/unsup
1003 token-ring-default              act/unsup
1004 fddinet-default                 act/unsup
1005 trnet-default                   act/unsup
```

VLAN 1 has all the features of any VLAN, except it cannot be renamed or deleted. By default, all Layer 2 control traffic is associated with VLAN 1.

## Native VLAN

A *native VLAN* is assigned to an 802.1Q trunk port. Trunk ports are the links between switches that support the transmission of traffic associated with more than one VLAN. An 802.1Q trunk port supports traffic coming from many VLANs (tagged traffic), as well as traffic that does not come from a VLAN (untagged traffic). Tagged traffic refers to traffic that has a 4-byte tag inserted within the original Ethernet frame header, specifying the VLAN to which the frame belongs. The 802.1Q trunk port places untagged traffic on the native VLAN, which by default is VLAN 1.

Native VLANs are defined in the IEEE 802.1Q specification to maintain backward compatibility with untagged traffic common to legacy LAN scenarios. A native VLAN serves as a common identifier on opposite ends of a trunk link.

It is a best practice to configure the native VLAN as an unused VLAN, distinct from VLAN 1 and other VLANs. In fact, it is not unusual to dedicate a fixed VLAN to serve the role of the native VLAN for all trunk ports in the switched domain.

## Data VLAN

A *data VLAN* is one that is configured to carry user-generated traffic. A VLAN carrying voice or management traffic would not be a data VLAN. It is common practice to separate voice and management traffic from data traffic. A data VLAN is sometimes referred to as a user VLAN. Data VLANs are used to separate the network into groups of users or devices.

## Management VLAN

A *management VLAN* is any VLAN configured to access the management capabilities of a switch. VLAN 1 is the management VLAN by default. To create the management VLAN, the switch virtual interface (SVI) of that VLAN is assigned an IP address and a subnet mask, allowing the switch to be managed via HTTP, Telnet, SSH, or SNMP. Because the out-of-the-box configuration of a Cisco switch has VLAN 1 as the default VLAN, VLAN 1 would be a bad choice for the management VLAN.

In the past, the management VLAN for a 2960 switch was the only active SVI. On 15.x versions of the Cisco IOS for Catalyst 2960 Series switches, it is possible to have more than one active SVI. Cisco IOS 15.x requires that the particular active SVI assigned for remote management be documented. While theoretically a switch can have more than one management VLAN, having more than one increases exposure to network attacks.

In Example 6-1, all ports are currently assigned to the default VLAN 1. No native VLAN is explicitly assigned, and no other VLANs are active; therefore, the network is designed with the native VLAN the same as the management VLAN. This is considered a security risk.

## Voice VLANs (6.1.1.4)

A separate VLAN is needed to support Voice over IP (VoIP). VoIP traffic requires:

- Assured bandwidth to ensure voice quality
- Transmission priority over other types of network traffic
- Ability to be routed around congested areas on the network
- Delay of less than 150 ms across the network

To meet these requirements, the entire network has to be designed to support VoIP. The details of how to configure a network to support VoIP are beyond the scope of this course, but it is useful to summarize how a *voice VLAN* works between a switch, a Cisco IP phone, and a computer.

In Figure 6-3, VLAN 150 is designed to carry voice traffic. The student computer PC5 is attached to the Cisco IP phone, and the phone is attached to switch S3. PC5 is in VLAN 20, which is used for student data.

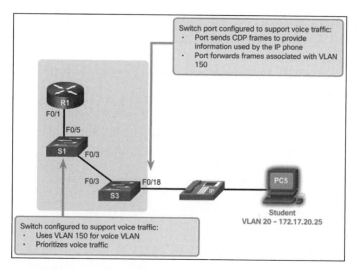

**Figure 6-3**   Voice VLAN

**Packet Tracer 6.1.1.5: Who Hears the Broadcast?**

Background/Scenario

In this activity, a 24-port Catalyst 2960 switch is fully populated. All ports are in use. You will observe broadcast traffic in a VLAN implementation and answer some reflection questions.

# VLANs in a Multiswitched Environment (6.1.2)

In this topic, you learn how a switch forwards frames based on VLAN configuration in a multiswitch environment.

## VLAN Trunks (6.1.2.1)

A trunk is a point-to-point link between two network devices that carries more than one VLAN. A *VLAN trunk* extends VLANs across an entire network. Cisco supports IEEE 802.1Q for coordinating trunks on Fast Ethernet, Gigabit Ethernet, and 10-Gigabit Ethernet interfaces.

VLANs would not be very useful without VLAN trunks. VLAN trunks allow all VLAN traffic to propagate between switches so that devices that are in the same VLAN, but connected to different switches, can communicate without the intervention of a router.

A VLAN trunk does not belong to a specific VLAN; rather, it is a conduit for multiple VLANs between switches and routers. A trunk could also be used between a network device and server or other device that is equipped with an appropriate 802.1Q-capable NIC. By default, on a Cisco Catalyst switch, all VLANs are supported on a trunk port.

In Figure 6-4, the links between switches S1 and S2, and S1 and S3, are configured to transmit traffic coming from VLANs 10, 20, 30, and 99 across the network. This network could not function without VLAN trunks.

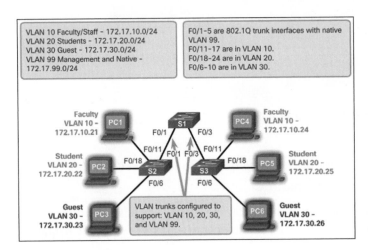

**Figure 6-4**   VLAN Trunks

## Controlling Broadcast Domains with VLANs (6.1.2.2)

Consider networks without VLANs and networks with VLANs.

### Network Without VLANs

In normal operation, when a switch receives a broadcast frame on one of its ports, it forwards the frame out all other ports except the port where the broadcast was received. As illustrated in Figure 6-5, the entire network is configured in the same subnet (172.17.40.0/24), and no VLANs are configured. As a result, when the faculty computer (PC1) sends out a broadcast frame, switch S2 sends that broadcast frame out all of its ports. Eventually the entire network receives the broadcast because the network is one broadcast domain.

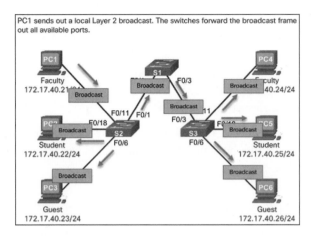

**Figure 6-5**   Broadcast Domain with no VLANs

In this example, all devices are on the same IPv4 subnet, but if there were devices from other IPv4 subnets attached to the switch, they would still receive the same broadcast frames not intended for them. Broadcasts such as an ARP request are intended only for devices on the same subnet.

## Network with VLANs

In Figure 6-6, the network has been segmented using two VLANs. Faculty devices are assigned to VLAN 10, and student devices are assigned to VLAN 20. As illustrated in the figure, a broadcast frame is sent from the faculty computer, PC1, to switch S2. The switch forwards that broadcast frame only to those switch ports configured to support VLAN 10.

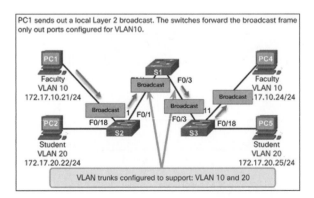

**Figure 6-6**   VLANs Segment Broadcast Domains

The ports that comprise the connection between switches S2 and S1 (ports F0/1), and between S1 and S3 (ports F0/3), are trunks that have been configured to support all the VLANs in the network.

When S1 receives the broadcast frame on port F0/1, S1 forwards that broadcast frame out of the only other port configured to support VLAN 10, which is port F0/3. When S3 receives the broadcast frame on port F0/3, it forwards that broadcast frame out the only other port configured to support VLAN 10, which is port F0/11. The broadcast frame arrives at the only other computer in the network configured in VLAN 10, which is faculty computer PC4.

When VLANs are implemented on a switch, the transmission of unicast, multicast, and broadcast traffic from a host in a particular VLAN are restricted to the devices that are in that VLAN.

### Tagging Ethernet Frames for VLAN Identification (6.1.2.3)

Catalyst 2960 Series switches are Layer 2 devices. They use the Ethernet frame header information to forward packets. They do not have routing tables. The standard Ethernet frame header does not contain information about the VLAN to which the frame belongs; thus, when Ethernet frames are placed on a trunk, information about the VLANs to which they belong must be added. This process, called tagging, is accomplished by using the *IEEE 802.1Q header*, specified in the *IEEE 802.1Q standard*. The 802.1Q header includes a 4-byte tag inserted within the original Ethernet frame header, specifying the VLAN to which the frame belongs.

When the switch receives a frame on a port configured in access mode and assigned a VLAN, the switch inserts a VLAN tag in the frame header, recalculates the Frame Check Sequence (FCS), and sends the tagged frame out of a trunk port.

### VLAN Tag Field Details

The *VLAN tag field* is shown in Figure 6-7.

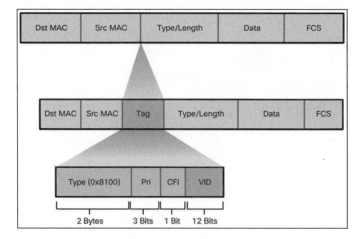

**Figure 6-7**    Fields in an Ethernet 802.1Q Frame

The VLAN tag field consists of a Type field, a Priority field, a *Canonical Format Identifier* field, and *VLAN ID* field:

- **Type**—A 2-byte value called the *tag protocol ID (TPID)* value. For Ethernet, it is set to hexadecimal 0x8100.

- *User priority*—A 3-bit value that supports level or service implementation.

- **Canonical Format Identifier (CFI)**—A 1-bit identifier that enables Token Ring frames to be carried across Ethernet links.

- **VLAN ID (VID)**—A 12-bit VLAN identification number that supports up to 4096 VLAN IDs.

After the switch inserts the Type and tag control information fields, it recalculates the FCS values and inserts the new FCS into the frame.

## Native VLANs and 802.1Q Tagging (6.1.2.4)

Some devices that support trunking add a VLAN tag to native VLAN traffic. Control traffic sent on the native VLAN should not be tagged. If an 802.1Q trunk port receives a tagged frame with the VLAN ID that is the same as the native VLAN, it drops the frame. Consequently, when configuring a switch port on a Cisco switch, configure devices so that they do not send tagged frames on the native VLAN. Devices from other vendors that support tagged frames on the native VLAN include IP phones, servers, routers, and non-Cisco switches.

When a Cisco switch trunk port receives *untagged frames* (which are unusual in a well-designed network), it forwards those frames to the native VLAN. If there are no devices associated with the native VLAN (which is not unusual) and there are no other trunk ports (which is not unusual), then the frame is dropped. The default native VLAN is VLAN 1. When configuring an 802.1Q trunk port, a default Port VLAN ID (PVID) is assigned the value of the native VLAN ID. All untagged traffic coming into or out of the 802.1Q port is forwarded based on the PVID value. For example, if VLAN 99 is configured as the native VLAN, the PVID is 99 and all untagged traffic is forwarded to VLAN 99. If the native VLAN has not been reconfigured, the PVID value is set to VLAN 1.

In Figure 6-8, PC1 is connected by a hub to an 802.1Q trunk link. PC1 sends untagged traffic, which the switches associate with the native VLAN configured on the trunk ports, and forward accordingly. Tagged traffic on the trunk received by PC1 is dropped.

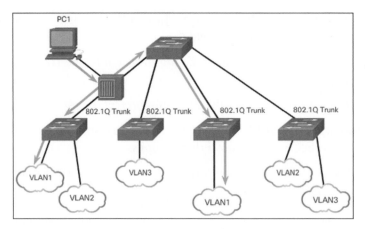

**Figure 6-8** Native VLAN on 802.1Q Trunk

This scenario reflects poor network design for several reasons: it uses a legacy hub, it has a host connected to a trunk link, and it implies that the switches have access ports assigned to the native VLAN. It also illustrates the motivation for the IEEE 802.1Q specification for native VLANs as a means of handling legacy scenarios.

## Voice VLAN Tagging (6.1.2.5)

Recall that to support VoIP, a separate voice VLAN is required.

An access port that is used to connect a Cisco IP phone can be configured to use two separate VLANs: one VLAN for voice traffic and another VLAN for data traffic from a device attached to the phone. The link between the switch and the IP phone acts as a trunk to carry both voice VLAN traffic and data VLAN traffic.

The Cisco IP Phone contains an integrated three-port 10/100 switch. The ports provide dedicated connections to these devices:

- Port 1 connects to the switch or other VoIP device.

- Port 2 is an internal 10/100 interface that carries the IP phone traffic.

- Port 3 (access port) connects to a PC or other device.

On the switch, the access is configured to send Cisco Discovery Protocol (CDP) packets that instruct an attached IP phone to send voice traffic to the switch in one of three ways, depending on the type of traffic:

- In a voice *VLAN tagged* with a Layer 2 *class of service (CoS)* priority value

- In an access VLAN tagged with a Layer 2 *CoS priority value*

- In an access VLAN, untagged (no Layer 2 CoS priority value)

In Figure 6-9, the student computer PC5 is attached to a Cisco IP phone, and the phone is attached to switch S3. VLAN 150 is designed to carry voice traffic, whereas PC5 is in VLAN 20, which is used for student data.

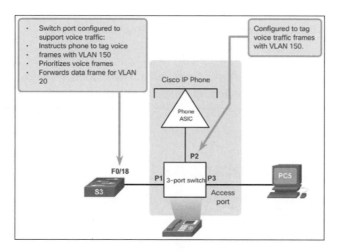

**Figure 6-9**  Voice VLAN Tagging

## Sample Configuration

Example 6-2 shows a sample output. Notice how the highlighted areas show that the F0/18 interface is configured to support a data VLAN (VLAN 20) and a voice VLAN (VLAN 150).

**Note**

A discussion of Cisco IOS voice commands is beyond the scope of this course.

**Example 6-2**  Verifying a Voice VLAN Configuration

```
S1# show interfaces fa0/18 switchport
Name: Fa0/18
Switchport: Enabled
Administrative Mode: static access
Operational Mode: down
Administrative Trunking Encapsulation: dot1q
Negotiation of Trunking: Off
Access Mode VLAN: 20 (student)
Trunking Native Mode VLAN: 1 (default)
Administrative Native VLAN tagging: enabled
Voice VLAN: 150 (voice)

<output omitted>
```

**Activity 6.1.2.6: Predict Switch Behavior**

Refer to the online course to complete this activity.

**Packet Tracer 6.1.2.7: Investigating a VLAN Implementation**

Background/Scenario

In this activity, you observe how broadcast traffic is forwarded by the switches when VLANs are configured and when VLANs are not configured.

# VLAN Implementations (6.2)

VLANs are used extensively in networks. Therefore, understanding how to properly implement VLANs in a corporate network is a required skill that all network administrators must possess.

In this section, you learn how to implement VLANs to segment a small-to medium-sized business network.

## VLAN Assignment (6.2.1)

In this topic, you configure a switch port to be assigned to a VLAN based on requirements.

### VLAN Ranges on Catalyst Switches (6.2.1.1)

Different Cisco Catalyst switches support various numbers of VLANs. The number of supported VLANs is large enough to accommodate the needs of most organizations. For example, the Catalyst 2960 and 3560 Series switches support more than 4,000 VLANs. *Normal range VLANs* on these switches are numbered 1 to 1005, and *extended range VLANs* are numbered 1006 to 4094. Example 6-3 illustrates the available VLANs on a Catalyst 2960 switch running Cisco IOS Release 15.x.

**Example 6-3** Normal Range VLANs

```
S1# show vlan brief

VLAN Name                             Status    Ports
---- -------------------------------  --------- ------------------------------
1    default                          active    Fa0/1,  Fa0/2,  Fa0/3,  Fa0/4
                                                Fa0/5,  Fa0/6,  Fa0/7,  Fa0/8
                                                Fa0/9,  Fa0/10, Fa0/11, Fa0/12
                                                Fa0/13, Fa0/14, Fa0/15, Fa0/16
                                                Fa0/17, Fa0/18, Fa0/19, Fa0/20
                                                Fa0/21, Fa0/22, Fa0/23, Fa0/24
                                                Gi0/1,  Gi0/2
1002 fddi-default                     act/unsup
1003 token-ring-default               act/unsup
1004 fddinet-default                  act/unsup
1005 trnet-default                    act/unsup
```

## Normal Range VLANs

- These are used in small- and medium-sized business and enterprise networks.

- They are identified by a VLAN ID between 1 and 1005.

- IDs 1002 through 1005 are reserved for Token Ring and Fiber Distributed Data Interface (FDDI) VLANs.

- IDs 1 and 1002 to 1005 are automatically created and cannot be removed.

- Configurations are stored within a VLAN database file, called *vlan.dat*. The vlan.dat file is located in the flash memory of the switch.

- The *VLAN Trunking Protocol (VTP)*, which helps manage VLAN configurations between switches, can only learn and store normal range VLANs.

## Extended Range VLANs

- These enable service providers to extend their infrastructure to a greater number of customers. Some global enterprises could be large enough to need extended range VLAN IDs.

- They are identified by a VLAN ID between 1006 and 4094.

- Configurations are not written to the vlan.dat file.

- They support fewer VLAN features than normal range VLANs.

- These are saved, by default, in the running configuration file.

- VTP does not learn extended range VLANs.

**Note**

4096 is the upper boundary for the number of VLANs available on Catalyst switches because there are 12 bits in the VLAN ID field of the IEEE 802.1Q header.

## Creating a VLAN (6.2.1.2)

When configuring normal range VLANs, the configuration details are stored in flash memory on the switch, in a file called vlan.dat. Flash memory is persistent and does not require the **copy running-config startup-config** command. However, because other details are often configured on a Cisco switch at the same time that VLANs are created, it is good practice to save running configuration changes to the startup configuration.

The management VLAN is created using the **vlan** *vlan_id* global configuration command. This creates the VLAN and enters VLAN configuration mode. The VLAN can now be assigned a unique name using the **name** *vlan_name* vlan configuration command.

Figure 6-10 shows how the student VLAN (VLAN 20) is configured on switch S1. In the topology example, the student computer (PC2) has not been associated with a VLAN yet, but it does have an IP address of 172.17.20.22.

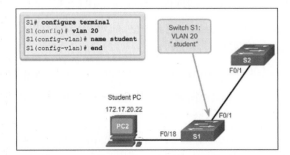

**Figure 6-10**   VLAN Configuration Example

Instead of creating one VLAN at a time, several VLANs can be created using one command. A series of VLAN IDs can be entered separated by commas (,), or a range of VLAN IDs can be entered separated by hyphens (-) using the **vlan** *vlan-id* command. In Example 6-4, VLANs 100, 102, and 105 through to 107 are created using one command.

**Example 6-4**  Creating Multiple VLANs

```
S1(config)# vlan 100,102,105-107
S1(config)#
```

## Assigning Ports to VLANs (6.2.1.3)

After creating a VLAN, the next step is to assign ports to the VLAN. An access port can belong to only one VLAN at a time. One exception to this rule is that of a port connected to an IP phone, in which case, there are two VLANs associated with the port: one for voice and one for data.

Access ports are most commonly assigned to VLANs. Although optional, it is strongly recommended as a security best practice that the port be assigned as an access port using the **switchport mode access** interface configuration command. With this command, the interface changes to permanent access mode. Next, assign the port to a VLAN using the **switchport access vlan** *vlan_id* interface command.

> **Note**
>
> Use the **interface range** command to simultaneously configure multiple interfaces.

In the example in Figure 6-11, VLAN 20 is assigned to port F0/18 on switch S1; therefore, the student computer (PC2) is in VLAN 20. VLANs are configured on the switch port, not on the device. PC2 is configured with an IPv4 address and subnet mask associated with the VLAN, which is configured on the switch port— VLAN 20 in this example. When VLAN 20 is configured on other switches, the network administrator knows to configure the other student computers to be in the same subnet as PC2 (172.17.20.0/24).

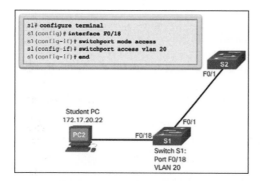

**Figure 6-11**    Assigning Ports Configuration Example

The **switchport access vlan** command forces the creation of a VLAN if it does not already exist on the switch. For example, VLAN 30 is not present in the **show vlan brief** output of the switch. If the **switchport access vlan 30** command is entered on any interface with no previous configuration, then the switch displays the following:

```
% Access VLAN does not exist. Creating vlan 30
```

## Changing VLAN Port Membership (6.2.1.4)

There are a number of ways to change VLAN port membership. To change a switch port back to VLAN 1, use the **no switchport access vlan** interface configuration mode command.

In Example 6-5, Interface F0/18 was previously assigned to VLAN 20. The **no switchport access vlan** command is entered for interface F0/18. Examine the output in the **show vlan brief** command that immediately follows.

**Example 6-5** Remove VLAN Assignment Configuration

```
S1(config)# int fa0/18
S1(config-if)# no switchport access vlan
S1(config-if)# end
S1#
S1# show vlan brief

VLAN Name                             Status    Ports
---- -------------------------------- --------- -------------------------------
1    default                          active    Fa0/1, Fa0/2, Fa0/3, Fa0/4
                                                Fa0/5, Fa0/6, Fa0/7, Fa0/8
                                                Fa0/9, Fa0/10, Fa0/11, Fa0/12
                                                Fa0/13, Fa0/14, Fa0/15, Fa0/16
                                                Fa0/17, Fa0/18, Fa0/19, Fa0/20
                                                Fa0/21, Fa0/22, Fa0/23, Fa0/24
                                                Gi0/1, Gi0/2
20   student                          active
1002 fddi-default                     act/unsup
1003 token-ring-default               act/unsup
1004 fddinet-default                  act/unsup
1005 trnet-default                    act/unsup
S1#
```

The **show vlan brief** command displays the VLAN assignment and membership type for all switch ports. It identifies the VLAN, the VLAN name, its status, and switch ports that are members of the VLAN.

Notice how VLAN 20 is still active, even though no ports are assigned to it.

In Example 6-6, the **show interfaces f0/18 switchport** output verifies that the access VLAN for interface F0/18 has been reset to VLAN 1.

**Example 6-6** Verify VLAN Is Removed

```
S1# sh interfaces fa0/18 switchport
Name: Fa0/18
Switchport: Enabled
Administrative Mode: static access
Operational Mode: down
Administrative Trunking Encapsulation: dot1q
Negotiation of Trunking: Off
Access Mode VLAN: 1 (default)
Trunking Native Mode VLAN: 1 (default)

<output omitted>
```

A port can easily have its VLAN membership changed. It is not necessary to first remove a port from a VLAN to change its VLAN membership. When an access port has its VLAN membership reassigned to another existing VLAN, the new VLAN membership simply replaces the previous VLAN membership. In Example 6-7, port F0/11 is assigned to VLAN 20.

**Example 6-7** Assign Port to VLAN

```
S1# config t
S1(config)# int fa0/11
S1(config-if)# switchport mode access
S1(config-if)# switchport access vlan 20
S1(config-if)# end
S1#
S1# show vlan brief

VLAN Name                             Status    Ports
---- -------------------------------- --------- -------------------------------
1    default                          active    Fa0/1, Fa0/2, Fa0/3, Fa0/4
                                                Fa0/5, Fa0/6, Fa0/7, Fa0/8
                                                Fa0/9, Fa0/10, Fa0/12, Fa0/13
                                                Fa0/14, Fa0/15, Fa0/16, Fa0/17
                                                Fa0/18, Fa0/19, Fa0/20, Fa0/21
                                                Fa0/22, Fa0/23, Fa0/24, Gi0/1
                                                Gi0/2
20   student                          active    Fa0/11
1002 fddi-default                     act/unsup
1003 token-ring-default               act/unsup
1004 fddinet-default                  act/unsup
1005 trnet-default                    act/unsup
S1#
```

## Deleting VLANs (6.2.1.5)

In Example 6-8, the **no vlan** *vlan-id* global configuration mode command is used to remove VLAN 20 from the switch. Switch S1 had a minimal configuration with all ports in VLAN 1 and an unused VLAN 20 in the VLAN database. The **show vlan brief** command verifies that VLAN 20 is no longer present in the vlan.dat file after using the **no vlan 20** command.

**Example 6-8** Delete a VLAN

```
S1# conf t
S1(config)# no vlan 20
S1(config)# end
S1#
S1# show vlan brief

VLAN Name                             Status    Ports
---- -------------------------------- --------- -------------------------------
1    default                          active    Fa0/1, Fa0/2, Fa0/3, Fa0/4
                                                Fa0/5, Fa0/6, Fa0/7, Fa0/8
                                                Fa0/9, Fa0/10, Fa0/12, Fa0/13
                                                Fa0/14, Fa0/15, Fa0/16, Fa0/17
                                                Fa0/18, Fa0/19, Fa0/20, Fa0/21
                                                Fa0/22, Fa0/23, Fa0/24, Gi0/1
                                                Gi0/2
1002 fddi-default                     act/unsup
1003 token-ring-default               act/unsup
1004 fddinet-default                  act/unsup
1005 trnet-default                    act/unsup
S1#
```

**Caution**

Before deleting a VLAN, reassign all member ports to a different VLAN. Any ports that are not moved to an active VLAN are unable to communicate with other hosts after the VLAN is deleted and until they are assigned to an active VLAN.

Alternatively, the entire vlan.dat file can be deleted using the **delete flash:vlan.dat** privileged EXEC mode command. The abbreviated command version (**delete vlan.dat**) can be used if the vlan.dat file has not been moved from its default location. After issuing this command and reloading the switch, the previously configured VLANs are no longer present. This effectively places the switch into its factory default condition with regard to VLAN configurations.

**Note**

For a Catalyst switch, the **erase startup-config** command must accompany the **delete vlan.dat** command prior to reload to restore the switch to its factory default condition.

## Verifying VLAN Information (6.2.1.6)

VLAN configurations can be validated using Cisco IOS **show** commands.

The command options available for the **show vlan** command are as follows:

```
show vlan [brief | id vlan-id | name vlan-name | summary]
```

Table 6-1 lists a description of each command option in the **show vlan** command.

**Table 6-1**   The **show vlan** Command Options

| Parameter | Description |
|---|---|
| brief | Display one line for each VLAN with the VLAN name, status, and its ports. |
| id *vlan-id* | Display information about a single VLAN identified by VLAN ID number. For *vlan-id*, the range is 1 to 4094. |
| name *vlan-name* | Display information about a single VLAN identified by VLAN name. The VLAN name is an ASCII string from 1 to 32 characters. |
| summary | Display information about a single VLAN identified by VLAN name. The VLAN name is an ASCII string from 1 to 32 characters. |

An example of the **show vlan brief** command is displayed in Example 6-8.

In Example 6-9, the **show vlan name student** command produces detailed output about the VLAN.

**Example 6-9** The **show vlan name** Command

```
S1# show vlan name student

VLAN Name                              Status    Ports
---- -------------------------------- --------- ------------------------------
20   student                          active    Fa0/11, Fa0/18

VLAN Type  SAID       MTU   Parent RingNo BridgeNo Stp  BrdgMode Trans1 Trans2
---- ----- ---------- ----- ------ ------ -------- ---- -------- ------ ------
20   enet  100020     1500  -      -      -        -    -        0      0

Remote SPAN VLAN
----------------
Disabled

Primary Secondary Type             Ports
------- --------- ---------------- ------------------------------------------
S1#
```

The **show vlan summary** command displays the count of all configured VLANs. The output in Example 6-10 shows seven VLANs.

**Example 6-10** The **show vlan summary** Command

```
S1# show vlan summary
Number of existing VLANs            : 7
 Number of existing VTP VLANs       : 7
 Number of existing extended VLANS  : 0

S1#
```

The **show interfaces** command can also be used to verify VLAN-related information using the **vlan** *vlan-id* parameter as follows:

```
show interfaces [interface-id | vlan vlan-id] | switchport
```

Table 6-2 lists a description of each command parameter.

**Table 6-2**   The **show interfaces** Command Options

| Parameter | Description |
|---|---|
| *interface-id* | Valid interfaces include physical ports (including type, module, and port number) and port channels. The port channel range is 1 to 16. |
| **vlan** *vlan-id* | VLAN identification. The range is 1 to 4094. |
| **switchport** | Display the administrative and operational status of a switching port, including port blocking and port protection settings. |

The important VLAN status information appears on the second line. In Example 6-11, the output indicates that VLAN 20 is down.

**Example 6-11**  The **show interfaces vlan** Command

```
S1# show interfaces vlan 20
Vlan20 is down, line protocol is down
  Hardware is EtherSVI, address is 0cd9.96e2.3d41 (bia 0cd9.96e2.3d41)
  MTU 1500 bytes, BW 1000000 Kbit/sec, DLY 10 usec,
     reliability 255/255, txload 1/255, rxload 1/255
  Encapsulation ARPA, loopback not set
  Keepalive not supported
  ARP type: ARPA, ARP Timeout 04:00:00
  Last input never, output never, output hang never
  Last clearing of "show interface" counters never
  Input queue: 0/75/0/0 (size/max/drops/flushes); Total output drops: 0
  Queueing strategy: fifo
  Output queue: 0/40 (size/max)
  5 minute input rate 0 bits/sec, 0 packets/sec
  5 minute output rate 0 bits/sec, 0 packets/sec
     0 packets input, 0 bytes, 0 no buffer
     Received 0 broadcasts (0 IP multicasts)
     0 runts, 0 giants, 0 throttles
     0 input errors, 0 CRC, 0 frame, 0 overrun, 0 ignored
     0 packets output, 0 bytes, 0 underruns
     0 output errors, 0 interface resets
     0 unknown protocol drops
     0 output buffer failures, 0 output buffers swapped out
S1#
```

An example of the **show interfaces** *interface-id* **switchport** command is displayed in Example 6-6.

Packet Tracer
☐ Activity

**Packet Tracer 6.2.1.7: Configuring VLANs**

Background/Scenario

VLANs are helpful in the administration of logical groups, allowing members of a group to be easily moved, changed, or added. This activity focuses on creating and naming VLANs and assigning access ports to specific VLANs.

# VLAN Trunks (6.2.2)

In this topic, you learn how to configure a trunk port on a LAN switch.

## Configuring IEEE 802.1Q Trunk Links (6.2.2.1)

A VLAN trunk is an OSI Layer 2 link between two switches that carries traffic for all VLANs (unless the allowed VLAN list is restricted manually or dynamically). To enable trunk links, configure the ports on either end of the physical link with parallel sets of commands.

To configure a switch port on one end of a trunk link, use the **switchport mode trunk** interface configuration command. With this command, the interface changes to permanent trunking mode. The port enters into a *Dynamic Trunking Protocol (DTP)* negotiation to convert the link into a trunk link even if the interface connecting to it does not agree to the change. In this course, the **switchport mode trunk** command is the only method implemented for trunk configuration.

> **Note**
>
> DTP is a Cisco proprietary protocol that is automatically enabled on Catalyst 2960 and Catalyst 3560 Series switches. DTP is beyond the scope of this course.

The native VLAN can also be changed. The Cisco IOS command syntax to specify a native VLAN (other than VLAN 1) is **switchport trunk native vlan** *vlan_id*.

Use the Cisco IOS **switchport trunk allowed vlan** *vlan-list* command to specify the list of VLANs to be allowed on the trunk link.

In the topology in Figure 6-12, VLANs 10, 20, and 30 support the Faculty, Student, and Guest computers (PC1, PC2, and PC3). The F0/1 port on switch S1 is configured as a trunk port and forwards traffic for VLANs 10, 20, and 30. VLAN 99 is configured as the native VLAN.

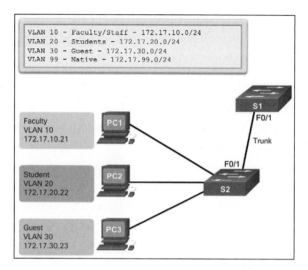

**Figure 6-12**  Trunk Configuration Topology

Example 6-12 displays the configuration of port F0/1 on switch S1 as a trunk port. The native VLAN is changed to VLAN 99, and the allowed VLAN list is restricted to 10, 20, 30, and 99.

**Example 6-12**  Trunk Configuration Example

```
S1(config)# interface FastEthernet0/1
S1(config-if)# switchport mode trunk
S1(config-if)# switchport trunk native vlan 99
S1(config-if)# switchport trunk allowed vlan 10,20,30,99
S1(config-if)# end
ES1#
```

**Note**

This configuration assumes the use of Cisco Catalyst 2960 switches, which automatically use 802.1Q encapsulation on trunk links. Other switches may require manual configuration of the encapsulation. Always configure both ends of a trunk link with the same native VLAN. If 802.1Q trunk configuration is not the same on both ends, Cisco IOS Software reports errors.

## Resetting the Trunk to Default State (6.2.2.2)

It may sometimes be necessary to reset a trunk to its default state or even disable trunking and turn the port to an access port.

To reset a trunk to allow all VLANs, use the **no switchport trunk allowed vlan** interface configuration command.

To reset the native VLAN to VLAN 1, use the **no switchport trunk native vlan** interface configuration command.

Example 6-13 shows the commands used to reset all trunking characteristics of a trunking interface to the default settings. The **show interfaces f0/1 switchport** command reveals that the trunk has been reconfigured to a default state.

**Example 6-13**  Resetting a Trunk Link Example

```
S1(config)# interface f0/1
S1(config-if)# no switchport trunk allowed vlan
S1(config-if)# no switchport trunk native vlan
S1(config-if)# end
S1#
S1# show interfaces f0/1 switchport
Name: Fa0/1
Switchport: Enabled
Administrative Mode: trunk
Operational Mode: trunk
Administrative Trunking Encapsulation: dot1q
Operational Trunking Encapsulation: dot1q
Negotiation of Trunking: On
Access Mode VLAN: 1 (default)
Trunking Native Mode VLAN: 1 (default)
Administrative Native VLAN tagging: enabled
<output omitted>
Administrative private-vlan trunk mappings: none
Operational private-vlan: none
Trunking VLANs Enabled: ALL
Pruning VLANs Enabled: 2-1001
<output omitted>
```

Finally, to set the port to a nontrunking port (that is, access mode), use the **switchport mode access** interface command.

In Example 6-14, the sample output shows the commands used to remove the trunk feature from the F0/1 switch port on switch S1. The **show interfaces f0/1 switchport** command reveals that the F0/1 interface is now in static access mode.

**Example 6-14**  Resetting a Port to Access Mode

```
S1(config)# interface f0/1
S1(config-if)# switchport mode access
S1(config-if)# end
S1#
S1# show interfaces f0/1 switchport
Name: Fa0/1
Switchport: Enabled
Administrative Mode: static access
Operational Mode: static access
Administrative Trunking Encapsulation: dot1q
Operational Trunking Encapsulation: native
Negotiation of Trunking: Off
Access Mode VLAN: 1 (default)
Trunking Native Mode VLAN: 1 (default)
Administrative Native VLAN tagging: enabled
<output omitted>
```

## Verifying Trunk Configuration (6.2.2.3)

Example 6-15 configures a trunk link with the native VLAN 99 on port F0/1 on switch S1. The configuration is verified with the **show interfaces** *interface-id* **switchport** command.

**Example 6-15**  Configure and Verify Trunking

```
S1(config)# interface f0/1
S1(config-if)# switchport mode trunk
S1(config-if)# switchport trunk native vlan 99
S1(config-if)# end
S1#
S1# show interfaces f0/1 switchport
Name: Fa0/1
Switchport: Enabled
Administrative Mode: trunk
Operational Mode: trunk
Administrative Trunking Encapsulation: dot1q
Operational Trunking Encapsulation: dot1q
Negotiation of Trunking: On
Access Mode VLAN: 1 (default)
Trunking Native Mode VLAN: 99 (VLAN0099)
Administrative Native VLAN tagging: enabled
Voice VLAN: none
```

```
Administrative private-vlan host-association: none
Administrative private-vlan mapping: none
Administrative private-vlan trunk native VLAN: none
Administrative private-vlan trunk Native VLAN tagging: enabled
Administrative private-vlan trunk encapsulation: dot1q
Administrative private-vlan trunk normal VLANs: none
Administrative private-vlan trunk associations: none
Administrative private-vlan trunk mappings: none
Operational private-vlan: none
Trunking VLANs Enabled: ALL
Pruning VLANs Enabled: 2-1001
<output omitted>
```

The top highlighted area shows that port F0/1 has its administrative mode set to **trunk**. The port is in trunking mode. The next highlighted area verifies that the native VLAN is VLAN 99. Further down in the output, the bottom highlighted area shows that all VLANs are enabled on the trunk.

Packet Tracer
☐ Activity

### Packet Tracer 6.2.2.4: Configuring Trunks

Background/Scenario

Trunks are required to pass VLAN information between switches. A port on a switch is either an access port or a trunk port. Access ports carry traffic from a specific VLAN assigned to the port. A trunk port, by default, is a member of all VLANs; therefore, it carries traffic for all VLANs. This activity focuses on creating trunk ports and assigning them to a native VLAN other than the default VLAN.

### Lab 6.2.2.5: Configuring VLANs and Trunking

In this lab, you will complete the following objectives:

- Part 1: Build the Network and Configure Basic Device Settings
- Part 2: Create VLANs and Assign Switch Ports
- Part 3: Maintain VLAN Port Assignments and the VLAN Database
- Part 4: Configure an 802.1Q Trunk Between the Switches
- Part 5: Delete the VLAN Database

# Troubleshoot VLANs and Trunks (6.2.3)

In this topic, you troubleshoot VLAN and trunk configurations in a switched network.

## IP Addressing Issues with VLAN (6.2.3.1)

Each VLAN must correspond to a unique IP subnet. If two devices in the same VLAN have different subnet addresses, they cannot communicate. This is a common problem, and it is easy to solve by identifying the incorrect configuration and changing the subnet address to the correct one.

In Figure 6-13, PC1 cannot connect to the Web/TFTP server shown.

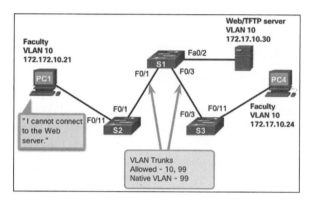

**Figure 6-13**   IP Issue Within VLAN

A check of the IPv4 configuration settings of PC1, shown in Example 6-16, reveals the most common error in configuring VLANs: an incorrectly configured IPv4 address. PC1 is configured with an IPv4 address of 172.172.10.21, but it should have been configured with 172.17.10.21.

**Example 6-16**  Problem: Incorrect IP Address

```
PC> ipconfig

    IP Address.....................: 172.172.10.21
    Subnet Mask....................: 255.255.0.0
    Default Gateway................: 0.0.0.0

PC>
```

In Figure 6-14, the PC1 Fast Ethernet configuration dialog box shows the updated IPv4 address of 172.17.10.21.

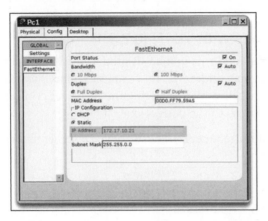

**Figure 6-14**   Solution: Change the IP Address

The output in Example 6-17 reveals that PC1 has regained connectivity to the Web/TFTP server found at IPv4 address 172.17.10.30.

**Example 6-17**   Verify Connectivity from PC1 to the Web/TFTP Server

```
PC> ping 172.17.10.30

Pinging 172.17.10.30 with 32 bytes of data:

Reply from 172.17.10.30: bytes=32 time=17ms TTL=255
Reply from 172.17.10.30: bytes=32 time=15ms TTL=255
Reply from 172.17.10.30: bytes=32 time=18ms TTL=255
Reply from 172.17.10.30: bytes=32 time=19ms TTL=255

Ping statistics for 172.17.10.30:
    Packets: Sent = 4, Received = 4, Lost = 0 (0% loss),
Approximate round trip times in milli-seconds:
    Minimum = 15ms, Maximum = 19ms, Average = 17ms

PC>
```

## Missing VLANs (6.2.3.2)

If there is still no connection between devices in a VLAN, but IP addressing issues have been ruled out, refer to the flowchart in Figure 6-15 to troubleshoot.

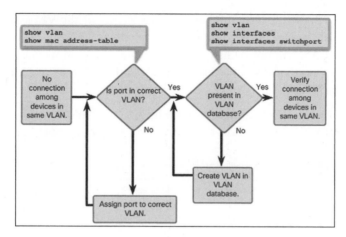

**Figure 6-15**  Flowchart: Troubleshooting Missing VLAN

**Step 1.**  The first step is to verify whether the port is in the correct VLAN. Use the **show vlan** command to check whether the port belongs to the expected VLAN.

Use the **show mac address-table** command to check which addresses were learned on a particular port of the switch and to which VLAN that port is assigned, as shown in Example 6-18.

**Example 6-18**  Verify VLAN Port Membership

```
S1# show mac address-table interface FastEthernet 0/1
          Mac Address Table
-------------------------------------------

Vlan      Mac Address        Type        Ports
----      -----------        --------    -----
  10      000c.296a.a21c     DYNAMIC     Fa0/1
  10      000f.34f9.9181     DYNAMIC     Fa0/1
Total Mac Addresses for this criterion: 2
S1#
```

The example shows MAC addresses that were learned on the F0/1 interface. It can be seen that MAC address 000c.296a.a21c was learned on interface F0/1 in VLAN 10. If the port is assigned to the wrong VLAN, use the **switchport access vlan** interface configuration command to correct the VLAN membership.

**Step 2.**  If the port is in the correct VLAN, then verify if the VLAN is present in the VLAN database.

Each port in a switch belongs to a VLAN. If the VLAN to which the port belongs is deleted, the port becomes inactive. The ports of a deleted VLAN will not be listed in the output of the **show vlan** command. All ports belonging to a deleted VLAN are unable to communicate with other hosts in the network.

Use the **show interfaces switchport** command to verify if the inactive VLAN is assigned to the port, as shown in Example 6-19.

**Example 6-19** Verify Whether Port Is Inactive

```
S1# show interfaces FastEthernet 0/1 switchport
Name: Fa0/1
Switchport: Enabled
Administrative Mode: static access
Operational Mode: static access
Administrative Trunking Encapsulation: dot1q
Operational Trunking Encapsulation: native
Negotiation of Trunking: Off
Access Mode VLAN: 10 (Inactive)
Trunking Native Mode VLAN: 1 (default)
Administrative Native VLAN tagging: enabled
Voice VLAN: none
S1#
```

If the port is inactive, it is not functional until the missing VLAN is created using the **vlan** *vlan-id* global configuration command or the VLAN is removed from the port with the **no switchport access vlan** *vlan-id* command.

## Introduction to Troubleshooting Trunks (6.2.3.3)

A common task of a network administrator is to troubleshoot trunk formation, or ports incorrectly behaving as trunk ports. Sometimes a switch port may behave like a trunk port even if it is not configured as a trunk port. For example, an access port might accept frames from VLANs different from the VLAN to which it is assigned. This is called *VLAN leaking*.

Figure 6-16 displays a flowchart of general trunk troubleshooting guidelines.

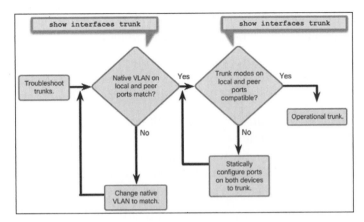

**Figure 6-16**   Flowchart: Troubleshooting Trunks

To troubleshoot issues when a trunk is not forming or when VLAN leaking is occurring, proceed as follows:

**Step 1.**   Verify whether there is a native VLAN mismatch. Use the **show interfaces trunk** command on the local switch and remote device to verify if the native VLANs match. If the native VLAN does not match on both sides, VLAN leaking occurs.

**Step 2.**   Verify whether the trunk modes on the local switch and remote device are compatible. Cisco Catalyst switch ports use DTP by default and attempt to negotiate a trunk link. However, it is recommended that trunk links be statically configured. Use the **show interfaces trunk** command to display the status of the trunk, the native VLAN used, and to verify trunk establishment.

## Common Problems with Trunks (6.2.3.4)

Trunking issues are usually associated with incorrect configurations, as summarized in Table 6-3.

**Table 6-3**   Common Problems with Trunks

| Problem | Result | Example |
|---|---|---|
| Native VLAN Mismatches | Poses a security risk and creates unintended results. | For example, one port is defined as VLAN 99 and the other is defined as VLAN 100. |
| Trunk Mode Mismatches | Causes loss of network connectivity. | For example, one side of the trunk is configured as an access port. |
| Allowed VLANs on Trunks | Causes unexpected traffic or no traffic to be sent over the trunk. | The list of allowed VLANs does not support current VLAN trunking requirements. |

When configuring VLANs and trunks on a switched infrastructure, the following types of configuration errors are the most common:

- *Native VLAN mismatches*—Trunk ports are configured with different native VLANs. This configuration error generates console notifications and can cause inter-VLAN routing issues, among other problems. This poses a security risk.

- *Trunk mode mismatches*—One trunk port is configured in a mode that is not compatible for trunking on the corresponding peer port. This configuration error causes the trunk link to stop working. Be sure both sides of the trunk are configured with the **switchport mode trunk** command. Other trunk configuration commands are beyond the scope of this course.

- **Allowed VLANs on trunks**—The list of allowed VLANs on a trunk has not been updated with the current VLAN trunking requirements. In this situation, unexpected traffic (or no traffic) is being sent over the trunk.

If an issue with a trunk is discovered and the cause is unknown, start troubleshooting by examining the trunks for a native VLAN mismatch. If that is not the cause, check for trunk mode mismatches. Finally, check for the allowed VLAN list on the trunk.

## Native VLAN Mismatches

When the native VLANs on interconnecting trunk links do not match, CDP generates notification messages. For instance, switch S1 in Example 6-20 was generating CDP notification messages regarding a native VLAN mismatch. Notice how the output in the message identifies that F0/1 is using VLAN 2 and that switch S2 F0/1 is using VLAN 99.

**Example 6-20** Trunk Verification Commands

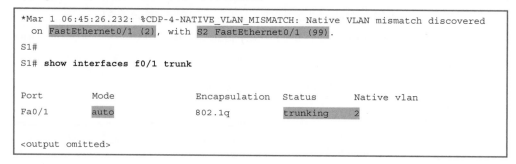

```
*Mar 1 06:45:26.232: %CDP-4-NATIVE_VLAN_MISMATCH: Native VLAN mismatch discovered
  on FastEthernet0/1 (2), with S2 FastEthernet0/1 (99).
S1#
S1# show interfaces f0/1 trunk

Port            Mode            Encapsulation  Status      Native vlan
Fa0/1           auto            802.1q         trunking        2

<output omitted>
```

The **show interfaces f0/1 trunk** command confirms the notification message information.

Because one end of the trunk is configured as native VLAN 99 and the other end is configured as native VLAN 2, a frame sent from VLAN 99 on one side is received on VLAN 2 on the other side. Therefore, VLAN 99 leaks into the VLAN 2 segment.

Connectivity issues occur in the network if a native VLAN mismatch exists. Data traffic for VLANs, other than the two native VLANs configured, successfully propagates across the trunk link, but data associated with either of the native VLANs does not successfully propagate across the trunk link.

Also notice that the native VLAN mismatch issue in Example 6-20 did not keep the trunk from forming as the status was "trunking."

To solve the native VLAN mismatch, configure the native VLAN to be the same VLAN on both sides of the link.

### Incorrect Port Mode (6.2.3.5)

Trunk links are normally configured statically with the **switchport mode trunk** command. Cisco Catalyst switch trunk ports use DTP to negotiate the state of the link. When a port on a trunk link is configured with a trunk mode that is incompatible with the neighboring trunk port, a trunk link fails to form between the two switches.

In the scenario illustrated in Figure 6-17, PC4 cannot connect to the internal web server. The topology indicates a valid configuration. Why is there a problem?

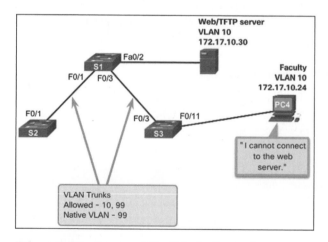

**Figure 6-17**    Incorrect Port Mode Scenario

Check the status of the trunk ports on switch S1 using the **show interfaces trunk** command. The output shown in Example 6-21 reveals that interfaces Fa0/1 and Fa0/3 on switch S1 are both currently trunking for VLANs 10 and 99.

**Example 6-21** S1: Mismatched Port Modes

```
S1# show interfaces trunk

Port          Mode                  Encapsulation  Status       Native vlan
Fa0/1         on                    802.1q         trunking     99
Fa0/3         on                    802.1q         trunking     99


Port          Vlans allowed on trunk
Fa0/1         10,99
Fa0/3         10,99


<output omitted>
S1#
S1# show interfaces fa0/3 switchport
Name: Fa0/3
Switchport: Enabled
Administrative Mode: trunk
<output omitted>
```

However, in Example 6-22, an examination of the trunks on switch S3 reveals that there are no active trunk ports. This is indicated by the lack of output being generated for the **show interfaces trunk** command.

Further checking reveals that the Fa0/3 interface is in static access mode. This is because the port was configured using the **switchport mode access** command. That explains why the trunk is down.

**Example 6-22** S3: Mismatched Port Modes

```
S3# show interfaces trunk

S3# show interface fa0/3 switchport
Name: Fa0/3
Switchport: Enabled
Administrative Mode: static access
<output omitted>
```

To resolve the issue, reconfigure the trunk mode of the F0/3 ports on switch S3, as shown in Example 6-23.

**Example 6-23** S3: Correct and Verify Trunk Mode

```
S3(config)# interface f0/3
S3(config-if)# switch mode trunk
S3(config-if)# end
S3#
S3# show interfaces f0/3 switchport
Name: Fa0/3
Switchport: Enabled
Administrative Mode: trunk
<output omitted>
S3#
S3# show interfaces trunk


Port            Mode                Encapsulation  Status        Native vlan
Fa0/3           on                  802.1q         trunking      99


Port            Vlans allowed on trunk
Fa0/3           10,99
<output omitted>
```

The output of the **show interfaces** commands indicates that the F0/3 is now a trunk and that it is trunking.

The output from PC4 in Example 6-24 indicates that it has regained connectivity to the Web/TFTP server found at IPv4 address 172.17.10.30.

**Example 6-24** Verify the PC Can Ping the Server

```
PC> ping 172.17.10.30

Pinging 172.17.10.30 with 32 bytes of data:

Reply from 172.17.10.30: bytes=32 time=17ms TTL=255
Reply from 172.17.10.30: bytes=32 time=15ms TTL=255
Reply from 172.17.10.30: bytes=32 time=18ms TTL=255
Reply from 172.17.10.30: bytes=32 time=19ms TTL=255

Ping statistics for 172.17.10.30:
    Packets: Sent = 4, Received = 4, Lost = 0 (0% loss),
Approximate round trip times in milli-seconds:
    Minimum = 15ms, Maximum = 19ms, Average = 17ms

PC>
```

## Incorrect VLAN List (6.2.3.6)

For traffic from a VLAN to be transmitted across a trunk, it must be allowed on the trunk. To do so, use the **switchport trunk allowed vlan** *vlan-id* command.

In Figure 6-18, VLAN 20 (Student) and PC5 have been added to the network. The documentation has been updated to show that the VLANs allowed on the trunk are 10, 20, and 99. In this scenario, PC5 cannot connect to the student email server.

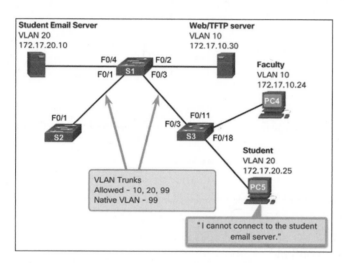

**Figure 6-18**   Incorrect VLAN List Scenario

Check the trunk ports on switch S1 using the **show interfaces trunk** command, as shown in Example 6-25. The **show interfaces trunk** command is an excellent tool for revealing common trunking problems.

**Example 6-25**  S1: Missing VLANs

```
S1# show interfaces trunk

Port         Mode             Encapsulation  Status       Native vlan
Fa0/1        on               802.1q         trunking     99
Fa0/3        on               802.1q         trunking     99


Port         Vlans allowed on trunk
Fa0/1        10,99
Fa0/3        10,99
<output omitted>
S1#
```

An examination of switch S1 reveals that interfaces F0/1 and F0/3 only allow VLANs 10 and 99. Someone updated the documentation but forgot to reconfigure the ports on the S1 switch.

In Example 6-26, the command reveals that the interface F0/3 on switch S3 is correctly configured to allow VLANs 10, 20, and 99. Therefore, the misconfiguration is on S1.

**Example 6-26**  S3: Missing VLANs

```
S3# show interfaces trunk

Port            Mode            Encapsulation  Status       Native vlan
Fa0/3           on              802.1q         trunking     99


Port            Vlans allowed on trunk
Fa0/3           10,20,99
<output omitted>
S3#
```

Reconfigure F0/1 and F0/3 on switch S1 using the **switchport trunk allowed vlan 10,20,99** command, as shown in Example 6-27.

**Example 6-27**  S1: Corrected VLAN List

```
S1(config)# interface fa0/1
S1(config-if)# switchport trunk allowed vlan 10,20,99
S1(config-if)# interface fa0/3
S1(config-if)# switchport trunk allowed vlan 10,20,99
S1(config-if)# end
S1#
S1# show interfaces trunk

Port            Mode            Encapsulation  Status       Native vlan
Fa0/1           on              802.1q         trunking     99
Fa0/3           on              802.1q         trunking     99


Port            Vlans allowed on trunk
Fa0/1           10,20,99
Fa0/3           10,20,99
<output omitted>
```

The output confirms that VLANs 10, 20, and 99 are now added to the F0/1 and F0/3 ports on switch S1.

As shown in Example 6-28, PC5 has regained connectivity to the student email server found at IPv4 address 172.17.20.10.

**Example 6-28** Verify the PC Can Ping the Server

```
PC> ping 172.17.20.30

Pinging 172.17.20.30 with 32 bytes of data:

Reply from 172.17.20.30: bytes=32 time=17ms TTL=255
Reply from 172.17.20.30: bytes=32 time=15ms TTL=255
Reply from 172.17.20.30: bytes=32 time=18ms TTL=255
Reply from 172.17.20.30: bytes=32 time=19ms TTL=255

Ping statistics for 172.17.20.30:
    Packets: Sent = 4, Received = 4, Lost = 0 (0% loss),
Approximate round trip times in milli-seconds:
    Minimum = 15ms, Maximum = 19ms, Average = 17ms

PC>
```

### Packet Tracer 6.2.3.7: Troubleshooting a VLAN Implementation—Scenario 1

Background/Scenario

In this activity, you troubleshoot connectivity problems between PCs on the same VLAN. The activity is complete when PCs on the same VLAN can ping each other. Any solution you implement must conform to the Addressing Table.

### Packet Tracer 6.2.3.8: Troubleshooting a VLAN Implementation—Scenario 2

Background/Scenario

In this activity, you troubleshoot a misconfigured VLAN environment. The initial network has errors. Your objective is to locate and correct the errors in the configurations and establish end-to-end connectivity. Your final configuration should match the Topology diagram and Addressing Table. The native VLAN for this topology is VLAN 56.

**Lab 6.2.3.9: Troubleshooting VLAN Configurations**

In this lab, you complete the following objectives:

- Part 1: Build the Network and Configure Basic Device Settings

- Part 2: Troubleshoot VLAN 10

- Part 3: Troubleshoot VLAN 20

# Inter-VLAN Routing Using Routers (6.3)

All hosts in a VLAN must be on the same network. What happens when traffic is destined to a host that is not in the same VLAN? The services of a router or Layer 3 switch must be used to forward traffic between VLANs.

In this section, you will configure routing between VLANs in a small-to medium-sized business network.

## Inter-VLAN Routing Operation (6.3.1)

In this topic, you learn about two options for configuring inter-VLAN routing.

### What Is Inter-VLAN Routing? (6.3.1.1)

VLANs are used to segment switched networks. Layer 2 switches, such as the Catalyst 2960 Series, can be configured with more than 4,000 VLANs. A VLAN is a broadcast domain, so computers on separate VLANs are unable to communicate without the intervention of a routing device. Layer 2 switches have limited IPv4 and IPv6 functionality and cannot perform the dynamic routing function of routers. Although Layer 2 switches are gaining more IP functionality, such as the ability to perform static routing, this is insufficient to handle these large numbers of VLANs.

Any device that supports Layer 3 routing, such as a router or a multilayer switch, can be used to perform the necessary routing functionality, as shown in Figure 6-19.

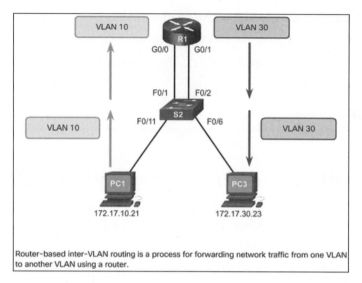

Router-based inter-VLAN routing is a process for forwarding network traffic from one VLAN to another VLAN using a router.

**Figure 6-19**    Inter-VLAN Routing Example

Regardless of the device used, the process of forwarding network traffic from one VLAN to another VLAN using routing is known as *inter-VLAN routing*.

There are three options for inter-VLAN routing:

- Legacy inter-VLAN routing

- Router-on-a-stick

- Layer 3 switching using SVIs

**Note**

This chapter focuses on the first two options. Layer 3 switching using SVIs is beyond the scope of this course.

## Legacy Inter-VLAN Routing (6.3.1.2)

Historically, the first solution for inter-VLAN routing relied on routers with multiple physical interfaces. Each interface had to be connected to a separate network and configured with a distinct subnet.

In this legacy approach, inter-VLAN routing is performed by connecting different physical router interfaces to different physical switch ports. The switch ports connected to the router are placed in access mode, and each physical interface is assigned to a different VLAN. Each router interface can then accept traffic from the VLAN associated with the switch interface that it is connected to, and traffic can be routed to the other VLANs connected to the other interfaces.

Figure 6-20 shows an example of *legacy inter-VLAN routing*.

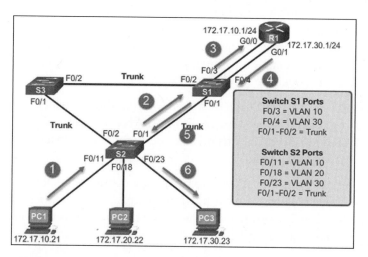

**Figure 6-20**    Legacy Inter-VLAN Routing Example

PC1 on VLAN 10 is communicating with PC3 on VLAN 30 through router R1.
PC1 and PC3 are on different VLANs and have IPv4 addresses on different subnets.
Router R1 has a separate interface configured for each of the VLANs.

1. PC1 sends unicast traffic destined for PC3 to switch S2 on VLAN 10.

2. S2 then forwards the unicast traffic out the trunk interface to switch S1.

3. Switch S1 then forwards the unicast traffic through its interface F0/3 to interface
   G0/0 on router R1.

4. The router routes the unicast traffic through its interface G0/1, which is
   connected to VLAN 30. The router forwards the unicast traffic to switch S1 on
   VLAN 30.

5. Switch S1 then forwards the unicast traffic to switch S2 through the active trunk
   link.

6. Switch S2 can then forward the unicast traffic to PC3 on VLAN 30.

In this example, the router was configured with two separate physical interfaces to
interact with the different VLANs and perform the routing.

**Note**

Legacy inter-VLAN routing is not efficient and is generally no longer implemented in switched
networks. It is discussed in this course for explanation purposes only.

## Router-on-a-Stick Inter-VLAN Routing (6.3.1.3)

Whereas legacy inter-VLAN routing requires multiple physical interfaces on both the router and the switch, a more common, present-day implementation of inter-VLAN routing does not. Instead, some router software permits configuring a router interface as a trunk link, meaning only one physical interface is required on the router and the switch to route packets between multiple VLANs.

"*Router-on-a-stick*" is a type of router configuration in which a single physical interface routes traffic between multiple VLANs on a network. The router interface is configured to operate as a trunk link and is connected to a switch port that is configured in trunk mode.

The router performs inter-VLAN routing by accepting VLAN-tagged traffic on the trunk interface coming from the adjacent switch, and then, internally routing between the VLANs using *subinterfaces*. The router then forwards the routed traffic, VLAN-tagged for the destination VLAN, out the same physical interface as it used to receive the traffic.

Subinterfaces are software-based virtual interfaces, associated with a single physical interface. Subinterfaces are configured in software on a router, and each subinterface is independently configured with an IP address and VLAN assignment. Subinterfaces are configured for different subnets corresponding to their VLAN assignment to facilitate logical routing. After a routing decision is made based on the destination VLAN, the data frames are VLAN tagged and sent back out the physical interface.

Figure 6-21 shows an example of router-on-a-stick inter-VLAN routing. PC1 on VLAN 10 is communicating with PC3 on VLAN 30 through router R1 using a single, physical router interface.

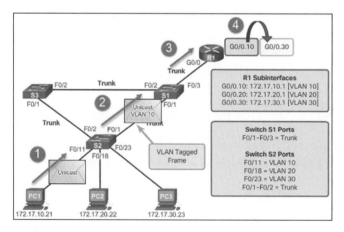

**Figure 6-21**   Unicast from VLAN 10 Is Routed to VLAN 30

1. PC1 sends its unicast traffic to switch S2.

2. Switch S2 tags the unicast traffic as originating on VLAN 10 and forwards the unicast traffic out its trunk link to switch S1.

3. Switch S1 forwards the tagged traffic out the other trunk interface on port F0/3 to the interface on router R1.

4. Router R1 accepts the tagged unicast traffic on VLAN 10 and routes it to VLAN 30 using its configured subinterfaces.

In Figure 6-22, R1 routes the traffic to the correct VLAN.

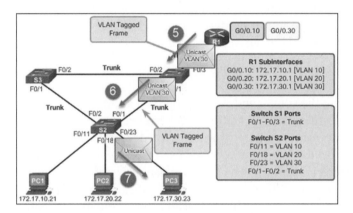

**Figure 6-22** Router Tags Unicast Frame with VLAN 30

1. The unicast traffic is tagged with VLAN 30 as it is sent out the router interface to switch S1.

2. Switch S1 forwards the tagged unicast traffic out the other trunk link to switch S2.

3. Switch S2 removes the VLAN tag of the unicast frame and forwards the frame out to PC3 on port F0/23.

**Note**

The router-on-a-stick method of inter-VLAN routing does not scale beyond 50 VLANs.

**Interactive Graphic**

**Activity 6.3.1.4: Identify the Types of Inter-VLAN Routing**

Refer to the online course to complete this activity.

# Configure Legacy Inter-VLAN Routing (6.3.2)

In this topic, you configure legacy inter-VLAN routing.

## Configure Legacy Inter-VLAN Routing: Preparation (6.3.2.1)

Legacy inter-VLAN routing requires routers to have multiple physical interfaces. The router accomplishes the routing by having each of its physical interfaces connected to a unique VLAN. Each interface is also configured with an IPv4 address for the subnet associated with the particular VLAN to which it is connected. By configuring the IPv4 addresses on the physical interfaces, network devices connected to each of the VLANs can communicate with the router using the physical interface connected to the same VLAN. In this configuration, network devices can use the router as a gateway to access the devices connected to the other VLANs.

The routing process requires the source device to determine if the destination device is local or remote to the local subnet. The source device accomplishes this by comparing the source and destination IPv4 addresses against the subnet mask. When the destination IPv4 address has been determined to be on a remote network, the source device must identify where it needs to forward the packet to reach the destination device. The source device examines the local routing table to determine where it needs to send the data. Devices use their default gateway as the Layer 2 destination for all traffic that must leave the local subnet. The default gateway is the route that the device uses when it has no other explicitly defined route to the destination network. The IPv4 address of the router interface on the local subnet acts as the default gateway for the sending device.

When the source device has determined that the packet must travel through the local router interface on the connected VLAN, the source device sends out an ARP request to determine the MAC address of the local router interface. When the router sends its ARP reply back to the source device, the source device can use the MAC address to finish framing the packet before it sends it out on the network as unicast traffic.

Because the Ethernet frame has the destination MAC address of the router interface, the switch knows exactly which switch port to forward the unicast traffic out of to reach the router interface for that VLAN. When the frame arrives at the router, the router removes the source and destination MAC address information to examine the destination IPv4 address of the packet. The router compares the destination address to entries in its routing table to determine where it needs to forward the data to reach its final destination. If the router determines that the destination network is a locally connected network, as is the case with inter-VLAN routing, the router sends an ARP request out the interface that is physically connected to the destination VLAN. The destination device responds to the router with its MAC address, which the router then uses to frame the packet. The router then sends the unicast traffic to the switch, which forwards it out the port where the destination device is connected.

Even though there are many steps in the process of inter-VLAN routing, when two devices on different VLANs communicate through a router, the entire process happens in a fraction of a second.

## Configure Legacy Inter-VLAN Routing: Switch Configuration (6.3.2.2)

To configure legacy inter-VLAN routing, start by configuring the switch.

As shown in Figure 6-23, router R1 is connected to switch ports F0/4 and F0/5, which have been configured for VLANs 10 and 30, respectively.

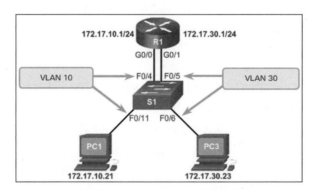

**Figure 6-23**   Legacy Inter-VLAN Routing Topology

Example 6-29 shows the legacy inter-VLAN routing configuration for switch S1.

**Example 6-29** Legacy Inter-VLAN Routing: Switch Configuration

```
S1(config)# vlan 10 , 30
S1(config-vlan)# exit
S1(config)#
S1(config)# interface f0/11
S1(config-if)# switchport access vlan 10
S1(config-if)# interface f0/4
S1(config-if)# switchport access vlan 10
S1(config-if)# interface f0/6
S1(config-if)# switchport access vlan 30
S1(config-if)# interface f0/5
S1(config-if)# switchport access vlan 30
S1(config-if)# end
*Mar 20 01:22:56.751: %SYS-5-CONFIG_I: Configured from console by console
S1#
S1# copy running-config startup-config
Destination filename [startup-config]?
Building configuration...
[OK]
```

Use the **vlan** *vlan_id* global configuration mode command to create VLANs. In this example, VLANs 10 and 30 were created on switch S1.

After the VLANs have been created, the switch ports are assigned to the appropriate VLANs. The **switchport access vlan** *vlan_id* command is executed from interface configuration mode on the switch for each interface to which the router connects.

In this example, interfaces F0/4 and F0/11 have been assigned to VLAN 10 using the **switchport access vlan 10** command. The same process is used to assign interface F0/5 and F0/6 on switch S1 to VLAN 30.

Finally, to protect the configuration so that it is not lost after a reload of the switch, the **copy running-config startup-config** command is executed to back up the running configuration to the startup configuration.

## Configure Legacy Inter-VLAN Routing: Router Interface Configuration (6.3.2.3)

Now the router can be configured to perform inter-VLAN routing.

Router interfaces are configured in a manner similar to configuring VLAN interfaces on switches. To configure a specific interface, change to interface configuration mode from global configuration mode.

As shown in Example 6-30, each interface is configured with an IPv4 address using the **ip address** *ip_address subnet_mask* command in interface configuration mode.

**Example 6-30** Legacy Inter-VLAN Routing: Router Configuration

```
R1(config)# interface g0/0
R1(config-if)# ip address 172.17.10.1 255.255.255.0
R1(config-if)# no shutdown
*Mar 20 01:42:12.951: %LINK-3-UPDOWN: Interface GigabitEthernet0/0, changed state
  to up
*Mar 20 01:42:13.951: %LINEPROTO-5-UPDOWN: Line protocol on Interface
  GigabitEthernet0/0, changed state to up
R1(config-if)# interface g0/1
R1(config-if)# ip address 172.17.30.1 255.255.255.0
R1(config-if)# no shutdown
*Mar 20 01:42:54.951: %LINK-3-UPDOWN: Interface GigabitEthernet0/1, changed state
  to up
*Mar 20 01:42:55.951: %LINEPROTO-5-UPDOWN: Line protocol on Interface
  GigabitEthernet0/1, changed state to up
R1(config-if)# end
R1# copy running-config startup-config
R1#
```

In the example, interface G0/0 is configured with IPv4 address 172.17.10.1 and subnet mask 255.255.255.0 using the **ip address 172.17.10.1 255.255.255.0** command.

Router interfaces are disabled by default and must be enabled using the **no shutdown** command before they are used. After the **no shutdown** interface configuration mode command has been issued, a notification displays, indicating that the interface state has changed to up. This indicates that the interface is now enabled.

The process is repeated for all router interfaces. Each router interface must be assigned to a unique subnet for routing to occur. In this example, the other router interface, G0/1, has been configured to use IPv4 address 172.17.30.1, which is on a different subnet than interface G0/0.

After the IPv4 addresses are assigned to the physical interfaces and the interfaces are enabled, the router is capable of performing inter-VLAN routing.

Examine the routing table using the **show ip route** command.

In Example 6-31, two routes are visible in the routing table. One route is to the 172.17.10.0 subnet, which is attached to the local interface G0/0. The other route is to the 172.17.30.0 subnet, which is attached to the local interface G0/1.

**Example 6-31** Verify the Routing Table Has VLAN Networks

```
R1# show ip route | begin Gateway
Gateway of last resort is not set


      172.17.0.0/16 is variably subnetted, 4 subnets, 2 masks
C        172.17.10.0/24 is directly connected, GigabitEthernet0/0
L        172.17.10.1/32 is directly connected, GigabitEthernet0/0
C        172.17.30.0/24 is directly connected, GigabitEthernet0/1
L        172.17.30.1/32 is directly connected, GigabitEthernet0/1


R1#
```

The router uses this routing table to determine where to send the traffic it receives. For example, if the router receives a packet on interface G0/0 destined for the 172.17.30.0 subnet, the router would identify that it should send the packet out interface G0/1 to reach hosts on the 172.17.30.0 subnet.

Notice the letter C to the left of each of the route entries for the VLANs. This letter indicates that the route is local for a connected interface, which is also identified in the route entry.

**Lab 6.3.2.4: Configuring Per-Interface Inter-VLAN Routing**

In this lab, you complete the following objectives:

- Part 1: Build the Network and Configure Basic Device Settings
- Part 2: Configure Switches with VLANs and Trunking
- Part 3: Verify Trunking, VLANs, Routing, and Connectivity

# Configure Router-on-a-Stick Inter-VLAN Routing (6.3.3)

In this topic, you configure router-on-a-stick inter-VLAN routing.

## Configure Router-on-a-Stick: Preparation (6.3.3.1)

Legacy inter-VLAN routing using physical interfaces has a significant limitation. Routers have a limited number of physical interfaces to connect to different VLANs. As the number of VLANs increases on a network, having one physical router interface per VLAN quickly exhausts the physical interface capacity of a router. An alternative in larger networks is to use VLAN trunking and subinterfaces. VLAN trunking allows a single physical router interface to route traffic for multiple VLANs. This technique is termed router-on-a-stick and uses virtual subinterfaces on the router to overcome the hardware limitations based on physical router interfaces.

Subinterfaces are software-based virtual interfaces that are assigned to physical interfaces. Each subinterface is configured independently with its own IP address and prefix length. This allows a single physical interface to simultaneously be part of multiple logical networks.

> **Note**
>
> The term "prefix length" can be used to refer to the IPv4 subnet mask when associated with an IPv4 address, and the IPv6 prefix length when associated with an IPv6 address.

When configuring inter-VLAN routing using the router-on-a-stick model, the physical interface of the router must be connected to a trunk link on the adjacent switch. On the router, subinterfaces are created for each unique VLAN on the network. Each subinterface is assigned an IP address specific to its subnet/VLAN and is configured to tag frames for that VLAN. This way, the router can keep the traffic from each subinterface separate as it traverses the trunk link back to the switch.

Functionally, the router-on-a-stick model is the same as using the legacy inter-VLAN routing model, but instead of using the physical interfaces to perform the routing, subinterfaces of a single physical interface are used.

Using trunk links and subinterfaces decreases the number of router and switch ports used. Not only can this save money, it can also reduce configuration complexity. Consequently, the router subinterface approach can scale to a much larger number of VLANs than a configuration with one physical interface per VLAN design.

### Configure Router-on-a-Stick: Switch Configuration (6.3.3.2)

To enable inter-VLAN routing using router-on-a stick, start by enabling trunking on the switch port that is connected to the router.

In Figure 6-24, router R1 is connected to switch S1 on trunk port F0/5.

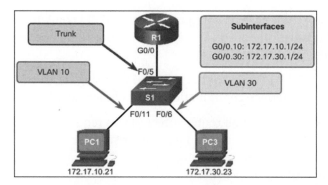

**Figure 6-24** Router-on-a-Stick Inter-VLAN Routing Topology

In Example 6-32, VLANs 10 and 30 are added to switch S1.

**Example 6-32** Router-on-a-Stick Inter-VLAN Routing: Switch Configuration

```
S1(config)# vlan 10
S1(config-vlan)# vlan 30
S1(config-vlan)# interface f0/5
S1(config-if)# switchport mode trunk
S1(config-if)# end
S1#
```

Because switch port F0/5 is configured as a trunk port, the port does not need to be assigned to a VLAN. To configure switch port F0/5 as a trunk port, execute the **switchport mode trunk** command in interface configuration mode for port F0/5.

The router can now be configured to perform inter-VLAN routing.

## Configure Router-on-a-Stick: Router Subinterface Configuration (6.3.3.3)

The router configuration using a router-on-a-stick configuration is different from legacy inter-VLAN routing. The router-on-a-stick model uses one physical interface that is configured logically for each VLAN using subinterfaces.

Each subinterface is created using the **interface** *interface_id.subinterface_id* global configuration mode command. The syntax for the subinterface is the physical interface, followed by a period and a subinterface number. The subinterface number can be any number but is typically configured to reflect the VLAN number, such as interface G0/0.10 and G0/0.20.

The subinterface must next be configured as an 802.1Q trunk for a specific VLAN using the **encapsulation dot1q** *vlan_id* [**native**] command. Use the **native** option only for the native VLAN.

Next, assign the IPv4 address for the subinterface using the **ip address** *ip_address subnet_mask* subinterface configuration mode command.

This process is repeated for all router subinterfaces required to route between the VLANs configured on the network. Each router subinterface must be assigned an IP address on a unique subnet for routing to occur. This IP address becomes the default gateway for all hosts in the VLAN.

Finally, the physical interface must be enabled. After a physical interface is enabled, subinterfaces are automatically enabled upon configuration. Subinterfaces do not need to be enabled with the **no shutdown** command at the subinterface configuration mode level of the Cisco IOS software.

**Note**

If the physical interface is disabled, all subinterfaces are disabled.

Individual subinterfaces can be administratively shut down with the **shutdown** command. Also, individual subinterfaces can be enabled independently with the **no shutdown** command in the subinterface configuration mode.

In Example 6-33, two subinterfaces are configured on interface G0/0 of R1. One subinterface is for VLAN 10 and the other for VLAN30.

**Example 6-33** Router-on-a-Stick Inter-VLAN Routing: Router Configuration

```
R1(config)# interface g0/0.10
R1(config-subif)# encapsulation dot1q 10
R1(config-subif)# ip address 172.17.10.1 255.255.255.0
R1(config-subif)# interface g0/0.30
R1(config-subif)# encapsulation dot1q 30
R1(config-subif)# ip address 172.17.30.1 255.255.255.0
R1(config-subif)# exit
R1(config)# interface g0/0
R1(config-if)# no shutdown
*Mar 20 00:20:59.299: %LINK-3-UPDOWN: Interface GigabitEthernet0/0, changed state
  to down
*Mar 20 00:21:02.919: %LINK-3-UPDOWN: Interface GigabitEthernet0/0, changed state
  to up
*Mar 20 00:21:03.919: %LINEPROTO-5-UPDOWN: Line protocol on Interface
  GigabitEthernet0/0, changed state to up
R1#
```

**Note**

In this example, the **native** keyword option was excluded to leave the native VLAN default as VLAN 1.

## Configure Router-on-a-Stick: Verifying Subinterfaces (6.3.3.4)

By default, Cisco routers are configured to route traffic between local subinterfaces. As a result, routing does not specifically need to be enabled.

In Example 6-34, the **show vlan** command displays information about the Cisco IOS VLAN subinterfaces. The output shows the two VLAN subinterfaces, GigabitEthernet0/0.10 and GigabitEthernet0/0.30.

**Example 6-34** Verify VLANs on R1

```
R1# show vlans
<output omitted>
Virtual LAN ID:  10 (IEEE 802.1Q Encapsulation)

   vLAN Trunk Interface:    GigabitEthernet0/0.10

   Protocols Configured:    Address:             Received:        Transmitted:
           IP               172.17.10.1               11                  18
<output omitted>
Virtual LAN ID:  30 (IEEE 802.1Q Encapsulation)
```

```
      vLAN Trunk Interface:    GigabitEthernet0/0.30


      Protocols Configured:    Address:            Received:          Transmitted:
            IP               172.17.30.1              11                     8
<output omitted>


R1#
```

Examine the routing table using the **show ip route** command, as shown in Example 6-35.

**Example 6-35** Verify the Routing Table on R1

```
R1# show ip route | begin Gateway
Gateway of last resort is not set


      172.17.0.0/16 is variably subnetted, 4 subnets, 2 masks
C        172.17.10.0/24 is directly connected, GigabitEthernet0/0.10
L        172.17.10.1/32 is directly connected, GigabitEthernet0/0.10
C        172.17.30.0/24 is directly connected, GigabitEthernet0/0.30
L        172.17.30.1/32 is directly connected, GigabitEthernet0/0.30
```

In the example, the routes defined in the routing table indicate that they are associated with specific subinterfaces, rather than separate physical interfaces. There are two routes in the routing table. One route is to the 172.17.10.0 subnet, which is attached to the local subinterface G0/0.10. The other route is to the 172.17.30.0 subnet, which is attached to the local subinterface G0/0.30.

The router uses this routing table to determine where to send the traffic it receives. For example, if the router received a packet on subinterface G0/0.10 destined for the 172.17.30.0 subnet, the router would identify that it should send the packet out subinterface G0/0.30 to reach hosts on the 172.17.30.0 subnet.

## Configure Router-on-a-Stick: Verifying Routing (6.3.3.5)

After the router and switch have been configured to perform inter-VLAN routing, the next step is to verify host-to-host connectivity. Access to devices on remote VLANs can be tested using the **ping** command.

### Ping Test

The **ping** command sends an ICMP echo request to the destination address. When a host receives an ICMP echo request, it responds with an ICMP echo reply to confirm that it received the ICMP echo request. The **ping** command calculates the elapsed time using the difference between the time the echo request was sent and the time the echo reply was received. This elapsed time is used to determine the latency of the connection. Successfully receiving a reply confirms that there is a path between the sending device and the receiving device.

## Tracert Test

Tracert is a useful utility for confirming the routed path taken between two devices. On UNIX systems, the utility is specified by **traceroute**. Tracert also uses ICMP to determine the path taken, but it uses ICMP echo requests with specific time-to-live values defined on the frame.

The time-to-live value determines exactly how many router hops away the ICMP echo is allowed to reach. The first ICMP echo request is sent with a time-to-live value set to expire at the first router on route to the destination device.

When the ICMP echo request times out on the first route, an ICMP message is sent back from the router to the originating device. The device records the response from the router and proceeds to send out another ICMP echo request, but this time with a greater time-to-live value. This allows the ICMP echo request to traverse the first router and reach the second device on route to the final destination. The process repeats recursively until finally the ICMP echo request is sent all the way to the final destination device. After the **tracert** utility finishes running, it displays a list of ingress router interfaces that the ICMP echo request reached on its way to the destination.

In Example 6-36, a **ping** and a **tracert** are initiated from PC1 to the destination address of PC3.

**Example 6-36** Verify Connectivity Between PCs on Different VLANs

```
PC> ping 172.17.30.23

Pinging 172.17.30.23 with 32 bytes of data:

Reply from 172.17.30.23: bytes=32 time=17ms TTL=255
Reply from 172.17.30.23: bytes=32 time=15ms TTL=255
Reply from 172.17.30.23: bytes=32 time=18ms TTL=255
Reply from 172.17.30.23: bytes=32 time=19ms TTL=255

Ping statistics for 172.17.30.23:
    Packets: Sent = 4, Received = 4, Lost = 0 (0% loss),
Approximate round trip times in milli-seconds:
    Minimum = 15ms, Maximum = 19ms, Average = 17ms
```

```
PC> tracert 172.17.10.30


Tracing route to 172.17.30.23 over a maximum of 30 hops:


  1    9 ms        7 ms        9 ms        172.17.10.1
  2   16 ms       15 ms       16 ms        172.17.30.23


Trace complete.
```

In the example, the **ping** utility was able to send an ICMP echo request to the IP address of PC3. Also, the **tracert** utility confirms that the path to PC3 is through the 172.17.10.1 subinterface IP address of router R1.

### Packet Tracer 6.3.3.6: Configuring Router-on-a-Stick Inter-VLAN Routing

In this activity, you check for connectivity prior to implementing inter-VLAN routing. You then configure VLANs and inter-VLAN routing. Finally, you enable trunking and verify connectivity between VLANs.

### Lab 6.3.3.7: Configuring 801.2Q Trunk-Based Inter-VLAN Routing

In this lab, you complete the following objectives:

- Part 1: Build the Network and Configure Basic Device Settings
- Part 2: Configure Switches with VLANs and Trunking
- Part 3: Configure Trunk-Based Inter-VLAN Routing

### Packet Tracer 6.3.3.8: Inter-VLAN Routing Challenge

In this activity, you troubleshoot a misconfigured VLAN environment. The initial network has errors. Your objective is to locate and correct the errors in the configurations and establish end-to-end connectivity. Your final configuration should match the Topology diagram and Addressing Table.

# Summary (6.4)

### Class Activity 6.4.1.1: The Inside Track

Your company has just purchased a three-level building. You are the network administrator and must design the company inter-VLAN routing network scheme to serve a few employees on each floor.

Floor 1 is occupied by the HR Department, Floor 2 is occupied by the IT Department, and Floor 3 is occupied by the Sales Department. All departments must be able to communicate with each other but at the same time have their own separate, working networks.

You brought three Cisco 2960 switches and a Cisco 1941 series router from the old office location to serve network connectivity in the new building. There is no budget available for new equipment.

### Packet Tracer 6.4.1.2: Skills Integration Challenge

In this activity, two switches are completely configured. On a third switch, you are responsible for assigning IP addressing to the SVI, configuring VLANs, assigning VLANs to interfaces, configuring trunking, and performing basic switch security.

This chapter introduced VLANS. VLANs are based on logical connections, instead of physical connections. VLANs are a mechanism to allow network administrators to create logical broadcast domains that can span across a single switch or multiple switches, regardless of physical proximity. This function is useful to reduce the size of broadcast domains or to allow groups or users to be logically grouped, without the need to be physically located in the same place.

There are several types of VLANs:

- Default VLAN
- Management VLAN
- Native VLAN
- User/Data VLAN
- Voice VLAN

The **switchport access vlan** command is used to create a VLAN on a switch. After creating a VLAN, the next step is to assign ports to the VLAN. The **show vlan brief** command displays the VLAN assignment and membership type for all switch ports. Each VLAN must correspond to a unique IP subnet.

Use the **show vlan** command to check whether the port belongs to the expected VLAN. If the port is assigned to the wrong VLAN, use the **switchport access vlan** command to correct the VLAN membership. Use the **show mac address-table** command to check which addresses were learned on a particular port of the switch and to which VLAN that port is assigned.

A port on a switch is either an access port or a trunk port. Access ports carry traffic from a specific VLAN assigned to the port. A trunk port by default is a member of all VLANs; therefore, it carries traffic for all VLANs.

VLAN trunks facilitate inter-switch communication by carrying traffic associated with multiple VLANs. IEEE 802.1Q frame tagging differentiates between Ethernet frames associated with distinct VLANs because they traverse common trunk links. To enable trunk links, use the **switchport mode trunk** command. Use the **show interfaces trunk** command to check whether a trunk has been established between switches.

Trunk negotiation is managed by the Cisco proprietary Dynamic Trunking Protocol (DTP), which operates on a point-to-point basis only, between network devices. DTP is automatically enabled on Catalyst 2960 and Catalyst 3560 Series switches.

To place a switch into its factory default condition with one default VLAN, use the commands **delete flash:vlan.dat** and **erase startup-config**.

This chapter also examined the configuration, verification, and troubleshooting of VLANs and trunks using the Cisco IOS CLI.

Inter-VLAN routing is the process of routing traffic between different VLANs, using either a dedicated router or a multilayer switch. Inter-VLAN routing facilitates communication between devices isolated by VLAN boundaries.

Legacy inter-VLAN routing depended on a physical router port being available for each configured VLAN. This has been replaced by the router-on-a-stick topology that relies on an external router with subinterfaces trunked to a Layer 2 switch. With the router-on-a-stick option, appropriate IP addressing and VLAN information must be configured on each logical subinterface, and a trunk encapsulation must be configured to match that of the trunking interface of the switch.

## Practice

The following activities provide practice with the topics introduced in this chapter. The Labs and Class Activities are available in the companion Routing and Switching Essentials v6 Labs & Study Guide (ISBN 9781587134265). The Packet Tracer Activities PKA files are found in the online course.

**Class Activities**

Class Activity 6.0.1.2: Vacation Station

Class Activity 6.4.1.1: The Inside Track

**Labs**

Lab 6.2.2.5: Configuring VLANs and Trunking

Lab 6.2.3.9: Troubleshooting VLAN Configurations

Lab 6.3.2.4: Configuring Per-Interface Inter-VLAN Routing

Lab 6.3.3.7: Configuring 802.1Q Trunk-Based Inter-VLAN Routing

**Packet Tracer Activities**

Packet Tracer 6.1.1.5: Who Hears the Broadcast

Packet Tracer 6.1.2.7: Investigating a VLAN Implementation

Packet Tracer 6.2.1.7: Configuring VLANs

Packet Tracer 6.2.2.4: Configuring Trunks

Packet Tracer 6.2.3.7: Troubleshooting a VLAN Implementation—Scenario 1

Packet Tracer 6.2.3.8: Troubleshooting a VLAN Implementation—Scenario 2

Packet Tracer 6.3.3.6: Configuring Router-on-a-Stick Inter-VLAN Routing

Packet Tracer 6.3.3.8: Inter-VLAN Routing Challenge

Packet Tracer 6.4.1.2: Skills Integration Challenge

# Check Your Understanding Questions

Complete all the review questions listed here to test your understanding of the topics and concepts in this chapter. The appendix "Answers to the 'Check Your Understanding' Questions" lists the answers.

1. Which three statements accurately describe VLAN types? (Choose three.)

   A. After the initial boot of an unconfigured switch, all ports are members of the default VLAN.

   B. An 802.1Q trunk port, with a native VLAN assigned, supports both tagged and untagged traffic.

C.  Voice VLANs are used to support user phone and email traffic on a network.

D.  VLAN 1 is always used as the management VLAN.

2.  Which type of VLAN is used to designate which traffic is untagged when crossing a trunk port?

A.  Data

B.  Default

C.  Native

D.  Management

E.  VLAN 1

3.  What are two primary benefits of using VLANs? (Choose two.)

A.  A reduction in the number of trunk links

B.  Cost reduction

C.  Improved IT staff efficiency

D.  No required configuration

E.  Reduced security

4.  Which command displays the encapsulation type, the voice VLAN ID, and the access mode VLAN for the Fa0/1 interface?

A.  **show interfaces Fa0/1 switchport**

B.  **show interfaces trunk**

C.  **show mac address-table interface Fa0/1**

D.  **show vlan brief**

5.  What must the network administrator do to remove Fast Ethernet port fa0/1 from VLAN 2 and assign it to VLAN 3?

A.  Enter the **no shutdown** command in interface configuration mode to return it to the default configuration and then configure the port for VLAN 3.

B.  Enter the **no vlan 2** and the **vlan 3** commands in global configuration mode.

C.  Enter the **switchport access vlan 3** command in interface configuration mode.

D.  Enter the **switchport trunk native vlan 3** command in interface configuration mode.

6. A Cisco Catalyst switch has been added to support the use of multiple VLANs as part of an enterprise network. The network technician finds it necessary to clear all VLAN information from the switch to incorporate a new network design. What should the technician do to accomplish this task?

   A. Delete the IP address that is assigned to the management VLAN and reboot the switch.

   B. Delete the startup configuration and the vlan.dat file in the flash memory of the switch and reboot the switch.

   C. Erase the running configuration and reboot the switch.

   D. Erase the startup configuration and reboot the switch.

7. Which two characteristics match extended range VLANs? (Choose two.)

   A. CDP can be used to learn and store these VLANs.

   B. They are commonly used in small networks.

   C. They are saved in the running-config file by default.

   D. VLAN IDs exist between 1006 and 4094.

   E. VLANs are initialized from flash memory.

8. What happens to switch ports after the VLAN to which they are assigned is deleted?

   A. The ports are assigned to VLAN1, the default VLAN.

   B. The ports are disabled.

   C. The ports are placed in trunk mode.

   D. The ports stop communicating with the attached devices.

9. A Cisco switch currently allows traffic tagged with VLANs 10 and 20 across trunk port Fa0/5. What is the effect of issuing a **switchport trunk allowed vlan 30** command on Fa0/5?

   A. It allows a native VLAN of 30 to be implemented on Fa0/5.

   B. It allows only VLAN 30 on Fa0/5.

   C. It allows VLANs 1 to 30 on Fa0/5.

   D. It allows VLANs 10, 20, and 30 on Fa0/5.

10. What VLANs are allowed across a trunk when the range of allowed VLANs is set to the default value?

   A. All VLANs will be allowed across the trunk.

   B. Only VLAN 1 will be allowed across the trunk.

   C. Only the native VLAN will be allowed across the trunk.

   D. The switches will negotiate via VTP which VLANs to allow across the trunk.

11. An administrator has determined that the traffic from a switch that corresponds to a VLAN is not being received on another switch over a trunk link. What could be the problem?

   A. Allowed VLANs on trunks

   B. Dynamic desirable mode on one of the trunk links

   C. Native VLAN mismatch

   D. Trunk mode mismatch

12. Which two modes does Cisco recommend when configuring a particular switch port? (Choose two.)

   A. Access

   B. FastEthernet

   C. Gigabit Ethernet

   D. IEEE 802.1Q

   E. ISL

   F. Trunk

# CHAPTER 7

# Access Control Lists

## Objectives

Upon completion of this chapter, you will be able to answer the following questions:

- How do ACLs filter traffic?

- How do ACLs use wildcard masks?

- How do you create ACLs?

- How do you place ACLs?

- How do you configure standard IPv4 ACLs to filter traffic to meet networking requirements?

- How do you use sequence numbers to edit existing standard IPv4 ACLs?

- How do you configure a standard ACL to secure vty access?

- How does a router process packets when an ACL is applied?

- How do you troubleshoot common standard IPv4 ACL errors using CLI commands?

## Key Terms

This chapter uses the following key terms. You can find the definitions in the Glossary.

# Introduction (7.0.1.1)

One of the most important skills a network administrator needs is mastery of *access control lists (ACL)*. ACLs provide security for a network.

Network designers use *firewalls* to protect networks from unauthorized use. Firewalls are hardware or software solutions that enforce network security policies. Consider a lock on a door to a room inside a building. The lock allows only authorized users with a key or access card to pass through the door. Similarly, a firewall filters unauthorized or potentially dangerous packets from entering the network.

On a Cisco router, you can configure a simple firewall that provides basic traffic-filtering capabilities using ACLs. Administrators use ACLs to stop traffic or permit only specified traffic on their networks.

This chapter explains how to configure and troubleshoot standard IPv4 ACLs on a Cisco router as part of a security solution. Included are tips, considerations, recommendations, and general guidelines on how to use ACLs. In addition, this chapter includes an opportunity to develop your mastery of ACLs with a series of lessons, activities, and lab exercises.

**Class Activity 7.0.1.2: Permit Me to Assist You**

Scenario

All individuals in the class will record five questions they would ask a candidate who is applying for a security clearance for a network assistant position within a small- to medium-sized business. The list of questions should be listed in order of importance to selecting a good candidate for the job. The preferred answers will also be recorded.

Two interviewers from the class will be selected. The interview process will begin. Candidates will be allowed or denied the opportunity to move to the next level of questions based on their answers to the interviewer's questions.

Refer to the accompanying PDF for further instructions for this activity.

The entire class will then get together and discuss their observations regarding the process to permit or deny them the opportunity to continue on to the next level of interviews.

# ACL Operation (7.1)

ACLs are used with other router features for a variety of tasks. A misconfigured ACL can cause connectivity problems in a network. For these reasons, it is important that you understand how ACLs operate and to carefully consider how they are implemented.

In this section, you learn about the purpose and operation of ACLs in small-to medium-sized business networks.

# Purpose of ACLs (7.1.1)

In this topic, you learn how ACLs filter traffic.

## What Is an ACL? (7.1.1.1)

An ACL is a series of IOS commands that control whether a router forwards or drops packets based on information found in the packet header. ACLs are among the most commonly used features of Cisco IOS software.

ACLs can be configured to perform the following tasks:

- Limit network traffic to increase network performance. For example, if corporate policy does not allow video traffic on the network, ACLs that block video traffic could be configured and applied. This would greatly reduce the network load and increase network performance.

- Provide traffic flow control. ACLs can restrict the delivery of routing updates to ensure that the updates are from a known source.

- Provide a basic level of security for network access. ACLs can allow one host to access a part of the network and prevent another host from accessing the same area. For example, access to the Human Resources network can be restricted to authorized users.

- Filter traffic based on traffic type. For example, an ACL can permit email traffic but block all Telnet traffic.

- Screen hosts to permit or deny access to network services. ACLs can permit or deny a user to access file types, such as FTP or HTTP.

By default, a router does not have ACLs configured; therefore, by default a router does not filter traffic. Traffic that enters the router is routed solely based on information within the routing table. However, when an ACL is applied to an interface, the router performs the additional task of evaluating all network packets as they pass through the interface to determine if the packet can be forwarded.

In addition to either permitting or denying traffic, ACLs can be used for selecting types of traffic to be analyzed, forwarded, or processed in other ways. For example, ACLs can be used to classify traffic to enable priority processing. This capability is similar to having a VIP pass at a concert or sporting event. The VIP pass gives selected guests privileges not offered to general admission ticket holders, such as priority entry or being able to enter a restricted area.

Figure 7-1 shows a sample topology with ACLs applied.

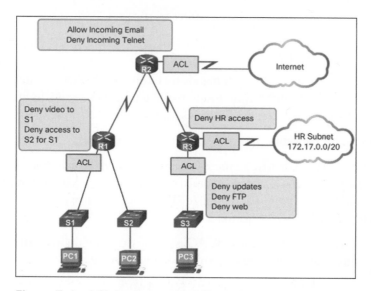

**Figure 7-1**   ACL Implementation Example

## Packet Filtering (7.1.1.2)

An ACL is a sequential list of permit or deny statements, known as *access control entries (ACE)*. ACEs are also commonly called ACL statements. When network traffic passes through an interface configured with an ACL, the router compares the information within the packet against each ACE, in sequential order, to determine if the packet matches one of the ACEs. This process is called *packet filtering*.

Packet filtering controls access to a network by analyzing the incoming and outgoing packets and forwarding them or discarding them based on given criteria. Packet filtering can occur at Layer 3 or Layer 4, as illustrated in Figure 7-2. *Standard ACLs* filter only at Layer 3. *Extended ACLs* filter at Layer 3 and Layer 4.

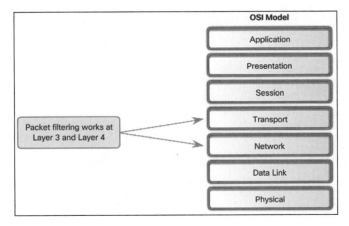

**Figure 7-2**   Packet Filtering

**Note**

Extended ACLs are beyond the scope of this course.

The source IPv4 address is the filtering criteria set in each ACE of a standard IPv4 ACL. A router configured with a standard IPv4 ACL extracts the source IPv4 address from the packet header. The router starts at the top of the ACL and compares the address to each ACE sequentially. When a match is made, the router carries out the instruction, either permitting or denying the packet. After a match is made, the remaining ACEs in the ACL, if any, are not analyzed. If the source IPv4 address does not match ACEs in the ACL, the packet is discarded.

The last statement of an ACL is always an *implicit deny*. This statement is automatically inserted at the end of each ACL even though it is not physically present. The implicit deny blocks all traffic. Because of this implicit deny, an ACL that does not have at least one permit statement blocks all traffic.

## ACL Operation (7.1.1.3)

ACLs define the set of rules that give added control for packets that enter inbound interfaces, packets that relay through the router, and packets that exit outbound interfaces of the router.

ACLs cannot filter packets that originate from the router itself.

ACLs can be configured to apply to inbound traffic and outbound traffic, as shown in Figure 7-3.

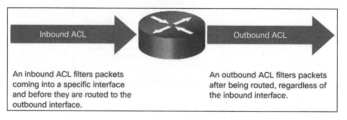

**Figure 7-3**  Inbound and Outbound ACLs

- *Inbound ACLs*—Incoming packets are processed before they are routed to the outbound interface. An inbound ACL is efficient because it saves the overhead of routing lookups if the packet is discarded. If the packet is permitted by the ACL, it is then processed for routing. Inbound ACLs are best used to filter packets when the network attached to an inbound interface is the only source of packets that need to be examined.

- *Outbound ACLs*—Incoming packets are routed to the outbound interface, and then they are processed through the outbound ACL. Outbound ACLs are best used when the same filter will be applied to packets coming from multiple inbound interfaces before exiting the same outbound interface.

Packet Tracer
☐ Activity

**Packet Tracer 7.1.1.4: ACL Demonstration**

In this activity, you observe how an ACL can be used to prevent a ping from reaching hosts on remote networks. After removing the ACL from the configuration, the pings are successful.

# Wildcard Masks in ACLs (7.1.2)

In this topic, you learn how ACLs use *wildcard masks*.

## Introducing ACL Wildcard Masking (7.1.2.1)

IPv4 ACEs include the use of wildcard masks. A wildcard mask is a string of 32 binary digits the router uses to determine which bits of the address to examine for a match.

As with subnet masks, the numbers 1 and 0 in the wildcard mask identify how to treat the corresponding IPv4 address bits. However, in a wildcard mask, these bits are used for different purposes and follow different rules.

Subnet masks use binary 1s and 0s to identify the network, subnet, and host portion of an IPv4 address. Wildcard masks use binary 1s and 0s to filter individual IPv4 addresses or groups of IPv4 addresses to permit or deny access to resources.

Wildcard masks and subnet masks differ in the way they match binary 1s and 0s. Wildcard masks use the following rules to match binary 1s and 0s:

- **Wildcard mask bit 0**—Match the corresponding bit value in the address.

- **Wildcard mask bit 1**—Ignore the corresponding bit value in the address.

Figure 7-4 shows how different wildcard masks filter IPv4 addresses. In the example, remember that binary 0 signifies a bit that must match, and binary 1 signifies a bit that can be ignored.

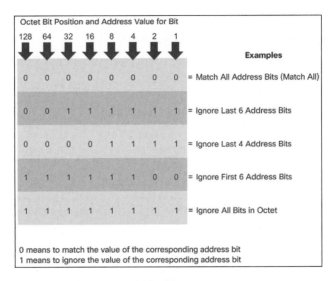

**Figure 7-4** Wildcard Masking

A wildcard mask is often referred to as an *inverse mask*. Unlike a subnet mask in which binary 1 is equal to a match and binary 0 is not a match, in a wildcard mask the reverse is true.

Table 7-1 shows the results of applying a 0.0.255.255 wildcard mask to a 32-bit IPv4 address. Remember that a binary 0 indicates a value that is matched.

**Table 7-1** Wildcard Mask Example

|  | **Decimal Address** | **Binary Address** |
|---|---|---|
| IP Address to Be Processed | 192.168.10.0 | 11000000.10101000.00001010.00000000 |
| Wildcard Mask | 0.0.255.255 | 00000000.00000000.11111111.11111111 |
| Resulting IP Address | 192.168.0.0 | 11000000.10101000.00000000.00000000 |

> **Note**
>
> Unlike IPv4 ACLs, IPv6 ACLs do not use wildcard masks. Instead, the prefix length is used to indicate how much of an IPv6 source or destination address should be matched. IPv6 ACLs are beyond the scope of this course.

## Wildcard Mask Examples (7.1.2.2)

Two of the ways wildcard masks can be used are to match IPv4 subnets and to match ranges.

### Wildcard Masks to Match IPv4 Subnets

Calculating the wildcard mask can take some practice. Tables 7-2 to 7-4 provide examples of using the 0.0.0.0 wildcard mask.

**Table 7-2**   Matching Hosts and Subnets—Example 1

| Example 1 | Decimal | Binary |
|---|---|---|
| IP Address | 192.168.1.1 | 11000000.10101000.00000001.00000001 |
| Wildcard Mask | 0.0.0.0 | 00000000.00000000.00000000.00000000 |
| Result | 192.168.1.1 | 11000000.10101000.00000001.00000001 |

In this example, the wildcard mask stipulates that every bit in the IPv4 192.168.1.1 must match exactly.

**Table 7-3**   Matching Hosts and Subnets—Example 2

| Example 2 | Decimal | Binary |
|---|---|---|
| IP Address | 192.168.1.1 | 11000000.10101000.00000001.00000001 |
| Wildcard Mask | 255.255.255.255 | 11111111.11111111.11111111.11111111 |
| Result | 0.0.0.0 | 00000000.00000000.00000000.00000000 |

In this example, the wildcard mask stipulates that anything will match.

**Table 7-4**   Matching Hosts and Subnets—Example 3

| Example 3 | Decimal | Binary |
|---|---|---|
| IP Address | 192.168.1.1 | 11000000.10101000.00000001.00000001 |
| Wildcard Mask | 0.0.0.255 | 00000000.00000000.00000000.11111111 |
| Result | 192.168.1.0 | 11000000.10101000.00000001.00000000 |

In this example, the wildcard mask stipulates that any host within the 192.168.1.0/24 network will match.

## Wildcard Masks to Match Ranges

The two examples in Tables 7-5 and 7-6 are more complex.

**Table 7-5**    Matching Ranges—Example 1

| Example 1 | Decimal | Binary |
|---|---|---|
| IP Address | 192.168.16.0 | 11000000.10101000.00010000.00000001 |
| Wildcard Mask | 0.0.15.255 | 00000000.00000000.00001111.11111111 |
| Result Range | 192.168.16.0 to 192.168.31.255 | 11000000.10101000.00010000.00000000 to 11000000.10101000.00011111.11111111 |

In this example, the first two octets and the first four bits of the third octet must match exactly. The last four bits in the third octet and the last octet can be any valid number. This results in a mask that checks for the range of networks 192.168.16.0 to 192.168.31.0.

**Table 7-6**    Matching Ranges—Example 2

| Example 2 | Decimal | Binary |
|---|---|---|
| IP Address | 192.168.1.0 | 11000000.10101000.00000001.00000000 |
| Wildcard Mask | 0.0.254.255 | 00000000.00000000.11111110.11111111 |
| Result | 192.168.1.0 | 11000000.10101000.00000001.00000000 |
| | All odd-numbered subnets in the 192.168.0.0 major network | |

This example shows a wildcard mask that matches the first two octets and the least significant bit in the third octet. The last octet and the first seven bits in the third octet can be any valid number. The result is a mask that would permit or deny all hosts from odd subnets from the 192.168.0.0 major network.

## Calculating the Wildcard Mask (7.1.2.3)

Calculating wildcard masks can be challenging. However, there is a simple shortcut method that can be used. It consists of simply subtracting the subnet mask from 255.255.255.255.

Refer to the three examples in Figure 7-5.

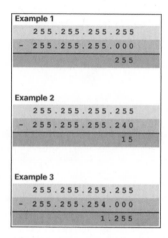

**Figure 7-5**   Wildcard Mask Calculation

## Wildcard Mask Calculation: Example 1

In the first example, assume you wanted to permit access to all users in the 192.168.3.0 network. Because the subnet mask is 255.255.255.0, you could take the 255.255.255.255 and subtract the subnet mask 255.255.255.0. The solution produces the wildcard mask 0.0.0.255.

## Wildcard Mask Calculation: Example 2

In the second example, assume you wanted to permit network access for the 14 users in the subnet 192.168.3.32/28. The subnet mask for the IPv4 subnet is 255.255.255.240; therefore, take 255.255.255.255 and subtract the subnet mask 255.255.255.240. The solution this time produces the wildcard mask 0.0.0.15.

## Wildcard Mask Calculation: Example 3

In the third example, assume you wanted to match only networks 192.168.10.0 and 192.168.11.0. Again, you take the 255.255.255.255 and subtract the regular subnet mask, which in this case would be 255.255.254.0. The result is 0.0.1.255.

You could accomplish the same result with statements like the two shown here:

```
R1(config)# access-list 10 permit 192.168.10.0
R1(config)# access-list 10 permit 192.168.11.0
R1(config)#
```

It is more efficient to configure the wildcard mask in the following way:

```
R1(config)# access-list 10 permit 192.168.10.0 0.0.1.255
R1(config)#
```

Consider an example in which you need to match networks in the range between 192.168.16.0/24 to 192.168.31.0/24. These networks would summarize to 192.168.16.0/20. In this case, 0.0.15.255 is the correct wildcard mask to configure one efficient ACL statement, as shown here:

```
R1(config)# access-list 10 permit 192.168.16.0 0.0.15.255
```

## Wildcard Mask Keywords (7.1.2.4)

Working with decimal representations of binary wildcard mask bits can be tedious. To simplify this task, the keywords **host** and **any** help identify the most common uses of wildcard masking. These keywords eliminate entering wildcard masks when identifying a specific host or an entire network. These keywords also make it easier to read an ACL by providing visual clues as to the source or destination of the criteria.

The **host** keyword substitutes for the 0.0.0.0 mask. This mask states that all IPv4 address bits must match to filter just one host address.

The **any** option substitutes for the IPv4 address and 255.255.255.255 mask. This mask says to ignore the entire IPv4 address or to accept any addresses.

Figure 7-6 explains how the host and any keywords work.

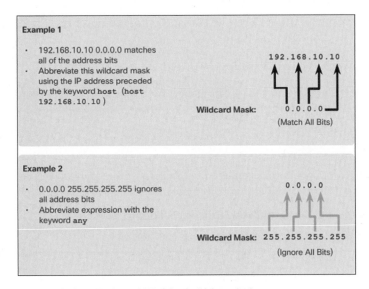

**Figure 7-6**   Wildcard Bit Mask Abbreviations

## Example 1: Wildcard Masking Process with a Single IPv4 Address

In Example 1, instead of entering **192.168.10.10 0.0.0.0**, you can use **host 192.168.10.10**.

## Example 2: Wildcard Masking Process with a Match Any IPv4 Address

In Example 2, instead of entering **0.0.0.0 255.255.255.255**, you can use the keyword **any** by itself.

### Wildcard Mask Keyword Examples (7.1.2.5)

Consider that an ACL is required to permit the host at IP address 192.168.10.10. The ACL could be entered as follows:

```
R1(config)# access-list 1 permit 192.168.10.10 0.0.0.0
```

However, the same can be accomplished by using the **host** keyword as follows:

```
R1(config)# access-list 1 permit host 192.168.10.10
```

The resulting ACL achieves the same result and makes it easier to read and understand what the ACE accomplishes.

An ACE with the IPv4 address 0.0.0.0 and wildcard mask of 255.255.255.255 matches all networks. The ACL could be entered as follows:

```
R1(config)# access-list 1 permit 0.0.0.0 255.255.255.255
```

However, the same can be accomplished by using the **any** keyword as follows:

```
R1(config)# access-list 1 permit any
```

**Note**

The syntax for configuring standard IPv4 ACLs is covered later in this chapter.

Interactive
Graphic

**Activity 7.1.2.6: Determine the Correct Wildcard Mask**

Refer to the online course to complete this activity.

Interactive
Graphic

**Activity 7.1.2.7: Determine the Permit or Deny**

Refer to the online course to complete this activity.

# Guidelines for ACL Creation (7.1.3)

In this topic, you learn how to create ACLs.

## General Guidelines for Creating ACLs (7.1.3.1)

Writing ACLs can be a complex task. For every interface, there may be multiple policies needed to manage the type of traffic allowed to enter or exit that interface. The router in Figure 7-7 has two interfaces configured for IPv4 and IPv6.

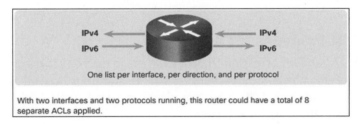

**Figure 7-7**   ACL Traffic Filtering on a Router

If you needed ACLs for both protocols, on both interfaces and in both directions, it would require eight separate ACLs. Each interface would have four ACLs: two ACLs for IPv4 and two ACLs for IPv6. For each protocol, one ACL is for inbound traffic and one for outbound traffic.

> **Note**
>
> ACLs do not have to be configured in both directions. The number of ACLs and their direction applied to the interface depend on the requirements being implemented.

Here are some guidelines for using ACLs:

- Use ACLs in firewall routers positioned between your internal network and an external network such as the Internet.

- Use ACLs on a router positioned between two parts of your network to control traffic entering or exiting a specific part of your internal network.

- Configure ACLs on border routers—that is, routers situated at the edges of your networks. This provides a basic buffer from the outside network, or between a less controlled area of your own network and a more sensitive area of your network.

- Configure ACLs for each network protocol configured on the border router interfaces.

You can configure one ACL per protocol, per direction, per interface:

- **One ACL per protocol**—To control traffic flow on an interface, an ACL must be defined for each protocol enabled on the interface.

- **One ACL per direction**—ACLs control traffic in one direction at a time on an interface. Two separate ACLs must be created to control inbound and outbound traffic.

- **One ACL per interface**—ACLs control traffic for an interface, such as GigabitEthernet 0/0.

## ACL Best Practices (7.1.3.2)

Using ACLs requires attention to detail and great care. Mistakes can be costly in terms of downtime, troubleshooting efforts, and poor network service. Before configuring an ACL, basic planning is required. Table 7-7 lists ACL best practice guidelines and their benefit.

**Table 7-7**  ACL Best Practices

| Guideline | Benefit |
| --- | --- |
| Base your ACLs on the security policy of the organization. | This ensures you implement organizational security guidelines. |
| Prepare a description of what you want your ACLs to do. | This helps you avoid inadvertently creating potential access problems. |
| Use a text editor to create, edit, and save ACLs. | This helps you create a library of reusable ACLs. |
| Test your ACLs on a development network before implementing them on a production network. | This helps you avoid costly errors. |

Interactive
Graphic

**Activity 7.1.3.3: ACL Operation**

Refer to the online course to complete this activity.

# Guidelines for ACL Placement (7.1.4)

In this topic, you learn where to place ACLs.

## Where to Place ACLs (7.1.4.1)

The proper placement of an ACL can make the network operate more efficiently. An ACL can be placed to reduce unnecessary traffic. For example, traffic that will be denied at a remote destination should not be forwarded using network resources along the route to that destination.

Every ACL should be placed where it has the greatest impact on efficiency, as shown in Figure 7-8.

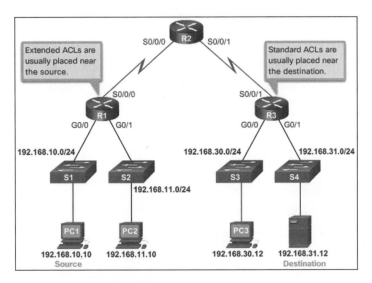

**Figure 7-8**   ACL Placement

The basic rules are as follows:

- **Extended ACLs**—Locate extended ACLs as close as possible to the source of the traffic to be filtered. This way, undesirable traffic is denied close to the source network without crossing the network infrastructure.

- **Standard ACLs**—Because standard ACLs do not specify destination addresses, place them as close to the destination as possible. Placing a standard ACL at the source of the traffic effectively prevents that traffic from reaching any other networks through the interface where the ACL is applied.

Placement of the ACL and therefore, the type of ACL used, may also depend on the following:

- **The extent of the network administrator's control**—Placement of the ACL can depend on whether or not the network administrator has control of both the source and the destination networks.

- **Bandwidth of the networks involved**—Filtering unwanted traffic at the source prevents transmission of the traffic before it consumes bandwidth on the path to a destination. This is especially important in low-bandwidth networks.

■ **Ease of configuration**—If a network administrator wants to deny traffic coming from several networks, one option is to use a single standard ACL on the router closest to the destination. The disadvantage is that traffic from these networks uses bandwidth unnecessarily. An extended ACL could be used on each router where the traffic originated. This saves bandwidth by filtering the traffic at the source but requires creating extended ACLs on multiple routers.

> **Note**
>
> Although extended ACLs are beyond the scope of the ICND1/CCENT exam, you should know the general guideline for placing both standard and extended ACLs. For CCNA certification, the general rule is that extended ACLs are placed as close as possible to the source, and standard ACLs are placed as close as possible to the destination.

## Standard ACL Placement (7.1.4.2)

To help understand where to place a standard ACL, refer to the topology in Figure 7-9.

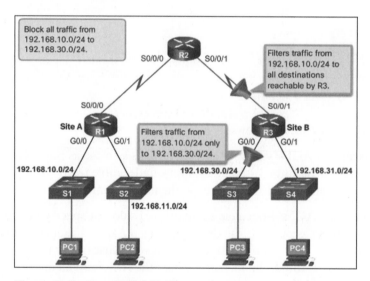

**Figure 7-9**   Standard ACL Placement

In this example, the administrator wants to prevent traffic originating in the 192.168.10.0/24 network from reaching the 192.168.30.0/24 network. This will be accomplished using a standard ACL.

The basic placement guideline for standard ACL is to place them close to the destination. As shown in the figure, the standard ACL could be applied to two interfaces on R3:

■ **R3 S0/0/1 interface**—Applying a standard ACL to prevent traffic from 192.168.10.0/24 from entering the S0/0/1 interface prevents this traffic from reaching 192.168.30.0/24. However, the ACL would prevent all traffic from reaching the 192.168.31.0/24 network as well. Because the intent of the ACL is to only filter traffic destined for 192.168.30.0/24, a standard ACL should not be applied to this interface.

- **R3 G0/0 interface**—Applying the standard ACL to traffic exiting the G0/0 interface filters packets from 192.168.10.0/24 to 192.168.30.0/24. This does not affect other networks reachable by R3. Packets from 192.168.10.0/24 are still able to reach 192.168.31.0/24.

Therefore, in this example, the standard ACL should be applied to the G0/0 interface on R3.

# Standard IPv4 ACLs (7.2)

Standard ACLs are used with a variety of features, and a misconfigured ACL can have a negative impact on a network. Therefore, it is important that you understand how to correctly create and apply ACLs.

In this section, you learn how to configure standard IPv4 ACLs to filter traffic in a small-to medium-sized business network.

## Configure Standard IPv4 ACLs (7.2.1)

In this topic, you configure standard IPv4 ACLs to filter traffic to meet networking requirements.

### Numbered Standard IPv4 ACL Syntax (7.2.1.1)

To use numbered standard ACLs on a Cisco router, you must first create the standard ACL and then activate the ACL on an interface.

The **access-list** global configuration command defines a standard ACL with a number in the range of 1 through 99. Cisco IOS Software Release 12.0.1 extended these numbers by allowing 1300 to 1999 to be used for standard ACLs. This allows for a maximum of 798 possible standard ACLs. These additional numbers are referred to as expanded IPv4 ACLs.

The full syntax of the standard ACL command is as follows:

```
Router(config)# access-list access-list-number {deny | permit | remark} source
  [source-wildcard] [log]
```

Table 7-8 provides a detailed explanation of the syntax for a standard ACL.

**Table 7-8**  Standard ACL Command Syntax

| Parameter | Description |
|---|---|
| *access-list-number* | Number of an ACL. This is a decimal number from 1 to 99, or 1300 to 1999 (for standard ACLs). |
| **deny** | Denies access if the conditions are matched. |
| **permit** | Permits access if the conditions are matched. |
| **remark** | Adds a remark about entries in an ACL to make it easier to read. |
| *source* | Number of the network or host from which the packet is being sent. There are two ways to specify the source:<br><br>■ Use a 32-bit quantity in four-part, dotted-decimal format<br><br>■ Use the keyword **any** as an abbreviation for a source and source-wildcard of 0.0.0.0 255.255.255.255 |
| *source-wildcard* | (Optional) 32-bit wildcard mask to be applied to the source. Places ones in the bit positions you want to ignore. |
| **log** | (Optional) Causes an informational logging message about the packet that matches the entry to be sent to the console. (The level of messages logged to the console is controlled by the logging console command.)<br><br>The message includes the ACL number, whether the packet was permitted or denied, the source address, and the number of packets. The message is generated for the first packet that matches, and then at five-minute intervals, including the number of packets permitted or denied in the prior five-minute interval. |

ACEs can permit or deny an individual host or a range of host addresses. For example, to create a host statement in numbered ACL 10 that permits a specific host with the IPv4 address 192.168.10.10, you would enter this:

```
R1(config)# access-list 10 permit host 192.168.10.10
```

To create a statement in numbered ACL 10 that permits all IPv4 addresses in the network 192.168.10.0/24, you would enter this:

```
R1(config)# access-list 10 permit 192.168.10.0 0.0.0.255
```

To remove the ACL, use the global configuration **no access-list** *access-list-number* global configuration command.

In Example 7-1, a standard ACL numbered 10 is created to permit all hosts on the 192.168.10.0/24 network. Notice how the **show access-lists** command is used to verify the content of configured ACLs.

**Example 7-1**  Adding an ACL

```
R1(config)# access-list 10 permit 192.168.10.0 0.0.0.255
R1(config)# exit
R1#
R1# show access-lists
Standard IP access list 10
    10 permit 192.168.10.0, wildcard bits 0.0.0.255
R1#
```

In Example 7-2, ACL 10 is removed from the configuration.

**Example 7-2**  Removing an ACL

```
R1(config)# no access-list 10
R1(config)# exit
R1#
R1# show access-lists
R1#
```

Typically, when an administrator creates an ACL, the purpose of each ACE is known and understood. However, to ensure that the administrator and others recall the purpose of a statement, remarks should be included.

The **remark** keyword is used for documentation and makes access lists a great deal easier to understand. Each remark is limited to 100 characters. The ACL in Example 7-3 demonstrates how the **remark** command is configured. Notice how the remark ACE in the **show running-config** output helps explain the purpose of the next ACE.

**Example 7-3**  Adding a Remark to an ACL

```
R1(config)# access-list 10 remark Permit hosts from 192.168.10.0 LAN
R1(config)# access-list 10 permit 192.168.10.0 0.0.0.255
R1(config)# exit
R1#
R1# show running-config | include access-list 10
access-list 10 remark Permit hosts from the 192.168.10.0 LAN
access-list 10 permit 192.168.10.0 0.0.0.255
R1#
```

## Applying Standard IPv4 ACLs to Interfaces (7.2.1.2)

After a standard IPv4 ACL is configured, it is linked to an interface using the **ip access-group** command in interface configuration mode:

```
Router(config-if)# ip access-group {access-list-number | access-list-name} {in | out}
```

To remove an ACL from an interface, first enter the **no ip access-group** command on the interface, and then enter the global **no access-list** command.

Consider the topology shown in Figure 7-10.

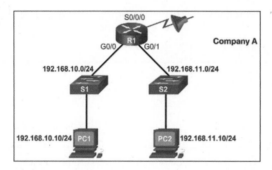

**Figure 7-10**   Permit a Specific Subnet Topology

Example 7-4 demonstrates how an ACL can be configured to permit traffic from a single network.

**Example 7-4** Permit a Specific Subnet Configuration

```
R1(config)# access-list 1 permit 192.168.10.0 0.0.0.255
R1(config)#
R1(config)# interface s0/0/0
R1(config-if)# ip access-group 1 out
R1(config-if)#
```

This ACL allows only traffic from source network 192.168.10.0 to be forwarded out of interface S0/0/0. Traffic from networks other than 192.168.10.0 is blocked.

The first line identifies the ACL as access-list 1. It permits traffic that matches the selected parameters. In this case, the IPv4 address and wildcard mask identifying the source network is 192.168.10.0 0.0.0.255. Recall that there is an implicit **deny all** statement that is equivalent to adding the line **access-list 1 deny 0.0.0.0 255.255.255.255** or **access-list deny any** to the end of the ACL.

The **ip access-group 1 out** interface configuration command links and ties ACL 1 to the Serial 0/0/0 interface as an outbound filter.

Therefore, ACL 1 only permits hosts from the 192.168.10.0/24 network to exit router R1. It denies any other network, including the 192.168.11.0 network.

## Numbered Standard IPv4 ACL Examples (7.2.1.3)

Example 7-5 demonstrates an ACL that permits a specific subnet except for a specific host on that subnet.

**Example 7-5**  Deny a Specific Host and Permit a Specific Subnet Configuration

```
R1(config)# no access-list 1
R1(config)#
R1(config)# access-list 1 deny host 192.168.10.10
R1(config)# access-list 1 permit 192.168.10.0 0.0.0.255
R1(config)#
R1(config)# interface s0/0/0
R1(config-if)# ip access-group 1 out
R1(config-if)#
```

The first command deletes the previous version of ACL 1. The next ACL statement denies the PC1 host located at 192.168.10.10. Every other host on the 192.168.10.0/24 network is then permitted. Again, the implicit deny statement matches every other network.

The ACL is reapplied to interface S0/0/0 in an outbound direction.

Figure 7-11 shows the topology with traffic filtering on the inbound G0/0 interface.

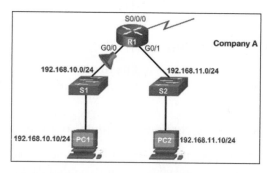

**Figure 7-11**    Deny a Specific Host Topology

Example 7-6 demonstrates an ACL that denies a specific host and replaces the previous example. This example still blocks traffic from host PC1 but permits all other traffic.

**Example 7-6** Deny a Specific Host Configuration

```
R1(config)# no access-list 1
R1(config)#
R1(config)# access-list 1 deny host 192.168.10.10
R1(config)# access-list 1 permit any
R1(config)#
R1(config)# interface g0/0
R1(config-if)# ip access-group 1 in
R1(config-if)#
```

The first two commands are the same as the previous example. The first command deletes the previous version of ACL 1, and the next ACL statement denies the PC1 host that is located at 192.168.10.10.

The third line is new and permits all other hosts. This means that all hosts from the 192.168.10.0/24 network will be permitted except for PC1, which was denied in the previous statement.

This ACL is applied to interface G0/0 in the inbound direction. Because the filter only affects the 192.168.10.0/24 LAN on G0/0, it is more efficient to apply the ACL to the inbound interface. The ACL could be applied to S0/0/0 in the outbound direction, but then R1 would have to examine packets from all networks including 192.168.11.0/24.

## Named Standard IPv4 ACL Syntax (7.2.1.4)

Naming an ACL makes it easier to understand its function. When you identify your ACL with a name instead of with a number, the configuration mode and command syntax are slightly different.

The command syntax and steps for configuring *named ACLs* are as follows:

Step 1.   Use the **ip access-list** [**standard** | **extended**] *name* global configuration command to create a named standard or extended ACL. ACL names are alphanumeric, case sensitive, and must be unique. An alphanumeric name string must be unique and cannot begin with a number.

**Note**

Numbered ACLs use the global configuration command **access-list**, whereas named IPv4 ACLs use the **ip access-list** command.

Specifically, this is the syntax to create a standard named ACL:

```
Router(config)# ip access-list standard name
Router(config-std-nacl)#
```

Notice that after entering the command, the router is in standard (std) named ACL (nacl) configuration mode.

**Step 2.**   From the named ACL configuration mode, use **permit** or **deny** statements to specify one or more conditions for determining whether a packet is forwarded or dropped. You can use **remark** to add a comment to the ACL. The syntax is as follows:

```
Router(config-std-nacl)# {permit | deny | remark} {source [source-wildcard]}
   [log]
```

**Step 3.**   Apply the ACL to an interface using the **ip access-group** *name* command. Specify whether the ACL should be applied to packets as they enter the interface (**in**) or applied to packets as they exit the interface (**out**).

```
Router(config-if)# ip access-group name [in | out]
```

Figure 7-12 shows the topology with traffic filtering on the outbound G0/0 interface.

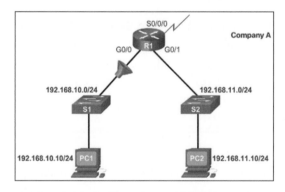

**Figure 7-12**   Named ACL Topology

In Example 7-7, a standard named ACL called NO_ACCESS that denies host 192.168.11.10 access to the 192.168.10.0 network is configured on router R1. The ACL is then applied outbound on interface G0/0.

**Example 7-7** Named ACL Configuration

```
R1(config)# ip access-list standard NO_ACCESS
R1(config-std-nacl)# deny host 192.168.11.10
R1(config-std-nacl)# permit any
R1(config-std-nacl)# exit
R1(config)#
R1(config)# interface g0/0
R1(config-if)# ip access-group NO_ACCESS out
R1(config-if)#
```

Capitalizing ACL names is recommended but not required. However, capitalizing ACL names makes them stand out when viewing the running-config output. It also makes it less likely that you will accidentally create two different ACLs with the same name but with different uses of capitalization.

**Activity 7.2.1.5: Configuring Standard IPv4 ACLs**

Refer to the online course to complete this activity.

**Packet Tracer 7.2.1.6: Configuring Numbered Standard IPv4 ACLs**

Standard ACLs are router configuration scripts that control whether a router permits or denies packets based on the source address. This activity focuses on defining filtering criteria, configuring standard ACLs, applying ACLs to router interfaces, and verifying and testing the ACL implementation. The routers are already configured, including IPv4 addresses and EIGRP routing.

**Packet Tracer 7.2.1.7: Configuring Named Standard IPv4 ACLs**

The senior network administrator has asked you to create a standard named ACL to prevent access to a file server. All clients from one network and one specific workstation from a different network should be denied access.

## Modify IPv4 ACLs (7.2.2)

In this topic, you will learn how to use sequence numbers to edit existing standard IPv4 ACLs.

## Method 1: Use a Text Editor (7.2.2.1)

After someone is familiar with creating and editing ACLs, it may be easier to construct the ACL using a text editor such as Microsoft Notepad. This allows you to create or edit the ACL and then paste it into the router interface. For an existing ACL, you can use the **show running-config** command to display the ACL, copy and paste it into the text editor, make the necessary changes, and paste it back into the router interface.

To demonstrate how to use a text editor, consider the ACL 1 configuration in Example 7-8.

**Example 7-8** ACL 1 Configuration

```
R1(config)# access-list 1 deny host 192.168.10.99
R1(config)# access-list 1 permit 192.168.0.0 0.0.255.255
R1(config)#
```

The ACL denies host 192.168.10.99 but permits all other hosts from that subnet. The problem is that the host IPv4 address 192.168.10.99 should have been 192.168.10.10. Entering a new ACE permitting the 192.168.10.10 host would not fix the problem because the ACE would be the third entry in the ACL (after all hosts have been permitted). The solution is to replace the incorrect ACE with a new one.

Here are the steps to edit and correct ACL 1:

**Step 1.**   Display the ACL using the **show running-config** command, as shown in Example 7-9.

**Example 7-9** Configure and Verify Initial ACL

```
R1# show running-config | include access-list 1
access-list 1 deny host 192.168.10.99
access-list 1 permit 192.168.0.0 0.0.255.255
```

**Step 2.**   Highlight the ACL, copy it, and then paste it into Microsoft Notepad. In Notepad, correct the host IP address. Next, highlight all of the ACL and copy it.

**Step 3.**   In global configuration mode, remove the access list using the **no access-list 1** command. Otherwise, the new statements would be appended to the existing ACL. Then paste and verify the corrected ACL as shown in Example 7-10.

**Example 7-10** Modify and Verify the ACL

```
R1(config)# no access-list 1
R1(config)#
R1(config)# access-list 1 deny host 192.168.10.10
R1(config)# access-list 1 permit 192.168.0.0 0.0.255.255
R1(config)# exit
R1#
R1# show running-config | include access-list 1
access-list 1 deny host 192.168.10.10
access-list 1 permit 192.168.0.0 0.0.255.255
```

**Step 4.**   Using the **show running-config** command, verify the changes.

It should be mentioned that when using the **no access-list** command, different IOS software releases act differently. If the ACL that has been deleted is still applied to an interface, some IOS versions behave as if no ACL is protecting your network, whereas others deny all traffic. For this reason, it is good practice to remove the reference to the access list from the interface before modifying the access list. If there is an error in the new list, disable it and troubleshoot the problem.

## Method 2: Use Sequence Numbers (7.2.2.2)

An alternate of correcting an ACL is to use the IOS sequence numbers. For example, using the same Example 7-9 as Method 1, the host ACE in ACL 1 incorrectly identified the host with IP address 192.168.10.99.

The host should have been configured as 192.168.10.10. To edit the ACL using sequence numbers, follow these steps:

**Step 1.**   Display the current ACL using the **show access-lists 1** command, as shown in Example 7-11.

**Example 7-11** Verify Initial ACL

```
R1# show access-lists 1
Standard IP access list 1
    10 deny    192.168.10.99
    20 permit 192.168.0.0, wildcard bits 0.0.255.255
R1#
```

The command produces output similar to the **show running-config** command with the exception that it also includes sequence numbers for every ACE. The sequence number is displayed at the beginning of each statement. The sequence number was automatically assigned when the access-list statement was entered. Notice that the misconfigured statement has the sequence number 10.

> **Note**
>
> The output from this command will be discussed in more detail later in this section.

**Step 2.**   Edit the ACL using sequence numbers. Numbered and named ACLs can be edited using the **ip access-list** command. Enter the **ip access-list standard** command and use ACL number 1 as the name.

ACEs cannot be overwritten using the same sequence number as an existing statement. The incorrect ACE must first be deleted and then reentered correctly, as shown in Example 7-12.

**Example 7-12**  Modify ACL Using Sequence Numbers

```
R1(config)# ip access-list standard 1
R1(config-std-nacl)# no 10
R1(config-std-nacl)# 10 deny host 192.168.10.10
R1(config-std-nacl)# end
R1#
```

**Step 3.**   Verify the changes using the **show access-lists** command.

Example 7-13 demonstrates this step.

**Example 7-13**  Verify the ACL Statements

```
R1# show access-lists
Standard IP access list 1
    10 deny    192.168.10.10
    20 permit 192.168.0.0, wildcard bits 0.0.255.255
R1#
```

As discussed previously, Cisco IOS implements an internal logic to standard access lists. The order in which standard ACEs are entered may not be the order in which they are stored, displayed, or processed by the router.

## Editing Standard Named ACLs (7.2.2.3)

In Example 7-12, sequence numbers were used to edit a standard numbered IPv4 ACL. By referring to the statement sequence numbers, individual statements can easily be inserted or deleted. This method can also be used to edit standard named ACLs.

Example 7-14 displays the ACEs for the named ACL NO_ACCESS.

**Example 7-14** Verify a Named ACL

```
R1# show access-lists
Standard IP access list NO_ACCESS
    10 deny    192.168.11.10
    20 permit 192.168.11.0, wildcard bits 0.0.0.255
R1#
```

ACE 10 specifically denies host 192.168.11.10. However, an additional host must now be added. In Example 7-15, a new ACE with sequence number 15 is inserted and verified.

**Example 7-15** Insert and Verify a New ACE

```
R1(config)# ip access-list standard NO_ACCESS
R1(config-std-nacl)# 15 deny host 192.168.11.11
R1(config-std-nacl)# end
R1#
R1# show access-lists
Standard IP access list NO_ACCESS
    10 deny    192.168.11.10
    15 deny    192.168.11.11
    20 permit 192.168.11.0, wildcard bits 0.0.0.255
R1#
```

The final **show** command output verifies that the new workstation is now also denied access.

> **Note**
>
> In named access-list configuration mode, use the **no** *sequence-number* command to quickly delete individual statements.

## Verifying ACLs (7.2.2.4)

As shown in Example 7-16, the **show ip interface** command is used to verify which ACL (if any) is configured on the interface.

**Example 7-16** Verifying Standard ACL Interfaces

```
R1# show ip interface s0/0/0
Serial0/0/0 is up, line protocol is up
  Internet address is 10.1.1.1/30
  <output omitted>
  Outgoing access list is 1
  Inbound  access list is not set
 <output omitted>

R1# show ip interface g0/0
GigabitEthernet0/1 is up, line protocol is up
  Internet address is 192.168.10.1/24
  <output omitted>
  Outgoing access list is NO_ACCESS
  Inbound  access list is not set
  <output omitted>
```

The output from this command includes the number or name of the access list and the direction in which the ACL was applied. The output shows router R1 has the access-list 1 applied to its S0/0/0 outbound interface and the access-list NO_ACCESS applied to its g0/0 interface, also in the outbound direction.

Example 7-17 shows the result of issuing the **show access-lists** command on router R1.

**Example 7-17** Verifying Standard ACL Statements

```
R1# show access-lists
Standard IP access list 1
    10 deny   192.168.10.10
    20 permit 192.168.0.0, wildcard bits 0.0.255.255
Standard IP access list NO_ACCESS
    15 deny   192.168.11.11
    10 deny   192.168.11.10
    20 permit 192.168.11.0, wildcard bits 0.0.0.255
R1#
```

To view an individual access list, use the **show access-lists** command followed by the access-list number or name. Notice that sequence number 15 is displayed prior to sequence number 10. This is a result of the router's internal process and is discussed later in this section.

## ACL Statistics (7.2.2.5)

After an ACL has been applied to an interface and some testing has occurred, the **show access-lists** command shows statistics for each statement that has been matched, as demonstrated in Example 7-18.

**Example 7-18** Verify ACL Statistics

```
R1# show access-lists
Standard IP access list 1
    10 deny   192.168.10.10 (4 match(es))
    20 permit 192.168.0.0, wildcard bits 0.0.255.255
Standard IP access list NO_ACCESS
    15 deny   192.168.11.11
    10 deny   192.168.11.10 (4 match(es))
    20 permit 192.168.11.0, wildcard bits 0.0.0.255
R1#
```

Notice how some of the ACEs have been "matched." When traffic is generated that should match an ACL statement, the matches shown in the **show access-lists** command output should increase. For instance, in this example, if a ping is issued from PC1 to PC3 or PC4, the output shows an increase in the matches for the **deny** statement of ACL 1, as demonstrated in Example 7-19.

**Example 7-19** ACL Statistics After a Match

```
R1# show access-lists
Standard IP access list 1
    10 deny   192.168.10.10 (8 match(es))
    20 permit 192.168.0.0, wildcard bits 0.0.255.255
Standard IP access list NO_ACCESS
    15 deny   192.168.11.11
    10 deny   192.168.11.10 (4 match(es))
    20 permit 192.168.11.0, wildcard bits 0.0.0.255
R1#
```

Both explicitly configured **permit** and **deny** statements track statistics for matched packets.

It should be noted that this is not true of the implied **deny any** statement. The implied **deny any** statement does not display matched packets unless it is explicitly configured as the last statement in an ACL.

It is sometimes advantageous to reset the matched counters when testing an ACL. The counters can be cleared using the **clear access-list counters** privileged EXEC command. This command can be used alone or with the number or name of a specific ACL.

In Example 7-20, the counters for ACL 1 are reset.

**Example 7-20** Clearing ACL Statistics

```
R1# show access-lists
Standard IP access list 1
    10 deny   192.168.10.10 (8 match(es))
    20 permit 192.168.0.0, wildcard bits 0.0.255.255
Standard IP access list NO_ACCESS
    15 deny   192.168.11.11
    10 deny   192.168.11.10 (4 match(es))
    20 permit 192.168.11.0, wildcard bits 0.0.0.255
R1#
R1# clear access-list counters 1
R1#
R1# show access-lists
Standard IP access list 1
    10 deny   192.168.10.10
    20 permit 192.168.0.0, wildcard bits 0.0.255.255
Standard IP access list NO_ACCESS
    15 deny   192.168.11.11
    10 deny   192.168.11.10 (4 match(es))
    20 permit 192.168.11.0, wildcard bits 0.0.0.255
```

**Lab 7.2.2.6: Configuring and Modifying Standard IPv4 ACLs**

In this lab, you complete the following objectives:

- Part 1: Set Up the Topology and Initialize Devices
- Part 2: Configure Devices and Verify Connectivity
- Part 3: Configure and Verify Standard Numbered and Named ACLs
- Part 4: Modify a Standard ACL

# Securing VTY Ports with a Standard IPv4 ACL (7.2.3)

In this topic, you configure a standard ACL to secure vty access.

## The access-class Command (7.2.3.1)

You can improve the security of administrative lines by restricting VTY access. Restricting VTY access is a technique that allows you to define which IP addresses are allowed remote access to the router EXEC process. Use this technique with SSH to further improve administrative access security.

You can specify which IP addresses are allowed remote access to your router with an ACL. However, instead of using the **ip access-group** interface command, use the **access-class** line vty configuration command to apply the ACL to the VTY lines. The **access-class** command configured in line configuration mode restricts incoming and outgoing connections between a particular VTY (into a Cisco device) and the addresses in an access list.

The following is the command syntax of the **access-class** command:

```
Router(config-line)# access-class access-list-number {in | out}
```

The parameter **in** restricts incoming connections between the addresses in the access list and the Cisco device, whereas the parameter **out** restricts outgoing connections between a particular Cisco device and the addresses in the access list.

Consider the topology in Figure 7-13.

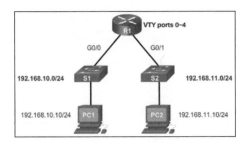

**Figure 7-13**   Applying an ACL to Restrict VTY Access

In Example 7-21, only hosts on network 192.168.10.0/24 are allowed SSH access to the VTY lines. Hosts from any other network are denied SSH access.

**Example 7-21** ACL VTY Configuration

```
R1(config)# access-list 21 permit 192.168.10.0 0.0.0.255
R1(config)# access-list 21 deny any
R1(config)#
R1(config)# line vty 0 4
R1(config-line)# login local
R1(config-line)# transport input ssh
R1(config-line)# access-class 21 in
R1(config-line)# exit
R1(config)#
```

The following should be considered when configuring access lists on VTYs:

- Both named and numbered access lists can be applied to VTYs.

- Identical restrictions should be set on all the VTYs because a user can attempt to connect to any of them.

**Note**

Access lists apply to packets that travel through a router. They are not designed to block packets that originate within the router. By default, an outbound ACL does not prevent remote access connections initiated from the router.

## Verifying the VTY Port Is Secured (7.2.3.2)

After the ACL to restrict access to the VTY lines is configured, it is important to verify that it is working as expected. Example 7-22 shows PC1 successfully accessing R1 using SSH.

**Example 7-22**  Allowed PC Verification

```
PC1> ssh 192.168.10.1

Login as: admin
Password: *****
R1>
```

Example 7-23 shows PC2 unsuccessfully attempting to access R1 using SSH.

**Example 7-23**  Denied PC Verification

```
PC2> ssh 192.168.11.1
ssh connect to host 192.168.11.1 port 22: Connection refused

PC2>
```

Examples 7-22 and 7-23 show the expected behavior, as the configured access list permits VTY access from the 192.168.10.0/24 network while denying all other devices.

The output in Example 7-24 for R1 shows the result of issuing the **show access-lists** command after the SSH attempts by PC1 and PC2.

**Example 7-24** Verifying ACL Statistics for VTY ACL

```
R1# show access-lists
Standard IP access list 21
    10 permit 192.168.10.0, wildcard bits 0.0.0.255 (2 matches)
    20 deny   any (1 match)
R1#
```

The match in the permit line of the output is a result of a successful SSH connection by PC1. The match in the deny statement is due to the failed attempt to create an SSH connection by PC2, a device on the 192.168.11.0/24 network.

**Packet Tracer 7.2.3.3: Configuring an IPv4 ACL on VTY Lines**

As the administrator of a network, you need to have remote access to your router. This access should not be available to other users of the network. Therefore, you will configure and apply an ACL that allows PC access to the Telnet lines but denies all other source IPv4 addresses.

**Lab 7.2.3.4: Configuring and Verifying VTY Restrictions**

In this lab, you complete the following objectives:

- Part 1: Configure Basic Device Settings
- Part 2: Configure and Apply the Access Control List on R1
- Part 3: Verify the Access Control List Using Telnet
- Part 4: Challenge—Configure and Apply the Access Control List on S1

# Troubleshoot ACLs (7.3)

Implementing ACLs correctly requires attention to detail because even a slight mistake can have disastrous results. It is imperative that you develop strong troubleshooting skills. Troubleshooting is a sought-after skill that is acquired through practice and experience.

In this section, you troubleshoot IPv4 ACL issues.

## Processing Packets with ACLs (7.3.1)

In this topic, you learn how a router processes packets when an ACL is applied.

## The Implicit Deny Any (7.3.1.1)

A single-entry ACL with only one deny entry has the effect of denying all traffic. At least one permit ACE must be configured in an ACL, or all traffic is blocked.

Consider the topology in Figure 7-14.

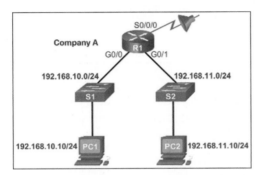

**Figure 7-14** ACL Configuration Topology

In Example 7-25, ACL 1 is using the implicit **deny any**, whereas ACL 2 is explicitly configured with the **deny any** statement.

**Example 7-25** Comparing Implicit and Explicit Deny ACLs

```
R1(config)# access-list 1 permit ip 192.168.10.0 0.0.0.255
R1(config)#
R1(config)# access-list 2 permit ip 192.168.10.0 0.0.0.255
R1(config)# access-list 2 deny any
R1(config)#
```

Applying either ACL 1 or ACL 2 to the S0/0/0 interface of R1 in the outbound direction has the same effect. Network 192.168.10.0 is permitted to access the networks reachable through S0/0/0, whereas 192.168.11.0 is not allowed to access those networks. In ACL 1, if a packet does not match the permit statement, it is discarded.

## The Order of ACEs in an ACL (7.3.1.2)

Cisco IOS applies an internal logic when accepting and processing standard ACEs. As discussed previously, ACEs are processed sequentially; therefore, the order in which ACEs are entered is important.

In Example 7-26, ACL 3 contains two ACEs. The first ACE uses a wildcard mask to deny a range of addresses, which includes all hosts in the 192.168.10.0/24 network.

The second ACE is a host statement that examines a specific host, 192.168.10.10, that belongs to the 192.168.10.0/24 network.

**Example 7-26** Host Statement Conflicts with Range Statement

```
R1(config)# access-list 3 deny 192.168.10.0 0.0.0.255
R1(config)# access-list 3 permit host 192.168.10.10
% Access rule can't be configured at higher sequence num as it is part of the
  existing rule at sequence num 10
R1(config)#
```

Notice how the IOS internal logic for standard access lists rejects the second statement and returns an error message because it is a subset of the previous statement.

The configuration in Example 7-27 of ACL 4 has the same two statements but in reverse order. This is a valid sequence of statements because the first statement refers to a specific host, not a range of hosts.

**Example 7-27** Host Statement Entered Before Range Statement

```
R1(config)# access-list 4 permit host 192.168.10.10
R1(config)# access-list 4 deny 192.168.10.0 0.0.0.255
R1(config)#
```

In Example 7-28, ACL 5 shows that a host statement can be configured after a statement that denotes a range of hosts. The host must not be within the range covered by a previous statement. The 192.168.11.10 host address is not a member of the 192.168.10.0/24 network, so this is a valid statement.

**Example 7-28** Host That Is Not Part of Range Configured After Range Statement

```
R1(config)# access-list 5 deny 192.168.10.0 0.0.0.255
R1(config)# access-list 5 permit host 192.168.11.10
R1(config)#
```

## Cisco IOS Reorders Standard ACLs (7.3.1.3)

The order in which standard ACEs are entered may not be the order that they are stored, displayed, or processed by the router.

Example 7-29 shows the configuration of a standard access list. Range statements that deny three networks are configured first, followed by five host statements. All the host statements are valid because their host IPv4 addresses are not part of the previously entered range statements.

**Example 7-29**  Configuring a Standard ACL

```
R1(config)# access-list 1 deny 192.168.10.0 0.0.0.255
R1(config)# access-list 1 deny 192.168.20.0 0.0.0.255
R1(config)# access-list 1 deny 192.168.30.0 0.0.0.255
R1(config)# access-list 1 permit 10.0.0.1
R1(config)# access-list 1 permit 10.0.0.2
R1(config)# access-list 1 permit 10.0.0.3
R1(config)# access-list 1 permit 10.0.0.4
R1(config)# access-list 1 permit 10.0.0.5
R1(config)# end
R1#
```

In Example 7-30, the **show running-config** command is used to verify the ACL configuration.

**Example 7-30**  Verifying ACL on R1

```
R1# show running-config | include access-list 1
access-list 1 permit 10.0.0.2
access-list 1 permit 10.0.0.3
access-list 1 permit 10.0.0.1
access-list 1 permit 10.0.0.4
access-list 1 permit 10.0.0.5
access-list 1 deny   192.168.10.0 0.0.0.255
access-list 1 deny   192.168.20.0 0.0.0.255
access-list 1 deny   192.168.30.0 0.0.0.255
R1#
```

Notice that the statements are listed in a different order than they were entered. The **show access-lists** command will be used to demonstrate the logic behind this.

In Example 7-31, the **show access-lists** command displays ACEs along with their sequence numbers.

**Example 7-31** Cisco IOS Changes Sequence Numbers After Reload

```
R1# show access-lists 1
Standard IP access list 1
    50 permit 10.0.0.2
    60 permit 10.0.0.3
    40 permit 10.0.0.1
    70 permit 10.0.0.4
    80 permit 10.0.0.5
    10 deny    192.168.10.0, wildcard bits 0.0.0.255
    20 deny    192.168.20.0, wildcard bits 0.0.0.255
    30 deny    192.168.30.0, wildcard bits 0.0.0.255
R1#
```

You might expect the order of the statements in the output to reflect the order in which they were entered. However, the **show access-lists** output shows that this is not the case.

The order in which the standard ACEs are listed is the sequence used by the IOS to process the list. Notice that the statements are grouped into two sections: host statements followed by range statements. The sequence number indicates the order that the statement was entered, not the order the statement will be processed.

The host statements are listed first, but not necessarily in the order that they were entered. The IOS puts host statements in an order using a special hashing function. The resulting order optimizes the search for a host ACL entry. The range statements are displayed after the host statements. These statements are listed in the order in which they were entered.

**Note**

The hashing function is applied only to host statements in an IPv4 standard access list. The details of the hashing function are beyond the scope of this course.

Recall that standard and numbered ACLs can be edited using sequence numbers. When inserting a new ACL statement, the sequence number affects only the location of a range statement in the list. Host statements are always put in order using the hashing function.

To reorder the sequence numbers correctly, the router configuration must be saved and the device rebooted.

In Example 7-32, R1 had its configuration saved and was rebooted. The output of the **show access-lists** command displays the sequence numbers in numerical order.

**Example 7-32**  Cisco IOS Changes Sequence Numbers After Reload

```
R1# show access-lists 1
Standard IP access list 1
    10 permit 10.0.0.2
    20 permit 10.0.0.3
    30 permit 10.0.0.1
    40 permit 10.0.0.4
    50 permit 10.0.0.5
    60 deny   192.168.10.0, wildcard bits 0.0.0.255
    70 deny   192.168.20.0, wildcard bits 0.0.0.255
    80 deny   192.168.30.0, wildcard bits 0.0.0.255
R1#
```

## Routing Processes and ACLs (7.3.1.4)

Figure 7-15 shows the logic of routing and ACL processes.

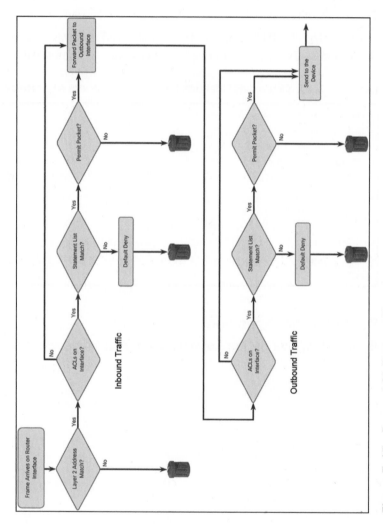

**Figure 7-15** Router ACL Process Flowchart

When a packet arrives at a router interface, the router process is the same, whether ACLs are used or not. As a frame enters an interface, the router checks to see whether the destination Layer 2 address matches its interface Layer 2 address, or whether the frame is a broadcast frame.

If the frame address is accepted, the frame information is stripped off and the router checks for an ACL on the inbound interface. If an ACL exists, the packet is tested against the statements in the list.

If the packet matches a statement, the packet is either permitted or denied. If the packet is accepted, it is then checked against routing table entries to determine the destination interface. If a routing table entry exists for the destination, the packet is then switched to the outgoing interface; otherwise, the packet is dropped.

Next, the router checks whether the outgoing interface has an ACL. If an ACL exists, the packet is tested against the statements in the list.

If the packet matches a statement, it is either permitted or denied.

If there is no ACL or the packet is permitted, the packet is encapsulated in the new Layer 2 protocol and forwarded out the interface to the next device.

## Common IPv4 Standard ACL Errors (7.3.2)

In this topic, you learn how to troubleshoot common standard IPv4 ACL errors using CLI commands.

### Troubleshooting Standard IPv4 ACLs—Example 1 (7.3.2.1)

The topology in Figure 7-16 will be used for the troubleshooting examples in this topic.

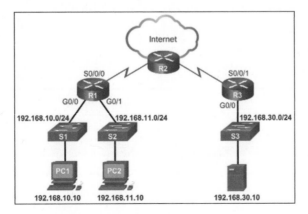

**Figure 7-16**   ACL Troubleshooting Topology

Using the **show** commands described earlier reveals most of the more common ACL errors. The most common errors are entering ACEs in the wrong order and not specifying adequate ACL rules. Other common errors include applying the ACL using the wrong direction, the wrong interface, or the wrong source addresses.

**Security Policy:** PC2 should not be able to access the file server.

Although PC2 cannot access the file server, neither can PC1. When viewing the output of the **show access-list** command in Example 7-33, only PC2 is explicitly denied.

**Example 7-33** Locate Example 1 Issue

```
R3# show access-list
Standard IP access list 10
    10 deny   192.168.11.10
R3#
```

However, there is no **permit** statement allowing other access.

**Solution:** All access out the G0/0 interface to the 192.168.30.0/24 LAN is currently implicitly denied. Add a statement to ACL 10 to permit all other traffic, as shown in Example 7-34.

**Example 7-34** Resolve Example 1 Issue

```
R3(config)# access-list 10 permit any
R3(config)# end
R3#
```

PC1 should now be able to access the file server. In Example 7-35, output from the **show access-list** command verifies that a ping from PC1 to the file server matches the **permit any** statement.

**Example 7-35** Verify Example 1

```
R3# show access-list
Standard IP access list 10
    10 deny   192.168.11.10
    20 permit any (4 match(es))
R3#
```

PC1 should now be able to access the file server. Output from the **show access-list** command verifies that a ping from PC1 to the file server matches the **permit any** statement.

## Troubleshooting Standard IPv4 ACLs—Example 2 (7.3.2.2)

**Security Policy:** The 192.168.11.0/24 network should not be able to access the 192.168.10.0/24 network.

PC2 cannot access PC1. Nor can it access the Internet through R2. In Example 7-36, the output of the **show access-list** command displays that packets are matching the **deny** statement.

**Example 7-36** Locate Example 2 Issue

```
R1# show access-list
Standard IP access list 20
    10 deny    192.168.11.0, wildcard bits 0.0.0.255 (8 match(es))
    20 permit any
R1#
```

ACL 20 seems to be configured correctly. You suspect that it must be incorrectly applied and view the interface configurations for R1. In Example 7-37, the output of the **show run** command is displayed.

**Example 7-37** Verify Interface Configuration

```
R1# show run | section interface
interface GigabitEthernet0/0
ip address 192.168.10.1 255.255.255.0
duplex auto
speed auto
interface GigabitEthernet0/1
ip address 192.168.11.1 255.255.255.0
ip access-group 20 in
duplex auto
speed auto

<output omitted>
```

The output reveals that ACL 20 was applied to the wrong interface and in the wrong direction. All traffic from the 192.168.11.0/24 is denied inbound access through the G0/1 interface.

**Solution:** To correct this error, remove ACL 20 from the G0/1 interface and apply it outbound on the G0/0 interface, as shown in Example 7-38.

**Example 7-38**  Resolve Example 2 Issue

```
R1(config)# interface g0/1
R1(config-if)# no ip access-group 20 in
R1(config-if)# exit
R1(config)#
R1(config)# interface g0/0
R1(config-if)# ip access-group 20 out
```

PC2 cannot access PC1 but can now access the Internet.

## Troubleshooting Standard IPv4 ACLs—Example 3 (7.3.2.3)

**Security Policy:** Only PC1 is allowed remote access to R1 using SSH.

PC1 is unable to remotely access R1 using an SSH connection.

In Example 7-39, the running configuration section for the VTY lines reveals that an ACL named PC1-SSH is correctly applied for inbound connections. The VTY lines are correctly configured to only allow SSH connections.

**Example 7-39**  Locate Example 3 Issue

```
R1# show run | section line vty
line vty 0 4
 access-class PC1-SSH in
 login
 transport input ssh
R1#
```

In Example 7-40, the output of the **show access-list** command is displayed.

**Example 7-40**  Locate and Resolve Example 3 Issue

```
R1# show access-list
Standard IP access list PC1-SSH
    10 permit 192.168.10.1
    20 deny   any (5 match(es))
R1#
```

Notice that the IPv4 address is the G0/0 interface for R1, not the IPv4 address of PC1. Also, notice that the administrator configured an explicit **deny any** statement in the ACL. This is helpful because, in this situation, you will see matches for failed attempts to remotely access R1.

**Solution:** Example 7-41 shows the process for correcting the error.

**Example 7-41** Resolve Example 3 Issue

```
R1(config)# ip access-list standard PC1-SSH
R1(config-std-nacl)# no 10
R1(config-std-nacl)# 10 permit host 192.168.10.10
R1(config-std-nacl)# end
R1#
R1# clear access-list counters
R1#
R1# show access-list
Standard IP access list PC1-SSH
    10 permit 192.168.10.10 (2 match(es))
    20 deny    any
R1#
```

Because the statement that needs to be corrected is the first one, you use the sequence number 10 to delete it by entering **no 10**. You then configure the correct IPv4 address for PC1. The **clear access-list counters** command resets the output to show only new matches. An attempt from PC2 to remotely access R1 is successful, as shown in the output for the **show access-list** command.

**Packet Tracer 7.3.2.4: Troubleshooting Standard IPv4 ACLs**

Scenario

Create a network that has the following three policies implemented:

- Hosts from the 192.168.0.0/24 network are unable to access any TCP service of Server3.

- Hosts from the 10.0.0.0/8 network are unable to access the HTTP service of Server1.

- Hosts from the 172.16.0.0/16 network are unable to access the FTP service of Server2.

**Lab 7.3.2.5: Troubleshooting Standard IPv4 ACL Configuration and Placement**

In this lab, you complete the following objectives:

- Part 1: Build the Network and Configure Basic Device Settings
- Part 2: Troubleshoot Internal Access
- Part 3: Troubleshoot Remote Access

# Summary (7.4)

**Class Activity 7.4.1.1: FTP Denied**

Scenario

It was recently reported that viruses are on the rise within your small- to medium-sized business network. Your network administrator has been tracking network performance and has determined that one particular host is constantly downloading files from a remote FTP server. This host may be the virus source perpetuating throughout the network.

Use Packet Tracer to complete this activity. Write a named ACL to deny the host access to the FTP server. Apply the ACL to the most effective interface on the router.

To complete the physical topology, you must use the following:

- One PC host station
- Two switches
- One Cisco 1941 series Integrated Services Router
- One server

Using the Packet Tracer text tool, record the ACL you prepared. Validate that the ACL works to deny access to the FTP server by trying to access the FTP server's address. Observe what happens while in simulation mode.

Save your file and be prepared to share it with another student or with the entire class.

**Packet Tracer 7.4.1.2: Skills Integration Challenge**

In this challenge activity, you finish the addressing scheme, configure routing, and implement named ACLs.

By default, a router does not filter traffic. Traffic that enters the router is routed solely based on information within the routing table.

Packet filtering controls access to a network by analyzing the incoming and outgoing packets and passing or dropping them based on criteria such as the source IP address, the destination IP addresses, and the protocol carried within the packet. A packet-filtering router uses rules to determine whether to permit or deny traffic. A router can also perform packet filtering at Layer 4, the transport layer.

An ACL is a sequential list of permit or deny statements. The last statement of an ACL is always an implicit deny, which blocks all traffic. To prevent the implied **deny any** statement at the end of the ACL from blocking all traffic, the **permit any** statement can be added.

When network traffic passes through an interface configured with an ACL, the router compares the information within the packet against each entry, in sequential order, to determine whether the packet matches one of the statements. If a match is found, the packet is processed accordingly.

ACLs are configured to apply to inbound traffic or to apply to outbound traffic.

Standard ACLs can be used to permit or deny traffic only from source IPv4 addresses. The destination of the packet and the ports involved are not evaluated. The basic rule for placing a standard ACL is to put it close to the destination.

Extended ACLs filter packets based on several attributes: protocol type, source or destination IPv4 address, and source or destination ports. The basic rule for placing an extended ACL is to put it as close to the source as possible.

The **access-list** global configuration command defines a standard ACL with a number in the range of 1 to 99. The **ip access-list standard** *name* is used to create a standard named ACL.

After an ACL is configured, it is linked to an interface using the **ip access-group** command in interface configuration mode. Remember these rules: one ACL per protocol, one ACL per direction, one ACL per interface.

To remove an ACL from an interface, first enter the **no ip access-group** command on the interface, and then enter the global **no access-list** command to remove the entire ACL.

The **show running-config** and **show access-lists** commands are used to verify ACL configuration. The **show ip interface** command is used to verify the ACL on the interface and the direction in which it was applied.

The **access-class** command configured in line configuration mode restricts incoming and outgoing connections between a particular VTY and the addresses in an access list.

## Practice

The following activities provide practice with the topics introduced in this chapter. The class, Lab, and Packet Tracer Activities are available in the companion *Routing and Switching Essentials v6 Labs & Study Guide* (ISBN 9781587134265). The Packet Tracer Activities PKA files are found in the online course.

**Class Activities**

Class Activity 7.0.1.2: Permit Me to Assist You

Class Activity 7.4.1.1: FTP Denied

**Labs**

Lab 7.2.2.6: Configuring and Modifying Standard IPv4 ACLs

Lab 7.2.3.4: Configuring and Verifying VTY Restrictions

Lab 7.3.2.5: Troubleshooting Standard IPv4 ACL Configuration and Placement

**Packet Tracer Activities**

Packet Tracer 7.1.1.4: ACL Demonstration

Packet Tracer 7.2.1.6: Packet Tracer Configuring Numbered Standard IPv4 ACLs

Packet Tracer 7.2.1.7: Configuring Named Standard IPv4 ACLs

Packet Tracer 7.2.3.3: Configuring an IPv4 ACL on VTY Lines

Packet Tracer 7.3.2.4: Troubleshooting Standard IPv4 ACLs

Packet Tracer 7.4.1.2: Skills Integration Challenge

# Check Your Understanding Questions

Complete all the review questions listed here to test your understanding of the topics and concepts in this chapter. The appendix "Answers to the 'Check Your Understanding' Questions" lists the answers.

1. Which three statements describe ACL processing of packets? (Choose three.)

    A. A packet can either be rejected or forwarded as directed by the ACE that is matched.

    B. A packet that does not match the conditions of any ACE will be forwarded by default.

    C. A packet that has been denied by one ACE can be permitted by a subsequent ACE.

    D. An implicit **deny any** rejects any packet that does not match any ACE.

E. Each packet is compared to the conditions of every ACE in the ACL before a forwarding decision is made.

F. Each statement is checked only until a match is detected or until the end of the ACE list.

2. What two functions describe uses of an access control list? (Choose two.)

A. ACLs assist the router in determining the best path to a destination.

B. ACLs can control which areas a host can access on a network.

C. ACLs can permit or deny traffic based upon the MAC address originating on the router.

D. ACLs provide a basic level of security for network access.

E. Standard ACLs can restrict access to specific applications and ports.

3. In which configuration would an outbound ACL placement be preferred over an inbound ACL placement?

A. When a router has more than one ACL

B. When an interface is filtered by an outbound ACL and the network attached to the interface is the source network being filtered within the ACL

C. When an outbound ACL is closer to the source of the traffic flow

D. When the ACL is applied to an outbound interface to filter packets coming from multiple inbound interfaces before the packets exit the interface

4. A network administrator needs to configure a standard ACL so that only the workstation of the administrator with the IP address 192.168.15.23 can access the virtual terminal of the main router. Which two configuration commands can achieve the task? (Choose two.)

A. R1(config)# access-list 10 permit 192.168.15.23 0.0.0.0

B. R1(config)# access-list 10 permit 192.168.15.23 0.0.0.255

C. R1(config)# access-list 10 permit 192.168.15.23 255.255.255.0

D. R1(config)# access-list 10 permit 192.168.15.23 255.255.255.255

E. R1(config)# access-list 10 permit host 192.168.15.23

5. What single access-list statement matches networks 192.168.16.0, 192.168.17.0, 192.168.18.0, and 192.168.19.0.

A. access-list 10 permit 192.168.0.0 0.0.15.255

B. access-list 10 permit 192.168.16.0 0.0.0.255

C. access-list 10 permit 192.168.16.0 0.0.3.255

D. access-list 10 permit 192.168.16.0 0.0.15.255

6. If a router has two interfaces and is routing both IPv4 and IPv6 traffic, how many ACLs could be created and applied to it?

    A.  4

    B.  6

    C.  8

    D.  12

    E.  16

7. Which three statements are generally considered to be best practices in the placement of ACLs? (Choose three.)

    A.  Filter unwanted traffic before it travels onto a low-bandwidth link.

    B.  For every inbound ACL placed on an interface, there should be a matching outbound ACL.

    C.  Place extended ACLs close to the destination IP address of the traffic.

    D.  Place extended ACLs close to the source IP address of the traffic.

    E.  Place standard ACLs close to the source IP address of the traffic.

    F.  Place standard ACLs close to the destination IP address of the traffic.

8. An administrator has configured an access list on R1 to allow SSH administrative access from host 172.16.1.100. Which command correctly applies the ACL?

    A.  R1(config-line)# **access-class 1 in**

    B.  R1(config-line)# access-class 1 out

    C.  R1(config-if)# ip access-group 1 in

    D.  R1(config-if)# ip access-group 1 out

9. Which statement describes a difference between the operation of inbound and outbound ACLs?

    A.  On a network interface, more than one inbound ACL can be configured, but only one outbound ACL can be configured.

    B.  Inbound ACLs are processed before the packets are routed, whereas outbound ACLs are processed after the routing is completed.

    C.  Inbound ACLs can be used in both routers and switches, but outbound ACLs can be used only on routers.

    D.  In contrast to outbound ALCs, inbound ACLs can be used to filter packets with multiple criteria.

# CHAPTER 8

# DHCP

## Objectives

Upon completion of this chapter, you will be able to answer the following questions:

- How does DHCPv4 operate in a small- to medium-sized business network?

- How do you configure a router as a DHCPv4 server?

- How do you configure a router as a DHCPv4 client?

- How do you troubleshoot a DHCP configuration for IPv4 in a switched network?

- Can you explain the operation of DHCPv6?

- How do you configure stateless DHCPv6 for a small-to medium-sized business?

- How do you configure stateful DHCPv6 for a small-to medium-sized business?

- How do you troubleshoot a DHCP configuration for IPv6 in a switched network?

## Key Terms

This chapter uses the following key terms. You can find the definitions in the Glossary.

# Introduction (8.0.1.1)

Every device that connects to a network needs a unique IP address. Network administrators assign static IP addresses to routers, servers, printers, and other network devices whose locations (physical and logical) are not likely to change. These are usually devices that provide services to users and devices on the network; therefore, the addresses assigned to them should remain constant. Additionally, static addresses enable administrators to manage these devices remotely. It is easier for network administrators to access a device when they can easily determine its IP address.

However, computers and users in an organization often change locations, physically and logically. It can be difficult and time consuming for administrators to assign new IP addresses every time an employee moves. Additionally, for mobile employees working from remote locations, manually setting the correct network parameters can be challenging. Even for desktop clients, the manual assignment of IP addresses and other addressing information presents an administrative burden, especially as the network grows.

Introducing a *DHCP* server to the local network simplifies IP address assignment to both desktop and mobile devices. Using a centralized DHCP server enables organizations to administer all dynamic IP address assignments from a single server. This practice makes IP address management more effective and ensures consistency across the organization, including branch offices.

DHCP is available for both IPv4 (*DHCPv4*) and for IPv6 (*DHCPv6*). This chapter explores the functionality, configuration, and troubleshooting of both DHCPv4 and DHCPv6.

# DHCPv4 (8.1)

All hosts in a network require an IP configuration. Although some devices will have their IP configuration statically assigned, most devices will use DHCP to acquire a valid IP configuration. Therefore, DHCP is a vital feature that must be managed and carefully implemented.

In this section, you learn how to implement DHCPv4 to operate across multiple LANs in a small-to medium-sized business network.

## DHCPv4 Operation (8.1.1)

In this topic, you learn how DHCPv4 operates in a small- to medium-sized business network.

## Introducing DHCPv4 (8.1.1.1)

DHCPv4 assigns IPv4 addresses and other network configuration information dynamically. As shown in Figure 8-1, the client requests an IP configuration from a DHCP server. The server replies and negotiates an IP configuration with the DHCP client.

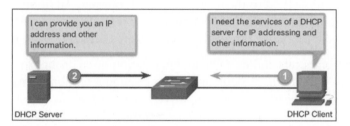

**Figure 8-1**   DHCP Overview

Because desktop clients typically make up the bulk of network nodes, DHCPv4 is an extremely useful and timesaving tool for network administrators. DHCP is scalable and relatively easy to manage.

Most organizations have dedicated DHCPv4 servers deployed. However, Cisco IOS software supports an optional, full-featured DHCPv4 server. In a small branch or SOHO location, a Cisco router can be configured to provide DHCPv4 services. This provides a cost saving because there is no need for a dedicated server.

The DHCPv4 server dynamically assigns, or leases, an IPv4 address from a pool of addresses for a limited period of time chosen by the server, or until the client no longer needs the address.

Clients *lease* the information from the server for an administratively defined period. Administrators configure DHCPv4 servers to set the leases to time out at different intervals. The lease is typically anywhere from 24 hours to a week or more. When the lease expires, the client must ask for another address, although the client is typically reassigned the same address.

## DHCPv4 Operation (8.1.1.2)

DHCPv4 works in a client/server mode. When a client communicates with a DHCPv4 server, the server assigns or leases an IPv4 address to that client. The client connects to the network with that leased IP address until the lease expires. The client must contact the DHCP server periodically to extend the lease. This lease mechanism ensures that clients that move or power off do not keep addresses that they no longer need. When a lease expires, the DHCP server returns the address to the pool where it can be reallocated as necessary.

## Lease Origination

Figure 8-2 illustrates the DHCPv4 lease operation process.

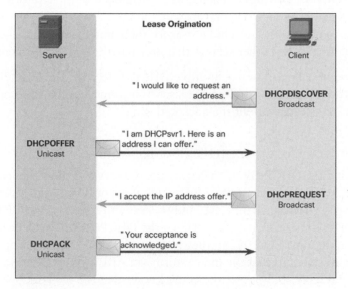

**Figure 8-2**   DCHPv4 Operation—Lease Origination

When the client boots (or otherwise wants to join a network), it begins a four-step process to obtain a lease. A client starts the process with a broadcast *DHCPDISCOVER message* that has its own MAC address to discover available DHCPv4 servers.

### DHCP Discover (DHCPDISCOVER)

The DHCPDISCOVER message finds DHCPv4 servers on the network. Because the client has no valid IPv4 information at bootup, it uses Layer 2 and Layer 3 broadcast addresses to communicate with the server.

### DHCP Offer (DHCPOFFER)

When the DHCPv4 server receives a DHCPDISCOVER message, it reserves an available IPv4 address to lease to the client. The server also creates an Address Resolution Protocol (ARP) entry consisting of the MAC address of the requesting client and the leased IPv4 address of the client. The DHCPv4 server sends the binding *DHCPOFFER message* to the requesting client. The DHCPOFFER message is sent as a unicast, using the Layer 2 MAC address of the server as the source address and the Layer 2 MAC address of the client as the destination.

## DHCP Request (DHCPREQUEST)

When the client receives the DHCPOFFER from the server, it sends back a *DHCPREQUEST message*. This message is used for both lease origination and lease renewal. When used for lease origination, the DHCPREQUEST serves as a binding acceptance notice to the selected server for the parameters it has offered and an implicit decline to any other servers that may have provided the client a binding offer.

Many enterprise networks use multiple DHCPv4 servers. The DHCPREQUEST message is sent in the form of a broadcast to inform this DHCPv4 server and any other DHCPv4 servers about the accepted offer.

## DHCP Acknowledgment (DHCPACK)

On receiving the DHCPREQUEST message, the server verifies the lease information with an ICMP ping to that address to ensure it is not being used already, creates a new ARP entry for the client lease, and replies with a unicast *DHCPACK message*. The DHCPACK message is a duplicate of the DHCPOFFER, except for a change in the message type field. When the client receives the DHCPACK message, it logs the configuration information and performs an ARP lookup for the assigned address. If there is no reply to the ARP, the client knows that the IPv4 address is valid and starts using it as its own.

## Lease Renewal

Figure 8-3 illustrates the DHCPv4 lease renewal process.

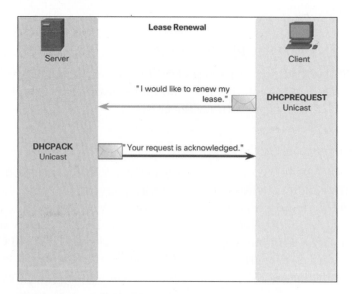

**Figure 8-3**  DCHPv4 Operation—Lease Renewal

## DHCP Request (DHCPREQUEST)

Before the lease expires, the client sends a DHCPREQUEST message directly to the DHCPv4 server that originally offered the IPv4 address. If a DHCPACK is not received within a specified amount of time, the client broadcasts another DHCPREQUEST so that one of the other DHCPv4 servers can extend the lease.

## DHCP Acknowledgment (DHCPACK)

On receiving the DHCPREQUEST message, the server verifies the lease information by returning a DHCPACK.

## DHCPv4 Message Format (8.1.1.3)

The DHCPv4 message format is used for all DHCPv4 transactions. DHCPv4 messages are encapsulated within the UDP transport protocol. DHCPv4 messages sent from the client use User Datagram Protocol (UDP) source port 68 and destination port 67. DHCPv4 messages sent from the server to the client use UDP source port 67 and destination port 68.

Figure 8-4 shows the format of a DHCPv4 message.

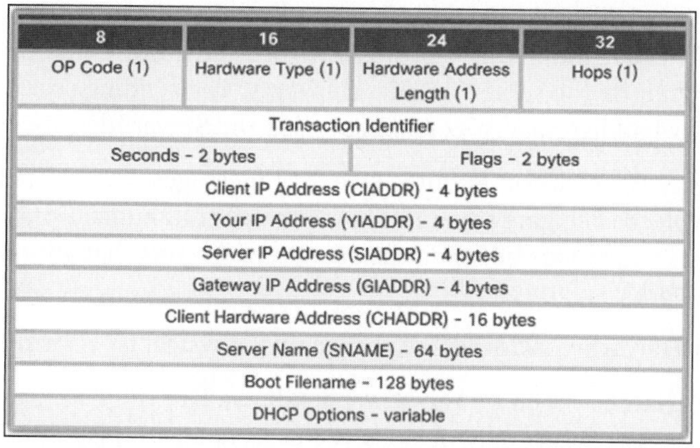

| 8 | 16 | 24 | 32 |
|---|---|---|---|
| OP Code (1) | Hardware Type (1) | Hardware Address Length (1) | Hops (1) |
| Transaction Identifier | | | |
| Seconds - 2 bytes | | Flags - 2 bytes | |
| Client IP Address (CIADDR) - 4 bytes | | | |
| Your IP Address (YIADDR) - 4 bytes | | | |
| Server IP Address (SIADDR) - 4 bytes | | | |
| Gateway IP Address (GIADDR) - 4 bytes | | | |
| Client Hardware Address (CHADDR) - 16 bytes | | | |
| Server Name (SNAME) - 64 bytes | | | |
| Boot Filename - 128 bytes | | | |
| DHCP Options - variable | | | |

**Figure 8-4**  DHCPv4 Message Format

The fields are as follows:

- **Operation (OP) Code**—Specifies the general type of message. A value of 1 indicates a request message; a value of 2 is a reply message.

- **Hardware Type**—Identifies the type of hardware used in the network. For example, 1 is Ethernet, 15 is Frame Relay, and 20 is a serial line. These are the same codes used in ARP messages.

- **Hardware Address Length**—Specifies the length of the address.

- **Hops**—Controls the forwarding of messages. Set to 0 by a client before transmitting a request.

- **Transaction Identifier**—Used by the client to match the request with replies received from DHCPv4 servers.

- **Seconds**—Identifies the number of seconds elapsed since a client began attempting to acquire or renew a lease. Used by DHCPv4 servers to prioritize replies when multiple client requests are outstanding.

- **Flags**—Used by a client that does not know its IPv4 address when it sends a request. Only one of the 16 bits—the broadcast flag—is used. A value of 1 in this field tells the DHCPv4 server or relay agent receiving the request that the reply should be sent as a broadcast.

- **Client IP Address**—Used by a client during lease renewal when the address of the client is valid and usable, not during the process of acquiring an address. The client puts its own IPv4 address in this field only if it has a valid IPv4 address while in the bound state; otherwise, it sets the field to 0.

- **Your IP Address**—Used by the server to assign an IPv4 address to the client.

- **Server IP Address**—Used by the server to identify the address of the server that the client should use for the next step in the bootstrap process, which may or may not be the server sending this reply. The sending server always includes its own IPv4 address in a special field called the Server Identifier DHCPv4 option.

- **Gateway IP Address**—Routes DHCPv4 messages when DHCPv4 relay agents are involved. The gateway address facilitates communications of DHCPv4 requests and replies between the client and a server that are on different subnets or networks.

- **Client Hardware Address**—Specifies the physical layer of the client.

- **Server Name**—Used by the server sending a DHCPOFFER or DHCPACK message. The server may optionally put its name in this field. This can be a simple text nickname or a Domain Name System (DNS) domain name, such as dhcpserver.netacad.net.

- **Boot Filename**—Optionally used by a client to request a particular type of boot file in a DHCPDISCOVER message. Used by a server in a DHCPOFFER to fully specify a boot file directory and filename.

- *DHCP Options*—Holds DHCP options, including several parameters required for basic DHCP operation. This field is variable in length. Both client and server may use this field.

## DHCPv4 Discover and Offer Messages (8.1.1.4)

If a client is configured to receive its IPv4 settings dynamically and wants to join the network, it requests addressing values from the DHCPv4 server. The client transmits a DHCPDISCOVER message on its local network when it boots or senses an active network connection. Because the client has no way of knowing the subnet to which it belongs, the DHCPDISCOVER message is an IPv4 broadcast (destination IPv4 address of 255.255.255.255). The client does not have a configured IPv4 address yet, so the source IPv4 address of 0.0.0.0 is used.

As shown in Figure 8-5, the *client IPv4 address (CIADDR)*, *default gateway address (GIADDR)*, and subnet mask are all marked to indicate that the address 0.0.0.0 is used.

**Note**

Unknown information is sent as 0.0.0.0.

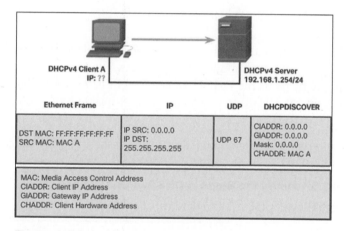

**Figure 8-5** DHCPv4 Discover Message

The DHCP client sends an IP broadcast with a DHCPDISCOVER packet. In this example, the DHCP server is on the same segment and will pick up this request. The server notes the GIADDR field is blank; therefore, the client is on the same segment. The server also notes the hardware address of the client in the request packet.

When the DHCPv4 server receives the DHCPDISCOVER message, it responds with a DHCPOFFER message. This message contains initial configuration information for the client, including the IPv4 address that the server offers, the subnet mask, the lease duration, and the IPv4 address of the DHCPv4 server making the offer.

The DHCPOFFER message can be configured to include other information, such as the lease renewal time and DNS address.

As shown in Figure 8-6, the DHCP server responds to the DHCPDISCOVER by assigning values to the CIADDR and subnet mask. The frame is constructed using the client hardware address (CHADDR) and sent to the requesting client.

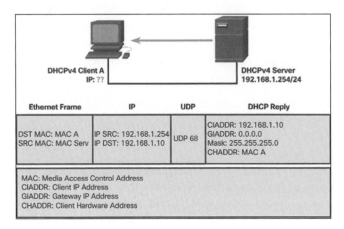

**Figure 8-6**   DHCPv4 Offer Message

The DHCP server picks an IP address from the available pool for that segment, as well as the other segment and global parameters. The DHCP server puts them into the appropriate fields of the DHCP packet. The DHCP server then uses the hardware address of A (in CHADDR) to construct an appropriate frame to send back to the client.

The client and server send acknowledgment messages, and the process is complete.

Interactive
Graphic

**Activity 8.1.1.5: Identify the Steps in DHCPv4 Operation**

Refer to the online course to complete this activity.

# Configuring a Basic DHCPv4 Server (8.1.2)

In this topic, you will learn how to configure a router as a DHCPv4 server.

### Configuring a Basic DHCPv4 Server (8.1.2.1)

A Cisco router running Cisco IOS software can be configured to provide DHCPv4 server services. The Cisco IOS DHCPv4 server assigns and manages IPv4 addresses from specified address pools within the router to DHCPv4 clients. The topology shown in Figure 8-7 is used to illustrate this functionality.

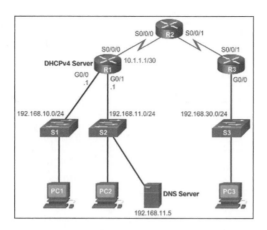

**Figure 8-7** DHCPv4 Configuration Topology

## Step 1. Excluding IPv4 Addresses

The router functioning as the DHCPv4 server assigns all IPv4 addresses in a DHCPv4 address pool unless configured to exclude specific addresses. Typically, some IPv4 addresses in a pool are assigned to network devices that require static address assignments. Therefore, these IPv4 addresses should not be assigned to other devices. Excluded addresses should include the addresses assigned to routers, servers, printers, and other devices that have been or will be manually configured.

To exclude specific addresses, use the **ip dhcp excluded-address** *low-address* [*high-address*] global configuration command. A single address or a range of addresses can be excluded by specifying the low address and high address of the range.

## Step 2. Configuring a DHCPv4 Pool

Configuring a DHCPv4 server involves defining a pool of addresses to assign. DHCP specifics are configured in DHCP configuration mode. Use the **ip dhcp pool** *pool-name* command to create a pool with the specified name and enter DHCPv4 configuration mode.

## Step 3. Configuring DHCP Specifics

Table 8-1 lists some of the DHCPv4 configuration commands. The **network** and **default-router** commands are typically configured. Most other commands are optionally configured depending on the network's specific DHCP requirements.

**Table 8-1**   DHCPv4 Server Command Syntax

| Command | Description |
| --- | --- |
| network *network-number* [mask | /*prefix-length*] | Define the address pool. |
| default-router *address* [*address2...address8*] | Define the default router or gateway. |
| dns-server *address* [*address2...address8*] | (Optional) Define a DNS server. |
| domain-name *domain* | (Optional) Define the domain name. |
| lease {*days* [*hours*] [*minutes*] | infinite} | (Optional) Define the duration of the DHCP lease. |
| netbios-name-server *address* [*address2...address8*] | (Optional) Legacy command to define a NetBIOS WINS server. |

The address pool and default gateway router must be configured. Use the **network** statement to define the range of available addresses.

Use the **default-router** command to define the default gateway router. Typically, the gateway is the LAN interface of the router closest to the client devices. One gateway is required, but you can list up to eight addresses if there are multiple gateways.

Other DHCPv4 pool commands are optional. For example, the IPv4 address of the DNS server that is available to a DHCPv4 client is configured using the **dns-server** command. The **domain-name** *domain* command defines the domain name. The duration of the DHCPv4 lease can be changed using the **lease** command. The default lease value is one day.

> **Note**
>
> Other DHCP command options are available but are beyond the scope of this chapter.

## DHCPv4 Example

A sample configuration with basic DHCPv4 parameters configured on router R1 is shown in Example 8-1. R1 is configured as a DHCPv4 server for the 192.168.10.0/24 and 192.168.11.0/24 LANs using the example topology from Figure 8-7.

**Example 8-1**  R1 DHCPv4 Server Configuration

```
R1(config)# ip dhcp excluded-address 192.168.10.1 192.168.10.9
R1(config)# ip dhcp excluded-address 192.168.10.254
R1(config)#
R1(config)# ip dhcp pool LAN-POOL-1
R1(dhcp-config)# network 192.168.10.0 255.255.255.0
R1(dhcp-config)# default-router 192.168.10.1
R1(dhcp-config)# dns-server 192.168.11.5
R1(dhcp-config)# domain-name example.com
R1(dhcp-config)# exit
R1(config)#
R1(config)# ip dhcp excluded-address 192.168.11.1 192.168.11.9
R1(config)# ip dhcp excluded-address 192.168.11.254
R1(config)#
R1(config)# ip dhcp pool LAN-POOL-2
R1(dhcp-config)# network 192.168.11.0 255.255.255.0
R1(dhcp-config)# default-router 192.168.11.1
R1(dhcp-config)# dns-server 192.168.11.5
R1(dhcp-config)# domain-name example.com
R1(dhcp-config)# end
R1#
```

## Disabling DHCPv4

The DHCPv4 service is enabled by default. To disable the service, use the **no service dhcp** global configuration mode command. Use the **service dhcp** global configuration mode command to re-enable the DHCPv4 server process. Enabling the service has no effect if the parameters are not configured.

## Verifying DHCPv4 (8.1.2.2)

Refer to Figure 8-7, in which R1 has been configured to provide DHCPv4 services. As shown in Example 8-2, the **show running-config | section dhcp** command output displays the DHCPv4 commands configured on R1. Notice how the **| section dhcp** command filter is useful because it only displays the commands associated with the DHCPv4 configuration.

For example, Figure 8-10 shows the default WAN setup page for a packet tracer wireless router.

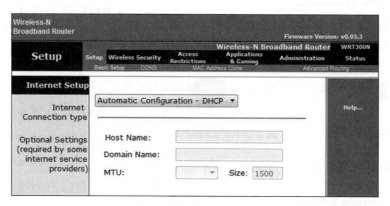

**Figure 8-10**    Wireless Router DHCPv4 Client Configuration

Notice that the Internet connection type is set to Automatic Configuration—DHCP. This selection is used when the router is connected to a DSL or cable modem and acts as a DHCPv4 client, requesting an IPv4 address from the ISP.

**Packet Tracer 8.1.3.3: Configuring DHCPv4 Using Cisco IOS**

A dedicated DHCP server is scalable and relatively easy to manage, but sometimes it is not cost effective. For example, in a small branch or SOHO location, a Cisco router can be configured to provide DHCPv4 services without the need for a dedicated server. Cisco IOS software supports an optional, full-featured DHCPv4 server. The DHCPv4 server leases configurations for 24 hours by default. As the network technician for your company, you are tasked with configuring a Cisco router as a DHCP server to provide dynamic allocation of addresses to clients on the network. You are also required to configure the edge router as a DHCP client so that it receives an IP address from the ISP network.

# Troubleshoot DHCPv4 (8.1.4)

In this topic, you learn how to troubleshoot a DHCP configuration for IPv4 in a switched network.

## Troubleshooting Tasks (8.1.4.1)

DHCPv4 problems can arise for a variety of reasons, such as software defects in operating systems, NIC drivers, or DHCP relay agents. However, the most common problems are related to configuration issues.

Because of the number of potentially problematic areas, a systematic approach to troubleshooting is required. The troubleshooting tasks are as follows:

1. Resolve conflicts.

2. Verify physical connectivity.

3. Test with a static IPv4 address.

4. Verify switch port configuration.

5. Test from the same subnet or VLAN.

## Troubleshooting Task 1: Resolve IPv4 Address Conflicts

An IPv4 address lease can expire on a client still connected to a network. If the client does not renew the lease, the DHCPv4 server can reassign that IPv4 address to another client. When the client reboots, it requests an IPv4 address. If the DHCPv4 server does not respond quickly, the client uses the last IPv4 address. The situation then arises in which two clients are using the same IPv4 address, creating a conflict.

The **show ip dhcp conflict** command displays all address conflicts recorded by the DHCPv4 server, as shown in Example 8-10.

**Example 8-10** Viewing DHCPv4 Conflicts

```
R1# show ip dhcp conflict
IP address Detection Method Detection time
192.168.10.32 Ping Feb 16 2013 12:28 PM
192.168.10.64 Gratuitous ARP Feb 23 2013 08:12 AM
```

This output displays IP addresses that have conflicts with the DHCP server. It shows the detection method and detection time for conflicting IP addresses that the DHCP server has offered.

When an address conflict is detected, the address is removed from the pool and not assigned until an administrator resolves the conflict.

## Troubleshooting Task 2: Verify Physical Connectivity

First, use the **show interfaces** *interface* command to confirm that the router interface acting as the default gateway for the client is operational. If the state of the interface is anything other than up, the port does not pass traffic, including DHCP client requests.

## Troubleshooting Task 3: Test Connectivity Using a Static IP Address

When troubleshooting any DHCPv4 issue, verify network connectivity by configuring static IPv4 address information on a client workstation. If the workstation is unable to reach network resources with a statically configured IPv4 address, the root cause of the problem is not DHCPv4, and the next step is to troubleshoot network connectivity.

## Troubleshooting Task 4: Verify Switch Port Configuration

If the DHCPv4 client is unable to obtain an IPv4 address from the DHCPv4 server on startup, attempt to obtain an IPv4 address from the DHCPv4 server by manually releasing and renewing the client to send a DHCPv4 request.

> **Note**
>
> If there is a switch between the client and the DHCPv4 server, and the client is unable to obtain the DHCP configuration, switch port configuration issues may be the cause.

## Troubleshooting Task 5: Test DHCPv4 Operation on the Same Subnet or VLAN

It is important to distinguish whether DHCPv4 is functioning correctly when the client is on the same subnet or VLAN as the DHCPv4 server. If DHCPv4 is working correctly when the client is on the same subnet or VLAN, the problem may be the DHCP relay agent. If the problem persists even with testing DHCPv4 on the same subnet or VLAN as the DHCPv4 server, the problem may actually be with the DHCPv4 server.

### Verify Router DHCPv4 Configuration (8.1.4.2)

When the DHCPv4 server is located on a separate LAN from the client, the router interface facing the client must be configured to relay DHCPv4 requests by configuring the IPv4 helper address. If the IPv4 helper address is not configured properly, client DHCPv4 requests are not forwarded to the DHCPv4 server.

Follow these steps to verify the router configuration:

**Step 1.** Verify that the **ip helper-address** command is configured on the correct interface. It must be present on the inbound interface of the LAN containing the DHCPv4 client workstations and must be directed to the correct DHCPv4 server. In Example 8-11, the output of the **show running-config** command verifies that the DHCPv4 relay IPv4 address is referencing the DHCPv4 server address at 192.168.11.6 and that the DHCP service has not been disabled on the router.

**Example 8-11** Verifying DHCPv4 Services

```
R1# show running-config interface GigabitEthernet0/0
interface GigabitEthernet0/0
 ip address 192.168.10.1 255.255.255.0
 ip helper-address 192.168.11.6
 duplex auto
 speed auto
R1#
R1# show running-config | include no service dhcp
R1#
```

The **show ip interface** command can also be used to verify the DHCPv4 relay on an interface.

Step 2.    Verify that the global configuration command **no service dhcp** has not been configured. This command disables all DHCP server and relay functionality on the router. The command **service dhcp** does not appear in the running-config because it is the default configuration.

Example 8-12 verifies whether DHCP services has been disabled.

**Example 8-12** Verifying DHCPv4 Services

```
R1# show running-config | include no service dhcp
R1#
```

The output verifies that the DHCPv4 service is enabled because there is no match for the **show running-config | include no service dhcp** command. If the service had been disabled, the **no service dhcp** command would be displayed in the output.

## Debugging DHCPv4 (8.1.4.3)

On routers configured as DHCPv4 servers, the DHCPv4 process fails if the router is not receiving requests from the client. To troubleshoot, verify that the router is receiving the DHCPv4 request from the client.

A good method to verify DHCP message exchanges between the router and clients involves configuring an extended ACL for debugging output and then enabling debugging of all IP packets that match the ACL.

In Example 8-13, an extended ACL is configured, and then debugging of IP packets matching the ACL is enabled.

**Example 8-13** Debugging DHCP Messages

```
R1(config)# access-list 100 permit udp any any eq 67
R1(config)# access-list 100 permit udp any any eq 68
R1(config)# end
R1#
R1# debug ip packet 100
IP packet debugging is on for access list 100
*IP: s=0.0.0.0 (GigabitEthernet0/1), d=255.255.255.255, len 333, rcvd 2
*IP: s=0.0.0.0 (GigabitEthernet0/1), d=255.255.255.255, len 333, stop process pak
  for forus packet
*IP: s=192.168.11.1 (local), d=255.255.255.255 (GigabitEthernet0/1), len 328,
  sending broad/multicast

<output omitted>
```

The extended ACL permits only packets with UDP destination ports of 67 or 68. These are the typical ports used by DHCPv4 clients and servers when sending DHCPv4 messages. The extended ACL is used with the **debug ip packet** command to display only DHCPv4 messages.

**Note**

Extended ACLs are beyond the scope of this course.

The output verifies that the router is receiving DHCP requests from the client. The source IP address is 0.0.0.0 because the client does not yet have an IP address. The destination is 255.255.255.255 because the DHCP discovery message from the client is sent as a broadcast. This output shows only a summary of the packet and not the DHCPv4 message itself. Nevertheless, the router did receive a broadcast packet with the source and destination IP and UDP ports that are correct for DHCPv4. The complete **debug** output shows all the packets in the DHCPv4 communications between the DHCPv4 server and client.

Another useful command for troubleshooting DHCPv4 operation is the **debug ip dhcp server events** command shown in Example 8-14.

**Example 8-14** Debugging DHCP Messages

```
R1# debug ip dhcp server events
DHCPD: returned 192.168.10.11 to address pool LAN-POOL-1
DHCPD: assigned IP address 192.168.10.12 to client 0100.0103.85e9.87.
DHCPD: checking for expired leases.
DHCPD: the lease for address 192.168.10.10 has expired.
DHCPD: returned 192.168.10.10 to address pool LAN-POOL-1
```

This command reports server events, such as address assignments and database updates.

**Lab 8.1.4.4: Troubleshooting DHCPv4**

In this lab, you complete the following objectives:

- Part 1: Build the Network and Configure Basic Device Settings
- Part 2: Troubleshoot DHCPv4 Issues

# DHCPv6 (8.2)

In IPv6, there are three ways a host can acquire its IPv6 configuration. By default, a host automatically generates its IPv6 configuration from an IPv6 enabled router. This is accomplished without the use of a DHCPv6 server. The other two methods require a DHCPv6 server. The second method is for the host to get its basic IPv6 configuration from an IPv6-enabled router and additional configuration information from a stateless DHCPv6 server. The third option is for a host to get its entire IPv6 configuration from a stateful DHCPv6 server.

In this section, you learn how to implement DHCPv6 to operate across multiple LANs in a small-to medium-sized business network.

## SLAAC and DHCPv6 (8.2.1)

In this topic, you learn about the operation of DHCPv6.

### Stateless Address Autoconfiguration (SLAAC) (8.2.1.1)

Similar to IPv4, IPv6 global unicast addresses can be configured manually or dynamically. As shown in Table 8-2, there are three methods in which IPv6 global unicast addresses can be assigned dynamically.

**Table 8-2**   Dynamic IPv6 Host Configuration Methods

| Option | Dynamic Method | Description |
|--------|----------------|-------------|
| 1 | SLAAC | The default method is enabled. |
| | | A host automatically obtains its IP configuration from an IPv6-enabled router using *stateless address autoconfiguration (SLAAC)*. |
| | | The host generates its own unique IPv6 address. |
| | | A DHCPv6 server is not required. |

| Option | Dynamic Method | Description |
|---|---|---|
| 2 | SLAAC and Stateless DHCPv6 | A host obtains some IP configuration information using SLAAC and additional information from a *stateless DHCPv6 server*. |
| | | The host generates its own unique IPv6 address. |
| 3 | *Stateful DHCPv6* | A host only obtains the default gateway from the router. |
| | | A host gets all remaining IPv6 configuration from a *stateful DHCPv6 server*. |
| | | The host is provided with a global unicast IPv6 address. |

## Introducing SLAAC

As illustrated in Figure 8-11, SLAAC is a method in which a host can obtain an IPv6 global unicast address without the services of a DHCPv6 server.

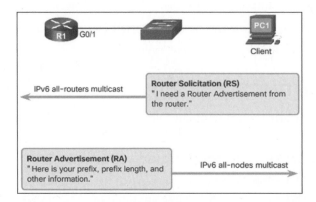

**Figure 8-11**    Obtaining an IPv6 Configuration Using SLAAC

At the core of SLAAC is *Internet Control Message Protocol version 6 (ICMPv6)*. ICMPv6 is similar to ICMPv4 but includes additional functionality and is a much more robust protocol.

SLAAC uses the following ICMPv6 messages to provide addressing information:

- *Router solicitation (RS) message*—When a client is configured to obtain its addressing information automatically using SLAAC, the client sends an RS message to the router. The RS message is sent to the IPv6 all-routers multicast address FF02::2.

■ *Router advertisement (RA) message*—RA messages are sent by routers to provide addressing information to clients configured to obtain their IPv6 addresses automatically. The RA message includes the prefix and prefix-length of the local segment. A client uses this information to create its own IPv6 global unicast address. A router sends an RA message periodically or in response to an RS message. By default, Cisco routers send RA messages every 200 seconds. RA messages are always sent to the IPv6 all-nodes multicast address FF02::1.

As the name indicates, SLAAC is stateless. A stateless service means there is no server that maintains network address information. Unlike DHCP, there is no SLAAC server that knows which IPv6 addresses are being used and which ones are available.

## SLAAC Operation (8.2.1.2)

A router must have IPv6 routing enabled before it can send RA messages. Use the **ipv6 unicast-routing** global configuration command to enable IPv6 routing.

Figure 8-12 illustrates how SLAAC operates.

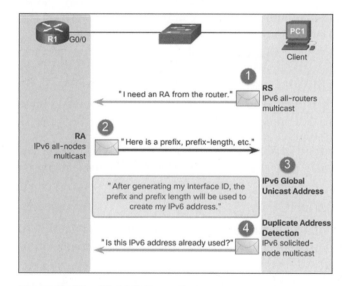

**Figure 8-12**   SLAAC Operation

1. PC1 is configured to obtain IPv6 address information automatically. Since booting, PC1 has not received an RA message, so it sends an RS message to the all-routers multicast address (FF02::2) to inform the local IPv6 router that it needs an RA.

2. R1 receives the RS message and responds with an RA message. Included in the RA message are the prefix and prefix-length of the network. The RA message is

sent to the IPv6 all-nodes multicast address FF02::1, with the link-local address of the router as the IPv6 source address.

3.  PC1 receives the RA message containing the prefix and the prefix-length for the local network. PC1 uses this information to create its own IPv6 global unicast address. PC1 now has a 64-bit network prefix but needs a 64-bit *interface ID (IID)* to create a global unicast address.

    PC1 can create its own unique IID in two ways:

    ○ *EUI-64*—Using the EUI-64 process, PC1 creates an IID using its 48-bit MAC address.

    ○ **Randomly generated**—The 64-bit IID can be a random number that the client operating system generates.

    PC1 can create a 128-bit IPv6 global unicast address by combining the 64-bit prefix with the 64-bit ID. PC1 uses the link-local address of the router as its IPv6 default gateway address.

4.  Because SLAAC is a stateless process, PC1 must verify that this newly created IPv6 address is unique before it can be used. PC1 sends an ICMPv6 *neighbor solicitation (NS) message* with a specially constructed multicast address, called a *solicited-node multicast address*, which duplicates the last 24 bits of PC1's IPv6 address. If no other devices respond with a *neighbor advertisement (NA) message*, then the address is virtually guaranteed to be unique and can be used by PC1. If PC1 receives an NA, the address is not unique and the operating system has to determine a new IID to use.

This process is part of ICMPv6 Neighbor Discovery and is known as *duplicate address detection (DAD)*. DAD specified by RFC 4443 is implemented using ICMPv6.

## SLAAC and DHCPv6 (8.2.1.3)

The decision of whether a client is configured to obtain its IPv6 address information automatically using only SLAAC, only DHCPv6, or a combination of both depends on the settings within the RA message.

The two flags are the *Managed Address Configuration flag (M flag)* and the *Other Configuration flag (O flag)*.

Using different combinations of the M and O flags, RA messages have one of three addressing options for the IPv6 device, as shown in Figure 8-13:

■  SLAAC (Router Advertisement only)

■  Stateless DHCPv6 (Router Advertisement and DHCPv6)

■  Stateful DHCPv6 (DHCPv6 only)

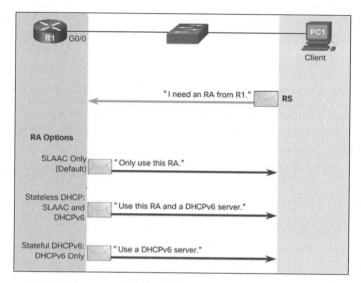

**Figure 8-13**    SLAAC and DHCPv6

Regardless of the option used, RFC 4861 states that IPv6 devices perform DAD.

Although the RA message specifies the process the client should use in obtaining an IPv6 address dynamically, the client operating system may choose to ignore the RA message and use the services of a DHCPv6 server exclusively.

## SLAAC Option (8.2.1.4)

SLAAC is the default option on Cisco routers. Both the M flag and the O flag are set to 0 in the RA, as shown in Figure 8-14.

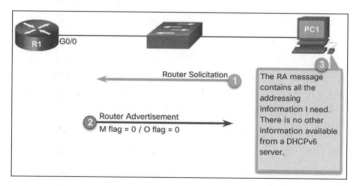

**Figure 8-14**    SLAAC Option

This option instructs the client to use the information in the RA message exclusively. This includes prefix, prefix-length, DNS server, MTU, and default gateway information. There is no further information available from a DHCPv6 server. The IPv6 global unicast address is created by combining the prefix from RA and an Interface ID using either EUI-64 or a randomly generated value.

RA messages are configured on an individual interface of a router. To re-enable an interface for SLAAC that might have been set to another option, the M and O flags need to be reset to their initial values of 0. To do so, use the **no ipv6 nd managed-config-flag** and **ipv6 nd other-config-flag** interface configuration mode commands.

## Stateless DHCPv6 Option (8.2.1.5)

Although DHCPv6 is similar to DHCPv4 in what it provides, the two protocols are independent of each other. DHCPv6 is defined in RFC 3315. There has been a lot of work done on this specification over the years, as indicated by the fact that DHCPv6 RFC has the highest revision number of any Internet draft.

The stateless DHCPv6 option is illustrated in Figure 8-15.

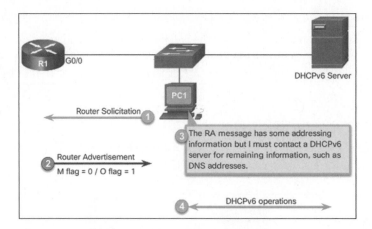

**Figure 8-15**   Stateless DHCPv6 Option

The stateless DHCPv6 option informs the client to use the information in the RA message for addressing, but additional configuration parameters are available from a stateless DHCPv6 server.

Using the prefix and prefix-length in the RA message, along with EUI-64 or a randomly generated IID, the client creates its IPv6 global unicast address.

The client then communicates with a stateless DHCPv6 server to obtain additional information not provided in the RA message. This may be a list of DNS server IPv6 addresses, for example. This process is known as stateless DHCPv6 because the server is not maintaining any client state information (i.e., a list of available and allocated IPv6 addresses). The stateless DHCPv6 server is only providing configuration parameters for clients, not IPv6 addresses.

For stateless DHCPv6, the O flag is set to 1 and the M flag is left at the default setting of 0. The O flag value of 1 is used to inform the client that additional configuration information is available from a stateless DHCPv6 server.

To modify the RA message sent on the interface of a router to indicate stateless DHCPv6, use the **ipv6 nd other-config-flag** interface configuration command.

## Stateful DHCPv6 Option (8.2.1.6)

The stateful DHCPv6 option, illustrated in Figure 8-16, is the most similar to DHCPv4.

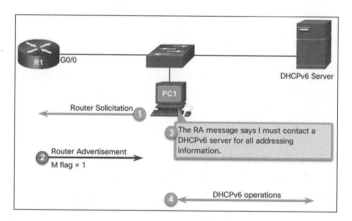

**Figure 8-16**   Stateful DHCPv6 Option

In stateful DHCPv6, the RA message informs the client not to use the information in the RA message. All addressing information and configuration information must be obtained from a stateful DHCPv6 server. This is known as stateful DHCPv6 because the DHCPv6 server maintains IPv6 state information. This is similar to a DHCPv4 server allocating addresses for IPv4.

The M flag indicates whether or not to use stateful DHCPv6. The O flag is not involved.

To signify stateful DHCPv6 and change the M flag from 0 to 1, use the **ipv6 nd managed-config-flag** interface configuration command.

## DHCPv6 Operations (8.2.1.7)

A summary of DHCPv6 operation is illustrated in Figure 8-17.

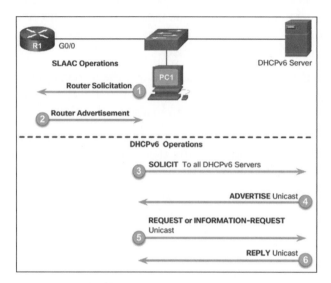

**Figure 8-17**    DHCPv6 Operations

Stateless or stateful DHCPv6, or both, begin with an ICMPv6 RA message from the router. The RA message might have been a periodic message or solicited by the device using an RS message.

If stateless or stateful DHCPv6 is indicated in the RA message, the device begins DHCPv6 client/server communications.

When stateless DHCPv6 or stateful DHCPv6 is indicated by the RA, DHCPv6 operation is invoked. DHCPv6 messages are sent over UDP. DHCPv6 messages from the server to the client use UDP destination port 546. The client sends DHCPv6 messages to the server using UDP destination port 547.

The client, now a DHCPv6 client, needs to locate a DHCPv6 server. The client sends a *DHCPv6 SOLICIT message* to the reserved IPv6 multicast all-DHCPv6-servers address FF02::1:2. This multicast address has link-local scope, which means routers do not forward the messages to other networks.

One or more DHCPv6 servers respond with a *DHCPv6 ADVERTISE unicast message*. The ADVERTISE message informs the DHCPv6 client that the server is available for DHCPv6 service.

The client responds with a *DHCPv6 REQUEST* message or a *DHCPv6 INFORMATION-REQUEST* unicast message to the server, depending on whether it is using stateful or stateless DHCPv6.

- *Stateless DHCPv6 client*—The client sends a DHCPv6 INFORMATION-REQUEST message to the DHCPv6 server requesting only configuration parameters, such as DNS server addresses. The client generated its own IPv6 address using the prefix from the RA message and a self-generated interface ID.

- *Stateful DHCPv6 client*—The client sends a DHCPv6 REQUEST message to the server to obtain an IPv6 address and all other configuration parameters from the server.

The server sends a ***DHCPv6 REPLY unicast message*** to the client containing the information requested in the DHCPv6 REQUEST or DHCPv6 INFORMATION-REQUEST message.

**Interactive Graphic**

**Activity 8.2.1.8: Identify the Steps in DHCPv6 Operation**

Refer to the online course to complete this activity.

# Stateless DHCPv6 (8.2.2)

In this topic, you learn how to configure stateless DHCPv6 for a small-to medium-sized business.

### Configuring a Router as a Stateless DHCPv6 Server (8.2.2.1)

There are four steps to configure a router as a DHCPv6 server:

**Step 1.**    **Enable IPv6 Routing.** The **ipv6 unicast-routing** command is required to enable IPv6 routing. This command is not necessary for the router to be a stateless DHCPv6 server, but it is required for the router to source ICMPv6 RA messages.

**Step 2.**    **Configure a DHCPv6 Pool.** The **ipv6 dhcp pool** *pool-name* command creates a pool and enters the router in DHCPv6 configuration mode, which is identified by the Router(config-dhcpv6)# prompt.

**Step 3.**    **Configure Pool Parameters.** During the SLAAC process, the client received the information it needed to create an IPv6 global unicast address. The client also received the default gateway information using the source IPv6 address from the RA message, which is the link-local address of the router. However, the stateless DHCPv6 server can be configured to provide other information that might not have been included in the RA message.

To include a DNS server address, use the **dns-server** *dns-server-address* DHCPv6 configuration mode command.

To include a domain name, use the **domain-name** *domain-name* DHCPv6 configuration mode command.

Step 4.   **Configure the DHCPv6 Interface.** The **ipv6 dhcp server** *pool-name* interface configuration mode command binds the DHCPv6 pool to the interface. The router responds to stateless DHCPv6 requests on this interface with the information contained in the pool.

The O flag needs to be changed from 0 to 1 using the **ipv6 nd other-config-flag** interface configuration command. RA messages sent on this interface indicate that additional information is available from a stateless DHCPv6 server.

Consider the topology in Figure 8-18.

**Figure 8-18**   Stateless DHCPv6 Server Topology

R1 needs to be configured as a stateless DHCPv6 server. R3 is configured as a DHCPv6 client to help verify the stateless DHCPv6 operations.

In Example 8-15, R1 is configured as a stateless DHCPv6 server.

**Example 8-15**   Stateless DHCPv6 Server Configuration on R1

```
R1(config)# ipv6 unicast-routing
R1(config)#
R1(config)# ipv6 dhcp pool IPV6-STATELESS
R1(config-dhcpv6)# dns-server 2001:db8:cafe:aaaa::5
R1(config-dhcpv6)# domain-name example.com
R1(config-dhcpv6)# exit
R1(config)#
R1(config)# interface g0/1
R1(config-if)# ipv6 address 2001:db8:cafe:1::1/64
R1(config-if)# ipv6 dhcp server IPV6-STATELESS
R1(config-if)# ipv6 nd other-config-flag
R1(config-if)#
```

## Configuring a Router as a Stateless DHCPv6 Client (8.2.2.2)

In Example 8-16, a Cisco router is used as the stateless DHCPv6 client. This is not a typical scenario and is used for demonstration purposes only. Typically, a stateless DHCPv6 client is a device, such as a computer, tablet, mobile device, or webcam.

**Example 8-16** Stateless DHCPv6 Client Configuration on R3

```
R3(config)# interface g0/1
R3(config-if)# ipv6 enable
R3(config-if)# ipv6 address autoconfig
R3(config-if)#
```

The client router needs an IPv6 link-local address on the interface to send and receive IPv6 messages, such as RS messages and DHCPv6 messages. The link-local address of a router is created automatically when IPv6 is enabled on the interface. This can happen when a global unicast address is configured on the interface or by using the **ipv6 enable** command. After the router receives a link-local address, it can participate in IPv6 neighbor discovery.

In this example, the **ipv6 enable** command is used because the router does not yet have a global unicast address.

The **ipv6 address autoconfig** command enables automatic configuration of IPv6 addressing using SLAAC. By assumption, the server router is configured for stateless DHCPv6, so it sends an RA message to inform the client router to use stateless DHCPv6 to obtain DNS information.

## Verifying Stateless DHCPv6 (8.2.2.3)

In Example 8-17, the **show ipv6 dhcp pool** command verifies the name of the DHCPv6 pool and its parameters.

**Example 8-17** Stateless DHCPv6 Server Verification

```
R1# show ipv6 dhcp pool
DHCPv6 pool: IPV6-STATELESS
  DNS server: 2001:DB8:CAFE:AAAA::5
  Domain name: example.com
  Active clients: 0
R1#
```

Notice how the number of active clients is 0. This is because the server is not maintaining a state.

The **show running-config** command can also be used to verify all the commands that were previously configured.

In Example 8-18, the **show ipv6 interface** command on R3 confirms that the interface has "Stateless address autoconfig enabled" and has an IPv6 global unicast address. The IPv6 global unicast address was created using SLAAC, which includes the prefix contained in the RA message. The IID was generated using EUI-64. DHCPv6 was not used to assign the IPv6 address.

**Example 8-18** Stateless DHCPv6 Client Verification

```
R3# show ipv6 interface g0/1
GigabitEthernet0/1 is up, line protocol is up
  IPv6 is enabled, link-local address is FE80::32F7:DFF:FE25:2DE1
  No Virtual link-local address(es):
  Stateless address autoconfig enabled
  Global unicast address(es):
    2001:DB8:CAFE:1:32F7:DFF:FE25:2DE1, subnet is 2001:DB8:CAFE:1::/64 [EUI/CAL/
      PRE]
      valid lifetime 2591935 preferred lifetime 604735
  Joined group address(es):
    FF02::1
    FF02::1:FF25:2DE1
  MTU is 1500 bytes
  ICMP error messages limited to one every 100 milliseconds
  ICMP redirects are enabled
  ICMP unreachables are sent
  ND DAD is enabled, number of DAD attempts: 1
  ND reachable time is 30000 milliseconds (using 30000)
  ND NS retransmit interval is 1000 milliseconds
  Default router is FE80::D68C:B5FF:FECE:A0C1 on GigabitEthernet0/1
R3#
```

The default router information is also from the RA message. This was the source IPv6 address of the packet that contained the RA message and the link-local address of the router.

The output from the **debug ipv6 dhcp detail** command in Example 8-19 shows the DHCPv6 messages exchanged between the client and the server.

**Example 8-19** Using Debug to View Stateless DHCPv6 Process

```
R3# debug ipv6 dhcp detail
    IPv6 DHCP debugging is on (detailed)
R3#
*Feb  3 02:39:10.454: IPv6 DHCP: Sending INFORMATION-REQUEST to FF02::1:2 on
  GigabitEthernet0/1
*Feb  3 02:39:10.454: IPv6 DHCP: detailed packet contents
*Feb  3 02:39:10.454:   src FE80::32F7:DFF:FE25:2DE1
*Feb  3 02:39:10.454:   dst FF02::1:2 (GigabitEthernet0/1)
*Feb  3 02:39:10.454:   type INFORMATION-REQUEST(11), xid 12541745
<output omitted>
```

```
*Feb  3 02:39:10.454: IPv6 DHCP: Adding server FE80::D68C:B5FF:FECE:A0C1
*Feb  3 02:39:10.454: IPv6 DHCP: Processing options
*Feb  3 02:39:10.454: IPv6 DHCP: Configuring DNS server 2001:DB8:CAFE:AAAA::5
*Feb  3 02:39:10.454: IPv6 DHCP: Configuring domain name example.com
*Feb  3 02:39:10.454: IPv6 DHCP: DHCPv6 changes state from INFORMATION-REQUEST to
  IDLE (REPLY_RECEIVED) on GigabitEthernet0/1
```

In this example, the command has been entered on the client. The INFORMATION-REQUEST message is shown because it is sent from a stateless DHCPv6 client. Notice that the client, router R3, is sending the DHCPv6 messages from its link-local address to the All_DHCPv6_Relay_Agents_and_Servers address FF02::1:2.

The **debug** output displays all the DHCPv6 messages sent between the client and the server, including the DNS server and domain name options that were configured on the server.

## Stateful DHCPv6 Server (8.2.3)

In this topic, you learn how to configure stateful DHCPv6 for a small-to medium-sized business.

### Configuring a Router as a Stateful DHCPv6 Server (8.2.3.1)

Configuring a stateful DHCPv6 server is similar to configuring a stateless server. The most significant difference is that a stateful server also includes IPv6 addressing information similar to a DHCPv4 server.

Step 1.    **Enable IPv6 Routing.** As shown in Figure 1, the **ipv6 unicast-routing** command is required to enable IPv6 routing. This command is not necessary for the router to be a stateful DHCPv6 server, but it is required for the router to source ICMPv6 RA messages.

Step 2.    **Configure a DHCPv6 Pool.** The **ipv6 dhcp pool** *pool-name* global configuration command creates a pool and enters the router in DHCPv6 configuration mode, which is identified by the Router(config-dhcpv6)# prompt.

Step 3.    **Configure Pool Parameters.** With stateful DHCPv6, the DHCPv6 server must assign all addressing and other configuration parameters.

Use the **address prefix** *prefix/length* [**lifetime** {*valid-lifetime* | **infinite**} {*preferred-lifetime* | **infinite**}] DHCPv6 configuration mode command to indicate the pool of addresses to be allocated by the server. The **lifetime** option indicates the valid and preferred lease times in seconds. As with stateless DHCPv6, the client uses the source IPv6 address from the packet containing the RA message.

Other information provided by the stateful DHCPv6 server typically includes the DNS server address and the domain name. To include a DNS server address, use the **dns-server** *dns-server-address* DHCPv6 configuration mode command. To include a domain name, use the **domain-name** *domain-name* DHCPv6 configuration mode command.

**Step 4.** **Interface Commands.** The **ipv6 dhcp server** *pool-name* interface command binds the DHCPv6 pool to the interface. The router responds to stateless DHCPv6 requests on this interface with the information contained in the pool. To change the M flag from 0 to 1, use the **ipv6 nd managed-config-flag** interface command. This informs the device not to use SLAAC but to obtain IPv6 addressing and all configuration parameters from a stateful DHCPv6 server.

Consider the topology in Figure 8-19.

**Figure 8-19**   Stateful DHCPv6 Server Topology

Example 8-20 shows a sample configuration of stateful DHCPv6 server commands for R1. Notice that a default gateway is not specified because the router automatically sends its own link-local address as the default gateway. Router R3 is configured as a client to help verify the stateful DHCPv6 operations.

**Example 8-20**  Stateful DHCPv6 Server Configuration on R1

```
R1(config)# ipv6 unicast-routing
R1(config)#
R1(config)# ipv6 dhcp pool IPV6-STATEFUL
R1(config-dhcpv6)# address prefix 2001:DB8:CAFE:1::/64 lifetime infinite infinite
R1(config-dhcpv6)# dns-server 2001:db8:cafe:aaaa::5
R1(config-dhcpv6)# domain-name example.com
R1(config-dhcpv6)# exit
R1(config)#
R1(config)# interface g0/1
R1(config-if)# ipv6 address 2001:db8:cafe:1::1/64
R1(config-if)# ipv6 dhcp server IPV6-STATEFUL
R1(config-if)# ipv6 nd managed-config-flag
R1(config-if)#
```

## Configuring a Router as a Stateful DHCPv6 Client (8.2.3.2)

As shown in Example 8-21, use the **ipv6 enable** interface configuration mode command to allow the router to receive a link-local address to send RS messages and participate in DHCPv6.

**Example 8-21** Stateful DHCPv6 Client Configuration on R3

```
R3(config)# interface g0/1
R3(config-if)# ipv6 enable
R3(config-if)# ipv6 address dhcp
R3(config-if)#
```

The **ipv6 address dhcp** interface configuration mode command enables the router to behave as a DHCPv6 client on this interface.

## Verifying Stateful DHCPv6 (8.2.3.3)

In Example 8-22, the **show ipv6 dhcp pool** command verifies the name of the DHCPv6 pool and its parameters. The number of active clients is 1, which reflects client R3 receiving its IPv6 global unicast address from this server.

**Example 8-22** Stateful DHCPv6 Server Verification on R1

```
R1# show ipv6 dhcp pool
DHCPv6 pool: IPV6-STATEFUL
  Address allocation prefix: 2001:DB8:CAFE:1::/64 valid 4294967295 preferred
    4294967295 (1 in use, 0 conflicts)
  DNS server: 2001:DB8:CAFE:AAAA::5
  Domain name: example.com
  Active clients: 1
R1#
R1# show ipv6 dhcp binding
Client: FE80::32F7:DFF:FE25:2DE1
  DUID: 0003000130F70D252DE0
  Username : unassigned
  IA NA: IA ID 0x00040001, T1 43200, T2 69120
    Address: 2001:DB8:CAFE:1:5844:47B2:2603:C171
            preferred lifetime INFINITY, , valid lifetime INFINITY,
R1#
```

The **show ipv6 dhcp binding** command in Example 8-22 displays the automatic binding between the link-local address of the client and the address that the server assigns. FE80::32F7:DFF:FE25:2DE1 is the link-local address of the client. In this example, this is the G0/1 interface of R3. This address is bound to the IPv6 global unicast address, 2001:DB8:CAFE:1:5844:47B2:2603:C171, which was assigned by R1, the DHCPv6 server. This information is maintained by a stateful DHCPv6 server and not by a stateless DHCPv6 server.

The output from the **show ipv6 interface** command shown in Example 8-23 verifies the IPv6 global unicast address on DHCPv6 client R3 that was assigned by the DHCPv6 server. The default router information is not from the DHCPv6 server, but it was determined by using the source IPv6 address from the RA message. Although the client does not use the information contained in the RA message, it is able to use the source IPv6 address for its default gateway information.

**Example 8-23** Stateful DHCPv6 Client Configuration on R3

```
R3# show ipv6 interface g0/1
GigabitEthernet0/1 is up, line protocol is up
  IPv6 is enabled, link-local address is FE80::32F7:DFF:FE25:2DE1
  No Virtual link-local address(es):
  Global unicast address(es):
    2001:DB8:CAFE:1:5844:47B2:2603:C171, subnet is 2001:DB8:CAFE:1:5844:47B2:
      2603:C171/128
  Joined group address(es):
    FF02::1
    FF02::1:FF03:C171
    FF02::1:FF25:2DE1
  MTU is 1500 bytes
  ICMP error messages limited to one every 100 milliseconds
  ICMP redirects are enabled
  ICMP unreachables are sent
  ND DAD is enabled, number of DAD attempts: 1
  ND reachable time is 30000 milliseconds (using 30000)
  ND NS retransmit interval is 1000 milliseconds
  Default router is FE80::D68C:B5FF:FECE:A0C1 on GigabitEthernet0/1
R3#
```

## Configuring a Router as a DHCPv6 Relay Agent (8.2.3.4)

If the DHCPv6 server is located on a different network than the client, the IPv6 router can be configured as a DHCPv6 relay agent. The configuration of a DHCPv6 relay agent is similar to the configuration of an IPv4 router as a DHCPv4 relay.

**Note**

Although the configuration of a DHCPv6 relay agent is similar to DHCPv4, IPv6 router or relay agents forward DHCPv6 messages slightly differently than DHCPv4 relays. The messages and the process are beyond the scope of this curriculum.

Figure 8-20 shows a sample topology in which a DHCPv6 server is located on the 2001:DB8:CAFE:1::/64 network. The network administrator wants to use this DHCPv6 server as a central, stateful DHCPv6 server to allocate IPv6 addresses to all clients. Therefore, clients on other networks such as PC1 on the 2001:DB8:CAFE:A::/64 network must communicate with the DHCPv6 server.

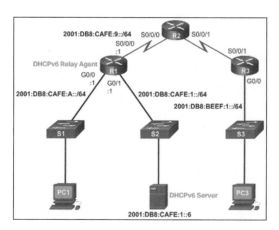

**Figure 8-20**   DHCPv6 Relay Agent Topology

DHCPv6 messages from clients are sent to the IPv6 multicast address FF02::1:2. All_DHCPv6_Relay_Agents_and_Servers address. This address has link-local scope, which means routers do not forward these messages. The router must be configured as a DHCPv6 relay agent to enable the DHCPv6 client and server to communicate.

As shown in Example 8-24, a DHCPv6 relay agent is configured using the **ipv6 dhcp relay destination** command. This command is configured on the interface facing the DHCPv6 client using the address of the DHCPv6 server as the destination.

**Example 8-24** DHCPv6 Relay Agent Configuration and Verification

```
R1(config)# interface g0/0
R1(config-if)# ipv6 dhcp relay destination 2001:db8:cafe:1::6
R1(config-if)# end
R1#
R1# show ipv6 dhcp interface g0/0
GigabitEthernet0/0 is in relay mode
  Relay destinations:
    2001:DB8:CAFE:1::6
R1#
```

The **show ipv6 dhcp interface** command verifies the G0/0 interface is in relay mode with 2001:DB8:CAFE:1::6 configured as the DHCPv6 server.

**Lab 8.2.3.5: Configuring Stateless and Stateful DHCPv6**

In this lab, you complete the following objectives:

- Part 1: Build the Network and Configure Basic Device Settings
- Part 2: Configure the Network for SLAAC
- Part 3: Configure the Network for Stateless DHCPv6
- Part 4: Configure the Network for Stateful DHCPv6

# Troubleshoot DHCPv6 (8.2.4)

In this topic, you learn how to troubleshoot a DHCP configuration for IPv6 in a switched network.

## Troubleshooting Tasks (8.2.4.1)

Troubleshooting DHCPv6 is similar to troubleshooting DHCPv4.

## Troubleshooting Task 1: Resolve Conflicts

Similar to IPv4 addresses, an IPv6 address lease can expire on a client that still needs to connect to the network. The **show ipv6 dhcp conflict** command displays any address conflicts logged by the stateful DHCPv6 server. If an IPv6 address conflict is detected, the client typically removes the address and generates a new one using either SLAAC or stateful DHCPv6.

## Troubleshooting Task 2: Verify Allocation Method

The **show ipv6 interface** *interface* command can verify the method of address allocation indicated in the RA message as indicated by the settings of the M and O flags. This information is displayed in the last lines of the output. If a client is not receiving its IPv6 address information from a stateful DHCPv6 server, it could be due to incorrect M and O flags in the RA message.

## Troubleshooting Task 3: Test with a Static IPv6 Address

When troubleshooting any DHCP issue, whether it is DHCPv4 or DHCPv6, network connectivity can be verified by configuring a static IP address on a client workstation. In the case of IPv6, if the workstation is unable to reach network resources with a statically configured IPv6 address, the root cause of the problem is not SLAAC or DHCPv6. At this point, network connectivity troubleshooting is required.

## Troubleshooting Task 4: Verify Switch Port Configuration

If the DHCPv6 client is unable to obtain information from a DHCPv6 server, verify that the switch port is enabled and is operating correctly.

---

**Note**

If there is a switch between the client and the DHCPv6 server, and the client is unable to obtain the DHCP configuration, switch port configuration issues may be the cause. These causes may include issues related to trunking, channeling, or spanning tree. PortFast and edge port configurations resolve the most common DHCPv6 client issues that occur with an initial installation of a Cisco switch.

---

## Troubleshooting Task 5: Test DHCPv6 Operation on the Same Subnet or VLAN

If the stateless or stateful DHCPv6 server is functioning correctly but is on a different IPv6 network or VLAN than the client, the problem may be with the DHCPv6 relay agent. The client-facing interface on the router must be configured with the **ipv6 dhcp relay destination** command.

### Verify Router DHCPv6 Configuration (8.2.4.2)

The router configurations for stateless and stateful DHCPv6 services have many similarities but also include significant differences.

### Stateless DHCPv6

Example 8-25 shows the configuration commands for a stateless DHCPv6 server.

**Example 8-25** Stateless DHCPv6 Server Configuration

```
R1(config)# ipv6 unicast-routing
R1(config)#
R1(config)# ipv6 dhcp pool IPV6-STATELESS
R1(config-dhcpv6)# dns-server 2001:db8:cafe:aaaa::5
R1(config-dhcpv6)# domain-name example.com
R1(config-dhcpv6)# exit
R1(config)#
R1(config)# interface g0/1
R1(config-if)# ipv6 address 2001:db8:cafe:1::1/64
R1(config-if)# ipv6 dhcp server IPV6-STATELESS
R1(config-if)# ipv6 nd other-config-flag
R1(config-if)#
```

For stateless DHCPv6 services, the **ipv6 nd other-config-flag** interface configuration mode command is used. This informs the device to use SLAAC for addressing information and a stateless DHCPv6 server for other configuration parameters.

## Stateful DHCPv6

Example 8-26 shows the configuration commands for a stateful DHCPv6 server.

**Example 8-26** Stateful DHCPv6 Server Configuration

```
R1(config)# ipv6 unicast-routing
R1(config)#
R1(config)# ipv6 dhcp pool IPV6-STATEFUL
R1(config-dhcpv6)# address prefix 2001:DB8:CAFE:1::/64 lifetime infinite infinite
R1(config-dhcpv6)# dns-server 2001:db8:cafe:aaaa::5
R1(config-dhcpv6)# domain-name example.com
R1(config-dhcpv6)# exit
R1(config)#
R1(config)# interface g0/1
R1(config-if)# ipv6 address 2001:db8:cafe:1::1/64
R1(config-if)# ipv6 dhcp server IPV6-STATEFUL
R1(config-if)# ipv6 nd managed-config-flag
R1(config-if)#
```

A router configured for stateful DHCPv6 services has the **address prefix** command to provide addressing information. For stateful DHCPv6 services, the **ipv6 nd managed-config-flag** interface configuration mode command is used. In this instance, the client ignores the addressing information in the RA message and communicates with a DHCPv6 server for both addressing and other information.

The **show ipv6 interface** command can be used to view the current configuration to determine the allocation method. The last line of the output indicates how clients obtain addresses and other parameters.

Example 8-27 displays the output when an interface is configured for SLAAC.

**Example 8-27** Verify SLAAC Method

```
R1# show ipv6 interface g0/1
GigabitEthernet0/1 is up, line protocol is up
  IPv6 is enabled, link-local address is FE80::D68C:B5FF:FECE:A0C1
  <output omitted>
  Hosts use stateless autoconfig for addresses.
R1#
```

Example 8-28 displays the output when an interface is configured for stateless DHCP.

**Example 8-28** Verify Stateless DHCPv6 Allocation Method

```
R1# show ipv6 interface g0/1
GigabitEthernet0/1 is up, line protocol is up
  IPv6 is enabled, link-local address is FE80::D68C:B5FF:FECE:A0C1
  <output omitted>
  Hosts use DHCP to obtain other configuration.
R1#
```

Example 8-29 displays the output when an interface is configured for stateful DHCP.

**Example 8-29** Verify Stateful DHCPv6 Allocation Method

```
R1# show ipv6 interface g0/1
GigabitEthernet0/1 is up, line protocol is up
  IPv6 is enabled, link-local address is FE80::D68C:B5FF:FECE:A0C1
  <output omitted>
  Hosts use DHCP to obtain routable addresses.
R1#
```

## Debugging DHCPv6 (8.2.4.3)

When the router is configured as a stateless or stateful DHCPv6 server, the **debug ipv6 dhcp detail** command is useful to verify the receipt and transmission of DHCPv6 messages. As shown in Example 8-30, a stateful DHCPv6 router has received a SOLICIT message from a client. The router is using the addressing information in its IPV6-STATEFUL pool for binding information.

**Example 8-30** Debug DHCPv6

```
R1# debug ipv6 dhcp detail
   IPv6 DHCP debugging is on (detailed)
R1#
*Feb  3 21:27:41.123: IPv6 DHCP: Received SOLICIT from FE80::32F7:DFF:FE25:2DE1 on
   GigabitEthernet0/1
*Feb  3 21:27:41.123: IPv6 DHCP: detailed packet contents
*Feb  3 21:27:41.123:   src FE80::32F7:DFF:FE25:2DE1 (GigabitEthernet0/1)
*Feb  3 21:27:41.127:   dst FF02::1:2
*Feb  3 21:27:41.127:   type SOLICIT(1), xid 13190645
*Feb  3 21:27:41.127:   option ELAPSED-TIME(8), len 2
*Feb  3 21:27:41.127:     elapsed-time 0
*Feb  3 21:27:41.127:   option CLIENTID(1), len 10
```

```
*Feb  3 21:27:41.127:      000
*Feb  3 21:27:41.127: IPv6 DHCP: Using interface pool IPV6-STATEFUL
*Feb  3 21:27:41.127: IPv6 DHCP: Creating binding for FE80::32F7:DFF:FE25:2DE1 in
  pool IPV6-STATEFUL
<output omitted>
```

### Lab 8.2.4.4: Troubleshooting DHCPv6

In this lab, you complete the following objectives:

- Part 1: Build the Network and Configure Basic Device Settings
- Part 2: Troubleshoot IPv6 Connectivity
- Part 3: Troubleshoot Stateless DHCPv6

# Summary (8.3)

### Class Activity 8.3.1.1: IoE and DHCP

This chapter presents the concept of using the DHCP process in a small- to medium-sized business network; however, DHCP also has other uses.

With the advent of the Internet of Everything (IoE), any device in your home capable of wired or wireless connectivity to a network will be able to be accessed from just about anywhere.

Using Packet Tracer for this modeling activity, perform the following tasks:

- Configure a Cisco 1941 router (or DHCP-server-capable ISR device) for IPv4 or IPv6 DHCP addressing.

- Think of five devices in your home that you would like to receive IP addresses from the router's DHCP service. Set the end devices to claim DHCP addresses from the DHCP server.

- Show output validating that each end device secures an IP address from the server. Save your output information via a screen capture program, or use the PrtScrn key command.

- Present your findings to a fellow classmate or to the class.

Packet Tracer
☐ Activity

### Packet Tracer 8.3.1.2: Skills Integration Challenge

In this culminating activity, you configure VLANs, trunks, DHCPv4 servers, DHCPv4 relay agents, and a router as a DHCP client.

All nodes on a network require a unique IP address to communicate with other devices. The static assignment of IP addressing information on a large network results in an administrative burden that can be eliminated by using DHCPv4 and DHCPv6 to dynamically assign IPv4 and IPv6 addressing information, respectively.

- DHCPv4 dynamically assigns, or leases, an IPv4 address from a pool of addresses for a limited period of time, as configured on the server, or until the client no longer needs the address.

DHCPv4 involves the exchange of several different packets between the DHCPv4 server and the DHCPv4 client resulting in the lease of valid addressing information for a predefined period of time.

Messages originating from the client (DHCPDISCOVER, DHCPREQUEST) are broadcast to allow all DHCPv4 servers on the network to hear the client request for, and receipt of, addressing information. Messages originating from the DHCPv4 server (DHCPOFFER, DHCPACK) are sent as unicasts directly to the client.

IPv6 global unicast addresses can be assigned dynamically in three ways:

- Stateless address autoconfiguration (SLAAC)
- SLAAC and stateless DHCP for IPv6 (stateless DHCPv6)
- Stateful DHCPv6

With SLAAC, the client uses information provided by the IPv6 RA message to automatically select and configure a unique IPv6 address. The stateless DHCPv6 option informs the client to use the information in the RA message for addressing, but additional configuration parameters are available from a DHCPv6 server.

Stateful DHCPv6 is similar to DHCPv4. In this case, the RA message informs the client not to use the information in the RA message. All addressing information and DNS configuration information is obtained from a stateful DHCPv6 server. The DHCPv6 server maintains IPv6 state information similar to a DHCPv4 server allocating addresses for IPv4.

If the DHCP server is located on a different network segment than the DHCP client, it is necessary to configure a relay agent. The relay agent forwards specific broadcast or multicast messages, including DHCP messages, originating from a host on a LAN segment and destined for a specific server located on a different LAN segment.

Troubleshooting issues with DHCPv4 and DHCPv6 involve the same tasks:

- Resolve address conflicts
- Verify physical connectivity
- Test connectivity using a static IP address
- Verify switch port configuration
- Test operation on the same subnet or VLAN

## Practice

The following activities provide practice with the topics introduced in this chapter. The Labs and Class Activities are available in the companion Routing and Switching Labs and Study Guide (ISBN 9781587134265). The Packet Tracer Activities PKA files are found in the online course.

**Class Activities**

Class Activity 8.3.1.1: IoE and DHCP

**Labs**

Lab 8.1.2.4: Configuring Basic DHCPv4 on a Router

Lab 8.1.2.5: Configuring Basic DHCPv4 on a Switch

Lab 8.1.4.4: Troubleshooting DHCPv4

Lab 8.2.3.5: Configuring Stateless and Stateful DHCPv6

Lab 8.2.4.4: Troubleshooting DHCPv6

**Packet Tracer Activities**

Packet Tracer 8.1.3.3: Configuring DHCPv4 Using Cisco IOS

Packet Tracer 8.3.1.2: Skills Integration Challenge

# Check Your Understanding Questions

Complete all the review questions listed here to test your understanding of the topics and concepts in this chapter. The appendix "Answers to the 'Check Your Understanding' Questions" lists the answers.

1. Which DHCPv4 message will a client send to accept an IPv4 address that is offered by a DHCP server?

    A. broadcast DHCPACK

    B. broadcast DHCPREQUEST

    C. unicast DHCPACK

    D. unicast DHCPREQUEST

2. Why is the DHCPREQUEST message sent as a broadcast during the DHCPv4 process?

    A. For hosts on other subnets to receive the information

    B. For routers to fill their routing tables with this new information

    C. To notify other DHCP servers on the subnet that the IP address was leased

    D. To notify other hosts not to request the same IP address

3. Which address does a DHCPv4 server target when sending a DHCPOFFER message to a client that makes an address request?

    A. Broadcast MAC address

    B. Client hardware address

    C.  Client IP address

    D.  Gateway IP address

4. As a DHCPv4 client lease is about to expire, what is the message that the client sends the DHCP server?

    A.  DHCPACK

    B.  DHCPDISCOVER

    C.  DHCPOFFER

    D.  DHCPREQUEST

5. What is an advantage of configuring a Cisco router as a relay agent?

    A.  It can forward both broadcast and multicast messages on behalf of clients.

    B.  It can provide relay services for multiple UDP services.

    C.  It reduces the response time from a DHCP server.

    D.  It allows DHCPDISCOVER messages to pass without alteration.

6. An administrator issues the **ip address dhcp** command on interface G0/1. What is the administrator trying to achieve?

    A.  Configuring the router to act as a DHCPv4 server

    B.  Configuring the router to act as a relay agent

    C.  Configuring the router to obtain IP parameters from a DHCPv4 server

    D.  Configuring the router to resolve IP address conflicts

7. Under which two circumstances would a router usually be configured as a DHCPv4 client? (Choose two.)

    A.  The administrator needs the router to act as a relay agent.

    B.  This is an ISP requirement.

    C.  The router has a fixed IP address.

    D.  The router is intended to be used as a SOHO gateway.

    E.  The router is meant to provide IP addresses to the hosts.

8. A host on the 10.10.100.0/24 LAN is not being assigned an IPv4 address by an enterprise DHCP server with the address 10.10.200.10/24. What is the best way for the network engineer to resolve this problem?

    A.  Issue the command **default-router 10.10.200.10** at the DHCP configuration prompt on the 10.10.100.0/24 LAN gateway router.

    B.  Issue the command **ip helper-address 10.10.100.0** on the router interface that is the 10.10.200.0/24 gateway.

C.  Issue the command **ip helper-address 10.10.200.10** on the router interface that is the 10.10.100.0/24 gateway.

D.  Issue the command **network 10.10.200.0 255.255.255.0** at the DHCP configuration prompt on the 10.10.100.0/24 LAN gateway router.

9.  A company uses the SLAAC method to configure IPv6 addresses for the employee workstations. Which address will a client use as its default gateway?

   A.  The all-routers multicast address

   B.  The global unicast address of the router interface that is attached to the network

   C.  The link-local address of the router interface that is attached to the network

   D.  The unique local address of the router interface that is attached to the network

10. A network administrator configures a router to send RA messages with M flag as 0 and O flag as 1. Which statement describes the effect of this configuration when a PC tries to configure its IPv6 address?

   A.  It should contact a DHCPv6 server for all the information that it needs.

   B.  It should contact a DHCPv6 server for the prefix, the prefix-length information, and an interface ID that is both random and unique.

   C.  It should use the information that is contained in the RA message and contact a DHCPv6 server for additional information.

   D.  It should use the information that is contained in the RA message exclusively.

11. A company implements the stateless DHCPv6 method for configuring IPv6 addresses on employee workstations. After a workstation receives messages from multiple DHCPv6 servers to indicate their availability for DHCPv6 service, which message does it send to a server for configuration information?

   A.  DHCPv6 ADVERTISE

   B.  DHCPv6 INFORMATION-REQUEST

   C.  DHCPv6 REQUEST

   D.  DHCPv6 SOLICIT

12. An administrator wants to configure hosts to automatically assign IPv6 addresses to themselves through the use of router advertisement messages, but also to obtain the DNS server address from a DHCPv6 server. Which address assignment method should be configured?

   A.  RA and EUI-64

   B.  SLAAC

    C. Stateful DHCPv6

    D. Stateless DHCPv6

13. How does an IPv6 client ensure that it has a unique address after it configures its IPv6 address using the SLAAC allocation method?

    A. It checks with the IPv6 address database that the SLAAC server hosts.

    B. It contacts the DHCPv6 server via a special formed ICMPv6 message.

    C. It sends an ARP message with the IPv6 address as the destination IPv6 address.

    D. It sends an ICMPv6 neighbor solicitation message with the IPv6 address as the target IPv6 address.

14. What is used in the EUI-64 process to create an IPv6 interface ID on an IPv6-enabled interface?

    A. A randomly generated 64-bit hexadecimal address

    B. An IPv4 address that is configured on the interface

    C. An IPv6 address that is provided by a DHCPv6 server

    D. The MAC address of the IPv6 enabled interface

15. A network administrator is implementing DHCPv6 for the company. The administrator configures a router to send RA messages with M flag as 1 by using the interface command **ipv6 nd managed-config-flag**. What effect will this configuration have on the operation of the clients?

    A. Clients must use all configuration information that is provided by a DHCPv6 server.

    B. Clients must use the information that is contained in RA messages.

    C. Clients must use the prefix and prefix-length that are provided by a DHCPv6 server and generate a random interface ID.

    D. Clients must use the prefix and prefix-length that are provided by RA messages and obtain additional information from a DHCPv6 server.

# CHAPTER 9

# NAT for IPv4

## Objectives

Upon completion of this chapter, you will be able to answer the following questions:

- What is the purpose and function of NAT?

- How do different types of NAT operate?

- What are the advantages and disadvantages of NAT?

- How do you configure static NAT?

- How do you configure dynamic NAT?

- How do you configure PAT?

- How do you configure port forwarding?

- How is NAT used with IPv6 networks?

- How do you troubleshoot NAT?

## Key Terms

This chapter uses the following key terms. You can find the definitions in the Glossary.

*network address translation (NAT)*   Page 418

*private IP addresses*   Page 418

*public IP addresses*   Page 418

*public IPv4 addresses*   Page 418

*private IPv4 addresses*   Page 418

*inside network*   Page 420

*outside network*   Page 420

*inside local address*   Page 421

*inside global address*   Page 421

*outside local address*   Page 421

*outside global address*   Page 421

*inside address*   Page 421

*outside address*   Page 421

*local address*   Page 421

*global address*   Page 421

*static address translation (static NAT)*   Page 424

*dynamic address translation (dynamic NAT)*   Page 424

*port address translation (PAT)*   Page 424

*NAT overloading*   Page 424

*IPsec*   Page 431

*port forwarding*   Page 451

*Internet Assigned Numbers Authority (IANA)*   Page 457

*regional Internet registry (RIR)   Page 457*

*Internet Architecture Board (IAB)
  Page 457*

*firewalls   Page 457*

*unique local addresses (ULA)   Page 457*

*dual-stack   Page 459*

*tunneling   Page 459*

*translation   Page 459*

*Network Address Translation-Protocol
  Translation (NAT-PT)   Page 459*

*NAT64   Page 459*

# Introduction (9.0.1.1)

All public IPv4 addresses that transverse the Internet must be registered with a regional Internet registry (RIR). Organizations can lease public addresses from a service provider. The registered holder of a public IP address can assign that address to a network device.

With a theoretical maximum of 4.3 billion addresses, IPv4 address space is severely limited. When Bob Kahn and Vint Cerf first developed the suite of TCP/IP protocols including IPv4 in 1981, they never envisioned what the Internet would become. At the time, the personal computer was mostly a curiosity for hobbyists, and the World Wide Web was still more than a decade away.

With the proliferation of personal computing and the advent of the World Wide Web, it soon became obvious that 4.3 billion IPv4 addresses would not be enough. The long-term solution was IPv6, but more immediate solutions to address exhaustion were required. For the short term, several solutions were implemented by the IETF, including network address translation (NAT) and RFC 1918 private IPv4 addresses. The chapter discusses how NAT, combined with the use of private address space, is used to both conserve and more efficiently use IPv4 addresses to provide networks of all sizes access to the Internet.

This chapter covers:

- NAT characteristics, terminology, and general operations

- The different types of NAT, including static NAT, dynamic NAT, and NAT with overloading

- The benefits and disadvantages of NAT

- The configuration, verification, and analysis of static NAT, dynamic NAT, and NAT with overloading

- How port forwarding can be used to access internal devices from the Internet

- Troubleshooting NAT using **show** and **debug** commands

- How NAT for IPv6 is used to translate between IPv6 addresses and IPv4 addresses

**Class Activity 9.0.1.2: Conceptual NAT**

Scenario

You work for a large university or school system.

Because you are the network administrator, many professors, administrative workers, and other network administrators need your assistance with their networks on a daily basis. They call you at all working hours of the day and, because of the number of telephone calls, you cannot complete your regular network administration tasks.

You need to find a way to limit when you take calls and from whom. You also need to mask your telephone number so that when you call someone, another number is displayed to the recipient.

This scenario describes a common problem for most small- to medium-sized businesses. Visit http://computer.howstuffworks.com/nat.htm/printable for an article titled "How Network Address Translation Works" and learn how the digital world handles these types of workday interruptions.

Use the PDF provided accompanying this activity to reflect further on how a process, known as NAT, could be the answer to this scenario's challenge.

# NAT Operation (9.1)

Almost all networks connecting to the Internet use the services of *network address translation (NAT)*. Typically, organizations assign inside hosts *private IP addresses*. When exiting the network, the private addresses are translated to *public IP addresses*. Return traffic to the public IP address is retranslated to the internal private IP address.

In this section, you learn how NAT provides IPv4 address scalability in a small-to medium-sized business network.

## NAT Characteristics (9.1.1)

In this topic, you explain the purpose and function of NAT.

### IPv4 Private Address Space (9.1.1.1)

There are not enough *public IPv4 addresses* to assign a unique address to each device connected to the Internet. Networks are commonly implemented using *private IPv4 addresses*, as defined in RFC 1918. Table 9-1 displays the classless inter-domain routing (CIDR) prefix and the range of addresses included in RFC 1918. It is likely that the computer that you use to view this course is assigned a private address.

**Table 9-1**   Private IPv4 Addresses

| Class | CIDR Prefix | RFC 1918 Internal Address Range |
| --- | --- | --- |
| A | 10.0.0.0/8 | 10.0.0.0 to 10.255.255.255 |
| B | 172.16.0.0/12 | 172.16.0.0 to 172.31.255.255 |
| C | 192.168.0.0/16 | 192.168.0.0 to 192.168.255.255 |

These private addresses are used within an organization or site to allow devices to communicate locally. However, because these addresses do not identify any single company or organization, private IPv4 addresses cannot be routed over the Internet. To allow a device with a private IPv4 address to access devices and resources outside of the local network, the private address must first be translated to a public address.

As illustrated in Figure 9-1, NAT provides the translation of private addresses to public addresses. This allows a device with a private IPv4 address to access resources outside of their private network, such as those found on the Internet.

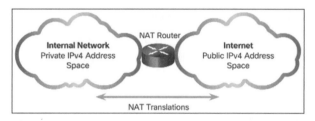

**Figure 9-1**    Translating Between Private and Public

NAT combined with private IPv4 addresses has proven to be a useful method of preserving public IPv4 addresses. A single, public IPv4 address can be shared by hundreds, even thousands, of devices, each configured with a unique private IPv4 address.

Without NAT, the exhaustion of the IPv4 address space would have occurred well before the year 2000. However, NAT has certain limitations, which will be explored later in this chapter. The solution to the exhaustion of IPv4 address space and the limitations of NAT is the eventual transition to IPv6.

## What Is NAT? (9.1.1.2)

NAT has many uses, but its primary use is to conserve public IPv4 addresses. It does this by allowing networks to use private IPv4 addresses internally and providing translation to a public address only when needed. NAT has an added benefit of adding a degree of privacy and security to a network because it hides internal IPv4 addresses from outside networks.

NAT-enabled routers can be configured with one or more valid public IPv4 addresses. These public addresses are known as the NAT pool. When an internal device sends traffic out of the network, the NAT-enabled router translates the internal IPv4 address of the device to a public address from the NAT pool. To outside devices, all traffic entering and exiting the network appears to have a public IPv4 address from the provided pool of addresses.

Notice that PC1 has different local and global addresses, whereas the web server has the same public IPv4 address for both. From the perspective of the web server, traffic originating from PC1 appears to have come from 209.165.200.226, the inside global address.

The NAT router, R2 in the figure, is the demarcation point between the inside and the outside networks and between local and global addresses.

The terms "inside" and "outside" are combined with the terms "local" and "global" to refer to specific addresses. In Figure 9-4, router R2 has been configured to provide NAT. It has a pool of public addresses to assign to inside hosts.

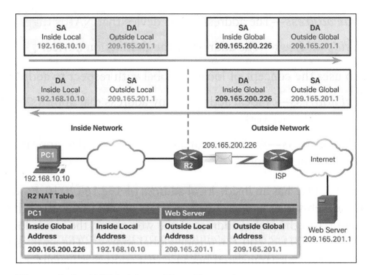

**Figure 9-4**   NAT Address Type Example

- **Inside local address**—The address of the source as seen from inside the network. In the figure, the IPv4 address 192.168.10.10 is assigned to PC1. This is the inside local address of PC1.

- **Inside global address**—The address of the source as seen from the outside network. In the figure, when traffic from PC1 is sent to the web server at 209.165.201.1, R2 translates the inside local address to an inside global address. In this case, R2 changes the IPv4 source address from 192.168.10.10 to 209.165.200.226. In NAT terminology, the inside local address of 192.168.10.10 is translated to the inside global address of 209.165.200.226.

- **Outside global address**—The address of the destination as seen from the outside network. It is a globally routable IPv4 address assigned to a host on the Internet. For example, the web server is reachable at IPv4 address 209.165.201.1. Most often the outside local and outside global addresses are the same.

- **Outside local address**—The address of the destination as seen from the inside network. In this example, PC1 sends traffic to the web server at the IPv4 address 209.165.201.1. Although uncommon, this address could be different from the globally routable address of the destination.

Figure 9-4 shows how traffic is addressed that is sent from an internal PC to an external web server, across the NAT-enabled router. It also shows how return traffic is initially addressed and translated.

**Note**

The use of the outside local address is outside the scope of this course.

## How NAT Works (9.1.1.5)

In Figure 9-5, PC1 with private address 192.168.10.10 wants to communicate with an outside web server with public address 209.165.201.1.

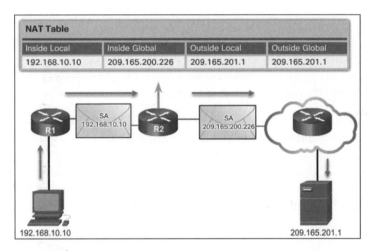

**Figure 9-5**   NAT in Action

PC1 sends a packet addressed to the web server. The packet is forwarded by R1 to R2.

When the packet arrives at R2, the NAT-enabled router for the network, R2 reads the source IPv4 address of the packet to determine if the packet matches the criteria specified for translation.

In this case, the source IPv4 address does match the criteria and is translated from 192.168.10.10 (inside local address) to 209.165.200.226 (inside global address). R2 adds this mapping of the local to global address to the NAT table.

R2 sends the packet with the translated source address toward the destination.

The web server responds with a packet addressed to the inside global address of PC1 (209.165.200.226).

R2 receives the packet with destination address 209.165.200.226. R2 checks the NAT table and finds an entry for this mapping. R2 uses this information and translates the inside global address (209.165.200.226) to the inside local address (192.168.10.10), and the packet is forwarded toward PC1.

**Interactive Graphic**

**Activity 9.1.1.6: Identify the NAT Terminology**

Refer to the online course to complete this activity.

# Types of NAT (9.1.2)

In this topic, you learn about the operation of different types of NAT.

## Static NAT (9.1.2.1)

There are three types of NAT translation:

- *Static network address translation (static NAT)*—One-to-one address mapping between local and global addresses.

- *Dynamic network address translation (dynamic NAT)*—Many-to-many address mapping between local and global addresses. Translations are made on an as-available basis; for example, if there are 100 inside local addresses and 10 inside global addresses, at any given time only 10 of the 100 inside local addresses can be translated. This limitation of dynamic NAT makes it much less useful for production networks than port address translation.

- *Port address translation (PAT)*—Many-to-one address mapping between local and global addresses. This method is also known as overloading (*NAT overloading*). For example, if there are 100 inside local addresses and 10 inside global addresses, PAT uses ports as an additional parameter to provide a multiplier effect, making it possible to reuse any one of the 10 inside global addresses up to 65,536 times (depending on whether the flow is based on UDP, TCP, or ICMP).

Static NAT uses a one-to-one mapping of local and global addresses. These mappings are configured by the network administrator and remain constant.

In Figure 9-6, R2 is configured with static mappings for the inside local addresses of Svr1, PC2, and PC3. When these devices send traffic to the Internet, their inside local addresses are translated to the configured inside global addresses. To outside networks, these devices have public IPv4 addresses.

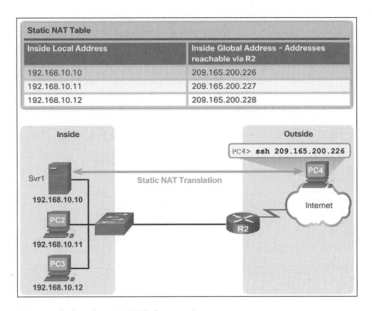

**Static NAT Table**

| Inside Local Address | Inside Global Address – Addresses reachable via R2 |
|---|---|
| 192.168.10.10 | 209.165.200.226 |
| 192.168.10.11 | 209.165.200.227 |
| 192.168.10.12 | 209.165.200.228 |

**Figure 9-6** Static NAT Scenario

Static NAT is particularly useful for servers or devices that must have a consistent address that is accessible from the Internet, such as a company web server. It is also useful for devices that must be accessible by authorized personnel when offsite, but not by the general public on the Internet. As illustrated in Figure 9-6, a network administrator using PC4 specifies the inside global address (209.165.200.226) of Svr1 to remotely connect to it using SSH. R2 translates this inside global address to the inside local address and connects the administrator's session to Svr1.

Static NAT requires that enough public addresses are available to satisfy the total number of simultaneous user sessions.

## Dynamic NAT (9.1.2.2)

Dynamic NAT uses a pool of public addresses and assigns them on a first-come, first-served basis. When an inside device requests access to an outside network, dynamic NAT assigns an available public IPv4 address from the pool.

In Figure 9-7, PC3 has accessed the Internet using the first available address in the dynamic NAT pool. The other addresses are still available for use. Similar to static NAT, dynamic NAT requires that enough public addresses are available to satisfy the total number of simultaneous user sessions.

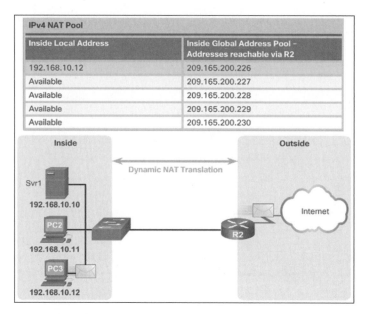

**Figure 9-7**   Dynamic NAT Scenario

## Port Address Translation (PAT) (9.1.2.3)

Port Address Translation (PAT), also known as NAT overloading, maps multiple private IPv4 addresses to a single public IPv4 address or a few addresses. This is what most home routers do. The ISP assigns one address to the router, yet several members of the household can simultaneously access the Internet. This is the most common form of NAT.

With PAT, multiple addresses can be mapped to one or to a few addresses because each private address is also tracked by a port number. When a device initiates a TCP/IP session, it generates a TCP or UDP source port value or a specially assigned query ID for ICMP to uniquely identify the session. When the NAT router receives a packet from the client, it uses its source port number to uniquely identify the specific NAT translation.

PAT ensures that devices use a different TCP port number for each session with a server on the Internet. When a response comes back from the server, the source port number, which becomes the destination port number on the return trip, determines to which device the router forwards the packets. The PAT process also validates that the incoming packets were requested, thus adding a degree of security to the session.

Figure 9-8 illustrates the PAT process. PAT adds unique source port numbers to the inside global address to distinguish between translations.

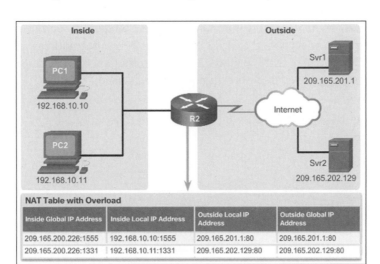

**Figure 9-8**    PAT Scenario

As R2 processes each packet, it uses a port number (1331 and 1555, in Figure 9-8) to identify the device from which the packet originated. The source address (SA) is the inside local address with the TCP/IP assigned port number added. The destination address (DA) is the outside local address with the service port number added. In this example, the service port is 80, which is HTTP.

For the source address, R2 translates the inside local address to an inside global address with the port number added. The destination address is not changed but is now referred to as the outside global IPv4 address. When the web server replies, the path is reversed.

## Next Available Port (9.1.2.4)

In the previous example, the client port numbers, 1331 and 1555, did not change at the NAT-enabled router. This is not a likely scenario because there is a good chance that these port numbers may have already been attached to other active sessions.

PAT attempts to preserve the original source port. However, if the original source port is already used, PAT assigns the first available port number starting from the beginning of the appropriate port group 0 to 511, 512 to 1,023, or 1,024 to 65,535. When there are no more ports available and there is more than one external address in the address pool, PAT moves to the next address to try to allocate the original source port. This process continues until there are no more available ports or external IPv4 addresses.

In Figure 9-9, PAT has assigned the next available port (1445) to the second host address. The hosts have chosen the same port number 1444. This is acceptable for the inside address because the hosts have unique private IPv4 addresses. However, at the NAT router, the port numbers must be changed; otherwise, packets from two different hosts would exit R2 with the same source address. The example in Figure 9-9 assumes that the first 420 ports in the range 1,024 to 65,535 are already in use, so the next available port number, 1445, is used.

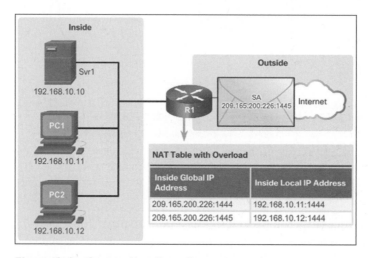

**Figure 9-9**   Source Port Reassignment

## Comparing NAT and PAT (9.1.2.5)

Summarizing the differences between NAT and PAT helps your understanding of each.

Table 9-2 shows how NAT translates IPv4 addresses on a 1:1 basis between private IPv4 addresses and public IPv4 addresses.

**Table 9-2**   NAT Translations

**NAT**

| Inside Local Address | Inside Global Address Pool |
| --- | --- |
| 192.168.10.10 | 209.165.200.226 |
| 192.168.10.11 | 209.165.200.227 |
| 192.168.10.12 | 209.165.200.228 |
| 192.168.10.13 | 209.165.200.229 |

However, Table 9-3 shows how PAT modifies both the address and the port number.

**Table 9-3**  PAT Translations

**PAT**

| Inside Local Address | Inside Global Address |
|---|---|
| 192.168.10.10:1444 | 209.165.200.226:1444 |
| 192.168.10.11:1444 | 209.165.200.226:1445 |
| 192.168.10.12:1555 | 209.165.200.226:1555 |
| 192.168.10.13:1555 | 209.165.200.226:1556 |

NAT forwards incoming packets to their inside destination by referring to the incoming source IPv4 address given by the host on the public network. With PAT, there is generally only one or a few publicly exposed IPv4 addresses. Incoming packets from the public network are routed to their destinations on the private network by referring to a table in the NAT router. This table tracks public and private port pairs. This is called connection tracking.

What about IPv4 packets carrying data other than a TCP or UDP segment? These packets do not contain a Layer 4 port number. PAT translates most common protocols carried by IPv4 that do not use TCP or UDP as a transport layer protocol. The most common of these is ICMPv4. Each of these types of protocols is handled differently by PAT. For example, ICMPv4 query messages, echo requests, and echo replies include a Query ID. ICMPv4 uses the Query ID to identify an echo request with its corresponding echo reply. The Query ID is incremented with each echo request sent. PAT uses the Query ID instead of a Layer 4 port number.

**Note**

Other ICMPv4 messages do not use the Query ID. These messages and other protocols that do not use TCP or UDP port numbers vary and are beyond the scope of this curriculum.

Packet Tracer
☐ Activity

**Packet Tracer 9.1.2.6: Investigating NAT Operation**

You know that as a frame travels across a network, the MAC addresses change. But IPv4 addresses can also change when a packet is forwarded by a device configured with NAT. This activity demonstrates what happens to IPv4 addresses during the NAT process.

# NAT Advantages (9.1.3)

In this topic, you learn about the advantages and disadvantages of NAT.

## Advantages of NAT (9.1.3.1)

NAT provides many benefits, including these:

- NAT conserves the legally registered addressing scheme by allowing the privatization of intranets. NAT conserves addresses through application port-level multiplexing. With NAT overload, internal hosts can share a single public IPv4 address for all external communications. In this type of configuration, few external addresses are required to support many internal hosts.

- NAT increases the flexibility of connections to the public network. Multiple pools, backup pools, and load-balancing pools can be implemented to ensure reliable public network connections.

- NAT provides consistency for internal network addressing schemes. On a network not using private IPv4 addresses and NAT, changing the public IPv4 address scheme requires the readdressing of all hosts on the existing network. The costs of readdressing hosts can be significant. NAT allows the existing private IPv4 address scheme to remain while allowing for easy change to a new public addressing scheme. This means an organization could change ISPs and not need to change any of its inside clients.

- NAT hides user IPv4 addresses. Using RFC 1918 IPv4 addresses, NAT provides the side effect of hiding users and other devices' IPv4 addresses. Some people consider this a security feature; however, most experts agree that NAT does not provide security. A stateful firewall is what provides security on the edge of the network.

## Disadvantages of NAT (9.1.3.2)

The disadvantages of NAT include the following:

- Performance is degraded.
- End-to-end functionality is degraded.
- End-to-end IP traceability is lost.
- Tunneling becomes more complicated.
- Initiating TCP connections can be disrupted.

NAT does have some drawbacks. The fact that hosts on the Internet appear to communicate directly with the NAT-enabled device, rather than with the actual host inside the private network, creates a number of issues.

One disadvantage of using NAT is related to network performance, particularly for real-time protocols such as VoIP. NAT increases forwarding delays because the translation of each IPv4 address within the packet headers takes time. The first packet is always process-switched going through the slower path. The router must look at every packet to decide whether it needs translation. The router must alter the IPv4 header and possibly alter the TCP or UDP header. The IPv4 header checksum, along with the TCP or UDP checksum, must be recalculated each time a translation is made. Remaining packets go through the fast-switched path if a cache entry exists; otherwise, they, too, are delayed.

Another disadvantage of using NAT is that end-to-end addressing is lost. Many Internet protocols and applications depend on end-to-end addressing from the source to the destination. Some applications do not work with NAT. For example, some security applications, such as digital signatures, fail because the source IPv4 address changes before reaching the destination. Applications that use physical addresses, instead of a qualified domain name, do not reach destinations that are translated across the NAT router. Sometimes this problem can be avoided by implementing static NAT mappings.

End-to-end IPv4 traceability is also lost. It becomes much more difficult to trace packets that undergo numerous packet address changes over multiple NAT hops, making troubleshooting challenging.

Using NAT also complicates the use of tunneling protocols, such as *IPsec*, because NAT modifies values in the headers, causing integrity checks to fail. Tunneling is discussed later in the chapter.

Services that require the initiation of TCP connections from the outside network, or stateless protocols, such as those using UDP, can be disrupted. Unless the NAT router has been configured to support such protocols, incoming packets cannot reach their destination. Some protocols can accommodate one instance of NAT between participating hosts (passive mode FTP, for example) but fail when both systems are separated from the Internet by NAT.

# Configure NAT (9.2)

Dynamic NAT, static NAT, and PAT are used extensively in networks. Therefore, it is important to understand how to properly configure the different types of NAT.

In this section, you learn how to configure NAT services on the edge router to provide IPv4 address scalability in a small-to medium-sized business network.

## Configuring Static NAT (9.2.1)

In this topic, you configure static NAT.

### Configure Static NAT (9.2.1.1)

Static NAT is a one-to-one mapping between an inside address and an outside address. Static NAT allows external devices to initiate connections to internal devices using the statically assigned public address. For instance, the web server with a private address in Figure 9-10 is mapped to a specific inside global address to make it accessible from outside hosts.

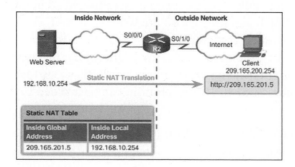

**Figure 9-10**   Static NAT Topology

Router R2 is configured with static NAT to allow devices on the outside network (Internet) to access the web server. The client on the outside network accesses the web server using a public IPv4 address. Static NAT translates the public IPv4 address to the private IPv4 address.

There are two basic steps when configuring static NAT translations.

**Step 1.**   The first task is to create a mapping between the inside local address and the inside global addresses using the **ip nat inside source static** *local-ip global-ip* global configuration command.

**Step 2.**   Next, the interfaces participating in the translation are configured as inside or outside relative to NAT. Inside interfaces are configured with the **ip nat inside** interface configuration command, whereas the outside interface is configured with the **ip nat outside** interface configuration command.

Example 9-1 shows the commands needed on R2 to create a static NAT mapping to the web server in Figure 9-10.

**Example 9-1** Static NAT Configuration

```
R2(config)# ip nat inside source static 192.168.10.254 209.165.201.5
R2(config)#
R2(config)# interface Serial0/0/0
R2(config-if)# ip address 10.1.1.2 255.255.255.252
R2(config-if)# ip nat inside
R2(config-if)# exit
R2(config)#
R2(config)# interface Serial0/1/0
R2(config-if)# ip address 209.165.200.225 255.255.255.224
R2(config-if)# ip nat outside
R2(config-if)#
```

Packets arriving on the inside interface of R2 (Serial 0/0/0) from the configured inside local IPv4 address 192.168.10.254 are translated to the inside global IP address of 209.165.201.5 and then forwarded to the outside network.

Packets arriving on the outside interface of R2 (Serial 0/1/0) addressed to the configured inside global IPv4 address 209.165.201.5 are translated to the inside local address 192.168.10.254 and forwarded to the inside network. Therefore, the Internet client can now direct web requests to the public IPv4 address 209.165.201.5, and R2 translates and forwards the traffic to the web server at 192.168.10.254.

## Analyzing Static NAT (9.2.1.2)

Using the previous configuration, Figure 9-11 illustrates the static NAT translation process between the client and the web server.

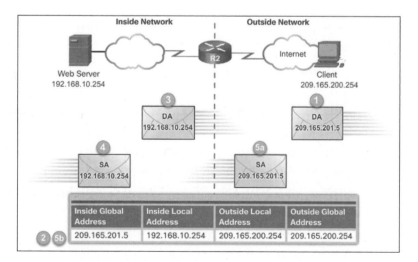

**Figure 9-11**    Static NAT Process

Usually static translations are used when clients on the outside network (Internet) need to reach servers on the inside (internal) network.

1. The client wants to open a connection to the web server. The client sends a packet to the web server using the public IPv4 destination address of 209.165.201.5. This is the inside global address of the web server.

2. The first packet that R2 receives from the client on its NAT outside interface causes R2 to check its NAT table. The destination IPv4 address is located in the NAT table and is translated.

3. R2 replaces the inside global address of 209.165.201.5 with the inside local address of 192.168.10.254. R2 then forwards the packet toward the web server.

4. The web server receives the packet and responds to the client using the inside local address, 192.168.10.254.

5a. R2 receives the packet from the web server on its NAT inside interface with the source address of the inside local address of the web server, 192.168.10.254.

5b. R2 checks the NAT table for a translation for the inside local address. The address is found in the NAT table. R2 translates the source address to the inside global address of 209.165.201.5 and forwards the packet toward the client.

6. The client receives the packet and continues the conversation. The NAT router performs Steps 2 to 5b for each packet. (Step 6 is not shown in the figure.)

## Verifying Static NAT (9.2.1.3)

A useful command to verify NAT operation is the **show ip nat translations** command, as shown in Example 9-2.

**Example 9-2** Static NAT Entry

```
R2# show ip nat translations
Pro Inside global       Inside local        Outside local       Outside global
--- 209.165.201.5       192.168.10.254      ---                 ---
R2#
```

This command displays active NAT translations. Static translations, unlike dynamic translations, are always present in the NAT table.

If the command is issued during an active session, the output also indicates the address of the outside device, as shown in Example 9-3.

**Example 9-3** Static NAT Entry During an Active Session

```
R2# show ip nat translations
Pro Inside global     Inside local      Outside local     Outside global
--- 209.165.201.5     192.168.10.254    209.165.200.254   209.165.200.254
R2#
```

Another useful command is the **show ip nat statistics** command, which displays information about the total number of active translations, the NAT configuration parameters, the number of addresses in the pool, and the number of addresses that have been allocated. To verify that the NAT translation is working, it is best to clear statistics from any past translations using the **clear ip nat statistics** command before testing.

In Example 9-4, the R2 NAT statistics are cleared and verified.

**Example 9-4** Verifying Static NAT Statistics

```
R2# clear ip nat statistics
R2#
R2# show ip nat statistics
Total active translations: 1 (1 static, 0 dynamic; 0 extended)
Peak translations: 0
Outside interfaces:
  Serial0/0/1
Inside interfaces:
  Serial0/0/0
Hits: 0  Misses: 0

<output omitted>
```

The output confirms that there is a static NAT entry and currently no hits.

In Example 9-5, a client has established a session with the web server. The **show ip nat statistics** command now confirms that the entry is being used because there are now five hits on the inside (Serial0/0/0) interface.

**Example 9-5** Verifying Static NAT Statistics

```
R2# show ip nat statistics
Total active translations: 1 (1 static, 0 dynamic; 0 extended)
Peak translations: 2, occurred 00:00:14 ago
Outside interfaces:
  Serial0/1/0
Inside interfaces:
  Serial0/0/0
Hits: 5  Misses: 0

<output omitted>
```

**Packet Tracer 9.2.1.4: Configuring Static NAT**

In IPv4 configured networks, clients and servers use private addressing. Before packets with private addressing can cross the Internet, they need to be translated to public addressing. Servers that are accessed from outside the organization are usually assigned both a public and a private static IPv4 address. In this activity, you configure static NAT so that outside devices can access an inside server at its public address.

# Configure Dynamic NAT (9.2.2)

In this topic, you configure dynamic NAT.

## Dynamic NAT Operation (9.2.2.1)

Although static NAT provides a permanent mapping between an inside local address and an inside global address, dynamic NAT allows the automatic mapping of inside local addresses to inside global addresses. These inside global addresses are typically public IPv4 addresses. Dynamic NAT uses a group, or pool of public IPv4 addresses, for translation.

Dynamic NAT, like static NAT, requires the configuration of the inside and outside interfaces participating in NAT. However, whereas static NAT creates a permanent mapping to a single address, dynamic NAT uses a pool of addresses.

**Note**

Translating between public and private IPv4 addresses is by far the most common use of NAT. However, NAT translations can occur between any pair of addresses.

The topology shown in Figure 9-12 has an inside network using addresses from the RFC 1918 private address space. Attached to router R1 are two LANs: 192.168.10.0/24 and 192.168.11.0/24. Router R2, the border router, is configured for dynamic NAT using a pool of public IPv4 addresses 209.165.200.226 through 209.165.200.240.

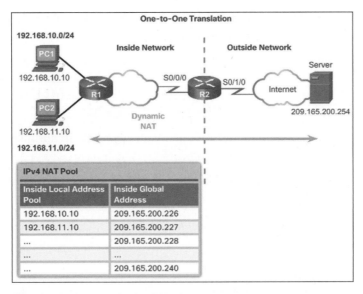

**Figure 9-12**   Dynamic NAT Topology: One-to-One Translation

The pool of public IPv4 addresses (inside global address pool) is available to any device on the inside network on a first-come first-served basis. With dynamic NAT, a single inside address is translated to a single outside address. With this type of translation, there must be enough addresses in the pool to accommodate all the inside devices needing access to the outside network at the same time. If all the addresses in the pool have been used, a device must wait for an available address before it can access the outside network.

## Configuring Dynamic NAT (9.2.2.2)

There are five steps when configuring dynamic NAT translations.

**Step 1.**   Define the pool of addresses to be used for translation. The pool is assigned a name to identify it. The pool of available addresses is defined by indicating the starting IPv4 address and the ending IPv4 address of the pool. This pool of addresses is typically a group of public addresses.

Use the **ip nat pool** *pool-name start-ip end-ip* {**netmask** *netmask* | **prefix-length** *prefix-length*} command. The **netmask** or **prefix-length** keywords indicate which address bits belong to the network and which bits belong to the host for the range of addresses.

**Step 2.**   Configure a standard ACL using the **access-list** *access-list-number* **permit** *source* [*source-wildcard*] command to identify (permit) addresses that can be translated. An ACL that is too permissive can lead to unpredictable results. Remember: there is an implicit **deny all** statement at the end of each ACL. Note that a named standard ACL could have been configured instead of a numbered standard ACL.

**Step 3.** Bind the ACL to the pool. Use the **ip nat inside source list** *access-list-number* **pool** *pool-name* global configuration command to bind the ACL to the pool. The router uses this configuration to identify and manage devices that can use the NAT addresses.

**Step 4.** Identify which interfaces are inside using the **ip nat inside** interface configuration command.

**Step 5.** Identify which interfaces are outside using the **ip nat outside** interface configuration command.

Example 9-6 configures R2 to provide dynamic NAT services for the hosts in Figure 9-12.

**Example 9-6** Dynamic NAT Configuration

```
R2(config)# ip nat pool NAT-POOL1 209.165.200.226 209.165.200.240 netmask
  255.255.255.224
R2(config)#
R2(config)# access-list 1 permit 192.168.0.0 0.0.255.255
R2(config)#
R2(config)# ip nat inside source list 1 pool NAT-POOL1
R2(config)#
R2(config)# interface Serial0/0/0
R2(config-if)# ip nat inside
R2(config-if)# exit
R2(config)#
R2(config)# interface Serial0/1/0
R2(config-if)# ip nat outside
R2(config-if)#
```

The configuration allows translation for all hosts on the 192.168.0.0/16 network, which includes the 192.168.10.0 and 192.168.11.0 LANs, when they generate traffic that enters S0/0/0 and exits S0/1/0. These hosts are translated to an available address in the pool in the range 209.165.200.226 to 209.165.200.240.

## Analyzing Dynamic NAT (9.2.2.3)

Figure 9-13 illustrates the dynamic NAT translation process between two clients and the web server. Specifically, the traffic flow from inside to outside is shown.

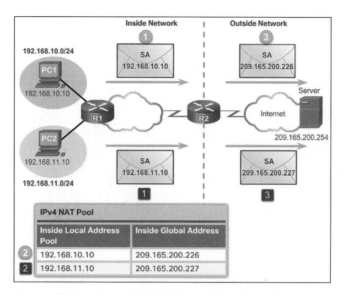

**Figure 9-13**   Dynamic NAT Process: Inside to Outside

1.  The hosts with the source IPv4 addresses (192.168.10.10 (PC1) and 192.168.11.10 (PC2)) send packets requesting a connection to the server at the public IPv4 address (209.165.200.254).

2.  R2 receives the first packet from host 192.168.10.10. Because this packet was received on an interface configured as an inside NAT interface, R2 checks the NAT configuration to determine if this packet should be translated. The ACL permits this packet, so R2 will translate the packet. R2 checks its NAT table. Because there is no translation entry for this IPv4 address, R2 determines that the source address 192.168.10.10 must be translated dynamically. R2 selects an available global address from the dynamic address pool and creates a translation entry, 209.165.200.226. The original source IPv4 address (192.168.10.10) is the inside local address, and the translated address is the inside global address (209.165.200.226) in the NAT table.

    For the second host, 192.168.11.10, R2 repeats the procedure, selects the next available global address from the dynamic address pool, and creates a second translation entry, 209.165.200.227.

3.  R2 replaces the inside local source address of PC1, 192.168.10.10, with the translated inside global address of 209.165.200.226 and forwards the packet. The same process occurs for the packet from PC2 using the translated address for PC2 (209.165.200.227).

In Figure 9-14, the traffic flow from outside to inside is shown.

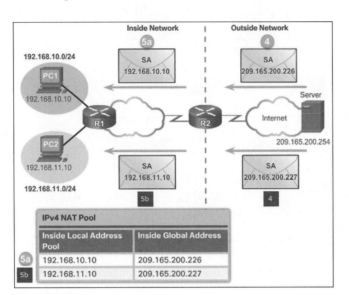

**Figure 9-14**  Dynamic NAT Process: Outside to Inside

4. The server receives the packet from PC1 and responds using the IPv4 destination address of 209.165.200.226. When the server receives the second packet, it responds to PC2 using the IPv4 destination address of 209.165.200.227.

5a. When R2 receives the packet with the destination IPv4 address of 209.165.200.226, it performs a NAT table lookup. Using the mapping from the table, R2 translates the address back to the inside local address (192.168.10.10) and forwards the packet toward PC1.

5b. When R2 receives the packet with the destination IPv4 address of 209.165.200.227, it performs a NAT table lookup. Using the mapping from the table, R2 translates the address back to the inside local address (192.168.11.10) and forwards the packet toward PC2.

6. PC1 at 192.168.10.10 and PC2 at 192.168.11.10 receive the packets and continue the conversation. The router performs Steps 2 to 5 for each packet. (Step 6 is not shown in the figure.)

## Verifying Dynamic NAT (9.2.2.4)

The output of the **show ip nat translations** command shown in Example 9-7 displays the details of the two previous NAT assignments. The command displays all static translations that have been configured and any dynamic translations that traffic has created.

**Example 9-7**  Verifying Dynamic NAT Translations

```
R2# show ip nat translations
Pro Inside global      Inside local      Outside local      Outside global
--- 209.165.200.226    192.168.10.10     ---                ---
--- 209.165.200.227    192.168.11.10     ---                ---
R2#
R2# show ip nat translations verbose
Pro Inside global      Inside local      Outside local      Outside global
--- 209.165.200.226    192.168.10.10     ---                ---
    create 00:17:25, use 00:01:54 timeout:86400000, left 23:58:05, Map-Id(In): 1,
      flags:
none, use_count: 0, entry-id: 32, lc_entries: 0
--- 209.165.200.227    192.168.11.10     ---                ---
    create 00:17:22, use 00:01:51 timeout:86400000, left 23:58:08, Map-Id(In): 1,
      flags:
none, use_count: 0, entry-id: 34, lc_entries: 0
R2#
```

Adding the **verbose** keyword displays additional information about each translation, including how long ago the entry was created and used.

By default, translation entries time out after 24 hours unless the timers have been reconfigured using the **ip nat translation timeout** *timeout-seconds* global configuration command.

It is useful to clear the dynamic entries when testing the NAT configuration. To clear dynamic entries before the timeout has expired, use the **clear ip nat translation** privileged EXEC mode command. Specific entries can be cleared to avoid disrupting active sessions. Use the **clear ip nat translation** * privileged EXEC command to clear all translations from the NAT table.

Table 9-4 displays variables and keyword options that can be used to control which entries are cleared.

**Table 9-4**  Options for Clearing NAT Translations

| Command | Description |
| --- | --- |
| clear ip nat translation * | Clears all dynamic translation entries for the NAT translation table |
| clear ip nat translation inside *global-ip local-ip* [outside *local-ip global-ip*] | Clears a simple dynamic translation entry containing and inside translation or both inside and outside translation |
| clear ip nat translation *protocol* inside *global-ip global-port local-ip local port* [outside *local-ip local-port global-ip global-port*] | Clears an extended dynamic translation entry |

**Note**

Only the dynamic translations are cleared from the table. Static translations cannot be cleared from the translation table.

In Example 9-8, the **show ip nat statistics** command is used to display information about the total number of active translations, NAT configuration parameters, number of addresses in the pool, and number of addresses that have been allocated.

**Example 9-8** Verifying Dynamic NAT Statistics

```
R2# show ip nat statistics
Total active translations: 2 (0 static, 2 dynamic; 0 extended)
Peak translations: 6, occurred 00:27:07 ago
Outside interfaces:
  Serial0/0/1
Inside interfaces:
  Serial0/1/0
Hits: 24   Misses: 0
CEF Translated packets: 24, CEF Punted packets: 0
Expired translations: 4
Dynamic mappings:
-- Inside Source
[Id: 1] access-list 1 pool NAT-POOL1 refcount 2
  pool NAT-POOL1: netmask 255.255.255.224
       start 209.165.200.226 end 209.165.200.240
      type generic, total addresses 15, allocated 2 (13%), misses 0

Total doors: 0
Appl doors: 0
Normal doors: 0
Queued Packets: 0
R2#
```

The output reveals that there are currently 2 dynamic NAT translations occurring. The translations are using the NAT-POOL1 addresses, and currently only 2 of the addresses have been allocated. The output also states that 13% of the available addresses have been allocated. There are 2 currently being used and 4 expired addresses for a total of 6 out of a possible 16 addresses available (therefore, 6 / 16 = 12.5 [or 13%].

When troubleshooting NAT, it may also be necessary to verify the running configuration file for NAT, ACL, interface, or pool command errors. Examine these carefully and correct any errors discovered.

**Packet Tracer 9.2.2.5: Configuring Dynamic NAT**

In this Packet Tracer, you complete the following objectives:

- Part 1: Configure Dynamic NAT
- Part 2: Verify NAT Implementation

**Lab 9.2.2.6: Configuring Dynamic and Static NAT**

In this lab, you complete the following objectives:

- Part 1: Build the Network and Verify Connectivity
- Part 2: Configure and Verify Static NAT
- Part 3: Configure and Verify Dynamic NAT

# Configure PAT (9.2.3)

In this topic, you configure PAT.

## Configuring PAT: Address Pool (9.2.3.1)

PAT (also called NAT overload) conserves addresses in the inside global address pool by allowing the router to use one inside global address for many inside local addresses. In other words, a single public IPv4 address can be used for hundreds, even thousands, of internal private IPv4 addresses. When this type of translation is configured, the router maintains enough information from higher-level protocols, TCP or UDP port numbers, for example, to translate the inside global address back into the correct inside local address. When multiple inside local addresses map to one inside global address, the TCP or UDP port numbers of each inside host distinguish between the local addresses.

### Note

The total number of internal addresses that can be translated to one external address could theoretically be as high as 65,536 per IPv4 address. However, the practical number of internal addresses that can be assigned a single IPv4 address is around 4,000.

There are two ways to configure PAT, depending on how the ISP allocates public IPv4 addresses. In the first instance, the ISP allocates more than one public IPv4 address to the organization, and in the other, it allocates a single public IPv4 address that is required for the organization to connect to the ISP.

If a site has been issued more than one public IPv4 address, these addresses can be part of a pool that is used by PAT. This is similar to dynamic NAT, except that there are not enough public addresses for a one-to-one mapping of inside to outside addresses. The small pool of addresses is shared among a larger number of devices.

There are five steps when configuring dynamic PAT translations. The five steps are identical to configuring dynamic NAT except for step 3.

**Step 1.** Define the pool of addresses that will be used for translation using the **ip nat pool** *pool-name start-ip end-ip* {**netmask** *netmask* | **prefix-length** *prefix-length*} command.

**Step 2.** Configure a standard ACL using the **access-list** *access-list-number* **permit** *source* [*source-wildcard*] command to identify (permit) addresses that can be translated.

**Step 3.** Bind the ACL to the pool. Use the **ip nat inside source list** *access-list-number* **pool** *pool-name* **overload** global configuration command to bind the ACL to the pool. This primary difference between PAT and NAT is that the **overload** keyword is used with this command.

**Step 4.** Identify which interfaces are inside using the **ip nat inside** interface configuration command.

**Step 5.** Identify which interfaces are outside using the **ip nat outside** interface configuration command.

Consider the topology in Figure 9-15.

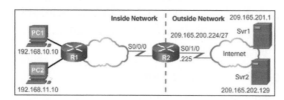

**Figure 9-15** PAT Topology

The configuration in Example 9-9 configures dynamic PAT on R2.

**Example 9-9** PAT Configuration

```
R2(config)# ip nat pool NAT-POOL2 209.165.200.226 209.165.200.240 netmask
  255.255.255.224
R2(config)#
R2(config)# access-list 1 permit 192.168.0.0 0.0.255.255
R2(config)#
R2(config)# ip nat inside source list 1 pool NAT-POOL2 overload
R2(config)#
R2(config)# interface Serial0/0/0
R2(config-if)# ip nat inside
R2(config-if)# exit
R2(config)#
R2(config)# interface Serial0/1/0
R2(config-if)# ip nat outside
R2(config-if)#
```

The configuration establishes overload translation for the NAT pool named NAT-POOL2, which contains addresses 209.165.200.226 to 209.165.200.240. Hosts in the 192.168.0.0/16 network are subject to translation. The S0/0/0 interface is identified as an inside interface, and the S0/1/0 interface is identified as an outside interface.

## Configuring PAT: Single Address (9.2.3.2)

Figure 9-16 displays the topology of a PAT implementation for a single public IPv4 address translation.

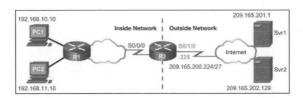

**Figure 9-16**    PAT with a Single Address Topology

All hosts from network 192.168.0.0/16 (matching ACL 1) that send traffic through router R2 to the Internet are translated to IPv4 address 209.165.200.225 (IPv4 address of interface S0/1/0). The traffic flows are identified by port numbers in the NAT table because the **overload** keyword was used.

There are four steps when configuring PAT with a single IPv4 address. The configuration is similar to dynamic PAT except there is no need to create a pool because only one IP address will be used. All inside addresses are translated to the single IPv4 address when leaving the outside interface.

Step 1.    Define the pool of addresses to be used for translation using the **ip nat pool** *pool-name start-ip end-ip* {**netmask** *netmask* | **prefix-length** *prefix-length*} command.

Step 2.    Bind the ACL to the pool. Use the **ip nat inside source list** *access-list-number* **interface** *type number* **overload** global configuration command to bind the ACL to the interface. Again, note that the **overload** keyword is required.

Step 3.    Identify which interfaces are inside using the **ip nat inside** interface configuration command.

Step 4.    Identify which interfaces are outside using the **ip nat outside** interface configuration command.

The configuration of PAT with a single address for Figure 9-16 is shown in Example 9-10.

**Example 9-10**  PAT with a Single Address Configuration

```
R2(config)# access-list 1 permit 192.168.0.0 0.0.255.255
R2(config)#
R2(config)# ip nat inside source list 1 interface serial 0/1/0 overload
R2(config)#
R2(config)# interface Serial0/0/0
R2(config-if)# ip nat inside
R2(config-if)# exit
R2(config)#
R2(config)# interface Serial0/1/0
R2(config-if)# ip nat outside
R2(config-if)#
```

## Analyzing PAT (9.2.3.3)

The process of NAT overload is the same whether a pool of addresses is used or a single address is used. Continuing with the previous PAT example, using a single public IPv4 address, PC1 wants to communicate with the web server, Svr1. At the same time, another client, PC2, wants to establish a similar session with the web server Svr2. Both PC1 and PC2 are configured with private IPv4 addresses, with R2 enabled for PAT.

The PC to server process is shown in Figure 9-17.

## Verifying PAT (9.2.3.4)

The same commands used to verify static and dynamic NAT are used to verify PAT.

For instance, assume that R2 was configured to support dynamic PAT as configured in Example 9-9. When the internal hosts exit router R2 to the Internet, they are translated to an IPv4 address from the PAT pool with a unique source port number.

In Example 9-11, two internal hosts are communicating with external web servers. The **show ip nat translations** command displays the translations of the two internal hosts to different external web servers.

**Example 9-11** Verify PAT Translations

```
R2# show ip nat translations
Pro  Inside global         Inside local        Outside local        Outside global
tcp  209.165.200.226:51839  192.168.10.10:51839  209.165.201.1:80     209.165.201.1:80
tcp  209.165.200.226:42558  192.168.11.10:42558  209.165.202.129:80
     209.165.202.129:80
R2#
```

Notice that the two inside hosts are allocated the same IPv4 address of 209.165.200.226 (inside global address). Only the source port numbers in the NAT table differentiate the two transactions.

As shown in Example 9-12, the **show ip nat statistics** command verifies the number and type of active translations, NAT configuration parameters, number of addresses in the pool, and number that have been allocated.

**Example 9-12** Verify PAT Statistics

```
R2# show ip nat statistics
Total active translations: 2 (0 static, 2 dynamic; 2 extended)
Peak translations: 2, occurred 00:00:05 ago
Outside interfaces:
  Serial0/0/1
Inside interfaces:
  Serial0/1/0
Hits: 4  Misses: 0
CEF Translated packets: 4, CEF Punted packets: 0
Expired translations: 0
Dynamic mappings:
-- Inside Source
```

```
[Id: 3] access-list 1 pool NAT-POOL2 refcount 2
pool NAT-POOL2: netmask 255.255.255.224
      start 209.165.200.226 end 209.165.200.240
      type generic, total addresses 15, allocated 1 (6%), misses 0

Total doors: 0
Appl doors: 0
Normal doors: 0
Queued Packets: 0
R2#
```

The output confirms that there are currently two dynamic extended NAT translations occurring and that the translations are sharing the one address allocated from the NAT-POOL2 pool.

**Activity 9.2.3.5: Identify the Address Information at Each Hop**

Refer to the online course to complete this activity.

**Packet Tracer 9.2.3.6: Implementing Static and Dynamic NAT**

In this packet tracer, you complete the following objectives:

- Part 1: Configure Dynamic NAT with PAT
- Part 2: Configure Static NAT
- Part 3: Verify NAT Implementation

**Lab 9.2.3.7: Configuring Port Address Translation (PAT)**

In this lab, you complete the following objectives:

- Part 1: Build the Network and Verify Connectivity
- Part 2: Configure and Verify NAT Pool Overload
- Part 3: Configure and Verify PAT

# Configure Port Forwarding (9.2.4)

In this topic, you configure port forwarding.

## Port Forwarding (9.2.4.1)

*Port forwarding* is the act of forwarding traffic addressed to a specific network port from one network node to another. This technique allows an external user to reach a port on a private IPv4 address (inside a LAN) from the outside, through a NAT-enabled router.

Typically, peer-to-peer file-sharing programs and operations, such as web serving and outgoing FTP, require that router ports be forwarded or opened to allow these applications to work, as shown in Figure 9-19. Because NAT hides internal addresses, peer-to-peer only works from the inside out where NAT can map outgoing requests against incoming replies.

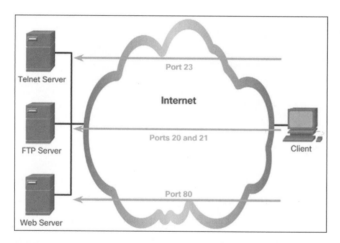

**Figure 9-19**   TCP and UDP Destination Ports

The problem is that NAT does not allow requests initiated from the outside. This situation can be resolved with manual intervention. Port forwarding can be configured to identify specific ports that can be forwarded to inside hosts.

Recall that Internet software applications interact with user ports that need to be open or available to those applications. Different applications use different ports. This makes it predictable for applications and routers to identify network services. For example, HTTP operates through the well-known port 80. When someone enters the http://cisco.com address, the browser displays the Cisco Systems, Inc. website. Notice that the user does not have to specify the HTTP port number for the page request because the application assumes port 80.

If a different port number is required, it can be appended to the URL separated by a colon (:). For example, if the web server is listening on port 8080, the user would type http://www.example.com:8080.

Port forwarding allows users on the Internet to access internal servers by using the WAN port address of the router and the matched external port number. The internal servers are typically configured with RFC 1918 private IPv4 addresses. When a request is sent to the IPv4 address of the WAN port via the Internet, the router forwards the request to the appropriate server on the LAN. For security reasons, broadband routers do not by default permit any external network request to be forwarded to an inside host.

Figure 9-20 shows a small business owner using a point of sale (PoS) server to track sales and inventories at the store.

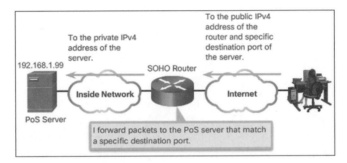

**Figure 9-20**  TCP and UDP Destination Ports

The server can be accessed within the store, but because it has a private IPv4 address, it is not publicly accessible from the Internet.

Enabling the local router for port forwarding allows the owner to access the PoS server from anywhere on the Internet. Port forwarding on the router is configured using the destination port number and the private IPv4 address of the PoS server. To access the server, the client software would use the public IPv4 address of the router and the destination port of the server.

## Wireless Router Example (9.2.4.2)

Figure 9-21 shows the Single Port Forwarding configuration window for a packet tracer wireless router. By default, port forwarding is not enabled on the router.

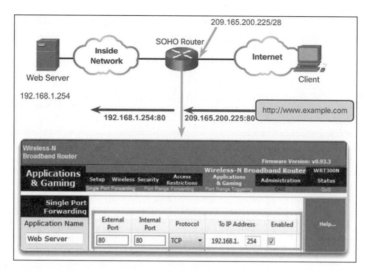

**Figure 9-21**   Configuring Single Port Forwarding

Port forwarding can be enabled for applications by specifying the inside local address that requests should be forwarded to. In the figure, HTTP service requests, coming into wireless router, are forwarded to the web server with the inside local address of 192.168.1.254. If the external WAN IPv4 address of the wireless router is 209.165.200.225, the external user can enter **http://www.example.com**, and the wireless router redirects the HTTP request to the internal web server at IPv4 address 192.168.1.254, using the default port number 80.

A port other than the default port 80 can be specified. However, the external user would have to know the specific port number to use. To specify a different port, the value of the external port in the Single Port Forwarding window would be modified.

The approach taken to configure port forwarding depends on the brand and model of the broadband router in the network. However, there are some generic steps to follow. If the instructions supplied by the ISP, or those that came with the router, do not provide adequate guidance, the website http://www.portforward.com provides guides for several broadband routers. You can follow the instructions to add or delete ports as required to meet the needs of any applications you want to allow or deny.

## Configuring Port Forwarding with IOS (9.2.4.3)

Implementing port forwarding with IOS commands is similar to the commands used to configure static NAT. Port forwarding is essentially a static NAT translation with a specified TCP or UDP port number.

To configure port forwarding, use the **ip nat inside source** {**static** {**tcp** | **udp** *local-ip local-port global-ip global-port*} [**extendable**] global configuration command.

Table 9-5 describes the command syntax used for configuring port forwarding.

**Table 9-5**   IOS Port Forwarding Command Syntax

| Parameter | Description |
|---|---|
| **tcp** or **udp** | This indicates whether this is a tcp or a udp port number. |
| *local-ip* | This is the IPv4 address assigned to the host on the inside network, typically from RFC 1918 private address space. |
| *local-port* | This sets the local TCP/UDP port in a range from 1 to 65535. This is the port number the server is listening on. |
| *global-ip* | This is the IPv4 globally unique IP address of an inside host. This is the IP address outside clients will use to reach the internal host. |
| *global-port* | This sets the global TCP/UDP port in a range from 1 to 65535. This is the port number the outside client will use to reach the internal server. |
| **extendable** | By default, the **extendable** option is applied automatically. It allows the user to configure several ambiguous static translations, where ambiguous translations are translations with the same local or global address. It allows the router to extend the translation to more than one port if necessary. |

Consider the topology in Figure 9-22.

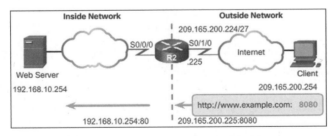

**Figure 9-22**   IOS Port Forwarding Topology

Example 9-13 demonstrates configuring port forwarding using IOS commands on router R2.

**Example 9-13** IOS Port Forwarding Configuration

```
R2(config)# ip nat inside source static tcp 192.168.10.254 80 209.165.200.225 8080
R2(config)#
R2(config)# interface Serial0/0/0
R2(config-if)# ip nat inside
R2(config-if)# exit
R2(config)#
R2(config)# interface Serial0/1/0
R2(config-if)# ip nat outside
R2(config-if)#
```

In the example, 192.168.10.254 is the inside local IPv4 address of the web server listening on port 80. Users access this internal web server using the global IPv4 address 209.165.200.225, a globally unique public IPv4 address. In this case, it is the address of the Serial 0/1/0 interface of R2. The global port is configured as 8080. This will be the destination port used, along with the global IPv4 address of 209.165.200.225 to access the internal web server.

Notice within the NAT configuration the following command parameters:

- *local-ip* = 192.168.10.254

- *local-port* = 80

- *global-ip* = 209.165.200.225

- *global-port* = 8080

When a well-known port number is not being used, the client must specify the port number in the application.

Like other types of NAT, port forwarding requires the configuration of both the inside and the outside NAT interfaces.

Similar to static NAT, the **show ip nat translations** command can be used to verify the port forwarding, as shown in Example 9-14.

**Example 9-14** Verifying IOS Port Forwarding

```
R2# show ip nat translations
Pro Inside global       Inside local      Outside local       Outside global
tcp 209.165.200.225:8080 192.168.10.254:80  209.165.200.254:46088
    209.165.200.254:46088
tcp 209.165.200.225:8080 192.168.10.254:80  ---                 ---
R2#
```

In the preceding output, R2 received a packet with the destination of the inside global IPv4 address of 209.165.200.225 and a TCP destination of port 8080. R2 performs a NAT table lookup matching that IP and port number. When it finds the entry, it changes the packet to destination IP 192.168.10.254 and destination port 80. R2 then forwards the packet to the web server. For return packets from the web server back to the client, this process is reversed.

**Packet Tracer 9.2.4.4: Configuring Port Forwarding on a Wireless Router**

Scenario

Your friend wants to play a game with you on your server. Both of you are at your respective homes, connected to the Internet. You need to configure your wireless router to port forward HTTP requests to your server so that your friend can access the game lobby web Page.

# NAT and IPv6 (9.2.5)

In this topic, you learn how NAT is used with IPv6 networks.

## NAT for IPv6? (9.2.5.1)

Since the early 1990s, the concern about the depletion of IPv4 address space has been a priority of the IETF. The combination of RFC 1918 private IPv4 addresses and NAT has been instrumental in slowing this depletion, as illustrated in Figure 9-23.

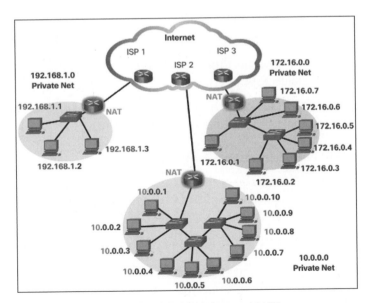

**Figure 9-23**   IPv4 Private Addresses and NAT

However, even the help of these solutions has not stopped the depletion of IPv4 addresses. In January 2011, the *Internet Assigned Numbers Authority (IANA)* allocated the last of its IPv4 addresses to a *regional Internet registry (RIR)*. It should be mentioned that RIRs may still have some IPv4 address blocks available by reclaiming and optimizing existing address blocks.

One of the unintentional benefits of NAT for IPv4 is that it hides the private network from the public Internet. NAT has the advantage of providing a perceived level of security by denying computers in the public Internet from accessing internal hosts. However, it should not be considered a substitute for proper network security, such as that provided by a firewall.

In RFC 5902, the *Internet Architecture Board (IAB)* included the following quote concerning IPv6 NAT:

"It is commonly perceived that a NAT box provides one level of protection because external hosts cannot directly initiate communication with hosts behind a NAT. However, one should not confuse NAT boxes with *firewalls*. As discussed [in] Section 2.2 in RFC4864, the act of translation does not provide security in itself. The stateful filtering function can provide the same level of protection without requiring a translation function."

IPv6, with a 128-bit address, provides 340 undecillion addresses. Therefore, address space is not an issue. IPv6 was developed with the intention of making NAT for IPv4 with its translation between public and private IPv4 addresses unnecessary. However, IPv6 does implement a form of NAT that includes a private address space and NAT. However, they are implemented differently than they are for IPv4.

## IPv6 Unique Local Addresses (9.2.5.2)

IPv6 *unique local addresses (ULA)* are similar to RFC 1918 private addresses in IPv4, but there are significant differences as well. The intent of ULA is to provide IPv6 address space for communications within a local site. ULA is not meant to provide additional IPv6 address space, nor is it meant to provide a level of security.

Figure 9-24 displays the structure of an IPv6 ULA packet.

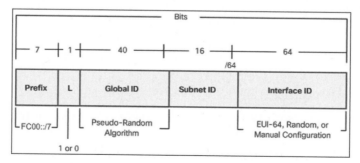

**Figure 9-24**   IPv6 Unique Local Address Structure

These first 64 bits consisting of Prefix, L (local flag), Global ID, and Subnet ID combine to make the ULA prefix. This remaining 64 bits identify the interface ID, or in IPv4 terms, the host portion of the address.

ULA addresses have the prefix FC00::/7, which results in a first hextet range of FC00 to FDFF. The next 1 bit is the local flag (L), which is usually set 1, indicating that the prefix was locally assigned. The next 40 bits is a global ID followed by a 16-bit Subnet ID. Recall that an organization uses the Subnet-ID to create various internal networks.

Unique local addresses are defined in RFC 4193. ULAs are also known as local IPv6 addresses (not to be confused with IPv6 link-local addresses) and have several characteristics including these:

- Allows sites to be combined or privately interconnected, without creating any address conflicts or requiring renumbering of interfaces that use these prefixes.

- Independent of any ISP and can be used for communications within a site without having any Internet connectivity.

- Not routable across the Internet, however, if accidentally leaked by routing or DNS, there is not conflict with other addresses.

ULA is not quite as straightforward as RFC 1918 addresses. Unlike private IPv4 addresses, it has not been the intention of the IETF to use a form of NAT to translate between unique local addresses and IPv6 global unicast addresses.

The implementation and potential uses for IPv6 unique local addresses are still being examined by the Internet community. For example, the IETF is considering allowing the option of having the 40-bit global ID centrally assigned when using the FC00::/8 ULA prefix, and the 40-bit global ID randomly generated, or perhaps manually assigned, when using the ULA prefix FD00::/8. The rest of the address remains the same. We still use 16 bits for the subnet ID and 64 bits for the interface ID.

**Note**

The original IPv6 specification allocated address space for site-local addresses, defined in RFC 3513. Site-local addresses have been deprecated by the IETF in RFC 3879 because the term "site" was somewhat ambiguous. Site-local addresses had the prefix range of FEC0::/10 and may still be found in some older IPv6 documentation.

## NAT for IPv6 (9.2.5.3)

NAT for IPv6 is used in a much different context than NAT for IPv4. NAT for IPv6 is not used as a form of private IPv6 address to global IPv6 address translation. NAT for IPv6 is used to interconnect IPv6 and IPv4 networks.

Ideally, IPv6 should be run natively wherever possible. This means IPv6 devices communicating with each other over IPv6 networks. However, to support the transition from IPv4 to IPv6, the IETF has developed several transition techniques to accommodate a variety of IPv4-to-IPv6 scenarios. These include:

- *Dual-stack*—A device interface is running both IPv4 and IPv6 protocols enabling it to communicate with either network.

- *Tunneling*—The process of encapsulating an IPv6 packet inside an IPv4 packet. This allows the IPv6 packet to be transmitted over an IPv4-only network.

- *Translation*—Implementing NAT to translate IPv6 to IPv4 addresses.

NAT for IPv6 should not be used as a long-term strategy, but as a temporary mechanism to assist in the migration from IPv4 to IPv6.

Over the years, there have been several types of NAT for IPv6 solutions developed. An early version was called ***Network Address Translation-Protocol Translation (NAT-PT)***. However, NAT-PT has been deprecated by IETF in favor of *NAT64*.

Figure 9-25 illustrates how NAT64 can translate between IPv6 nd IPv4 networks.

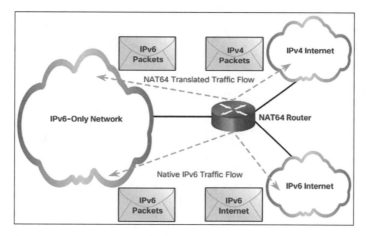

**Figure 9-25**   NAT64 Scenario

NAT64 is beyond the scope of this curriculum.

# Troubleshoot NAT (9.3)

Correctly implementing NAT should be fairly straightforward using a documented systematic approach. However, mistakes do happen. It is imperative that you develop strong troubleshooting skills. Troubleshooting is a sought-after skill that is acquired through practice and experience.

In this section, you learn how to troubleshoot NAT issues in a small-to medium-sized business network.

## NAT Troubleshooting Commands (9.3.1)

In this topic, you will troubleshoot NAT.

### The show ip nat Commands (9.3.1.1)

When there are IPv4 connectivity problems in a NAT environment, it may be difficult to determine the cause of the problem.

Consider the topology in Figure 9-26. In this example, in this example, R2 is enabled for dynamic PAT using the pool of addresses from the 209.165.200.226 to 209.165.200.240 range.

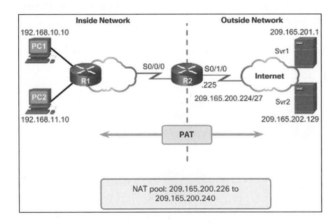

**Figure 9-26** Troubleshooting NAT

Follow these steps to verify that NAT is operating as expected:

Step 1. To help troubleshoot and observe the NAT process, clear NAT statistics and NAT translations using the **clear ip nat statistics** and **clear ip nat translations** commands.

Step 2. Test NAT and then verify that correct translations exist in the translation table using the **show ip nat translations** command.

Step 3. Check NAT statistics using the **show ip nat statistics** command.

Step 4. Observe the NAT process using **debug ip nat** command.

Step 5. Review in detail what is happening to the packet, and verify that routers have the correct routing information to move the packet.

Example 9-15 clears the NAT statistics and translations on the NAT-enabled router, R2.

**Example 9-15** Clearing NAT Statistics to Troubleshoot

```
R2# clear ip nat statistics
R2# clear ip nat translation *
R2#
```

Next, NAT is verified and the internal host (192.168.10.10) telnets to the outside server (209.165.201.1) to generate a NAT entry.

Example 9-16 verifies the NAT statistics and NAT translation table to see if the host generated a NAT entry.

**Example 9-16** Using NAT Statistics to Troubleshoot

```
R2# show ip nat statistics
Total active translations: 1 (0 static, 1 dynamic; 1 extended)
Peak translations: 1, occurred 00:00:09 ago
Outside interfaces:
  Serial0/0/1
Inside interfaces:
  Serial0/0/0
Hits: 31  Misses: 0
CEF Translated packets: 31, CEF Punted packets: 0
Expired translations: 0
Dynamic mappings:
-- Inside Source
[Id: 5] access-list 1 pool NAT-POOL2 refcount 1
 pool NAT-POOL2: netmask 255.255.255.224
      start 209.165.200.226 end 209.165.200.240
      type generic, total addresses 15, allocated 1 (6%), misses 0

<output omitted>

R2# show ip nat translations
Pro Inside global         Inside local        Outside local      Outside global
tcp 209.165.200.226:19005 192.168.10.10:19005 209.165.201.1:23   209.165.201.1:23
R2#
```

The preceding output verifies that NAT is operational.

If the output gave unexpected results, check the NAT configuration using the **show running-config | include nat**. If the NAT pool, binding, and interface commands look accurate, verify that the ACL referenced in the NAT command is permitting all of the necessary networks.

Example 9-17 verifies the currently configured ACLs on R2.

**Example 9-17**  Verifying the NAT ACL

```
R2# show access-lists
Standard IP access list 1
    10 permit 192.168.0.0, wildcard bits 0.0.255.255 (29 matches)
R2#
```

Notice that in this example, only 192.168.0.0/16 addresses are eligible to be translated. R2 does not translate packets from the inside network destined for the Internet with source addresses that are not explicitly permitted by ACL 1.

## The debug ip nat Command (9.3.1.2)

In a simple network environment, it is useful to monitor NAT statistics with the **show ip nat statistics** command. The **show ip nat statistics** command displays information about the total number of active translations, the NAT configuration parameters, the number of addresses in the pool, and the number that have been allocated.

However, in a more complex NAT environment, with several translations taking place, this command may not clearly identify the issue. It may be necessary to run **debug** commands on the router.

Use the **debug ip nat** command to verify the operation of the NAT feature by displaying information about every packet that the router translates.

The **debug ip nat detailed** command generates a description of each packet considered for translation. This command also provides information about certain errors or exception conditions, such as the failure to allocate a global address. Note that the **debug ip nat detailed** command generates more overhead than the **debug ip nat** command. However, it can provide the detail that may be needed to troubleshoot the NAT problem.

> **Note**
>
> Regardless of which **debug** command is used, always disable debugging when finished.

Example 9-18 shows a sample **debug ip nat** output.

**Example 9-18** Debugging NAT

```
R2# debug ip nat
IP NAT debugging is on
R2#

*Feb 15 20:01:311.670: NAT*: s=192.168.10.10->209.165.200.226, d=209.165.201.1
  [2817]
*Feb 15 20:01:311.682: NAT*: s=209.165.201.1, d=209.165.200.226->192.168.10.10
  [4180]
*Feb 15 20:01:311.698: NAT*: s=192.168.10.10->209.165.200.226, d=209.165.201.1
  [2818]
*Feb 15 20:01:311.702: NAT*: s=192.168.10.10->209.165.200.226, d=209.165.201.1
  [2819]
*Feb 15 20:01:311.710: NAT*: s=192.168.10.10->209.165.200.226, d=209.165.201.1
  [2820]
*Feb 15 20:01:311.710: NAT*: s=209.165.201.1, d=209.165.200.226->192.168.10.10
  [4181]
*Feb 15 20:01:311.722: NAT*: s=209.165.201.1, d=209.165.200.226->192.168.10.10
  [4182]
*Feb 15 20:01:311.726: NAT*: s=192.168.10.10->209.165.200.226, d=209.165.201.1
  [2821]
*Feb 15 20:01:311.730: NAT*: s=209.165.201.1, d=209.165.200.226->192.168.10.10
  [4183]
*Feb 15 20:01:311.734: NAT*: s=192.168.10.10->209.165.200.226, d=209.165.201.1
  [2822]
*Feb 15 20:01:311.734: NAT*: s=209.165.201.1, d=209.165.200.226->192.168.10.10
  [4184]
<Output omitted>
```

The output shows that the inside host (192.168.10.10) initiated traffic to the outside host (209.165.201.1), and the source address was translated to address 209.165.200.226.

When decoding the **debug** output, note what the following symbols and values indicate:

- *—The asterisk (*) next to NAT indicates that the translation is occurring in the fast-switched path. The first packet in a conversation is always process-switched, which is slower. The remaining packets go through the fast-switched path if a cache entry exists.

- s=—The s= symbol refers to the source IPv4 address.

- a.b.c.d--->w.x.y.z—This value indicates that source address a.b.c.d is translated (->) to w.x.y.z.

- **d=**—The **d=** symbol refers to the destination IPv4 address.

- **[xxxx]**—The value in brackets is the IPv4 identification number. This information may be useful for debugging in that it enables correlation with other packet traces from protocol analyzers.

## NAT Troubleshooting Scenario (9.3.1.3)

In Figure 9-27, hosts from the 192.168.0.0/16 LANs (PC1, and PC2) cannot ping servers (Svr1 and Svr2) on the outside network.

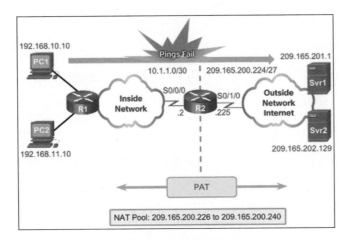

**Figure 9-27**  NAT Troubleshooting Scenario

To begin troubleshooting the problem, use the **show ip nat translations** command to see whether any translations are currently in the NAT table.

Example 9-19 verifies the NAT translations.

**Example 9-19**  Use **show** Commands to Discover Issue

```
R2# show ip nat translations
R2#
```

The output reveals that no translations are in the table.

The **show ip nat statistics** command is used to determine whether any translations have taken place. It also identifies the interfaces that translation should be occurring between.

In Example 9-20, the NAT counters are at 0, verifying that no translation has occurred.

**Example 9-20** Verify NAT Statistics

```
R2# show ip nat statistics
Total active translations: 0 (0 static, 0 dynamic; 0 extended)
Peak translations: 0
Outside interfaces:
  Serial0/0/0
Inside interfaces:
  Serial0/1/0
Hits: 0  Misses: 0
<Output omitted>
R2(config)#
```

By comparing the output with the topology shown in Figure 9-27, notice that the router interfaces are incorrectly defined as NAT inside or NAT outside. The incorrect configuration can also be verified using the **show running-config** command.

The current NAT interface configuration must be deleted from the interfaces before applying the correct configuration.

Example 9-21 deletes the NAT interface configuration and applies the correct configuration.

**Example 9-21** Resolve NAT Interface Issue

```
R2(config)# interface serial 0/0/0
R2(config-if)# no ip nat outside
R2(config-if)# ip nat inside
R2(config-if)# exit
R2(config)#
R2(config)# interface serial 0/0/1
R2(config-if)# no ip nat inside
R2(config-if)# ip nat outside
R2(config-if)#
```

Assume that a test ping from PC1 to Svr1 still fails. Also, the **show ip nat translations** command does not display translations, and the **show ip nat statistics** command does not display changes.

Determine whether the ACL that the NAT command references is permitting all of the necessary networks.

Example 9-22 verifies the NAT ACL.

**Example 9-22**  Display Configured ACLs

```
R2# show access-lists
Standard IP access list 1
    10 permit 192.168.0.0, wildcard bits 0.0.0.255
R2#
```

Examining the output indicates that an incorrect wildcard bit mask has been used in the ACL that defines the addresses needing to be translated. The wildcard mask (0.0.0.255) is only permitting the 192.168.0.0/24 subnet. To permit the 192.168.0.0/16 subnet, the wildcard mask should be 0.0.255.255.

Example 9-23 removes the ACL and then reconfigures it using the correct wildcard mask.

**Example 9-23**  Resolve ACL Issue

```
R2(config)# no access-list 1
R2(config)#
R2(config)# access-list 1 permit 192.168.0.0 0.0.255.255
R2(config)#
```

After configurations are corrected, another ping is generated from PC1 to Svr1, and this time the ping succeeds. Next verify that the NAT translation is occurring.

Example 9-24 displays the output of the **show ip nat statistics** and **show ip nat translations** commands.

**Example 9-24**  Verify NAT Operation

```
R2# show ip nat statistics
Total active translations: 1 (0 static, 1 dynamic; 1 extended)
Peak translations: 1, occurred 00:37:58 ago
Outside interfaces:
  Serial0/0/1
Inside interfaces:
  Serial0/1/0
Hits: 20  Misses: 0
CEF Translated packets: 20, CEF Punted packets: 0
Expired translations: 1
```

```
Dynamic mappings:
-- Inside Source
[Id: 5] access-list 1 pool NAT-POOL2 refcount 1
 pool NAT-POOL2: netmask 255.255.255.224
    start 209.165.200.226 end 209.165.200.240
    type generic, total addresses 15, allocated 1 (6%), misses 0
<Output omitted>


R2# show ip nat translations
Pro Inside global      Inside local     Outside local      Outside global
icmp 209.165.200.226:38 192.168.10.10:38  209.165.201.1:38   209.165.201.1:38
R2#
```

The output confirms that NAT is now operational and outside connectivity has been established.

**Packet Tracer 9.3.1.4: Verifying and Troubleshooting NAT Configurations**

A contractor restored an old configuration to a new router running NAT. But the network has changed, and a new subnet was added after the old configuration was backed up. It is your job to get the network working again.

**Lab 9.3.1.5: Troubleshooting NAT Configurations**

In this lab, you complete the following objectives:

- Part 1: Build the Network and Configure Basic Device Settings
- Part 2: Troubleshoot Static NAT
- Part 3: Troubleshoot Dynamic NAT

## Summary (9.4)

### Class Activity 9.4.1.1: NAT Check

Scenario

Network address translation is not currently included in your company's network design. It has been decided to configure some devices to use NAT services for connecting to the mail server.

Before deploying NAT live on the network, you prototype it using a network simulation program.

For further instructions, refer to the PDF that accompanies this activity.

### Packet Tracer 9.4.1.2: Skills Integration Challenge

Scenario

This culminating activity includes many of the skills that you have acquired during this course. First, you complete the documentation for the network, so make sure you have a printed version of the instructions. During implementation, you configure VLANs, trunking, port security, and SSH remote access on a switch. Then you implement inter-VLAN routing and NAT on a router. Finally, you use your documentation to verify your implementation by testing end-to-end connectivity.

This chapter has outlined how NAT is used to help alleviate the depletion of IPv4 address space. NAT for IPv4 allows network administrators to use RFC 1918 private address space while providing connectivity to the Internet, using a single or limited number of public addresses.

NAT conserves public address space and saves considerable administrative overhead in managing adds, moves, and changes. NAT and PAT can be implemented to conserve public address space without affecting the ISP connection. However, NAT has drawbacks in terms of its negative effects on device performance, mobility, and end-to-end connectivity and should be considered a short-term implementation for address exhaustion, with the long-term solution being IPv6.

This chapter discussed NAT for IPv4, including these topics:

- NAT characteristics, terminology, and general operations
- The different types of NAT, including static NAT, dynamic NAT, and PAT
- The benefits and disadvantages of NAT

- The configuration, verification, and analysis of static NAT, dynamic NAT, and PAT
- How port forwarding can be used to access an internal device from the Internet
- Why NAT is available but not integral to IPv6 networking
- Troubleshooting NAT using **show** and **debug** commands

## Practice

The following activities provide practice with the topics introduced in this chapter. The labs and class activities are available in the companion Routing and Switching Essentials v6 Labs & Study Guide (ISBN 9781587134265). The packet tracer activities PKA files are found in the online course.

**Class Activities**

Class Activity 9.0.1.2: Conceptual NAT

Class Activity 9.4.1.1: NAT Check

**Labs**

Lab 9.2.2.6: Configuring Dynamic and Static NAT

Lab 9.2.3.7: Configuring Port Address Translation (PAT)

Lab 9.3.1.5: Troubleshooting NAT Configurations

Packet Tracer
☐ Activity

**Packet Tracer Activities**

Packet Tracer 9.1.2.6: Investigating NAT Operation

Packet Tracer 9.2.1.4: Configuring Static NAT

Packet Tracer 9.2.2.5: Configuring Dynamic NAT

Packet Tracer 9.2.3.6: Implementing Static and Dynamic NAT

Packet Tracer 9.2.4.4: Configuring Port Forwarding on a Wireless Router

Packet Tracer 9.3.1.4: Verifying and Troubleshooting NAT Configurations

Packet Tracer 9.4.1.2: Skills Integration Challenge

# Check Your Understanding Questions

Complete all the review questions listed here to test your understanding of the topics and concepts in this chapter. The appendix "Answers to the 'Check Your Understanding' Questions" lists the answers.

1. Typically, which network device is used to perform NAT for a corporate environment?

   A. Switch

   B. Server

   C. DHCP server

   D. Router

   E. Host device

2. When NAT is employed in a small office, which address type is typically used for hosts on the local LAN?

   A. Both private and public IP addresses

   B. Global public IP addresses

   C. Internet-routable addresses

   D. Private IP addresses

3. Which version of NAT allows many hosts inside a private network to simultaneously use a single inside global address for connecting to the Internet?

   A. Dynamic NAT

   B. PAT

   C. Port forwarding

   D. Static NAT

4. Which type of NAT maps a single inside local address to a single inside global address?

   A. Dynamic

   B. Overloading

   C. Port address translation

   D. Static

5. What is a disadvantage of NAT?

   A. The costs of readdressing hosts can be significant for a publicly addressed network.

   B. The internal hosts have to use a single public IPv4 address for external communication.

C. There is no end-to-end addressing.

D. The router does not need to alter the checksum of the IPv4 packets.

6. How can NAT cause IPsec to fail?

A. End-to-end IPv4 traceability is lost.

B. Header values are modified, which causes issues with integrity checks.

C. Network performance is degraded even more than with just NAT.

D. Troubleshooting is made impossible.

7. Which statement accurately describes dynamic NAT?

A. It always maps a private IP address to a public IP address.

B. It dynamically provides IP addressing to internal hosts.

C. It provides a mapping of internal host names to IP addresses.

D. It provides an automated mapping of inside local to inside global IP addresses.

8. A network administrator configures the border router with the **ip nat inside source list 4 pool** NAT-POOL global configuration command. What is required to be configured for this particular command to be functional?

A. A VLAN named NAT-POOL to be enabled and active and routed by R1

B. A NAT pool named NAT-POOL that defines the starting and ending public IP addresses

C. An access list named NAT-POOL that defines the private addresses that are affected by NAT

D. An access list numbered 4 that defines the starting and ending public IP addresses

E. **ip nat outside** to be enabled on the interface that connects to the LAN affected by the NAT

9. When dynamic NAT without overloading is being used, what happens if seven users attempt to access a public server on the Internet when only six addresses are available in the NAT pool?

A. All users can access the server.

B. No users can access the server.

C. The first user is disconnected when the seventh user makes the request.

D. The request to the server for the seventh user fails.

10. What is the purpose of port forwarding?

    A. Port forwarding allows for translating inside local IP addresses to outside local addresses.

    B. Port forwarding allows users to reach servers on the Internet that are not using standard port numbers.

    C. Port forwarding allows an internal user to reach a service on a public IPv4 address that is located outside a LAN.

    D. Port forwarding allows an external user to reach a service on a private IPv4 address that is located inside a LAN.

11. What is a characteristic of unique local addresses?

    A. Their implementation depends on ISPs providing the service.

    B. They allow sites to be combined without creating address conflicts.

    C. They are defined in RFC 3927.

    D. They are designed to improve the security of IPv6 networks.

12. Which prefix is used for IPv6 ULAs?

    A. FC00::/7

    B. FF02::1:FF00:0/104

    C. 2001:DB8:1:2::/64

    D. 2001:7F8::/29

13. Which technology would be used on a router that is running both IPv4 and IPv6?

    A. Dynamic NAT

    B. Dual stack

    C. NAT for IPv6

    D. Static NAT

14. Which configuration would be appropriate for a small business that has the public IP address of 209.165.200.225/30 assigned to the external interface on the router that connects to the Internet?

    A. **access-list 1 permit 10.0.0.0 0.255.255.255**

       **ip nat pool NAT-POOL 192.168.2.1 192.168.2.8 netmask 255.255.255.240**

       **ip nat inside source list 1 pool NAT-POOL**

B.  access-list 1 permit 10.0.0.0 0.255.255.255

ip nat pool NAT-POOL 192.168.2.1 192.168.2.8 netmask 255.255.255.240

ip nat inside source list 1 pool NAT-POOL overload

C.  access-list 1 permit 10.0.0.0 0.255.255.255

ip nat inside source list 1 interface serial 0/0/0 overload

D.  access-list 1 permit 10.0.0.0 0.255.255.255

ip nat pool NAT-POOL 192.168.2.1 192.168.2.8 netmask 255.255.255.240

ip nat inside source list 1 pool NAT-POOL overload

ip nat inside source static 10.0.0.5 209.165.200.225

15. What are two of the required steps to configure PAT? (Choose two.)

A.  Create a standard access list to define applications that should be translated.

B.  Define a pool of global addresses to be used for overload translation.

C.  Define the hello and interval timers to match the adjacent neighbor router.

D.  Define the range of source ports to be used.

E.  Identify the inside interface.

16. What is the group of public IPv4 addresses used on a NAT-enabled router known as?

A.  Inside global addresses

B.  Inside local addresses

C.  Outside global addresses

D.  Outside local addresses

# CHAPTER 10

# Device Discovery, Management, and Maintenance

## Objectives

Upon completion of this chapter, you will be able to answer the following questions:

- How do you use CDP to map a network topology?

- How do you use LLDP to map a network topology?

- How do you implement NTP between an NTP client and an NTP server?

- How does syslog operate?

- How do you configure syslog servers and clients?

- How do you use commands to back up and restore an IOS configuration file?

- How do you explain the IOS image naming conventions implemented by Cisco?

- How do you upgrade an IOS system image?

- How do you explain the licensing process for Cisco IOS software in a small- to medium-sized business network?

- How do you configure a router to install an IOS software image license?

## Key Terms

This chapter uses the following key terms. You can find the definitions in the Glossary.

Cisco Discovery Protocol (CDP)    Page 477

Link Layer Discovery Protocol (LLDP)    Page 483

syslog    Page 486

Network Time Protocol (NTP)    Page 486

NTP client    Page 487

NTP server    Page 487

software clock    Page 487

stratum    Page 488

authoritative time source    Page 488

severity level    Page 493

facility    Page 493

ROMMON mode    Page 511

configuration register    Page 511

Services on Demand    Page 514

universal Cisco IOS Software image    Page 514

Product Activation Key (PAK)    Page 515

# Introduction (10.0.0.1)

In this chapter, you will explore the tools network administrators can use for device discovery, device management, and device maintenance. Both Cisco Discovery Protocol (CDP) and Link Layer Discover Protocol (LLDP) are capable of discovering information about directly connected devices.

Network Time Protocol (NTP) can be effectively used to synchronize the time across all your networking devices, which is especially important when trying to compare log files from different devices. The syslog protocol generates those log files. Syslog messages can be captured and sent to a syslog server to aid in device management tasks.

Device maintenance includes ensuring that Cisco IOS images and configuration files are backed up in a safe location in the event that the device memory is corrupted or erased, either maliciously or inadvertently. Maintenance also includes keeping the IOS image up to date. The "Device Maintenance" section of the chapter includes topics for file maintenance, image management, and software licensing.

# Device Discovery (10.1)

It is often useful to discover which neighboring devices are connected. Device discovery identifies the type of devices connecting and specifics about those devices. Device discovery also validates that Layers 1 and 2 are operational, which can be useful when troubleshooting network connectivity problems.

In this section, you use discovery protocols to map a network topology.

## Device Discovery with CDP (10.1.1)

In this topic, you learn how to use CDP to map a network topology.

### CDP Overview (10.1.1.1)

*Cisco Discovery Protocol (CDP)* is a Cisco proprietary Layer 2 protocol that gathers information about Cisco devices sharing the same data link. CDP is media and protocol independent and runs on all Cisco devices, such as routers, switches, and access servers.

The device sends periodic CDP advertisements to connected devices, as shown in Figure 10-1.

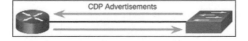

**Figure 10-1**    CDP Operation

These advertisements share information about the type of devices and IOS versions, the name of the devices, and the number and type of the interfaces.

Because most network devices are connected to other devices, CDP can assist in network design decisions, troubleshooting, and changes to equipment. CDP can also be used as a network discovery tool to determine the information about the neighboring devices. This information gathered from CDP can help build a logical topology of a network when documentation is missing or lacking in detail.

## Configure and Verify CDP (10.1.1.2)

For Cisco devices, CDP is enabled by default. However, an attacker can use CDP to gather valuable insight about the network layout, such as types of devices, IP addresses, and IOS versions. Therefore, for security reasons, it may be desirable to disable CDP on a network device globally, or per interface.

To disable CDP for all the interfaces on the device, enter the **no cdp run** global configuration command.

In Example 10-1, CDP is disabled globally for all interfaces using the **no cdp run** command.

**Example 10-1** CDP Globally Disabled

```
R1(config)# no cdp run
R1(config)# exit
R1#
R1# show cdp

R1#
```

The **show cdp** command verifies the status and displays information about CDP.

To enable CDP globally for all the supported interfaces on the device, enter **cdp run** in the global configuration mode.

In Example 10-2, CDP is enabled globally using the **cdp run** command.

**Example 10-2** CDP Globally Enabled

```
R1(config)# cdp run
R1(config)# exit
R1#
R1# show cdp
Global CDP information:
        Sending CDP packets every 60 seconds
        Sending a holdtime value of 180 seconds
        Sending CDPv2 advertisements is  enabled
R1#
```

CDP can also be enabled or disabled on select interfaces. For example, CDP should be disabled on the edge router interface connecting to the ISP.

To disable CDP on a specific interface, use the **no cdp enable** interface configuration command. This command only affects CDP on that interface. CDP is still enabled on the device. To enable CDP on the specific interface again, enter the **cdp enable** interface configuration command as shown in Example 10-3.

**Example 10-3** CDP Configuration Command

```
R1(config)# interface gigabitethernet 0/1
R1(config-if)# cdp enable
R1(config-if)#
```

To verify the status of CDP and display a list of neighbors, use the **show cdp neighbors** privileged EXEC mode command. The command displays important information about the CDP neighbors.

Example 10-4 displays output generated by the **show cdp neighbors** command.

**Example 10-4** Listing CDP Neighbors

```
R1# show cdp neighbors
Capability Codes: R - Router, T - Trans Bridge, B - Source Route Bridge
                  S - Switch, H - Host, I - IGMP, r - Repeater, P - Phone,
                  D - Remote, C - CVTA, M - Two-port Mac Relay


Device ID        Local Intrfce      Holdtme    Capability  Platform  Port ID

Total cdp entries displayed : 0
```

Currently, R1 does not have neighbors because it is not physically connected to any devices, as indicated by the results.

Use the **show cdp interface** command to display the interfaces that are CDP enabled on a device. The status of each interface is also displayed. Example 10-5 shows that five interfaces are CDP enabled on the router with only one active connection to another device.

**Example 10-5** Displaying Enable CDP Interfaces

```
R1# show cdp interface
Embedded-Service-Engine0/0 is administratively down, line protocol is down
  Encapsulation ARPA
  Sending CDP packets every 60 seconds
  Holdtime is 180 seconds
```

```
GigabitEthernet0/0 is administratively down, line protocol is down
  Encapsulation ARPA
  Sending CDP packets every 60 seconds
  Holdtime is 180 seconds
GigabitEthernet0/1 is up, line protocol is up
  Encapsulation ARPA
  Sending CDP packets every 60 seconds
  Holdtime is 180 seconds
Serial0/0/0 is administratively down, line protocol is down
  Encapsulation HDLC
  Sending CDP packets every 60 seconds
  Holdtime is 180 seconds
Serial0/0/1 is administratively down, line protocol is down
  Encapsulation HDLC
  Sending CDP packets every 60 seconds
  Holdtime is 180 seconds
```

## Discover Devices Using CDP (10.1.1.3)

With CDP enabled on the network, the **show cdp neighbors** command can be used to determine the network layout.

For example, consider the lack of documentation in the topology shown in Figure 10-2. No information is available regarding the rest of the network.

**Figure 10-2**   Initial Topology

The **show cdp neighbors** command in Example 10-6 provides helpful information about each CDP neighbor device, including the following:

- **Device identifiers**—The host name of the neighbor device.

- **Port identifier**—The name of the local and remote port.

- **Capabilities list**—Whether the device is a router (R) or a switch (S). Note that I is for Internet Group Management Protocol (IGMP), which is beyond scope for this course.

- **Platform**—The hardware platform of the device.

**Example 10-6** Discovering S1

```
R1# show cdp neighbors
Capability Codes: R - Router, T - Trans Bridge, B - Source Route Bridge
                  S - Switch, H - Host, I - IGMP, r - Repeater, P - Phone,
                  D - Remote, C - CVTA, M - Two-port Mac Relay


Device ID          Local Intrfce      Holdtme      Capability  Platform  Port ID
S1                 Gig 0/1            122               S I    WS-C2960- Fas 0/5
```

The output reveals that the G0/1 interface on R1 is connected to the Fa/05 interface on a Catalyst 2960 switch named S1.

If more information is needed, the **show cdp neighbors detail** command can also provide information, such as the neighbors' IOS version and IPv4 address, as displayed in Example 10-7.

**Example 10-7** Discovering Detail Information About S1

```
R1# show cdp neighbors detail
-------------------------
Device ID: S1
Entry address(es):
  IP address: 192.168.1.2
Platform: cisco WS-C2960-24TT-L,  Capabilities: Switch IGMP
Interface: GigabitEthernet0/1,  Port ID (outgoing port): FastEthernet0/5
Holdtime : 136 sec

Version :
Cisco IOS Software, C2960 Software (C2960-LANBASEK9-M), Version 15.0(2)SE7, RELEASE
  SOFTWARE (fc1)
Technical Support: http://www.cisco.com/techsupport
Copyright (c) 1986-2014 by Cisco Systems, Inc.
Compiled Tue 30-Aug-16 14:49 by prod_rel_team

advertisement version: 2
Protocol Hello:  OUI=0x00000C, Protocol ID=0x0112; payload len=27, value=00000000FF
  FFFFFF010221FF000000000000002291210380FF0000
VTP Management Domain: ''
Native VLAN: 1
Duplex: full
Management address(es):
  IP address: 192.168.1.2


Total cdp entries displayed : 1
```

Figure 10-3 shows the topology now with S1 added.

**Figure 10-3**   Topology with S1 Added

By accessing S1 either remotely through SSH or physically through the console port, a network administrator can determine which other devices are connected to S1.

The output of the **show cdp neighbors** on S1 is displayed in Example 10-8.

**Example 10-8** Discovering Device Connected to S1

```
S1# show cdp neighbors

Capability Codes: R - Router, T - Trans Bridge, B - Source Route Bridge
                  S - Switch, H - Host, I - IGMP, r - Repeater, P - Phone,
                  D - Remote, C - CVTA, M - Two-port Mac Relay


Device ID        Local Intrfce     Holdtme    Capability Platform  Port ID
S2               Fas 0/4           ¬158              S I WS-C2960-  Fas 0/4
R1               Fas 0/5           136         R B S I CISCO1941   Gig 0/1
```

Another switch, S2, is revealed in the output. Figure 10-4 shows the topology with S2 added.

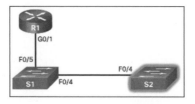

**Figure 10-4**   Topology with S2 Added

The network administrator then accesses S2 and displays its CDP neighbors, as shown in Example 10-9.

**Example 10-9** Discovering Device Connected to S2

```
S2#
Capability Codes: R - Router, T - Trans Bridge, B - Source Route Bridge
                  S - Switch, H - Host, I - IGMP, r - Repeater, P - Phone,
                  D - Remote, C - CVTA, M - Two-port Mac Relay

Device ID          Local Intrfce      Holdtme    Capability  Platform  Port ID
S1                 Fas 0/4            173         S I         WS-C2960- Fas 0/4
```

The only device connected to S2 is S1. Therefore, there are no more devices to discover in the topology. The network administrator can now update the documentation to reflect the discovered devices.

**Packet Tracer 10.1.1.4: Map a Network Using CDP**

A senior network administrator requires you to map the Remote Branch Office network and discover the name of a recently installed switch that still needs an IPv4 address to be configured. Your task is to create a map of the branch office network. To map the network, you will use SSH for remote access and the Cisco Discovery Protocol (CDP) to discover information about neighboring network devices, such as routers and switches.

# Device Discovery with LLDP (10.1.2)

In this topic, you learn how to use LLDP to map a network topology.

## LLDP Overview (10.1.2.1)

Cisco devices also support *Link Layer Discovery Protocol (LLDP)*, as shown in Figure 10-5, which is a vendor-neutral neighbor discovery protocol similar to CDP. LLDP works with network devices, such as routers, switches, and wireless LAN access points. Like CDP, LLDP advertises its identity and capabilities to other devices and receives the information from a physically connected Layer 2 device.

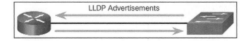

**Figure 10-5**    LLDP Overview

## Configure and Verify LLDP (10.1.2.2)

Depending on the device, LLDP may be enabled by default. To enable LLDP globally on a Cisco network device, enter the **lldp run** global configuration command. To disable LLDP, enter the **no lldp run** command in the global configuration mode.

Similar to CDP, LLDP can be configured on specific interfaces. However, LLDP must be configured separately to transmit and receive LLDP packets, as shown in Example 10-10.

**Example 10-10**  Configure and Verify LLDP

```
S1(config)# lldp run
S1(config)#
S1(config)# interface gigabitethernet 0/1
S1(config-if)# lldp transmit
S1(config-if)# lldp receive
S1(config-if)# end
S1#
S1# show lldp

Global LLDP Information:
    Status: ACTIVE
    LLDP advertisements are sent every 30 seconds
    LLDP hold time advertised is 120 seconds
    LLDP interface reinitialisation delay is 2 seconds
```

To verify LLDP has been enabled on the device, enter the **show lldp** command in the privileged EXEC mode.

## Discover Devices Using LLDP (10.1.2.3)

With LLDP enabled, device neighbors can be discovered using the **show lldp neighbors** command. For example, consider the lack of documentation in the topology shown in Figure 10-6.

**Figure 10-6**  Initial Topology

The network administrator only knows that S1 is connected to two devices. Using the **show lldp neighbors** command, as shown in Example 10-11, the network administrator discovers that S1 has a router and a switch as neighbors.

**Example 10-11**  Discovering R1 and S2

```
S1# show lldp neighbors
Capability codes:
    (R) Router, (B) Bridge, (T) Telephone, (C) DOCSIS Cable Device
    (W) WLAN Access Point, (P) Repeater, (S) Station, (O) Other

Device ID            Local Intf     Hold-time  Capability      Port ID
R1                   Fa0/5          99         R               Gi0/1
S2                   Fa0/4          120        B               Fa0/4

Total entries displayed: 2
```

> **Note**
>
> The letter B under capability for S2 represents a bridge. For this output, the word "bridge" can also mean switch.

From the results of **show lldp neighbors**, a topology from switch S1 can be constructed, as depicted in Figure 10-7.

**Figure 10-7**  Topology with R1 and S2 Added

When more details about the neighbors are needed, the **show lldp neighbors detail** command shown in Example 10-12 can provide information, such as the IOS version, IP address, and device capability of the neighboring device.

**Example 10-12**  Discovering Detail Information About R1 and S2

```
S1# show lldp neighbors detail
------------------------------------------------
Chassis id: fc99.4775.c3e0
Port id: Gi0/1
Port Description: GigabitEthernet0/1
System Name: R1

System Description:
Cisco IOS Software, C1900 Software (C1900-UNIVERSALK9-M), Version 15.4(3)M2,
  RELEASE SOFTWARE (fc2)
Technical Support: http://www.cisco.com/techsupport
Copyright (c) 1986-2015 by Cisco Systems, Inc.
Compiled Tue 30-Aug-16 17:01 by prod_rel_team
```

```
Time remaining: 101 seconds
System Capabilities: B,R
Enabled Capabilities: R
Management Addresses:
    IP: 192.168.1.1
Auto Negotiation - not supported
Physical media capabilities - not advertised
Media Attachment Unit type - not advertised
Vlan ID: - not advertised


----------------------------------------------
Chassis id: 0cd9.96d2.3f80
Port id: Fa0/4
Port Description: FastEthernet0/4
System Name: S2

<output omitted>
```

**Interactive Graphic**

**Activity 10.1.2.4: Compare CDP and LLDP**

Refer to the online course to complete this activity.

**Lab 10.1.2.5: Configure CDP and LLDP**

In this lab, you will complete the following objectives:

- Build the Network and Configure Basic Device Settings
- Network Discovery with CDP
- Network Discovery with LLDP

# Device Management (10.2)

Routers and switches periodically generate informational console messages. However, it is unmanageable to console into each device to read the informational messages. For this reason, network devices typically use a *syslog* server to capture all console-related messages on a central device.

Devices must also have their time synchronized. Although it is possible to set the times manually on each device, it would be impossible to have them all synch up to a millisecond. For this reason, *Network Time Protocol (NTP)* is typically enabled on a network to ensure all devices have their time synchronized.

In this section, you learn how to configure NTP and syslog in a small-to medium-sized business network.

# NTP (10.2.1)

In this topic, you learn how to implement NTP between an *NTP client* and an *NTP server*.

## Setting the System Clock (10.2.1.1)

The *software clock* on a router or switch starts when the system boots and is the primary source of time for the system. It is important to synchronize the time across all devices on the network because all aspects of managing, securing, troubleshooting, and planning networks require accurate timestamping. When the time is not synchronized between devices, it will be impossible to determine the order of the events and the cause of an event.

Typically, the date and time settings on a router or switch can be set using one of two methods:

- Manually configure the date and time, as shown in Example 10-13
- Configure the NTP

**Example 10-13** The **clock** Command

```
R1# clock set 20:36:00 aug 30 2016
R1#
*Aug 30 20:36:00.000: %SYS-6-CLOCKUPDATE: System clock has been updated from
  21:32:31 UTC Tue Aug 30 2016 to 20:36:00 UTC Tue Aug 30 2016, configured from
  console by console.
```

As a network grows, it becomes difficult to ensure that all infrastructure devices are operating with synchronized time. Even in a smaller network environment, the manual method is not ideal. If a router reboots, how will it get an accurate date and timestamp?

A better solution is to configure the NTP on the network. This protocol allows routers on the network to synchronize their time settings with an NTP server. A group of NTP clients that obtain time and date information from a single source have more consistent time settings. When NTP is implemented in the network, it can be set up to synchronize to a private master clock, or it can synchronize to a publicly available NTP server on the Internet.

NTP uses UDP port 123 and is documented in RFC 1305.

## NTP Operation (10.2.1.2)

NTP networks use a hierarchical system of time sources. Each level in this hierarchical system is called a *stratum*. The stratum level is defined as the number of hop counts from the *authoritative time source*. The synchronized time is distributed across the network using NTP. Figure 10-8 displays a sample NTP network.

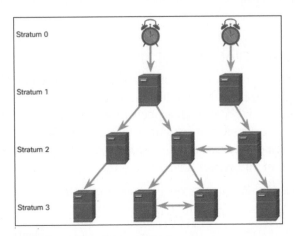

**Figure 10-8**   NTP Stratum Levels

NTP servers are arranged in three levels showing the three strata. Stratum 1 is connected to Stratum 0 clocks.

## Stratum 0

An NTP network gets the time from authoritative time sources. These authoritative time sources, also referred to as stratum 0 devices, are high-precision timekeeping devices assumed to be accurate and with little or no delay associated with them. Stratum 0 devices are represented by the clock in the figure.

## Stratum 1

The stratum 1 devices are directly connected to the authoritative time sources. They act as the primary network time standard.

## Stratum 2 and Lower

The stratum 2 servers are connected to stratum 1 devices through network connections. Stratum 2 devices, such as NTP clients, synchronize their time using the NTP packets from stratum 1 servers. They can also act as servers for stratum 3 devices.

Smaller stratum numbers indicate that the server is closer to the authorized time source than larger stratum numbers. The larger the stratum number, the lower the stratum level.

The max hop count is 15. Stratum 16, the lowest stratum level, indicates that a device is unsynchronized. Time servers on the same stratum level can be configured to act as a peer with other time servers on the same stratum level for backup or verification of time.

## Configure and Verify NTP (10.2.1.3)

To help explain how NTP is configured, consider the topology in Figure 10-9.

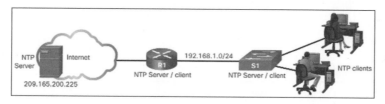

**Figure 10-9**   NTP Client/Server Topology

In this topology, an NTP server is reachable at IP 201.165.200.225. R1 will be a client of the NTP server; R1 also will serve as the NTP master for S1. S1 is an NTP client of R1 and will be the NTP server for hosts connecting to S1.

Before NTP is configured on the network, verify the current time on the software clock using the **show clock [detail]** command, as demonstrated in Example 10-14. The **detail** keyword also displays the time source.

**Example 10-14** Verify Time Source

```
R1# show clock detail
20:55:10.207 UTC Tue Aug 30 2016


R1#
```

The software clock in the example has been manually configured.

To identify the NTP server for R1, use the **ntp server** *ip-address* global configuration command with the IP address 209.165.200.225. To verify the NTP time source, use the **show clock detail** command again.

In Example 10-15, the NTP server IP address is configured on R1, and then the time source is verified.

**Example 10-15** Configure Stratum 2 NTP Server

```
R1(config)# ntp server 209.165.200.225
R1(config)# end
R1#
R1# show clock detail
21:01:34.563 UTC Tue Aug 30 2016
Time source is NTP
```

The output of the **show** command confirms that NTP was used to set the time.

In Example 10-16, R1 is verified to see if it is synchronized with the NTP server at 209.165.200.225 using the **show ip ntp associations** and **show ntp status** commands.

**Example 10-16** Verify NTP Server Configuration

```
R1# show ntp associations

  address         ref clock       st   when   poll reach  delay  offset    disp
*~209.165.200.225 .GPS.           1     61     64   377   0.481   7.480   4.261
 * sys.peer, # selected, + candidate, - outlyer, x falseticker, ~ configured


R1#
R1# show ntp status
Clock is synchronized, stratum 2, reference is 209.165.200.225
nominal freq is 250.0000 Hz, actual freq is 249.9995 Hz, precision is 2**19
ntp uptime is 589900 (1/100 of seconds), resolution is 4016
reference time is DA088DD3.C4E659D3 (13:21:23.769 PST Tue Aug 30 2016)
clock offset is 7.0883 msec, root delay is 99.77 msec
root dispersion is 13.43 msec, peer dispersion is 2.48 msec
loopfilter state is 'CTRL' (Normal Controlled Loop), drift is 0.000001803 s/s
system poll interval is 64, last update was 169 sec ago.
```

Notice that R1 is synchronized with a stratum 1 NTP server at 209.165.200.225, which is synchronized with a GPS clock. The **show ntp status** command displays that R1 is now a stratum 2 device synchronized with the NTP server at 209.165.220.225.

In Example 10-17, S1 is configured to synchronize to R1 using NTP.

**Example 10-17**  Configure Stratum 3 NTP Server

```
S1(config)# ntp server 192.168.1.1
S1(config)# end
S1#
S1# show ntp associations

  address          ref clock        st    when    poll reach  delay  offset   disp
*~192.168.1.1      209.165.200.225  2      12      64   377   1.066  13.616   3.840
 * sys.peer, # selected, + candidate, - outlyer, x falseticker, ~ configured

S1#
S1# show ntp status
Clock is synchronized, stratum 3, reference is 192.168.1.1
nominal freq is 119.2092 Hz, actual freq is 119.2088 Hz, precision is 2**17
reference time is DA08904B.3269C655 (13:31:55.196 PST Tue Aug 30 2016)
clock offset is 18.7764 msec, root delay is 102.42 msec
root dispersion is 38.03 msec, peer dispersion is 3.74 msec
loopfilter state is 'CTRL' (Normal Controlled Loop), drift is 0.000003925 s/s
system poll interval is 128, last update was 178 sec ago.
```

Output from the **show ntp associations** command verifies that the clock on S1 is now synchronized with R1 at 192.168.1.1 via NTP. R1 is a stratum 2 device and NTP server to S1. Now S1 is a stratum 3 device that can provide NTP service to other devices in the network, such as end devices.

Packet Tracer
☐ Activity

**Packet Tracer 10.2.1.4: Configure and Verify NTP**

NTP synchronizes the time of day among a set of distributed time servers and clients. Although several applications require synchronized time, this lab focuses on the need to correlate events when listed in the systems system logs and other time-specific events from multiple network devices.

# Syslog Operation (10.2.2)

In this topic, you learn about the operation of syslog.

## Introduction to Syslog (10.2.2.1)

When certain events occur on a network, networking devices have trusted mechanisms to notify the administrator with detailed system messages. These messages can be either noncritical or significant. Network administrators have a variety of options for storing, interpreting, and displaying these messages and for being alerted to those messages that could have the greatest impact on the network infrastructure.

The most common method of accessing system messages is to use a protocol called syslog.

Syslog is a term that describes a standard. It also describes the protocol developed for that standard. The syslog protocol was developed for UNIX systems in the 1980s but was first documented as RFC 3164 by IETF in 2001.

The syslog protocol allows networking devices to send their system messages across the network to syslog servers. As illustrated in Figure 10-10, devices use syslog to send event notification messages generated by devices over an IP network to a syslog server. The syslog server serves as an event message collector. Syslog messages are sent using UDP port 514.

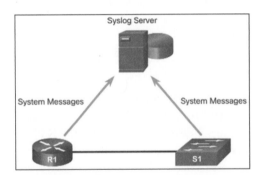

**Figure 10-10**   Syslog Topology

Many networking devices support syslog, including routers, switches, application servers, firewalls, and other network appliances.

Several syslog server software packages exist for Windows and UNIX. Many of them are freeware.

The syslog logging service provides three primary functions:

- The ability to gather logging information for monitoring and troubleshooting
- The ability to select the type of logging information that is captured
- The ability to specify the destinations of captured syslog messages

### Syslog Operation (10.2.2.2)

On Cisco network devices, the syslog protocol starts by sending system messages and **debug** output to a local logging process internal to the device. How the logging process manages these messages and outputs is based on device configurations. For example, syslog messages may be sent across the network to an external syslog server. These messages can be retrieved without the need of accessing the actual device. Log messages and outputs stored on the external server can be pulled into various reports for easier reading.

Alternatively, syslog messages may be sent to an internal buffer. Messages sent to the internal buffer are only viewable through the command-line interface (CLI) of the device.

Finally, the network administrator may specify that only certain types of system messages are sent to various destinations. For example, the device may be configured to forward all system messages to an external syslog server. However, debug-level messages are forwarded to the internal buffer and are only accessible by the administrator from the CLI.

As shown in Figure 10-11, popular destinations for syslog messages include these:

- Logging buffer (RAM inside a router or switch)

- Console line

- Terminal line

- Syslog server

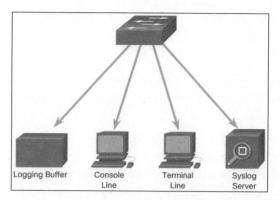

**Figure 10-11**   Syslog Message Destination Options

It is possible to remotely monitor system messages by viewing the logs on a syslog server or accessing the device through Telnet, SSH, or the console port.

## Syslog Message Format (10.2.2.3)

Cisco devices produce syslog messages as a result of network events. Every syslog message contains a *severity level* and a *facility*.

The smaller numerical levels are the more critical syslog alarms. The severity level of the messages can be set to control where each type of message is displayed (that is, on the console or the other destinations). The complete list of syslog levels is shown in Table 10-1.

**Table 10-1**   Syslog Severity Level

| Severity Level | Severity Name | Explanation |
| --- | --- | --- |
| Level 0 | Emergency | System unusable |
| Level 1 | Alert | Immediate action needed |
| Level 2 | Critical | Critical condition |
| Level 3 | Error | Error condition |
| Level 4 | Warning | Warning condition |
| Level 5 | Notification | Normal but significant condition |
| Level 6 | Informational | Informational message |
| Level 7 | Debugging | Debugging message |

Each syslog level has its own meaning:

- **Emergency Level 0—Warning Level 4**—These messages are error messages about software or hardware malfunctions. Level 0 to 4 messages indicate that the functionality of the device is affected. The severity of the issue determines the actual syslog level applied.

- **Notification Level 5**—The notifications level generates normal but significant system messages, such as interface up or down transitions and system restart messages.

- **Informational Level 6**—The informational level generates system messages that do not affect device functionality. For example, when a Cisco device is booting, you might see the following informational message:

```
%LICENSE-6-EULA_ACCEPT_ALL: The Right to Use End User License Agreement is accepted.
```

- **Debugging Level 7**—The debugging level generates output generated from issuing various **debug** commands.

In addition to specifying the severity, syslog messages contain information on the facility. Syslog facilities are service identifiers that recognize and categorize system state data for error and event message reporting. The logging facility options that are available are specific to the networking device. For example, Cisco 2960 Series switches running Cisco IOS Release 15.0(2) and Cisco 1941 routers running Cisco

IOS Release 15.2(4) support 24 facility options that are categorized into 12 facility types.

Following are some common syslog message facilities reported on Cisco IOS routers:

- IP

- OSPF protocol

- SYS operating system

- IP security (IPsec)

- Interface IP (IF)

By default, the format of syslog messages on the Cisco IOS Software is as follows:

```
seq no: timestamp: %facility-severity-MNEMONIC: description
```

The fields contained in the Cisco IOS Software syslog message are explained in Table 10-2.

**Table 10-2**   Syslog Message Format

| Field | Explanation |
|---|---|
| seq no | Stamps log messages with a sequence number only if the **service sequence-numbers** global configuration command is configured |
| timestamp | Date and time of the message or event, which appears only if the **service timestamps** global configuration command is configured |
| facility | The facility to which the message refers |
| severity | Single-digit code from 0 to 7 that indicates the severity of the message |
| MNEMONIC | Text string that uniquely describes the message |
| description | Text string containing information about the event being reported |

For example, sample output on a Cisco switch for an EtherChannel link changing state to up follows:

```
00:00:46: %LINK-3-UPDOWN: Interface Port-channel1, changed state to up
```

Here the facility is LINK and the severity level is 3, with a MNEMONIC of UPDOWN.

The most common messages are link up and down messages and messages that a device produces when it exits from configuration mode. If ACL logging is configured, the device generates syslog messages when packets match a parameter condition.

## Service Timestamp (10.2.2.4)

By default, log messages are not timestamped. In Example 10-18, the R1 GigabitEthernet 0/0 interface is shutdown.

**Example 10-18** Generating a Syslog Notification Message with No Timestamp

```
R1(config)# interface g0/0
R1(config-if)# shutdown
%LINK-5-CHANGED: Interface GigabitEthernet0/0, changed state to administratively
  down
%LINEPROTO-5-UPDOWN: Line protocol on Interface GigabitEthernet0/0, changed state
  to down
R1(config-if)# exit
R1(config)#
```

Notice how the message logged to the console does not identify when the interface state was changed. By default, messages do not include a timestamp. However, log messages should be timestamped to record when they were generated. This is especially helpful when forwarding messages to a syslog server.

Example 10-19 enables syslog message timestamps, and then interface G0/0 is shut down to generate a syslog notification message.

**Example 10-19** Adding a Timestamp to Syslog Messages

```
R1(config)# service timestamps log datetime
R1(config)#
R1(config)# interface g0/0
R1(config-if)# no shutdown
*Aug  1 11:52:42: %LINK-3-UPDOWN: Interface GigabitEthernet0/0, changed state to
  down
*Aug  1 11:52:45: %LINK-3-UPDOWN: Interface GigabitEthernet0/0, changed state to up
*Aug  1 11:52:46: %LINEPROTO-5-UPDOWN: Line protocol on Interface
  GigabitEthernet0/0, changed state to up
R1(config-if)#
```

As shown in the output, the **service timestamps log datetime** global configuration command is configured to force logged events to display the date and time.

---

**Note**

When using the **datetime** keyword, the clock on the networking device must be set, either manually or through NTP.

---

**Activity 10.2.2.5: Interpret Syslog Output**

Refer to the online course to complete this activity.

# Syslog Configuration (10.2.3)

In this topic, you configure syslog servers and clients.

## Syslog Server (10.2.3.1)

To view syslog messages, a syslog server must be installed on a workstation in the network. There are several freeware and shareware versions of syslog, as well as enterprise versions for purchase.

The syslog server provides a relatively user-friendly interface for viewing syslog output. The server parses the output and places the messages into predefined columns for easy interpretation. If timestamps are configured on the networking device sourcing the syslog messages, the date and time of each message are included in the syslog server output, as shown in the example in Figure 10-12.

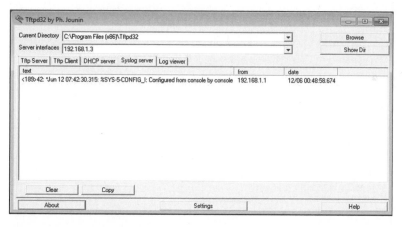

**Figure 10-12**   Syslog Server

Network administrators can easily navigate the large amount of data compiled on a syslog server. One advantage of viewing syslog messages on a syslog server is the ability to perform granular searches through the data. Also, a network administrator can quickly delete unimportant syslog messages from the database.

## Default Logging (10.2.3.2)

By default, Cisco routers and switches send log messages for all severity (levels Level 0 through 7) to the console. On some IOS versions, the device also buffers log messages by default. To enable these two settings, use the **logging console** and **logging buffered** global configuration commands, respectively.

The **show logging** command displays the default logging service settings on a Cisco router, as demonstrated in Example 10-20. The first lines of output list information about the logging process, with the end of the output listing log messages.

**Example 10-20** Default Logging Service Settings

```
R1# show logging
Syslog logging: enabled (0 messages dropped, 2 messages rate-limited, 0 flushes, 0
  overruns, xml disabled, filtering disabled)


No Active Message Discriminator.


No Inactive Message Discriminator.


    Console logging: level debugging, 32 messages logged, xml disabled,
                    filtering disabled
    Monitor logging: level debugging, 0 messages logged, xml disabled,
                    filtering disabled
    Buffer logging:  level debugging, 32 messages logged, xml disabled,
                    filtering disabled
    Exception Logging: size (4096 bytes)
    Count and timestamp logging messages: disabled
    Persistent logging: disabled

No active filter modules.

    Trap logging: level informational, 34 message lines logged
        Logging Source-Interface:       VRF Name:


Log Buffer (8192 bytes):

*Aug  2 00:00:02.527: %LICENSE-6-EULA_ACCEPT_ALL: The Right to Use End User License
  Agreement is accepted
*Aug  2 00:00:02.631: %IOS_LICENSE_IMAGE_APPLICATION-6-LICENSE_LEVEL: Module name =
  c1900 Next reboot level = ipbasek9 and License = ipbasek9
*Aug  2 00:00:02.851: %IOS_LICENSE_IMAGE_APPLICATION-6-LICENSE_LEVEL: Module name =
  c1900 Next reboot level = securityk9 and License = securityk9
*Aug 12 17:46:01.619: %IFMGR-7-NO_IFINDEX_FILE: Unable to open nvram:/ifIndex-table
  No such file or directory
<output omitted>
```

The first highlighted line states that this router logs to the console and includes debug messages. This actually means that all debug-level messages, as well as any lower-level messages (such as notification level messages), are logged to the console. On most Cisco IOS routers, the default severity level is 7, debugging. The output also notes that 32 such messages have been logged.

The second highlighted line states that this router logs to an internal buffer. Because this router has enabled logging to an internal buffer, the **show logging** command also lists the messages in that buffer. You can view some of the system messages that have been logged at the end of the output.

## Router and Switch Commands for Syslog Clients (10.2.3.3)

There are three steps to configuring the router to send system messages to a syslog server where they can be stored, filtered, and analyzed:

**Step 1.** Use the **logging** global configuration command to configure the destination hostname or IPv4 address of the syslog server.

**Step 2.** Use the **logging trap** *level* global configuration command to select the desired severity level to send to the syslog server. For example, to limit the messages to levels 4 and lower (0 to 4), use the **logging trap 4** global configuration command. This sends Level 0 through 4 severity messages.

**Step 3.** Optionally, configure the source interface with the **logging source-interface** *interface-type interface-number* global configuration mode command. This specifies that syslog packets contain the IPv4 or IPv6 address of a specific interface, regardless of which interface the packet uses to exit the router.

In Example 10-21, R1 is configured to send log messages of levels 4 and lower to the syslog server at 192.168.1.3. The source interface is set as the G0/0 interface. A loopback interface is created, shut down, and then brought back up. The console output reflects these actions.

**Example 10-21** Syslog Configuration

```
R1(config)# logging 192.168.1.3
R1(config)# logging trap 4
R1(config)# logging source-interface GigabitEthernet 0/0
R1(config)# interface loopback 0
R1(config-if)#
*Jun 12 22:06:02.902: %LINK-3-UPDOWN: Interface Loopback0, changed state to up
*Jun 12 22:06:03.902: %LINEPROTO-5-UPDOWN: Line protocol on Interface Loopback0,
  changed state to up
```

```
*Jun 12 22:06:03.902: %SYS-6-LOGGINGHOST_STARTSTOP: Logging to host 192.168.1.3
  port 514 started - CLI initiated
R1(config-if)# shutdown
R1(config-if)#
*Jun 12 22:06:49.642: %LINK-5-CHANGED: Interface Loopback0, changed state to
  administratively down
*Jun 12 22:06:50.642: %LINEPROTO-5-UPDOWN: Line protocol on Interface Loopback0,
  changed state to down
R1(config-if)# no shutdown
R1(config-if)#
*Jun 12 22:09:18.210: %LINK-3-UPDOWN: Interface Loopback0, changed state to up
*Jun 12 22:09:19.210: %LINEPROTO-5-UPDOWN: Line protocol on Interface Loopback0,
  changed state to up
R1(config-if)#
```

Figure 10-13 displays a screenshot of the Tftpd32 syslog server application running on a Windows host with IPv4 address 192.168.1.3.

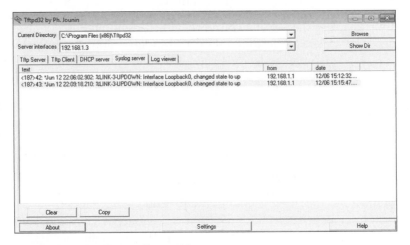

**Figure 10-13**   Syslog Server Output

As you can see, the only messages that appear on the syslog server are those with severity level of 4 or lower (more severe). The messages with severity level of 5 or higher (less severe) appear on the router console output but do not appear on the syslog server output because the logging trap command limits the syslog messages sent to the syslog server based on severity.

## Verifying Syslog (10.2.3.4)

You can use the **show logging** command to view any logged messages. When the logging buffer is large, it is helpful to use the pipe option (|) with the **show logging** command. The pipe option allows the administrator to specifically state which messages should be displayed. For example, you can use the pipe to filter only messages that have changed to an "up" state, as shown in Example 10-22.

**Example 10-22** Viewing Logged Syslog Messages

```
R1# show logging | include changed state to up
*Jun 12 17:46:26.143: %LINK-3-UPDOWN: Interface GigabitEthernet0/1, changed state
  to up
*Jun 12 17:46:26.143: %LINK-3-UPDOWN: Interface Serial0/0/1, changed state to up
*Jun 12 17:46:27.263: %LINEPROTO-5-UPDOWN: Line protocol on Interface
  GigabitEthernet0/1, changed state to up
*Jun 12 17:46:27.263: %LINEPROTO-5-UPDOWN: Line protocol on Interface Serial0/0/1,
  changed state to up
*Jun 12 20:28:43.427: %LINK-3-UPDOWN: Interface GigabitEthernet0/0, changed state
  to up
*Jun 12 20:28:44.427: %LINEPROTO-5-UPDOWN: Line protocol on Interface
  GigabitEthernet0/0, changed state to up
*Jun 12 22:04:11.862: %LINEPROTO-5-UPDOWN: Line protocol on Interface Loopback0,
  changed state to up
*Jun 12 22:06:02.902: %LINK-3-UPDOWN: Interface Loopback0, changed state to up
*Jun 12 22:06:03.902: %LINEPROTO-5-UPDOWN: Line protocol on Interface Loopback0,
  changed state to up
*Jun 12 22:09:18.210: %LINK-3-UPDOWN: Interface Loopback0, changed state to up
*Jun 12 22:09:19.210: %LINEPROTO-5-UPDOWN: Line protocol on Interface Loopback0,
  changed state to up
*Jun 12 22:35:55.926: %LINK-3-UPDOWN: Interface Loopback0, changed state to up
*Jun 12 22:35:56.926: %LINEPROTO-5-UPDOWN: Line protocol on Interface Loopback0,
  changed state to up
```

To view only the messages that were logged to the buffer on or after Jun 12 10:35 PM, you would use the filter **begin June 12 22:35**, as shown in Example 10-23.

**Example 10-23** Viewing Logged Syslog Messages

```
R1# show logging | begin Jun 12 22:35
*Jun 12 22:35:46.206: %LINK-5-CHANGED: Interface Loopback0, changed state to
  administratively down
*Jun 12 22:35:47.206: %LINEPROTO-5-UPDOWN: Line protocol on Interface Loopback0,
  changed state to down
*Jun 12 22:35:55.926: %LINK-3-UPDOWN: Interface Loopback0, changed state to up
*Jun 12 22:35:56.926: %LINEPROTO-5-UPDOWN: Line protocol on Interface Loopback0,
  changed state to up
*Jun 12 22:49:52.122: %SYS-5-CONFIG_I: Configured from console by console
*Jun 12 23:15:48.418: %SYS-5-CONFIG_I: Configured from console by console
R1#
```

**Packet Tracer 10.2.3.5: Configuring Syslog and NTP**

Background/Scenario

In this activity, you enable and use the syslog service and the NTP service so that the network administrator is able to monitor the network more effectively.

**Lab 10.2.3.6: Configuring Syslog and NTP**

In this lab, you complete the following objectives:

- Part 1: Configure Basic Device Settings
- Part 2: Configure NTP
- Part 3: Configure Syslog

# Device Maintenance (10.3)

Routers and switches can fail and for this reason, it is important to have backup copies of IOS image files and individual device configuration files. As well, the IOS is often updated by Cisco and network administrators must understand how IOS licensing works and how to correctly upgrade their devices with newer IOS images.

In this section, you learn how to maintain router and switch configuration and IOS files.

## Router and Switch File Maintenance (10.3.1)

In this topic, you use commands to back up and restore an IOS configuration file.

### Router File Systems (10.3.1.1)

The Cisco IOS File System (IFS) allows the administrator to navigate to different directories, list the files in a directory, and create subdirectories in flash memory or on a disk. The directories available depend on the device.

Example 10-24 displays the output of the **show file systems** command, which lists all of the available file systems on a Cisco 1941 router. This command provides useful information such as the amount of available and free memory, the type of file system, and its permissions. Permissions include read only (ro), write only (wo), and read and write (rw), shown in the Flags column of the command output.

**Example 10-24**  The **show file systems** Command on a Router

```
R1# show file systems
File Systems:

        Size(b)         Free(b)         Type    Flags   Prefixes
              -               -          opaque    rw    archive:
              -               -          opaque    rw    system:
              -               -          opaque    rw    tmpsys:
              -               -          opaque    rw    null:
              -               -         network    rw    tftp:
*     256487424       183234560            disk    rw    flash0: flash:#
              -               -            disk    rw    flash1:
         262136          254779           nvram    rw    nvram:
              -               -          opaque    wo    syslog:
              -               -          opaque    rw    xmodem:
              -               -          opaque    rw    ymodem:
              -               -         network    rw    rcp:
              -               -         network    rw    http:
              -               -         network    rw    ftp:
              -               -         network    rw    scp:
              -               -          opaque    ro    tar:
              -               -         network    rw    https:
              -               -          opaque    ro    cns:
R1#
```

Although there are several file systems listed, of interest to us will be the tftp, flash, and nvram file systems.

Notice that the flash file system also has an asterisk preceding it. This indicates that flash is the current default file system. The bootable IOS is located in flash; therefore, the pound symbol (#) is appended to the flash listing, indicating that it is a bootable disk.

## The Flash File System

Example 10-25 displays the output from the **dir** (directory) command. Because flash is the default file system, the **dir** command lists the contents of flash. Several files are located in flash, but of specific interest is the last listing. This is the name of the current Cisco IOS file image that is running in RAM.

**Example 10-25** Viewing Flash Contents

```
R1# dir
Directory of flash0:/


    1   -rw-          2903    Sep 7 2012 06:58:26 +00:00   cpconfig-19xx.cfg
    2   -rw-       3000320    Sep 7 2012 06:58:40 +00:00   cpexpress.tar
    3   -rw-          1038    Sep 7 2012 06:58:52 +00:00   home.shtml
    4   -rw-        122880    Sep 7 2012 06:59:02 +00:00   home.tar
    5   -rw-       1697952    Sep 7 2012 06:59:20 +00:00   securedesktop-ios-3.1.1.
    45-k9.pkg
    6   -rw-        415956    Sep 7 2012 06:59:34 +00:00   sslclient-win-1.1.4.176.pkg
    7   -rw-      67998028    Sep 26 2012 17:32:14 +00:00  c1900-universalk9-mz.
    SPA.152-4.M1.bin


256487424 bytes total (183234560 bytes free)
R1#
```

## The NVRAM File System

To view the contents of NVRAM, you must change the current default file system using the **cd** (change directory) command, as shown in Example 10-26.

**Example 10-26** Viewing NVRAM Contents

```
R1# cd nvram:
R1#
R1# pwd
nvram:/
R1#
R1# dir
Directory of nvram:/

  253   -rw-          1156                  <no date>   startup-config
  254   ----             5                  <no date>   private-config
  255   -rw-          1156                  <no date>   underlying-config
    1   -rw-          2945                  <no date>   cwmp_inventory
    4   ----            58                  <no date>   persistent-data
    5   -rw-            17                  <no date>   ecfm_ieee_mib
    6   -rw-           559                  <no date>   IOS-Self-Sig#1.cer


262136 bytes total (254779 bytes free)
R1#
```

The **pwd** (present working directory) command verifies that you are viewing the NVRAM directory. Finally, the **dir** command lists the contents of NVRAM. Although several configuration files are listed, of specific interest is the startup-configuration file.

## Switch File Systems (10.3.1.2)

With the Cisco 2960 switch flash file system, you can copy configuration files and archive (upload and download) software images.

The command to view the file systems on a Catalyst switch is the same as on a Cisco router. Example 10-27 displays the file system on a Catalyst 2960 switch.

**Example 10-27** The **show file system** Command on a Switch

```
S1# show file systems
File Systems:

      Size(b)       Free(b)        Type   Flags   Prefixes
*    32514048      20887552        flash     rw    flash:
            -             -      opaque     rw    vb:
            -             -      opaque     ro    bs:
            -             -      opaque     rw    system:
            -             -      opaque     rw    tmpsys:
        65536         48897        nvram     rw    nvram:
            -             -      opaque     ro    xmodem:
            -             -      opaque     ro    ymodem:
            -             -      opaque     rw    null:
            -             -      opaque     ro    tar:
            -             -      network     rw    tftp:
            -             -      network     rw    rcp:
            -             -      network     rw    http:
            -             -      network     rw    ftp:
            -             -      network     rw    scp:
            -             -      network     rw    https:
            -             -      opaque     ro    cns:
S1#
```

## Backing Up and Restoring Using Text Files (10.3.1.3)

Configuration files can be saved/archived to a text file using Tera Term, as shown in Figure 10-14. Once saved, the text file can restore the configuration, if necessary.

**Figure 10-14**  Saving a Text File in Tera Term

## Backing Up to a Text File

The steps to save a configuration using Tera Term follow:

**Step 1.**  On the File menu, click **Log**.

**Step 2.**  Choose the location to save the file. Tera Term begins capturing text.

**Step 3.**  After capture has been started, execute the **show running-config** or **show startup-config** command at the privileged EXEC prompt. Text displayed in the terminal window is directed to the chosen file.

**Step 4.**  When the capture is complete, select **Close** in the Tera Term: Log window.

**Step 5.**  View the file to verify that it was not corrupted.

## Restoring from a Text File

A configuration can be copied from a file to a device. When copied from a text file and pasted into a terminal window, the IOS executes each line of the configuration text as a command. This means that the file requires editing to ensure that encrypted passwords are in plain text and that noncommand text such as "--More--" and IOS messages are removed.

Further, at the CLI, the device must be set at the global configuration mode to receive the commands from the text file being pasted into the terminal window.

When using Tera Term, follow these steps:

**Step 1.**  On the File menu, click **Send file**.

**Step 2.**  Locate the file to be copied into the device and click **Open**.

**Step 3.**  Tera Term pastes the file into the device.

The text in the file is applied as commands in the CLI and become the running configuration on the device. This is a convenient method for manually configuring a router.

### Backing Up and Restoring TFTP (10.3.1.4)

You can use a service like Trivial File Transfer Protocol (TFTP) to remotely back up and restore files.

### Backup Configurations with TFTP

Copies of configuration files should be stored as backup files in the event of a problem. Configuration files can be stored on a TFTP server or a USB drive. A configuration file should also be included in the network documentation.

Follow these steps to back up the running configuration to a TFTP server:

**Step 1.**   Enter the **copy running-config tftp** command.

**Step 2.**   Enter the IP address of the host where the configuration file will be stored.

**Step 3.**   Enter the name to assign to the configuration file.

**Step 4.**   Press **Enter** to confirm each choice.

Example 10-28 copies the running configuration file to a TFTP server located at IP address 192.168.10.254.

**Example 10-28**  Backing Up Running Config to TFTP

```
R1# copy running-config tftp
Address or name of remote host []? 192.168.10.254
Destination filename [r1-confg]? R1-Jan-2016
Write file R1-Jan-2016 to 192.168.10.254? [confirm]
Writing R1-Jan-2016 !!!!!! [OK]
```

### Restoring Configurations with TFTP

To restore the running configuration or the startup configuration from a TFTP server, use either the **copy tftp running-config** or the **copy tftp startup-config** command.

Use these steps to restore the running configuration from a TFTP server:

**Step 1.**   Enter the **copy tftp running-config** command.

**Step 2.**   Enter the IP address of the TFTP server where the configuration file is stored.

**Step 3.**    Enter the name assigned to the configuration file. For example, in Example 10-28 the file was assigned the name R1-Jan-2016.

**Step 4.**    Press **Enter** to confirm.

## Using USB Ports on a Cisco Router (10.3.1.5)

The Universal Serial Bus (USB) storage feature enables certain models of Cisco routers to support USB flash drives, as shown in Figure 10-15.

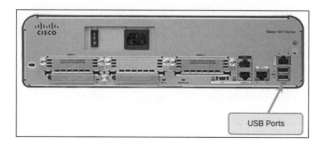

**Figure 10-15**    Cisco 1941 Router USB Port

The USB flash feature provides an optional secondary storage capability and an additional boot device. Images, configurations, and other files can be copied to or from the Cisco USB flash memory with the same reliability as storing and retrieving files using the Compact Flash card. In addition, modular integrated services routers can boot any Cisco IOS Software image saved on USB flash memory. Ideally, USB flash can hold multiple copies of the Cisco IOS and multiple router configurations.

Use the **dir** command to view the contents of the USB flash drive, as shown in Example 10-29.

**Example 10-29** Displaying the Contents of a USB Flash Drive

```
R1# dir usbflash0:
Directory of usbflash0:/
1 -rw- 30125020 Dec 22 2032 05:31:32 +00:00 c3825-entservicesk9-mz.123-14.T
63158272 bytes total (33033216 bytes free)
```

## Backing Up and Restoring Using a USB (10.3.1.6)

You can use a USB flash drive to remotely back up and restore files.

## Backup Configurations with a USB Flash Drive

When backing up to a USB port, it is a good idea to issue the **show file systems** command to verify that the USB drive is there and confirm the name, as shown in Example 10-30.

**Example 10-30** Verifying the USB Drive Is Available

```
R1# show file systems
File Systems:


        Size(b)        Free(b)        Type    Flags    Prefixes
              -              -        opaque     rw     archive:
              -              -        opaque     rw     system:
              -              -        opaque     rw     tmpsys:
              -              -        opaque     rw     null:
              -              -        network    rw     tftp:
*      256487424      184819712       disk       rw     flash0: flash:#
              -              -        disk       rw     flash1:
         262136         249270       nvram      rw     nvram:
              -              -        opaque     wo     syslog:
              -              -        opaque     rw     xmodem:
              -              -        opaque     rw     ymodem:
              -              -        network    rw     rcp:
              -              -        network    rw     http:
              -              -        network    rw     ftp:
              -              -        network    rw     scp:
              -              -        opaque     ro     tar:
              -              -        network    rw     https:
              -              -        opaque     ro     cns:
     4050042880     3774152704       usbflash   rw     usbflash0:
R1#
```

Next, use the **copy run usbflash0:/** command to copy the configuration file to the USB flash drive. Be sure to use the name of the flash drive, as indicated in the file system. The slash is optional but indicates the root directory of the USB flash drive.

The IOS prompts for the filename, as shown in Example 10-31.

**Example 10-31** Backing Up Running Config to USB Drive

```
R1# copy running-config usbflash0:
Destination filename [running-config]? R1-Config
5024 bytes copied in 0.736 secs (6826 bytes/sec)
```

If the filename already existed, the device generates a warning message stating that there is a file already existing with this name and prompts the user to overwrite the file.

Use the **dir** command to see the file on the USB drive and the **more** command to see the contents, as seen in Example 10-32.

**Example 10-32** Viewing the Saved File on the USB Drive

```
R1# dir usbflash0:/
Directory of usbflash0:/

    1  drw-             0   Oct 15 2010 16:28:30 +00:00   Cisco
   16  -rw-          5024   Jan 7 2013 20:26:50 +00:00   R1-Config

4050042880 bytes total (3774144512 bytes free)

R1# more usbflash0:/R1-Config
!
! Last configuration change at 20:19:54 UTC Mon Jan 7 2013 by admin
version 15.2
service timestamps debug datetime msec
service timestamps log datetime msec
no service password-encryption
!
hostname R1
!
boot-start-marker
boot-end-marker
!
!
logging buffered 51200 warnings
!
no aaa new-model
!
no ipv6 cef
<output omitted>
```

## Restore Configurations with a USB Flash Drive

To copy the file back, it is necessary to edit the USB R1-Config file with a text editor. Assuming the filename is **R1-Config**, use the command **copy usbflash0:/R1-Config** *running-config* to restore a running configuration.

## Password Recovery (10.3.1.7)

Passwords on devices are used to prevent unauthorized access. For encrypted passwords, such as the enable secret passwords, the passwords must be replaced after recovery. Depending on the device, the detailed procedure for password recovery varies; however, all the password recovery procedures follow the same principle:

**Step 1.**    Enter the *ROMMON mode*. This mode displays a basic boot loader command line that enables an administrator to access files stored in flash memory, format the flash file system, reinstall the operating system software, or recover a lost password. It also enables an administrator to change the *configuration register* settings that instruct the router how to boot up.

**Step 2.**    Change the configuration register to 0x2142. This setting informs the router to ignore the startup config file on bootup.

**Step 3.**    Make necessary changes to the original startup config file.

**Step 4.**    Save the new configuration.

Physical access to the device is required. Password recovery cannot be accomplished remotely.

Console access to the device using terminal emulator software on a PC is also required for password recovery. With console access, a user can access the ROMMON mode by using a break sequence during the bootup process or removing the external flash memory when the device is powered off.

> **Note**
>
> The break sequence for PuTTY is Ctrl+Break. A list of standard break key sequences for other terminal emulators and operating systems can be found at http://www.cisco.com/c/en/us/support/docs/routers/10000-series-routers/12818-61.html.

The ROMMON software supports some basic commands, such as **confreg**. The **confreg 0x2142** command allows the user to set the configuration register to 0x2142. With the configuration register at 0x2142, the device ignores the startup config file during startup. The startup config file is where the forgotten passwords are stored.

After setting the configuration register to 0x2142, type **reset** at the prompt to restart the device. Enter the break sequence while the device is rebooting and decompressing the IOS.

Example 10-33 displays the terminal output of a 1941 router in the ROMMON mode after using a break sequence during the bootup process.

**Example 10-33** ROMMON Mode on a 1941 Router

```
Readonly ROMMON initialized

monitor: command "boot" aborted due to user interrupt
rommon 1 > confreg 0x2142
rommon 2 > reset

System Bootstrap, Version 15.0(1r)M9, RELEASE SOFTWARE (fc1)
Technical Support: http://www.cisco.com/techsupport
Copyright (c) 2010 by cisco Systems, Inc.
<output omitted>
```

After the device has finished rebooting, copy the startup configuration file to the running configuration file, as displayed in Example 10-34.

**Example 10-34** Recovering the Startup Configuration

```
Router# copy startup-config running-config
Destination filename [running-config]?

1450 bytes copied in 0.156 secs (9295 bytes/sec)
R1#
```

**CAUTION**

Do *not* enter **copy running-config startup-config**. This command erases your original startup configuration.

Because you are in privileged EXEC mode, you can now configure all the necessary passwords. After the new passwords are configured, change the configuration register back to 0x2102 using the **config-register 0x2102** global configuration mode command, save the running-config to startup-config, and then reload the device, as shown in Example 10-35.

**Example 10-35** Changing Password and Resetting Configuration Register Setting

```
R1(config)# enable secret cisco
R1(config)# config-register 0x2102
R1(config)# end
R1#
R1# copy running-config startup-config
Destination filename [startup-config]?
Building configuration...
[OK]
R1# reload
```

**Note**

The password **cisco** is not a strong password and is used here only as an example.

The device now uses the newly configured passwords for authentication. Be sure to use **show** commands to verify that all the configurations are still in place. For example, verify that the appropriate interfaces are not shut down after password recovery.

The following link provides detailed instructions for the password recovery procedure for a specific device:

http://www.cisco.com/c/en/us/support/docs/ios-nx-os-software/ios-software-releases-121-mainline/6130-index.html

### Packet Tracer 10.3.1.8: Backing Up Configuration Files

This activity is designed to show how to restore a configuration from a backup and then perform a new backup. Due to an equipment failure, a new router has been put in place. Fortunately, backup configuration files have been saved to a TFTP Server. You are required to restore the files from the TFTP Server to get the router back online with as little downtime as possible.

### Lab 10.3.1.9: Managing Router Configuration Files with Tera Term

In this lab, you complete the following objectives:

- Part 1: Configure Basic Device Settings
- Part 2: Use Terminal Emulation Software to Create a Backup Configuration File
- Part 3: Use a Backup Configuration File to Restore a Router

### Lab 10.3.1.10: Managing Device Configuration Files Using TFTP, Flash, and USB

In this lab, you complete the following objectives:

- Part 1: Build the Network and Configure Basic Device Settings
- Part 2: (Optional) Download TFTP Server Software
- Part 3: Use TFTP to Back Up and Restore the Switch Running Configuration
- Part 4: Use TFTP to Back Up and Restore the Router Running Configuration
- Part 5: Back Up and Restore Running Configurations Using Router Flash Memory
- Part 6: (Optional) Use a USB Drive to Back Up and Restore the Running Configuration

**Lab 10.3.1.11: Researching Password Recovery Procedures**

In this lab, you complete the following objectives:

- Part 1: Research the Configuration Register
- Part 2: Document the Password Recovery Procedure for a Specific Cisco Router

# IOS System Files (10.3.2)

In this topic, you learn about the IOS image naming conventions implemented by Cisco.

## IOS 15 System Image Packaging (10.3.2.1)

Cisco Integrated Services Routers Generation Two (ISR G2) 1900, 2900, and 3900 Series support services on demand through the use of software licensing. The *Services on Demand* process enables customers to realize operational savings through ease of software ordering and management. When an order is placed for a new ISR G2 platform, the router is shipped with a single *universal Cisco IOS Software image*, and a license is used to enable the specific feature set packages, as shown in Figure 10-16.

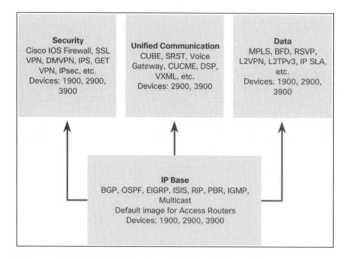

**Figure 10-16**    IOS Packaging Model for ISR G2 Routers

Two types of universal images are supported in ISR G2:

- **Universal images with the "universalk9" designation in the image name**—This universal image offers all of the Cisco IOS Software features, including strong payload cryptography features, such as IPsec VPN, SSL VPN, and Secure Unified Communications.

- Universal images with the "universalk9_npe" designation in the image name—The strong enforcement of encryption capabilities provided by Cisco Software Activation satisfies requirements for the export of encryption capabilities. However, some countries have import requirements mandating that the platform does not support strong cryptography functionality, such as payload cryptography. To satisfy the import requirements of those countries, the npe universal image does not support strong payload encryption.

With the ISR G2 devices, IOS image selection has been made easier because all features are included within the universal image. Features are activated through licensing. Each device ships with the universal Cisco IOS Software image. The technology packages IP Base, Data, UC (Unified Communications), and SEC (Security) are enabled in the universal image using Cisco Software Activation licensing keys. Each licensing key is unique to a particular device and is obtained from Cisco by providing the product ID and serial number of the router and a *Product Activation Key (PAK)*. Cisco provides the PAK at the time of software purchase. The IP Base is installed by default.

## IOS Image Filenames (10.3.2.2)

When selecting or upgrading a Cisco IOS router, it is important to choose the proper IOS image with the correct feature set and version. The Cisco IOS image file is based on a special naming convention. The name for the Cisco IOS image file contains multiple parts, each with a specific meaning. It is important to understand this naming convention when upgrading and selecting a Cisco IOS Software.

As shown in Example 10-36, the **show flash** command displays the files stored in flash memory, including the system image files.

**Example 10-36** Displaying the IOS Image

```
R1# show flash0:
-# - --length-- -----date/time------ path

<Output omitted>

8   68831808   Apr 2 2013 21:29:58 +00:00 c1900-universalk9-mz.SPA.152-4.M3.bin

182394880 bytes available (74092544 bytes used)

R1#
```

Figure 10-17 illustrates the different parts of an IOS 15 system image file on an ISR G2 device.

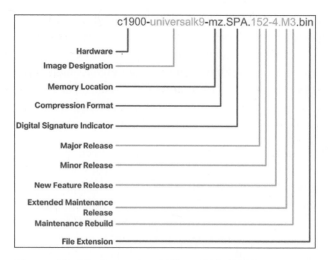

**Figure 10-17**  Example of Cisco IOS 15.2 Image

Specifically, the different parts are identified as follows:

- **Image Name (c1900)**—Identifies the platform on which the image runs. In this example, the platform is a Cisco 1900 router.

- **universalk9**—Specifies the image designation. The two designations for an ISR G2 are universalk9 and universalk9_npe. Universalk9_npe does not contain strong encryption and is meant for countries with encryption restrictions. Features are controlled by licensing and can be divided into four technology packages. These are IP Base, Security, Unified Communications, and Data.

- **mz**—Indicates where the image runs and if the file is compressed. In this example, mz indicates that the file runs from RAM and is compressed.

- **SPA**—Designates that the file is digitally signed by Cisco.

- **152-4.M3**—Specifies the filename format for the image 15.2(4)M3. This is the version of IOS, which includes the major release, minor release, maintenance release, and maintenance rebuild numbers. The M indicates this is an extended maintenance release.

- **bin**—The file extension. This extension indicates that this file is a binary executable file.

The most common designation for memory location and compression format is mz. The first letter indicates the location where the image is executed on the router. The locations can include the following:

- **f**—flash

- **m**—RAM

- r—ROM

- l—relocatable

The compression format can be either z for zip or x for mzip. Zipping is a method Cisco uses to compress some run-from-RAM images that is effective in reducing the size of the image. It is self-unzipping, so when the image is loaded into RAM for execution, the first action is to unzip.

**Note**

The Cisco IOS Software naming conventions, field meaning, image content, and other details are subject to change.

On most Cisco routers, including the integrated services routers, the IOS is stored in compact flash as a compressed image and loaded into DRAM during bootup. The Cisco IOS Software Release 15.0 images available for the Cisco 1900 and 2900 ISR require 256 MB of flash and 512 MB of RAM. The 3900 ISR requires 256 MB of flash and 1 GB of RAM. For complete details, refer to the product data sheet for the specific router.

## IOS Image Management (10.3.3)

In this topic, you learn how to upgrade an IOS system image.

### TFTP Servers as a Backup Location (10.3.3.1)

As a network grows, Cisco IOS Software images and configuration files can be stored on a central TFTP server, as shown in Figure 10-18. This helps to control the number of IOS images and the revisions to those IOS images, as well as the configuration files that must be maintained.

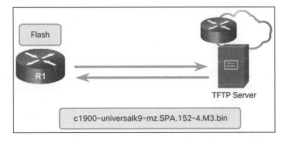

**Figure 10-18**   Central TFTP Server IPv4 Topology

Production internetworks usually span wide areas and contain multiple routers. For any network, it is good practice to keep a backup copy of the Cisco IOS Software image in case the system image in the router becomes corrupted or accidentally erased.

Widely distributed routers need a source or backup location for Cisco IOS Software images. Using a network TFTP server allows image and configuration uploads and downloads over the network. The network TFTP server can be another router, a workstation, or a host system.

## Steps to Back Up IOS Image to TFTP Server (10.3.3.2)

To maintain network operations with minimum down time, it is necessary to have procedures in place for backing up Cisco IOS images. This allows the network administrator to quickly copy an image back to a router in case of a corrupted or erased image.

In Figure 10-18, the network administrator wants to create a backup of the current image file on the router (c1900-universalk9-mz.SPA.152-4.M3.bin) to the TFTP server at 172.16.1.100.

To create a backup of the Cisco IOS image to a TFTP server, perform the following three steps:

Step 1.    Ensure that there is access to the network TFTP server. Ping the TFTP server to test connectivity, as shown in Example 10-37.

**Example 10-37**  Verify Connectivity to the Server

```
R1# ping 172.16.1.100
Type escape sequence to abort.
Sending 5, 100-byte ICMP Echos to 172.16.1.100, timeout is 2 seconds:
!!!!!
Success rate is 100 percent (5/5), round-trip min/avg/max = 56/56/56 ms
R1#
```

Step 2.    Verify that the TFTP server has sufficient disk space to accommodate the Cisco IOS Software image. Use the **show flash0:** command on the router to determine the size of the Cisco IOS image file. In Example 10-38, the file size is 68,831,808 bytes.

**Example 10-38**  Verify the IOS Size

```
R1# show flash0:
-# - --length-- -----date/time------ path
8    68831808    Apr 2 2013 21:29:58   +00:00 c1900-universalk9-mz.SPA.152-4.M3.bin
<Output omitted>
R1#
```

Step 3.    Copy the image to the TFTP server using the **copy** *source-url destination-url* command, as shown in Example 10-39.

**Example 10-39**  Copy the Image to the TFTP Server

```
R1# copy flash0: tftp:
Source filename []? c1900-universalk9-mz.SPA.152-4.M3.bin
Address or name of remote host []? 172.16.1.100
Destination filename [c1900-universalk9-mz.SPA.152-4.M3.bin]?
Writing c1900-universalk9-mz.SPA.152-4.M3.bin...
!!!!!!!!!!!!!!!!!!!!
<output omitted>
68831808 bytes copied in 363.468 secs (269058 bytes/sec)
R1#
```

After issuing the command using the specified source and destination URLs, the user is prompted for the source filename, IP address of the remote host, and destination filename. The transfer then begins.

## Steps to Copy an IOS Image to a Device (10.3.3.3)

Cisco consistently releases new Cisco IOS software versions to address new security threats, resolve caveats, and provide new features.

Figure 10-19 illustrates copying a Cisco IOS software image from a TFTP server. A new image file (c1900-universalk9-mz.SPA.152-4.M3.bin) will be copied from the TFTP server at 2001:DB8:CAFE:100::99 to the router.

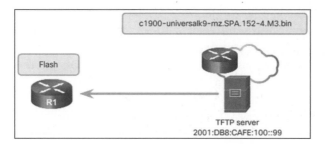

**Figure 10-19**   Central TFTP Server IPv6 Topology

This example uses IPv6 for the transfer to show that TFTP can also be used across IPv6 networks. Follow these steps to upgrade the software on the Cisco router:

**Step 1.**    Select a Cisco IOS image file that meets the requirements in terms of platform, features, and software. Download the file from cisco.com and transfer it to the TFTP server.

**Step 2.**    Verify connectivity to the TFTP server. Ping the TFTP server from the router. The output in Example 10-40 shows the TFTP server is accessible from the router.

**Example 10-40** Verify Connectivity to the Server

```
R1# ping 2001:DB8:CAFE:100::99
Type escape sequence to abort.
Sending 5, 100-byte ICMP Echos to 2001:DB8:CAFE:100::99, timeout is 2 seconds:
!!!!!
Success rate is 100 percent (5/5), round-trip min/avg/max = 56/56/56 ms
R1#
```

**Step 3.**    Ensure that there is sufficient flash space on the router that is being upgraded. The amount of free flash can be verified using the **show flash0:** command. Compare the free flash space with the new image file size. The free flash size in Example 10-41 is 182,394,880 bytes.

**Example 10-41** Verify Flash Has Free Space

```
R1# show flash0:
-# - --length-- -----date/time------ path
<Output omitted>

182394880 bytes available (74092544 bytes used)

R1#
```

**Step 4.**    Copy the IOS image file from the TFTP server to the router using the **copy** command shown in Example 10-42. After issuing this command with specified source and destination URLs, the user is prompted for the IP address of the remote host, the source filename, and the destination filename. The transfer of the file then begins.

**Example 10-42** Copy the Image from the TFTP Server

```
R1# copy tftp: flash0:
Address or name of remote host []? 2001:DB8:CAFE:100::99
Source filename []? c1900-universalk9-mz.SPA.152-4.M3.bin
Destination filename []? c1900-universalk9-mz.SPA.152-4.M3.bin
Accessing tftp://2001:DB8:CAFE:100::99/c1900-universalk9-mz.SPA.152-4.M3.bin...
Loading c1900-universalk9-mz.SPA.152-4.M3.bin from 2001:DB8:CAFE:100::99 (via
  GigabitEthernet0/0): !!!!!!!!!!!!!!!!!!!!!
<Output omitted>
[OK - 68831808 bytes]
68831808 bytes copied in 368.128 secs (265652 bytes/sec)
```

## The boot system Command (10.3.3.4)

To upgrade to the copied IOS image after that image is saved on the router's flash memory, configure the router to load the new image during bootup using the **boot system** command, as shown in Example 10-43. Save the configuration. Reload the router to boot the router with the new image.

> **Note**
>
> Failure to do this step will result with the router consistently rebooting using the older image.

**Example 10-43** Set the Image to Boot and Reload System

```
R1(config)# boot system flash0://c1900-universalk9-mz.SPA.152-4.M3.bin
R1(config)# exit
R1#
R1# copy running-config startup-config
R1#
R1# reload
```

After the router has booted, to verify the new image has loaded, use the **show version** command, as shown in Example 10-44.

**Example 10-44** Verifying the Configured Image Loaded

```
R1# show version
Cisco IOS Software, C1900 Software (C1900-UNIVERSALK9-M), Version 15.2(4)M3,
   RELEASE SOFTWARE (fc2)
Technical Support: http://www.cisco.com/techsupport
Copyright (c) 1986-2013 by Cisco Systems, Inc.
Compiled Tue 26-Feb-13 02:11 by prod_rel_team


ROM: System Bootstrap, Version 15.0(1r)M15, RELEASE SOFTWARE (fc1)


R1 uptime is 1 hour, 2 minutes
System returned to ROM by power-on
System image file is "flash0:c1900-universalk9-mz.SPA.152-4.M3.bin"
R#
```

During startup, the bootstrap code parses the startup configuration file in NVRAM for the **boot system** commands that specify the name and location of the Cisco IOS Software image to load. Several **boot system** commands can be entered in sequence to provide a fault-tolerant boot plan.

If there are no **boot system** commands in the configuration, the router defaults to loading the first valid Cisco IOS image in flash memory and running it.

**Packet Tracer 10.3.3.5: Using a TFTP Server to Upgrade a Cisco IOS Image**

Background/Scenario

A TFTP server can help manage the storage of IOS images and revisions to IOS images. For any network, it is good practice to keep a backup copy of the Cisco IOS Software image in case the system image in the router becomes corrupted or accidentally erased. A TFTP server can also be used to store new upgrades to the IOS and then deployed throughout the network where it is needed. In this activity, you upgrade the IOS images on Cisco devices by using a TFTP server. You also back up an IOS image with the use of a TFTP server.

**Video Demonstration 10.3.3.6: Managing Cisco IOS Images**

Refer to the online course to complete this activity.

## Software Licensing (10.3.4)

In this topic, you learn about the licensing process for Cisco IOS software in a small- to medium-sized business network.

### Licensing Overview (10.3.4.1)

Beginning with Cisco IOS Software release 15.0, Cisco modified the process to enable new technologies within the IOS feature sets. Cisco IOS Software release 15.0 incorporates cross-platform feature sets to simplify the image selection process. It does this by providing similar functions across platform boundaries. Each device ships with the same universal image. Technology packages are enabled in the universal image via *Cisco IOS Software Activation* licensing keys. The Cisco IOS Software Activation feature allows the user to enable licensed features and register licenses. The Cisco IOS Software Activation feature is a collection of processes and components used to activate Cisco IOS software feature sets by obtaining and validating Cisco software licenses.

Figure 10-16 showed the technology packages that are available. The *technology package licenses* include the following features:

- **IP Base**—Offers features found in IP Base IOS image on ISR 1900, 2900, and 3900 + Flexible Netflow + IPv6 parity for IPv4 features present in IP Base. Some of the key features are AAA, BGP, OSPF, EIGRP, IS-IS, RIP, PBR, IGMP, Multicast, DHCP, HSRP, GLBP, NHRP, HTTP, HQF, QoS, ACL, NBAR, GRE,

CDP, ARP, NTP, PPP, PPPoA, PPPoE, RADIUS, TACACS, SCTP, SMDS, SNMP, STP, VLAN, DTP, IGMP, Snooping, SPAN, WCCP, ISDN, ADSL over ISDN, NAT-Basic X.25, RSVP, NTP, and Flexible Netflow.

- **Data**—Data features found in SP Services and Enterprise Services IOS image on ISR 1900, 2900, and 3900, such as MPLS, BFD, RSVP, L2VPN, L2TPv3, Layer 2 Local Switching, Mobile IP, Multicast Authentication, FHRP-GLBP, IP SLAs, PfR, DECnet, ALPS, RSRB, BIP, DLSw+, FRAS, Token Ring, ISL, IPX, STUN, SNTP, SDLC, and QLLC.

- **Unified Communications**—Offers the UC Features found in IPVoice IOS image on ISR 1900, 2900, and 3900, such as TDM/PSTN Gateway, Video Gateway [H320/324], Voice Conferencing, Codec Transcoding, RSVP Agent (voice), FAX T.37/38, CAC/QOS, and Hoot-n-Holler.

- **Security**—Offers the security features found in Advanced Security IOS image on ISR 1900, 2900, and 3900, such as IKE v1/IPsec/PKI, IPsec/GRE, Easy VPN w/ DVTI, DMVPN, Static VTI, Firewall, Network Foundation Protection, and GETVPN.

**Note**

Refer to cisco.com for more information on the features listed.

**Note**

The IP Base license is a prerequisite for installing the Data, Security, and Unified Communications licenses. For earlier router platforms that can support Cisco IOS Software release 15.0, a universal image is not available. It is necessary to download a separate image that contains the desired features.

**Note**

You are not required to memorize all the features of each package. However, you should have a general understanding of the differences between each.

Technology package licenses are supported on Cisco ISR G2 platforms (Cisco 1900, 2900, and 3900 Series routers). The Cisco IOS universal image contains all packages and features in one image. Each package is a grouping of technology-specific features. Multiple technology package licenses can be activated on the Cisco 1900, 2900, and 3900 series ISR platforms.

**Note**

Use the **show license feature** command to view the technology package licenses and feature licenses supported on the router.

## Licensing Process (10.3.4.2)

When a new router is shipped, it comes preinstalled with the software image and the corresponding *permanent licenses* for the customer-specified packages and features. A permanent license is a license that never expires.

The router also comes with the *evaluation license*, known as a temporary license, for most packages and features supported on the specified router. This allows customers to try a new software package or feature by activating a specific evaluation license. If customers want to permanently activate a software package or feature on the router, they must get a new software license.

Figure 10-20 shows the three steps to permanently activate a new software package or feature on the router.

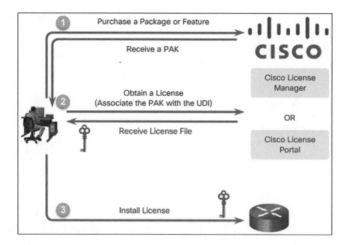

**Figure 10-20**   Licensing Overview

## Step 1. Purchase the Software Package or Feature to Install (10.3.4.3)

The first step is to purchase the software package or feature needed. This may be adding a package to IP Base, such as Security.

Software Claim Certificates are used for licenses that require software activation. The claim certificate provides the Product Activation Key (PAK) for the license and important information regarding the Cisco *End User License Agreement (EULA)*. In most instances, Cisco or the Cisco channel partner will have already activated the licenses ordered at the time of purchase and no Software Claim Certificate is provided.

In either instance, customers receive a PAK with their purchase. The PAK serves as a receipt and is used to obtain a license. A PAK is an 11-digit alphanumeric key created by Cisco manufacturing. It defines the Feature Set associated with the PAK. A PAK is not tied to a specific device until the license is created. A PAK can be purchased that generates any specified number of licenses. As shown in Figure 10-21, a separate license is required for each package, IP Base, Data, UC, and SEC.

**Figure 10-21**    Purchasing a License for a Feature

## Step 2. Obtain a License (10.3.4.4)

The second step is to obtain the license, which is actually a license file. A license file, also known as a Software Activation License, is obtained using one of the following options:

- *Cisco License Manager (CLM)*—This is a free software application available at http://www.cisco.com/go/clm. Cisco License Manager is a standalone application from Cisco that helps network administrators rapidly deploy multiple Cisco software licenses across their networks. Cisco License Manager can discover network devices, view their license information, and acquire and deploy licenses from Cisco. The application provides a GUI that simplifies installation and helps automate license acquisition, as well as perform multiple licensing tasks from a central location. CLM is free of charge and can be downloaded from CCO.

- *Cisco License Registration Portal*—This is the web-based portal for getting and registering individual software licenses, available at http://www.cisco.com/go/license.

Both of these processes require a PAK number and a *unique device identifier (UDI)*.

The PAK is received during purchase.

The UDI is a combination of the Product ID (PID), the Serial Number (SN), and the hardware version. The SN is an 11-digit number that uniquely identifies a device. The PID identifies the type of device. Only the PID and the SN are used for license creation. This UDI can be displayed using the **show license udi** command shown in Example 10-45.

**Example 10-45**  Displaying the UDI

```
R1# show license udi
Device#    PID                  SN             UDI
----------------------------------------------------------------------
*0         CISCO1941/K9         FTX1636848Z    CISCO1941/K9:FTX1636848Z

R1#
```

This information is also available on a pull-out label tray found on the device. Figure 10-22 shows an example of the pull-out label on a Cisco 1941 router.

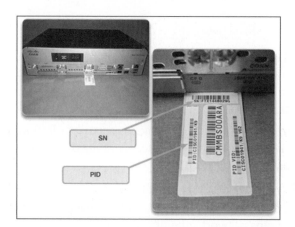

**Figure 10-22**  Displaying the UDI (PID/SN) on a Pull-Out Label

After entering the appropriate information, the customer receives an email containing the license information to install the license file. The license file is an XML text file with a .lic extension.

## Step 3. Install the License (10.3.4.5)

After the license has been purchased, the customer receives a license file. Installing a permanent license requires two steps:

**Step 1.**    Use the **license install** *stored-location-url* privileged EXEC mode command to install a license file.

**Step 2.**    Reboot the router using the **reload** privileged EXEC command. A reload is not required if an evaluation license is active.

Example 10-46 shows the configuration for installing the permanent license for the Security package on the router.

**Example 10-46** Permanent License Installation

```
R1# license install flash0:seck9-C1900-SPE150_K9-FHH12250057.xml
Installing licenses from "seck9-c1900-SPE150_K9-FHH12250057.xml"
Installing...Feature:seck9...Successful:Supported
1/1 licenses were successfully installed
0/1 licenses were existing licenses
0/1 licenses were failed to install
R1#
*Jul 7 17:24:57.391: %LICENSE-6-INSTALL: Feature seck9 1.0 was installed in this
  device. UDI=1900-SPE150/K9:FHH12250057; StoreIndex=15:Primary License Storage
*Jul 7 17:24:57.615: %IOS_LICENSE_IMAGE_APPLICATION-6-LICENSE_LEVEL: Module
  name = c1900 Next reboot level = seck9 and License = seck9
R1# reload
```

**Note**

Unified Communications is not supported on 1941 routers.

After a permanent license is installed on a router, it is good for that particular feature set for the life of the router, even across IOS versions. For example, when a UC, SEC, or Data license is installed on a router, the subsequent features for that license are activated even if the router is upgraded to a new IOS release. A permanent license is the most common license type used when a feature set is purchased for a device.

**Note**

Cisco manufacturing preinstalls the appropriate permanent license on the ordered device for the purchased feature set. No customer interaction with the Cisco IOS Software Activation processes is required to enable that license on new hardware.

## License Verification and Management (10.3.5)

In this topic, you configure a router to install an IOS software image license.

### License Verification (10.3.5.1)

After a new license has been installed, the router must be rebooted using the **reload** command. Use the **show version** command after the router is reloaded to verify that the license has been installed.

As shown in Example 10-47, R1 has the Security license permanently installed.

**Example 10-47** Permanent License Verification

```
R1# show version
<Output omitted>
License Info:
License UDI:
--------------------------------------------------
Device#    PID                    SN
--------------------------------------------------
*0         CISCO1941/K9           FTX1636848Z
Technology Package License Information for Module:'c1900'
-------------------------------------------------------------
Technology    Technology-package         Technology-package
              Current      Type          Next reboot
-------------------------------------------------------------
ipbase        ipbasek9     Permanent     ipbasek9
security      seck9        Permanent     seck9
uc            None         None          None
data          None         None          None
R1#
```

The **show license** command in Example 10-48 displays additional information about Cisco IOS software licenses.

**Example 10-48** Displaying Software License Information

```
R1# show license
Index 1 Feature: ipbasek9
      Period left: Life time
      License Type: Permanent
      License State: Active, In Use
      License Count: Non-Counted
      License Priority: Medium
Index 2 Feature: securityk9
      Period left: Life time
      License Type: Permanent
      License State: Active, In Use
      License Count: Non-Counted
      License Priority: Medium
```

```
Index 3 Feature: datak9
      Period left: Not Activated
      Period Used: 0  minute  0  second
      License Type: EvalRightToUse
      License State: Not in Use, EULA not accepted
      License Count: Non-Counted
      License Priority: None
<Output omitted>
R1#
```

This command displays license information used to help with troubleshooting issues related to Cisco IOS software licenses. This command displays all the licenses installed in the system. In this example, both the IP Base and Security licenses have been installed. This command also displays the features that are available, but not licensed to execute, such as the Data feature set. Output is grouped according to how the features are stored in license storage.

The following is a brief description of the **show license** output:

- **Feature**—Name of the feature.

- **License Type**—Identifies if the license is permanent or evaluation.

- **License State**—Identifies if the status of the license is Active or In Use.

- **License Count**—Number of licenses available and in use, if counted. If noncounted is indicated, the license is unrestricted.

- **License Priority**—Identifies the priority of the license as either high or low.

### Activate an Evaluation Right-to-Use License (10.3.5.2)

Evaluation licenses are replaced with *Evaluation Right-to-Use licenses (RTU)* after 60 days. An Evaluation license is good for a 60-day evaluation period. After the 60 days, this license automatically transitions into an RTU license. These licenses are available on the honor system and require the customer's acceptance of the EULA. The EULA is automatically applied to all Cisco IOS software licenses.

The **license accept end user agreement** global configuration mode command is used to configure a one-time acceptance of the EULA for all Cisco IOS software packages and features. After the command is issued and the EULA accepted, the EULA is automatically applied to all Cisco IOS software licenses and the user is not prompted to accept the EULA during license installation.

Example 10-49 configures the one-time acceptance of the EULA using the **license accept end user agreement** global configuration command.

**Example 10-49** Accept the EULA

```
R1(config)# license accept end user agreement
R1(config)#
```

Example 10-50 activates the Data Evaluation RTU license using the **license boot module** *module-name* **technology-package** *package-name* privileged EXEC mode command.

**Example 10-50** Activating the Evaluation License

```
R1(config)# license boot module c1900 technology-package datak9
% use 'write' command to make license boot config take effect on next boot
R1(config)#
*Apr 25 23:15:01.874: %IOS_LICENSE_IMAGE_APPLICATION-6-LICENSE_LEVEL: Module name =
  c1900 Next reboot level = datak9 and License = datak9
*Apr 25 23:15:02.502: %LICENSE-6-EULA_ACCEPTED: EULA for feature datak9 1.0 has
  been accepted. UDI=CISCO1941/K9:FTX1636848Z; StoreIndex=1:Built-In License
  Storage
R1(config)#
```

Use the **?** in place of the arguments to determine which module names and supported software packages are available on the router. Technology package names for Cisco ISR G2 platforms follow:

- **ipbasek9**—IP Base technology package

- **securityk9**—Security technology package

- **datak9**—Data technology package

- **uck9**—Unified Communications package (not available on 1900 series)

**Note**

A reload using the **reload** command is required to activate the software package.

Evaluation licenses are temporary and are used to evaluate a feature set on new hardware. Temporary licenses are limited to a specific usage period (for example, 60 days).

Reboot the router after a license is successfully installed using the **reload** command. The **show license** command in Example 10-51 verifies that the license has been installed.

**Example 10-51** Evaluation License Verification

```
R1# show license
Index 1 Feature: ipbasek9
      Period left: Life time
      License Type: Permanent
      License State: Active, In Use
      License Count: Non-Counted
      License Priority: Medium
Index 2 Feature: securityk9
      Period left: Life time
      License Type: Permanent
      License State: Active, In Use
      License Count: Non-Counted
      License Priority: Medium
Index 3 Feature: datak9
      Period left: 8   weeks 4   days
      Period Used: 0   minute   0   second
      License Type: EvalRightToUse
      License State: Active, Not in Use, EULA accepted
      License Count: Non-Counted
      License Priority: Low
<Output omitted>
R1#
```

## Back Up the License (10.3.5.3)

The **license save** command is used to copy all licenses in a device and store them in a format required by the specified storage location. Saved licenses are restored by using the **license install** command.

The command to back up a copy of the licenses on a device is **license save** *file-sys://lic-location* privileged EXEC.

Example 10-52 backs up the license to flash with the name **all_licenses.lic**.

**Example 10-52** Backing Up the License

```
R1# license save flash0:all_licenses.lic
license lines saved ..... to flash0:all_licenses.lic

R1#
```

Use the **show flash0:** privileged EXEC command to verify that the licenses have been saved, as shown in Example 10-53.

**Example 10-53**  Verify Saved License

```
R1# show flash0:
-# - --length-- -----date/time------ path
<Output omitted>
8      68831808 Apr 2 2013 21:29:58 +00:00 c1900-universalk9-mz.SPA.152-4.M3.bin
9          1153 Apr 26 2013 02:24:30 +00:00 all_licenses.lic

182390784 bytes available (74096640 bytes used)

R1#
```

The license storage location can be a directory or a URL that points to a file system. Use the **?** command to see the storage locations a device supports.

## Uninstall the License (10.3.5.4)

To clear an active permanent license from the Cisco 1900 series, 2900 series, and 3900 series routers, perform the following steps:

## Step 1. Disable the technology package.

- Disable the active license with the **license boot module** *module-name* **technology-package** *package-name* **disable** global configuration command.

- Reboot the router using the **reload** command. A reload is required to make the software package inactive.

## Step 2. Clear the license.

- Clear the technology package license from license storage using the **license clear** *feature-name* privileged EXEC command.

- Remove the **license boot module** command configured in Step 1 using the **no license boot module** *module-name* **technology-package** *package-name* **disable** global configuration command.

**Note**

Some licenses, such as built-in licenses, cannot be cleared. Only licenses that have been added by using the **license install** command are removed. Evaluation licenses are not removed.

Example 10-54 disables the Security technology package license.

**Example 10-54**  Disabling an Active and Permanent License

```
R1(config)# license boot module c1900 technology-package seck9 disable
R1(config)# exit
R1# reload
```

In Example 10-55, the technology package license is cleared from license storage.

**Example 10-55**  Clearing an Active and Permanent License

```
R1# license clear seck9
R1#
R1# configure terminal
R1(config)# no license boot module c1900 technology-package seck9 disable
R1(config)# exit
R1# reload
```

Video

**Video Demonstration 10.3.5.5: Working with IOS 15 Image Licenses**

Refer to the online course to complete this activity.

# Summary (10.4)

**Packet Tracer 10.4.1.1: Skills Integration Challenge**

In this challenge activity, you finish the addressing scheme, configure routing, and implement named access control lists.

---

In this chapter, you learned and practiced skills that network administrators use for device discovery, management, and maintenance.

CDP is a Cisco proprietary protocol for network discovery on the data link layer. It can share information such as device names and IOS versions with other physically connected Cisco devices. LLDP is a vendor-neutral protocol on the data link layer for network discovery. The network devices advertise information, such as their identities and capabilities, to their neighbors.

NTP synchronizes the time of day among a set of distributed time servers and clients. This allows networking devices to agree on the time a specific event occurred, such as the loss of connectivity between a router and a switch. Syslog messages can be trapped and sent to a syslog server, where the network administrator can investigate when the link failed.

Device maintenance includes the tasks of backing up, restoring, and upgrading IOS images and configuration files. Upgrading an IOS image also includes tasks related to software licensing.

# Practice

The following activities provide practice with the topics introduced in this chapter. The labs and packet tracer activities are available in the companion Routing and Switching Essentials v6 Labs & Study Guide (ISBN 9781587134265). The packet tracer activities PKA files are found in the online course.

**Labs**

Lab 10.1.2.5: Configure CDP and LLDP

Lab 10.2.3.6: Configuring Syslog and NTP

Lab 10.3.1.9: Managing Router Configuration Files with Terminal Emulation Software

Lab 10.3.1.10: Managing Device Configuration Files Using TFTP, Flash, and USB

Lab 10.3.1.11: Configure and Verify Password Recovery

---

**Packet Tracer Activities**

Packet Tracer 10.1.1.4: Map a Network Using CDP

Packet Tracer 10.2.1.4: Configure and Verify NTP

Packet Tracer 10.2.3.5: Configuring Syslog and NTP

Packet Tracer 10.3.1.8: Backing Up Configuration Files

Packet Tracer 10.3.3.5: Using a TFTP Server to Upgrade a Cisco IOS Image

Packet Tracer 10.4.1.1: Skills Integration Challenge

# Check Your Understanding Questions

Complete all the review questions listed here to test your understanding of the topics and concepts in this chapter. The appendix "Answers to the 'Check Your Understanding' Questions" lists the answers.

1. What is a difference between CDP and LLDP?

   A. CDP can gather information from routers, switches, and wireless APs, whereas LLDP can only gather information from routers and switches.

   B. CDP can obtain both Layer 2 and Layer 3 information, whereas LLDP can only obtain Layer 2 information.

   C. CDP is a proprietary protocol, whereas LLDP is a vendor-neutral protocol.

   D. CDP is enabled on an interface using two commands, whereas LLDP requires only one command.

2. A network administrator wants to configure a router so that only a specific interface will send and receive CDP information. Which two configuration steps accomplish this? (Choose two.)

   A. R1(config)# **no cdp enable**

   B. R1(config)# **no cdp run**

   C. R1(config-if)# **cdp enable**

   D. R1(config-if)# **cdp run**

   E. R1(config-if)# **cdp receive**

   F. R1(config-if)# **cdp transmit**

3. What information can be gathered about a neighbor device from the **show cdp neighbors detail** command that cannot be found with the **show cdp neighbors** command?

   A. The capabilities of the neighbor

   B. The hostname of the neighbor

   C. The IP address of the neighbor

   D. The platform that is used by the neighbor

4. What is the configuration command to globally enable LLDP on a Cisco Catalyst switch?

   A. **enable lldp**

   B. **feature lldp**

   C. **lldp enable**

   D. **lldp run**

5. Which option correctly enables LLDP on an interface?

   A. R1(config-if)# **lldp enable**

   B. R1(config-if)# **lldp enable**
      R1(config-if)# **lldp receive**

   C. R1(config-if)# **lldp receive**
      R1(config-if)# **lldp transmit**

   D. R1(config-if)# **lldp enable**
      R1(config-if)# **lldp receive**
      R1(config-if)# **lldp transmit**

6. What are the most common syslog messages?

   A. Error messages about hardware or software malfunctions

   B. Link up and link down messages

   C. Output messages that are generated from **debug** output

   D. Those that occur when a packet matches a parameter condition in an access control list

7. When logging is used, which severity level indicates that a device is unusable?

   A. Level 0—Emergency

   B. Level 1—Alert

   C. Level 2—Critical

   D. Level 3—Error

8. Which protocol or service allows network administrators to receive system messages that are provided by network devices?

   A. NTP

   B. NetFlow

   C. SNMP

   D. Syslog

9. Which syslog message type is accessible only to an administrator via the Cisco CLI?

   A. Alerts

   B. Debugging

   C. Emergency

   D. Errors

10. Which destination do Cisco routers and switches use by default when sending syslog messages for all severity levels?

    A. RAM

    B. NVRAM

    C. Nearest syslog server

    D. Console

11. A network administrator has issued the **logging trap 4** global configuration mode command. What is the result of this command?

    A. The syslog client sends to the syslog server any event message that has a severity level of 4 and lower.

    B. The syslog client sends to the syslog server event messages with an identification trap level of only 4.

    C. The syslog client sends to the syslog server any event message that has a severity level of 4 and higher.

    D. After four events, the syslog client sends an event message to the syslog server.

12. The command **ntp server 10.1.1.1** is issued on router R1. What impact does this command have?

    A. Identifies the NTP server that R1 will use to send system log messages to

    B. Identifies the NTP server that R1 will use to store backup configurations

    C. Identifies R1 as the NTP server using IP address 10.1.1.1

    D. Synchronizes the clock of R1 with the timeserver at IP address 10.1.1.1

13. Which two statements are true about NTP servers in an enterprise network? (Choose two.)

   A.  All NTP servers synchronize directly to a stratum 1 time source.

   B.  NTP servers at stratum 1 are directly connected to an authoritative time source.

   C.  NTP servers control the mean time between failures (MTBF) for key network devices.

   D.  NTP servers ensure an accurate time stamp on logging and debugging information.

   E.  There can be only one NTP server on an enterprise network.

14. What can a network administrator do to access a router if the password has been lost?

   A.  Access the router remotely through Telnet, and use the **show running-config** command.

   B.  Boot the router into ROMMON mode and reinstall the IOS from a TFTP server.

   C.  From ROMMON mode, configure the router to ignore the startup configuration when the router initializes.

   D.  Reboot the router and use the break key sequence to bypass the password during IOS bootup.

15. An administrator issues the command **confreg 0x2142** at the rommon 1> prompt. What is the effect when this router is rebooted?

   A.  Contents in NVRAM will be erased.

   B.  Contents in NVRAM will be ignored.

   C.  Contents in RAM will be erased.

   D.  Contents in RAM will be ignored.

16. A network technician is attempting a password recovery on a router. From ROMMON mode, which command must be entered to bypass the startup configuration file?

   A.  rommon> **config-register 0x2102**

   B.  rommon> **confreg 0x2102**

   C.  rommon> **config-register 0x2142**

   D.  rommon> **confreg 0x2142**

17. What must an administrator have in order to reset a lost password on a router?

    A. A crossover cable

    B. A TFTP server

    C. Access to another router

    D. Physical access to the router

18. In the IOS image named c1900-universalk9-mz.SPA.152-3.T.bin, which part identifies the major release number?

    A. 1900

    B. 15

    C. 52

    D. 2

    E. 3

19. What statement describes a Cisco IOS image with the "universalk9_npe" designation for Cisco ISR G2 routers?

    A. It is an IOS version that, at the request of some countries, removes any strong cryptographic functionality.

    B. It is an IOS version that can only be used in the United States of America.

    C. It is an IOS version that offers all of the Cisco IOS Software feature sets.

    D. It is an IOS version that provides only the IPBase feature set.

20. A network engineer is upgrading the Cisco IOS image on a 2900 series ISR. What command could the engineer use to verify the total amount of flash memory as well as how much flash memory is currently available?

    A. **show boot memory**

    B. **show flash0:**

    C. **show interfaces**

    D. **show startup-config**

    E. **show version**

21. Which two conditions should the network administrator verify before attempting to upgrade a Cisco IOS image using a TFTP server? (Choose two.)

    A. Verify connectivity between the router and TFTP server using the **ping** command.

    B. Verify that the checksum for the image is valid using the **show version** command.

C. Verify that the TFTP server is running using the **tftpdnld** command.

D. Verify the name of the TFTP server using the **show hosts** command.

E. Verify that there is enough flash memory for the new Cisco IOS image using the **show flash** command.

22. Beginning with the Cisco IOS Software Release 15.0, which license is a prerequisite for installing additional technology pack licenses?

A. DATA

B. IPBase

C. SEC

D. UC

23. A network technician is troubleshooting problems with a router that is running IOS 15. Which command displays the features activated for the licenses that are installed on the router?

A. **show boot memory**

B. **show flash0:**

C. **show license**

D. **show startup-config**

E. **show version**

24. How long is the evaluation license period for Cisco IOS Release 15.0 software packages?

A. 10 days

B. 15 days

C. 30 days

D. 60 days

E. 120 days

25. Which command is used to configure a one-time acceptance of the EULA for all Cisco IOS software packages and features?

A. **license accept end user agreement**

B. **license boot module** *module-name*

C. **license save**

D. **show license**

# Answers to the "Check Your Understanding" Questions

## Chapter 1

1. B. Availability is the likelihood that the network is available for use when it is required. Scalability indicates how easily the network can accommodate more users and data transmission requirements. Reliability indicates the dependability of the components that make up the network, such as the routers, switches, PCs, and servers, and is often measured as a probability of failure or as the mean time between failures (MTBF). Usability is a software characteristic, not a network characteristic.

2. A and C. A switch controls the flow of data using Layer 2 addresses. Routers create more but smaller broadcast domains, and switches manage VLAN databases.

3. A and C. Routers first install directly connected routes. Only RIP uses the hop count metric. The metric varies depending on the routing protocol used. This is true for IPv4 and IPv6. The administrator can alter the administrative distance.

4. A, E, and F. A host can use its IP address and subnet mask to determine if a destination is on the same network or on a remote network. If it is on a remote network, the host will need a configured default gateway to send packets to the remote destination. DNS servers translate names into IP addresses, and DHCP servers are used to automatically assign IP addressing information to hosts. Neither of these servers has to be configured for basic remote connectivity.

5. A. The loopback interface is a logical interface internal to the router and is automatically placed in an "up" state, as long as the router is functioning. It is not assigned to a physical port and can therefore never be connected to another device. Multiple loopback interfaces can be enabled on a router.

6. A and B. The command **show ip interface brief** shows the IP address of each interface, as well as the operational status of the interfaces at both Layer 1 and Layer 2. To see interface descriptions and speed and duplex settings, use the command **show running-config interface**. Next-hop addresses are displayed in the routing table with the command **show ip route**, and the MAC address of an interface can be seen with the command **show interfaces**.

7. B and F. The source and destination IP addresses normally remain constant when sending data from one computer in a company to a remote computer in the same company. The port numbers also normally stay the same. The MAC addresses change as the packet moves in one router interface to an outbound router Ethernet interface. ARP tables are constantly changing as entries age and are removed.

8. B and E. The result of ANDing any IP address with a subnet mask is a network number. If the source network number is the same as the destination network number, the data stays on the local

network. If the destination network number is different, the packet is sent to the default gateway (the router that will send the packet onward toward the destination network).

9. D. After a router determines the destination network by ANDing the destination IP address with the subnet mask, the router examines the routing table for the resulting destination network number. When a match is found, the packet is sent to the interface associated with the network number. When no routing table entry is found for the particular network, the default gateway or Gateway of Last Resort (if configured or known) is used. If there is no Gateway of Last Resort, the packet is dropped. In this instance, the 192.168.12.224 network is not found in the routing table and the router uses the Gateway of Last Resort. The Gateway of Last Resort is the IP address of 209.165.200.226. The router knows this is an IP address associated with the 209.165.200.224 network. The router then proceeds to transmit the packet out the Serial0/0/0 interface, or the interface that is associated with 209.165.200.224.

10. A and C. EIGRP uses bandwidth, delay, load, and reliability as metrics for selecting the best path to reach a network.

11. A. The most believable route or the route with the lowest administrative distance is one that is directly connected to a router.

12. A. The Serial0/0/0 indicates the outgoing interface on R1 that is used to send packets for the 10.1.1.0/24 destination network.

13. D and E. IPv6 address 2001:DB8:ACAD:2::12 is not in the routing table. FF00::/8 is not a static route. Packets destined to network 2001:DB8:ACAD:1::/64 will be forwarded through G0/0 and not through G0/1 as stated. Packets destined to network 2001:DB8:ACAD:2::/64 will be forwarded through G0/1. R1 only knows about directly connected networks and the multicast network (FF00::/8). It does not know routes to remote networks.

14. A. A directly connected network will be added to the routing table when these three conditions are met: (1) the interface is configured with a valid IP address; (2) it is activated with the **no shutdown** command; and (3) it receives a carrier signal from another device that is connected to the interface. An incorrect subnet mask for an IPv4 address will not prevent its appearance in the routing table, although the error may prevent successful communications.

15. D. The command **ip route 0.0.0.0 0.0.0.0** *<next hop>* adds a default route to the routing table of a router. When the router receives a packet and does not have a specific route toward the destination, it forwards the packet to the next hop indicated in the default route. A route created with the **ip route** command is a static route, not a dynamic route. There is no network 0.0.0.0; therefore, option C is incorrect.

16. B and E. There are two common types of static routes in a routing table: namely, a static route to a specific network and a default static route. A static route configured on a router can be distributed by the router to other neighboring routers. However, the distributed static route will be a little different in the routing table on neighboring routers.

17. D. To enable IPv6 on a router you must use the **ipv6 unicast-routing** global configuration command or use the **ipv6 enable** interface configuration command. This is equivalent to entering **ip routing** to enable IPv4 routing on a router when it has been turned off. Keep in mind that IPv4 is enabled on a router by default. IPv6 is not enabled by default.

# Chapter 2

1. A and E. Static routing requires a thorough understanding of the entire network for proper implementation. It can be prone to errors and does not scale well for large networks. Static routing uses fewer router resources because no computing is required for updating routes. Static routing can also be more secure because it does not advertise over the network.

2. A. A static default route is a catch-all route for all unmatched networks.

3. C. By default, dynamic routing protocols have a higher AD than static routes. Configuring a static route with a higher AD than that of the dynamic routing protocol will result in the dynamic route being used instead of the static route. However, should the dynamically learned route fail, then the static route will be used as a backup.

4. D. Floating static routes are used as backup routes, often to routes learned from dynamic routing protocols. To be a floating static route, the configured route must have a higher AD than the primary route. For example, if the primary route is learned through OSPF, then a floating static route that serves as a backup to the OSPF route must have an AD greater than 110. In this example, the AD of 120 is put at the end of the static route: ip route 209.165.200.228 255.255.255.248 10.0.0.1 120.

5. B. When only the exit interface is used, the route is a directly connected static route. When the next-hop IP address is used, the route is a recursive static route. When both are used, it is a fully specified static route.

6. C. The route will appear in the routing with a code of S (Static).

7. B and E. A fully specified static route can be used to avoid recursive routing table lookups by the router. A fully specified static route contains both the IP address of the next-hop router and the ID of the exit interface.

8. B. A floating static is a backup route that only appears in the routing table when the interface used with the primary route is down. To test a floating static route, the route must be in the routing table. Therefore, shutting down the interface used as a primary route would allow the floating static route to appear in the routing table.

9. A, C, and D. The **ping, show ip route**, and **show ip interface brief** commands provide information to help troubleshoot static routes. The **show version** command does not provide routing information. The **tracert** command is used at the Windows command prompt and is not an IOS command.

The **show arp** command displays learned IP address to MAC address mappings contained in the ARP table.

10. C. When the interface associated with a static route goes down, the router will remove the route because it is no longer valid.

# Chapter 3

1. C and E. Routing protocols are responsible for discovering local and remote networks and for maintaining and updating the routing table.

2. D. By default, dynamic routing protocols forward messages across a network without authenticating the receiver or originator of traffic. Static routes increase in configuration complexity as the network grows larger and are more suitable for smaller networks. Static routes also require manual intervention when a network topology changes or links become disabled.

3. A. BGP is a protocol developed to interconnect different levels of ISPs as well as ISPs and some of their larger private clients.

4. A and E. Classless routing updates include subnet mask information and support VLSM.

5. A. A passive interface does not send routing updates or hello packets; however, it is still advertised to other routers connected to nonpassive interfaces.

6. B. The command that the engineer is entering will cause RIPv2 to activate on the interface for the 192.168.10.0 network. If RIPv1 is configured, the router will send only version 1 updates but will listen for both version 1 and version 2 updates. If RIPv2 is configured, the router will send and listen to only version 2 updates.

7. B. Routes in a routing table are manually created or dynamically learned. Letter D indicates that the route was learned dynamically through the EIGRP routing protocol.

8. C and D. An ultimate route is a routing table entry that contains either a next-hop IP address (another path) or an exit interface, or both. This means that directly connected and link-local routes are ultimate routes. A default route is a level 1 ultimate route, but not all ultimate routes are default routes. Routing table entries that are subnetted are level 1 parent routes but do not meet either of the two requirements to be ultimate routes. Ultimate routes do not have to be classful network entries.

9. B. The selection of both IPv6 routes and IPv4 routes is based on the longest matching prefix. In this example, option B is the longest match.

10. D. When Cisco Express Forwarding (CEF) is not being used on a router, a recursive lookup must be performed when a route using a next-hop IP address is selected as the best pathway to forward data.

11. A. Routers running IOS release 15 have link local routing table entries for both IPv4 and IPv6. The selection of both IPv6 routes and IPv4 routes is based on the longest matching prefix. The routing tables of both IPv6 and IPv4 use directly connected interfaces, static routes, and dynamically learned routes.

# Chapter 4

1. C. One of the basic functions of the distribution layer of the Cisco Borderless Architecture is to perform routing between different VLANs. Acting as a backbone and aggregating campus blocks are functions of the core layer. Providing access to end user devices is a function of the access layer.

2. A and E. A hierarchical design for switches helps network administrators when planning and deploying a network expansion, performing fault isolation when a problem occurs, and providing resiliency when traffic levels are high. A good hierarchical design has redundancy when it can be afforded so that one switch does not cause all networks to be down.

3. D. A collapsed core design is appropriate for a small, single-building business. This type of design uses two layers (the collapsed core and distribution layers consolidated into one layer and the access layer). Larger businesses use the traditional three-tier switch design model.

4. A and B. A converged network provides a single infrastructure that combines voice, video, and data. Analog phones, user data, and point-to-point video traffic are contained within the single network infrastructure of a converged network.

5. D. Maintaining three separate network tiers is not always required or cost-efficient. All network designs require an access layer, but a two-tier design can collapse the distribution and core layers into one layer to serve the needs of a small location with few users.

6. A. A fixed-configuration switch would meet all of the requirements of the law firm.

7. A and D. Fixed-configuration switches, although lower in price, have a designated number of ports and no ability to add ports. They also typically provide fewer high-speed ports. To scale switching on a network that consists of fixed-configuration switches, more switches need to be purchased. This increases the number of power outlets that need to be used. Modular switches can be scaled simply by purchasing additional line cards.

8. A. A switch builds a MAC address table of MAC addresses and associated port numbers by examining the source MAC address found in inbound frames. To forward a frame onward, the switch examines the destination MAC address, looks in the MAC address for a port number associated with that destination MAC address, and sends it to the specific port. If the destination MAC address is not in the table, the switch forwards the frame out all ports except the inbound port that originated the frame.

9. B. Cisco LAN switches use the MAC address table to make decisions of traffic forwarding. The decisions are based on the ingress port and the destination MAC address of the frame. The ingress port information is important because it carries the VLAN to which the port belongs.

10. D. A switch provides microsegmentation so that no other device competes for the same Ethernet network bandwidth.

11. D. When a switch receives a frame with a source MAC address that is not in the MAC address table, the switch adds that MAC address to the table and maps that address to a specific port. Switches do not use IP addressing in the MAC address table.

**12.** D and F. A switch can create temporary point-to-point connections between the directly attached transmitting and receiving network devices. The two devices have full-bandwidth full duplex connectivity during the transmission. Segmenting adds collision domains to reduce collisions.

**13.** B. When a LAN switch with the microsegmentation feature is used, each port represents a segment that in turns forms a collision domain. If each port is connected with an end user device, there will be no collisions. However, if multiple end devices are connected to a hub and the hub is connected to a port on the switch, some collisions will occur in that particular segment, but not beyond it.

**14.** converged

# Chapter 5

**1.** D. Interface VLAN 1 is the default management SVI.

**2.** A and B. The prompt occurs after a switch boots normally but does not have or has failed to load a startup configuration file.

**3.** A and E. In full duplex operation, the NIC does not process frames any faster, the data flow is bidirectional, and there are no collisions.

**4.** C. The port speed LED indicates that the port speed mode is selected. When selected, the port LEDs will display colors with different meanings. If the LED is off, the port is operating at 10 Mb/s. If the LED is green, the port is operating at 100 Mb/s. If the LED is blinking green, the port is operating at 1000 Mb/s.

**5.** B. The switch boot loader environment is presented when the switch cannot locate a valid operating system. The boot loader environment provides a few basic commands that allow a network administrator to reload the operating system or provide an alternate location of the operating system.

**6.** C. The **show interfaces** command is useful to detect media errors, to see if packets are being sent and received, and to determine if any runts, giants, CRCs, interface resets, or other errors have occurred. Problems with reachability to a remote network would likely be caused by a misconfigured default gateway or other routing issue, not a switch issue. The **show mac address-table** command shows the MAC address of a directly attached device.

**7.** B. SSH provides security for remote management connections to a network device. SSH does so through encryption for session authentication (username and password) as well as for data transmission. Telnet sends a username and password in plain text, which can be targeted to obtain the username and password through data capture. Both Telnet and SSH use TCP, support authentication, and connect to hosts in CLI.

**8.** B. When a violation occurs on a switch port that is configured for port security with the shutdown violation action, it is put into the err-disabled state. It can be brought back up by shutting down the interface and then issuing the **no shutdown** command.

**9.** B and C.

10. B. In port security implementation, an interface can be configured for one of three violation modes: Protect—a port security violation causes the interface to drop packets with unknown source addresses and no notification is sent that a security violation has occurred. Restrict—a port security violation causes the interface to drop packets with unknown source addresses and to send a notification that a security violation has occurred. Shutdown—a port security violation causes the interface to immediately become error-disabled and turns off the port LED. No notification is sent that a security violation has occurred.

## Chapter 6

1. A and B. Voice VLANs do not carry email traffic and the management VLAN is not always VLAN 1.

2. C. A native VLAN is the VLAN that does not receive a VLAN tag in the IEEE 802.1Q frame header. Cisco best practices recommend the use of an unused VLAN (not a data VLAN, the default VLAN of VLAN 1, or the management VLAN) as the native VLAN whenever possible.

3. B and C. Cost reduction and improved IT staff efficiency are benefits of using VLANs, along with higher performance, broadcast storm mitigation, and simpler project and application management. End users are not usually aware of VLANs, and VLANs do require configuration. Because VLANs are assigned to access ports, they do not reduce the number of trunk links. VLANs increase security by segmenting traffic.

4. A. The **show interfaces switchport** command displays the following information for a given port: Switchport, Administrative Mode, Operational Mode, Administrative Trunking Encapsulation, Operational Trunking Encapsulation, Negotiation of Trunking, Access Mode VLAN, Trunking Native Mode VLAN, Administrative Native VLAN tagging, and Voice VLAN

5. C. There is no need to enter the **no shutdown** command or remove VLAN 2 using the **no vlan 2** command. The **switchport trunk** command is not used on an access port.

6. B. There is no need to delete the IP address or erase the running configuration file. The startup configuration and the vlan.dat should both be deleted.

7. C and D. Extended range VLANs are stored in the running-configuration file by default and must be saved after being configured. Extended VLANs use the VLAN IDs from 1006 to 4094.

8. D. The affected ports must be reconfigured for an active VLAN.

9. B. The **switchport trunk allowed vlan 30** command allows traffic that is tagged with VLAN 30 across the trunk port. Any VLAN that is not specified in this command will not be allowed on this trunk port.

10. A. By default, all VLANs, including the native VLAN and untagged traffic, are allowed across a trunk link.

11. A. The list of allowed VLANs on a trunk is configured by the administrator by issuing the **switch-port trunk allowed vlan** command.

12. A and F. Some Cisco switches are automatically configured for auto negotiation of a trunk. A best practice for configuring a port is to manually configure the port for either access mode or trunking mode.

# Chapter 7

1. A, D, and F. Packets not matching an ACE are implicitly denied. After a packet matches an ACE, it is no longer processed by the ACL.

2. B and D.

3. D. An outbound ACL should be utilized when the same ACL filtering rules will be applied to packets coming from more than one inbound interface before exiting a single outbound interface. The outbound ACL will be applied on the single outbound interface.

4. A and E. To permit or deny one specific IP address, either the wildcard mask 0.0.0.0 (used after the IP address) or the wildcard mask keyword host (used before the IP address) can be used.

5. C. The ACL statement access-list 10 permit 192.168.16.0 0.0.3.255 will match all four network prefixes. All four prefixes have the same 22 high-order bits. These 22 high-order bits are matched by the network prefix and wildcard mask of 192.168.16.0 0.0.3.255.

6. C. In calculating how many ACLs can be configured, use the rule of "three Ps": one ACL per protocol, per direction, per interface. In this case, 2 interfaces times 2 protocols times 2 directions yields 8 possible ACLs.

7. A, D, and F. Extended ACLs should be placed as close as possible to the source IP address so that traffic that needs to be filtered does not cross the network and use network resources. Because standard ACLs do not specify a destination address, they should be placed as close to the destination as possible. Placing a standard ACL close to the source may filter all traffic and limit services to other hosts. Filtering unwanted traffic before it enters low-bandwidth links preserves bandwidth and supports network functionality. Decisions on placing ACLs inbound or outbound are dependent on the requirements to be met.

8. A. Administrative access over SSH to the router is through the vty lines. Therefore, the ACL must be applied to those lines in the inbound direction. This is accomplished by entering line configuration mode and issuing the **access-class** command.

9. B. With an inbound ACL, incoming packets are processed before they are routed. With an outbound ACL, packets are first routed to the outbound interface; then they are processed. Thus, processing inbound is more efficient from the router perspective. The structure, filtering methods, and limitations (on an interface, only one inbound and one outbound ACL can be configured) are the same for both types of ACLs.

# Chapter 8

1. B. When a DHCP client receives DHCPOFFER messages, it sends a broadcast DHCPREQUEST message for two purposes. First, it indicates to the offering DHCP server that it would like to accept the offer and bind the IP address. Second, it notifies any other responding DHCP servers that their offers are declined.

2. C. The DHCPREQUEST message is broadcast to inform other DHCP servers that an IP address has been leased.

3. B. When a DHCPv4 client does not have an IPv4 address, a DHCPv4 server sends a DHCPOFFER message back to the client hardware address of the requesting DHCPv4 client.

4. D. When a DHCP client lease is about to expire, the client sends a DHCPREQUEST message to the DHCPv4 server that originally provided the IPv4 address. This allows the client to request that the lease be extended.

5. B. By default, the **ip helper-address** command forwards the following eight UDP services:
   - Port 37: Time
   - Port 49: TACACS
   - Port 53: DNS
   - Port 67: DHCP/BOOTP client
   - Port 68: DHCP/BOOTP server
   - Port 69: TFTP
   - Port 137: NetBIOS name service
   - Port 138: NetBIOS datagram service

6. C. The **ip address dhcp command** activates the DHCPv4 client on a given interface. By doing this, the router obtains the IP parameters from a DHCPv4 server.

7. B and D. The ISP frequently requires SOHO routers to be configured as DHCPv4 clients to be connected to the provider.

8. C. The DHCP server is not on the same network as the hosts, so a DHCP relay agent is required. This is achieved by issuing the **ip helper-address** command on the interface of the router that contains the DHCPv4 clients to direct DHCP messages to the DHCPv4 server IP address.

9. C. When a PC is configured to use the SLAAC method for configuring IPv6 addresses, it uses the prefix and prefix-length information that is contained in the RA message, combined with a 64-bit interface ID (obtained by using the EUI-64 process or by using a random number that is generated by the client operating system), to form an IPv6 address. It uses the link-local address of the router interface that is attached to the LAN segment as its IPv6 default gateway address.

10. C. ICMPv6 RA messages contain two flags to indicate whether a workstation should use SLAAC, a DHCPv6 server, or a combination to configure its IPv6 address. These two flags are M flag and O flag. When both flags are 0 (by default), a client must use only the information in the RA message. When M flag is 0 and O flag is 1, a client should use the information in the RA message and look for the other configuration parameters (such as DNS server addresses) on DHCPv6 servers.

11. B. In stateless DHCPv6 configuration, a client configures its IPv6 address by using the prefix and prefix length in the RA message, combined with a self-generated interface ID. It then contacts a DHCPv6 server for additional configuration information via an INFORMATION-REQUEST message. The DHCPv6 SOLICIT message is used by a client to locate a DHCPv6 server. DHCPv6 servers use the DHCPv6 ADVERTISE message to indicate their availability for DHCPv6 service. The DHCPv6 REQUEST message is used by a client, in the stateful DHCPv6 configuration, to request all configuration information from a DHCPv6 server.

12. D. Stateless DHCPv6 allows clients to use ICMPv6 router advertisement (RA) messages to automatically assign IPv6 addresses to themselves but then allows these clients to contact a DHCPv6 server to obtain additional information such as the domain name and address of DNS servers. SLAAC does not allow the client to obtain additional information through DHCPv6, and stateful DHCPv6 requires that the client receive its interface address directly from a DHCPv6 server. RA messages, when combined with an EUI-64 interface identifier, are used to automatically create an interface IPv6 address and are part of both SLAAC and stateless DHCPv6.

13. D. SLAAC is a stateless allocation method and does not use a DHCP server to manage the IPv6 addresses. When a host generates an IPv6 address, it must verify that it is unique. The host sends an ICMPv6 neighbor solicitation message with its own IPv6 address as the target. As long as no other device responds with a neighbor advertisement message, the address is unique.

14. D. The EUI-64 process uses the MAC address of an interface to construct an interface ID (IID). Because the MAC address is only 48 bits in length, 16 additional bits (FF:FE) must be added to the MAC address to create the full 64-bit IID.

15. A. Under stateful DHCPv6 configuration, which is indicated by setting M flag as 1 (through the interface command **ipv6 nd managed-config-flag**), the DHCPv6 server manages the dynamic IPv6 address assignments. Clients must obtain all configuration information from a DHCPv6 server.

# Chapter 9

1. D. Typically, the translation from private IP addresses to public IP addresses is performed on routers in corporate environments. In a home environment, this device might be an access point that has routing capability or the DSL or cable router.

2. D. It is common practice to configure addresses from the 10.0.0.0/8, 172.16.0.0/12, and 192.168.0.0/16 ranges.

3. B. PAT allows many hosts on a private network to share a single public address by mapping sessions to TCP/UDP port numbers.

4. D. A one-to-one mapping of an inside local address to an inside global address is accomplished through static NAT.

5. C. Many Internet protocols and applications depend on end-to-end addressing from the source to the destination. Because parts of the header of the IP packets are modified, the router needs to alter the checksum of the IPv4 packets. Using a single public IP address allows for the conservation of legally registered IP addressing schemes. If an addressing scheme needs to be modified, it is cheaper to use private IP addresses.

6. B. IPsec and other tunneling protocols do integrity checks. NAT must modify IP headers to translate private IP addresses to public addresses. Disadvantages of using NAT include causing end-to-end IPv4 traceability to be lost, complicating troubleshooting, and slowing down traffic such as VoIP, which cannot tolerate much delay.

7. D. Dynamic NAT provides a dynamic mapping of inside local to inside global IP addresses. NAT is merely the one-to-one mapping of one address to another address without taking into account whether the address is public or private. DHCP is automatic assignment of IP addresses to hosts. DNS is mapping host names to IP addresses.

8. B. For the **ip nat inside source list 4 pool** NAT-POOL command to work, the following procedure needs to be used beforehand:

   - Create an access list that defines the private IP addresses affected by NAT.

   - Establish a NAT pool of starting and ending public IP addresses by using the **ip nat pool** command.

   - Use the **ip nat inside source list** command to associate the access list with the NAT pool.

   - Apply NAT to internal and external interfaces by using the **ip nat inside** and **ip nat outside** commands.

9. D. If all the addresses in the NAT pool have been used, a device must wait for an available address before it can access the outside network.

10. D. Port forwarding allows a user or program from outside to reach services inside a private network. It is not a technique that allows for using services with nonstandard port numbers. NAT or PAT convert inside IP addresses to outside local addresses.

11. B. Link-local addresses are defined in RFC 3927. Unique local addresses are independent of any ISP and are not meant to improve the security of IPv6 networks.

12. A. Unique local addresses (ULA) are similar to private addresses within IPv4. These addresses cannot be routed across the Internet.

13. B. Dual stack is used when a router has protocols associated with both IPv4 and IPv6 that it must process. Static and dynamic NAT are technologies used in IPv4 to translate private to public addresses. NAT for IPv6 is a generic term that is used when describing the transition of going from IPv4 to IPv6.

14. C. With the **ip nat inside source list 1 interface serial 0/0/0 overload** command, the router is configured to translate internal private IP addresses in the range of 10.0.0.0/8 to a single public IP address, 209.165.200.225/30. The other options will not work because the IP addresses defined in the pool, 192.168.2.0/28, are not routable on the Internet.

15. B and E. The steps that are required to configure PAT are to define a pool of global addresses to be used for overload translation, to configure source translation by using the keywords interface and overload, and to identify the interfaces that are involved in the PAT.

16. A. An inside local address is the address of the source as seen from the inside of the network. An outside global address is the address of the destination as seen from the outside network.

# Chapter 10

1. C. CDP only operates on Cisco IOS devices. LLDP is an open standard, defined in IEEE 802.1AB, to support non-Cisco devices and to allow for interoperability between other devices.

2. B and C. Option A and D through F are invalid commands.

3. C. Both commands provide information for options A, B, and D. However, only **show cdp neighbors detail** provides the IP address.

4. D. Options A through C are invalid commands. The option to enable LLDP on interfaces is **lldp transmit** and **lldp receive**.

5. C. The option to enable LLDP on interfaces is **lldp transmit** and **lldp receive**.

6. These are all syslog messages, but the most common are link up and link down messages.

7. A. The smaller the level numbers, the more critical the alarms. Emergency—Level 0 messages indicate that the system is unusable. This would be an event that has halted the system. Alert—Level 1 messages indicate that immediate action is needed, such as a failed connection to the ISP. Critical—Level 2 messages indicate a critical condition. An example would be the failure of a backup connection to the ISP. Error—Level 3 messages indicate an error condition, such as an interface that is down.

8. D. Syslog is used to access and store system messages. Cisco developed NetFlow for the purpose of gathering statistics on packets flowing through Cisco routers and multilayer switches. SNMP can be used to collect and store information about a device. NTP is used to allow network devices to synchronize time settings.

9. B. Syslog messages can be sent to the logging buffer, the console line, the terminal line, or a syslog server. However, debug-level messages are only forwarded to the internal buffer and only accessible through the Cisco CLI.

10. D. Syslog messages for Cisco routers and switches can be sent to memory, the console, a tty line, or a syslog server.

11. A. The logging trap level allows a network administrator to limit event messages that are being sent to a syslog server based on severity.

12. D. Option A is for syslog, B is for TFTP, and the explanation for C is incorrect.

13. B and D. A is incorrect. NTP have nothing to do with MTBF, and multiple NTP servers can be identified for redundancy.

14. C. The logging trap level allows a network administrator to limit event messages that are being sent to a syslog server based on severity.

15. B.

16. D. Options A and C are global configuration commands, whereas Option B restores it to its default and looks for the configuration file.

17. D. Physical access to the device along with a console connection is required to perform password recovery.

18. B. The part of the image name 152-3 indicates that the major release is 15, the minor release is 2, and the new feature release is 3.

19. A. To support Cisco ISR G2 platforms, Cisco provides two types of universal images. The images with the "universalk9_npe" designation in the image name do not support any strong cryptography functionality such as payload cryptography to satisfy the import requirements of some countries. The "universalk9_npe" images include all other Cisco IOS software features.

20. B. The **show flash0:** command displays the amount of flash available (free) and the amount of flash used. The command also displays the files stored in flash, including their size and when they were copied.

21. A and E.

22. B. Cisco IOS Software release 15.0 incorporates four technology packs. They are IPBase, DATA, UC (unified Communications), and SEC (Security). Having the IPBase license installed is a prerequisite for installing the other technology packs.

23. C. The **show license** command displays all licenses that are installed on the system and both the activated and not activated features that are available.

24. D. Valuation licenses are good for a 60-day period. After 60 days, the evaluation license automatically changes to a Right-to-Use license.

25. A. The **license save** command is used to back up a copy of the licenses on a device. The **show license** command is used to display additional information about Cisco IOS software licenses. The **license boot module** *module-name* command activates an Evaluation Right-to-Use license. To configure a one-time acceptance of the End User License Agreement (EULA) covering all Cisco IOS packages and features, use the **license accept end user agreement** command.

# A

**access control entries (ACE)**   A single line in an ACL. ACEs are also commonly called ACL statements. When network traffic passes through an interface configured with an ACL, the router compares the information within the packet against each ACE, in sequential order, to determine if the packet matches one of the ACEs.

**access control list (ACL)**   A series of IOS commands that controls whether a router forwards or drops packets based on information found in the packet header.

**access layer**   A tier in the two- and three-layer hierarchical network design model where devices connect to the network and include services such as power to network end points.

**adjacency table**   A table in a router that contains a list of the relationship formed between selected neighboring routers and end nodes for the purpose of exchanging routing information. Adjacency is based on the use of a common media segment.

**administrative distance (AD)**   The metric that routers use to select the best path when there are two or more different routes to the same destination from two different routing protocols. The AD represents the "trustworthiness" or reliability of the route.

**algorithm**   Well-defined rule or process for arriving at a solution to a problem. Algorithms consist of a finite list of steps used to accomplish a task. Routing protocols use algorithms for

facilitating routing information and for best path determination.

**application-specific-integrated circuits (ASIC)**   Electronics added to a switch that allowed it to have more ports without degrading performance.

**authoritative time source**   A high-precision timekeeping device assumed to be accurate and with little or no delay associated with it. Also referred to as a stratum 0 device.

**automated attendant**   Converged network telephony feature that routes calls directly to the right individual or department without the intervention of a receptionist.

**automatic medium-dependent interface crossover (auto-MDIX)**   A detection on a switch port or hub port to detect the type of cable used between switches or hubs. Once the cable type is detected, the port is connected and configured accordingly. With auto-MDIX, a crossover or a straight-through cable can be used for connections to a copper 10/100/1000 port on the switch, regardless of the type of device on the other end of the connection.

**automatic summarization**   A routing feature that summarizes networks at major network boundaries by default.

**autonegotiate**   Ethernet feature in which two interconnecting devices automatically negotiate duplex and speed settings.

**availability**   A measure of the probability that the network is available for use when it is required.

# B

**BOOT environment variable**   A configurable setting on a device that identifies where the IOS image file is located. The boot loader software uses the image file identified by this variable.

**boot loader command line**   Basic device command line that supports commands to recover a lost or forgotten password, format the flash file system, and reinstall the IOS. The Catalyst 2960 boot loader command line prompt is switch: whereas a Cisco 2901 ISR2 prompt is rommon>.

**boot loader software**   A small program stored in ROM that runs immediately after POST successfully completes. It is used to initialize a network device such as a router or a switch. The boot loader locates and launches the operating system.

**Border Gateway Protocol (BGP)**   Routing protocol used between Internet service providers (ISP) and their larger private clients to exchange routing information.

**broadcast domains**   All nodes that are part of a network segment, VLAN, or subnet, and all devices on the LAN receive broadcast frames from a host within the LAN. A broadcast domain is bounded by a Layer 3 device. A Layer 3 device such as a router sets the boundary of the broadcast domain.

**buffer**   An area of memory that temporarily stores data.

# C

**call control**   IP telephony feature that provides telephone call processing, caller ID, call transfer, hold, and conference.

**Canonical Format Identifier (CFI)**   A field in the VLAN tag field consisting of a 1-bit flag. When set to 1, it enables legacy Token Ring frames to be carried across Ethernet links. Other fields in the 802.1Q VLAN tag frame are the Type field, Priority field, and VLAN ID field.

**Cisco Borderless Network**   Cisco Borderless Networks are designed to help IT balance demanding business challenges and changing business models promoted by the influx of consumer devices into the business world. Cisco Borderless Networks can help IT evolve its infrastructure to deliver secure, reliable, and seamless user experiences in a world with many new and shifting borders.

**Cisco Discovery Protocol (CDP)**   A media and protocol-independent device-discovery protocol that runs on Cisco equipment such as routers, access servers, bridges, and switches. With CDP enabled, a device can advertise its existence to other directly connected devices and receive information about other devices on the same LAN or on the remote side of a WAN.

**Cisco Express Forwarding (CEF)**   A Layer 3 switching method. It defines the fastest method by which a Cisco router or Layer 3 switch forwards packets from ingress to egress interfaces.

**Cisco IOS helper address**   DHCP feature that enables a router to forward DHCPv4 broadcasts to the DHCPv4 server. When a router forwards address assignment/parameter requests, it is acting as a DHCPv4 relay agent.

**Cisco IOS Software Activation** Cisco licensing feature required to enable technology features and register licenses in IOS 15. The Cisco IOS Software Activation feature is a collection of processes and components used to activate Cisco IOS software feature sets by obtaining and validating Cisco software licenses.

**Cisco License Manager (CLM)** A free, downloadable standalone application from Cisco that helps network administrators discover network devices, view their license information, and acquire and deploy licenses from a central location.

**Cisco License Registration Portal** The web-based portal for getting and registering individual Cisco software technology licenses.

**Cisco StackPower** Cisco StackWise feature that enables power sharing among stack members. See *Cisco StackWise*.

**Cisco StackWise** Cisco technology that allows the interconnection of up to nine switches in a daisy chain fashion. The stacked switches effectively operate as a single larger switch. Stackable switches use a special port and cable for interconnections.

**class of service (CoS)** A 3-bit field in an 802.1Q VLAN tagged Ethernet frame. It is used to specify how the frame should be handled when quality of service (QoS) is enabled. The 3-bit field identifies the CoS priority value.

**classful routing protocol** A routing protocol that does not carry subnet mask information in its routing updates.

**classless routing protocol** A routing protocol that carries subnet mask information in its routing updates. Classless routing protocols can take advantage of VLSM and supernet routes.

**client IPv4 address (CIADDR)** Field in a DHCP message exchange that identifies the client IP address in the message.

**collapsed core layer model** A hierarchical network design model that collapses the core and distribution layers into a single layer that connects to the access layer where wired and wireless end devices attach. Also called a two-tier campus network design.

**collision domains** A network segment that shares the same bandwidth between the devices, such as between a switch and a PC. Each port on a switch is its own collision domain. Every device connected to a hub is within a single collision domain, meaning that when two devices attempt communication simultaneously, collisions occur.

**configuration register** Hexadecimal value used to change the booting behavior and connection settings of a Cisco router. Common settings include 0x2102 (normal boot) and 0x2142 (bypass startup configuration for password recovery.)

**content addressable memory (CAM) table** Table in memory that stores source MAC addresses and port numbers learned from frames entering the switch. Also called the MAC address table.

**converged network** Convergence means several things in networking: (1) combining voice and video with the traditional data network, (2) providing a loop-free Layer 2 topology for a switched LAN through the use of spanning tree, and (3) providing a stable Layer 3 network where the routers have completed providing each other updates and the routing tables are complete.

**core layer** A tier in the three-layer hierarchical network design model that creates the network backbone. All traffic to and from peripheral networks must pass through the core layer. It includes high-speed switching devices that can handle relatively large amounts of traffic. In a two-layer hierarchical design model, the core layer is combined with the distribution layer for small-to-medium-sized business networks.

**CoS priority value**   The value in the 3-bit field in an 802.1Q VLAN tagged Ethernet frame that specifies how the frame should be handled when quality of service (QoS) is enabled. Higher values mean higher priority.

**CPU subsystem**   Consists of the CPU, the DRAM, and the portion of the flash device that makes up the flash file system. POST checks the CPU subsystem upon bootup of the device.

**CRC errors**   See *cyclic redundancy check (CRC)*.

**cut-through switching**   A method used inside a switch where, after the destination MAC address has been received, the frame is processed without waiting for the complete frame to arrive.

**cyclic redundancy check (CRC)**   A process to check for errors within the Layer 2 frame. The sending device generates a CRC and includes this value in the frame check sequence (FCS) field. The receiving device generates a CRC and compares it to the received CRC to look for errors. If the calculations match, no error has occurred. If the calculations do not match, the frame is dropped. CRC errors on Ethernet and serial interfaces usually mean a media or a cable problem.

# D

**data structures**   A group of data elements that are stored under one name. Routing protocols typically use tables or databases for their operations. The adjacency database, link-state database, and forwarding database are all examples of data structures. This information is kept in RAM.

**data VLAN**   A VLAN that is configured to carry only user-generated traffic. In particular, a data VLAN does not carry voice-based traffic or traffic used to manage a switch.

**default gateway address (GIADDR)**   Field in a DHCP message exchange that identifies the default gateway address.

**default static route**   A route that matches all packets and identifies the gateway IP address to which the router sends all packets that it does not have a learned or static route for.

**default VLAN**   The VLAN that all the ports on a switch are members of when a switch is reset to factory defaults or new. All switch ports are members of the default VLAN after the initial boot of the switch. On a Cisco switch, VLAN 1 is the default VLAN.

**DHCP**   A protocol used to dynamically assign IP configurations to hosts. The services defined by the protocol are used to request and assign an IP address, default gateway, and DNS server address to a network host.

**DHCP Options**   Provides a framework for passing configuration information to hosts on a TCP/IP network. It can be used to deliver parameters in addition to the traditional IP address, subnet mask, default gateway, and DNS server address.

**DHCPACK message**   A unicast message sent by a DHCP server in response to a device that sends a DHCPREQUEST. The DHCPACK message is used by the DHCP server to complete the DHCP process.

**DHCPDISCOVER message**   A broadcast message sent by a network device to discover an IPv4 DHCP server.

**DHCPOFFER message**   A unicast message returned by a DHCP server in response to a client device sending a DHCPDISCOVER broadcast message. The DHCPOFFER message typically contains an IP address, subnet mask, default gateway address, and other information.

**DHCPREQUEST message**   A broadcast message sent by a network device in response to a DHCPOFFER made by a DHCP server that sent a DHCPOFFER message. The device uses the DHCPREQUEST message to accept the IP addressing offer made by the DHCP server.

**DHCPv4**   The IPv4 version of DHCP. A method of deploying IP address-related information to IPv4 devices. DHCPv4 uses four types of messages: DHCP discover, DHCP offer, DHCP request, and DHCP acknowledgment.

**DHCPv4 relay agent**   Allows relaying DHCP messages between a DHCP client and a DHCP server located on a different network.

**DHCPv6**   The IPv6 version of DHCP. IPv6 network devices can obtain IPv6 addressing information using one of three options: SLAAC, stateless DHCPv6, and stateful DHCPv6.

**DHCPv6 ADVERTISE unicast message**   A DHCPv6 message sent by a DHCPv6 server to inform the DHCPv6 client that the server is available for DHCPv6 service. It is generated in response to a DHCPv6 SOLICIT message.

**DHCPv6 INFORMATION-REQUEST message**   A DHCPv6 message sent by a stateless client to the DHCPv6 server requesting only configuration parameters, such as DNS

server address. The client generated its own IPv6 address using the prefix from the RA message and a self-generated Interface ID.

**DHCPv6 REPLY unicast message**   The DHCPv6 message unicast message that the DHCPv6 server sends to the client. The DHCPv6 message contains the information requested in the DHCPv6 REQUEST or DHCPv6 INFORMATION-REQUEST message.

**DHCPv6 REQUEST message**   A DHCPv6 message that a stateful client sends to the DHCPv6 server to obtain an IPv6 address and all other configuration parameters from the server.

**DHCPv6 SOLICIT message**   A DHCPv6 message that the DHCPv6 client sends to the reserved IPv6 multicast all-DHCPv6-servers address FF02::1:2. This multicast address has link-local scope, which means routers do not forward the messages to other networks.

**directly connected interfaces**   The interfaces on a router.

**directly connected routes**   The active IP networks connected to the router interfaces.

**directly connected static route**   A static route in which only the router exit interface is specified.

**discontiguous networks**   A discontiguous network has two or more nonadjacent subnetworks of a classful network connected by different classful networks.

**distribution layer**   A tier in the three-layer hierarchical network design model that connects the access layer to the core layer. The distribution layer aggregates connectivity from multiple access layer devices, Layer 2 broadcast domains, and Layer 3 routing boundaries. In a two-layer hierarchical design model, the distribution layer is combined with the core layer for small-to-medium-sized business networks.

**dual-stack**   An IPv4 to IPv6 migration technique in which a device is enabled for both IPv4 and IPv6 protocols. It is a transition mechanism used when converting from IPv4 to IPv6. When using a dual stack, a router runs both IPv4 and IPv6. Other IPv6 migration techniques translation and tunneling.

**duplex mismatch**   Half-duplex communication relies on unidirectional data flow where sending and receiving data are not performed at the same time. In full-duplex communication, data flow is bidirectional, so data can be sent and received at the same time. A duplex mismatch is when one end of a connection is set to half duplex while the other end is set to full duplex.

**duplicate address detection (DAD)**   A process that IPv6 devices employing an ICMPv6 Neighbor Solicitation message use to verify whether any other device has the same IPv6 address.

**dynamic network address translation (dynamic NAT)**   A type of network address translation (NAT) in which many local addresses (normally private IP addresses) are mapped to many global IP addresses (which are normally public IP addresses).

**dynamic routing protocols**   A remote network in a routing table that has been automatically learned using a dynamic routing protocol such as EIGRP or OSPF.

**dynamic secure MAC addresses**   Port security feature in which MAC addresses are dynamically learned and stored only in the address table. MAC addresses configured in this way are removed when the switch restarts.

**Dynamic Trunking Protocol (DTP)**   A Cisco-proprietary protocol that negotiates both the status and the encapsulation of trunk ports.

# E

**edge router**   Router connecting the inside network to the outside network (typically the Internet).

**egress**   The exit or the way out.

**egress port**   The port through which a frame exits a switch.

**End User License Agreement (EULA)**   A legal contract between a software application and the user of the application.

**Enhanced IGRP (EIGRP)**   An advanced version of IGRP that Cisco developed. It provides superior convergence properties and operating efficiency and combines the advantages of link-state protocols with those of distance vector protocols.

**equal cost load balancing**   When a router utilizes multiple paths with the same administrative distance and cost to a destination.

**Ethernet bridges**   Early versions of a switch. In the 1990s, advancements in integrated circuit technologies allowed for Ethernet LAN switches to replace Ethernet bridges.

**EUI-64**   The Extended Unique Identifier (EUI-64) is an IPv6 process that uses a client's 48-bit Ethernet MAC address and inserts another 16 bits in the middle of the 48-bit MAC address to create a 64-bit Interface ID for an IPv6 global unicast address.

**evaluation license**   Also known as a temporary license, it allows a client to try a new software package or feature by activating a specific evaluation license. If customers want to permanently activate a software package or feature on the router, they must get a new software license.

**Evaluation Right-to-Use licenses (RTU)**    Evaluation licenses are replaced with Evaluation Right-to-Use licenses (RTU) after 60 days. These licenses are available on the honor system and require the customer's acceptance of the EULA. The EULA is automatically applied to all Cisco IOS software licenses.

**exit interface**    The interface through which frames leave a device.

**extended ACLs**    Filter traffic based upon multiple attributes including protocol type, source IPv4 addresses, destination IPv4 addresses, source ports, and destination ports.

**extended range VLANs**    Extended range VLANs are numbered 1006 to 4094, and they enable service providers to extend their infrastructure to a greater number of customers. Some global enterprises could be large enough to need extended range VLAN IDs. In contrast, normal range VLANs on these switches are numbered 1 to 1005.

# F

**facility**    Syslog facilities are service identifiers that identify and categorize system state data for error and event message reporting. The logging facility options that are available are specific to the networking device.

**fast switching**    In fast switching, the first packet is copied to packet memory, and the destination network or host is found in the fast-switching cache. The frame is rewritten and sent to the

outgoing interface that services the destination. Subsequent packets for the same destination use the same switching path.

**fast-switching cache**    Section of memory used by the fast switching process to temporarily store next-hop frame forwarding information.

**firewalls**    Routers or access servers designated as buffers between any connected public network and a private network. A firewall router uses access lists and other methods to ensure the security of the private network.

**fixed configuration switch**    A type of switch commonly used in the access layer of the hierarchical network design model that supports only the features and options shipped with the switch. This type of switch is not upgradable. Contrast this with a modular configuration switch.

**flash**    A removable component that has memory space for storage. Used on the router or switch for storing the compressed operating system image.

**floating static route**    Static route used to provide a backup path to a primary static or dynamic route in the event of a link failure. Used only when the primary route is not available.

**form factors**    An aspect of hardware design including the size, shape, and other physical specifications of components, particularly in consumer electronics and electronic packaging. Switch form factors include fixed configuration and modular configuration switch.

**Forwarding Information Base (FIB)**    Used with CEF to provide optimized lookups for more efficient packet forwarding.

**fragment free**    Refers to a form of cut-through switching called fragment free switching in which only error-free frames are processed. See *fragment-free switching.*

**fragment-free switching**   A modified form of cut-through switching in which the switch waits for the collision window (64 bytes) to pass before forwarding the frame. This means each frame is checked into the data field to make sure no fragmentation has occurred. Fragment-free switching provides better error checking than cut-through, with practically no increase in latency.

**frame buffers**   Sections of memory used to store frames on congested ports.

**frame-check-sequence (FCS)**   A checksum value found in the last field of a datagram that the switch uses to validate that the frame is free of errors.

**full duplex**   Both devices can transmit and receive on the media at the same time.

**fully specified static route**   A static route in which both the output interface and the next-hop address are identified.

# G

**Gateway of Last Resort**   Used to direct packets addressed to networks not explicitly listed in the routing table. Also known as a default route.

**giants**   Problematic Ethernet frames of excess size caused by a malfunctioning NIC or an improperly terminated or unterminated cable.

**global address**   NAT term used to describe any address that appears on the outside portion of the network.

# H

**half duplex**   Both devices can transmit and receive on the media but cannot do so simultaneously.

**hierarchical network addressing**   Network addressing scheme in which IP network numbers are applied to network segments or VLANs in an orderly fashion that takes the network as a whole into consideration. Blocks of contiguous network addresses are reserved for and configured on devices in a specific area of the network.

**high port density**   Switches have high port densities: 24- and 48-port switches are often just a single rack unit and operate at speeds of 100 Mb/s, 1 Gb/s, and 10 Gb/s. Large enterprise switches may support many hundreds of ports.

**High-Speed WAN Interface Card (HWIC) slots**   Slot on a router used to install a high-speed WAN interface card.

**host route**   An IPv4 address with a 32-bit mask or an IPv6 address with a 128-bit mask. Host routes can be added to the routing table.

# I

**ICMPv6 Neighbor Solicitation and Neighbor Advertisement messages**   Similar to IPv4 ARP, IPv6 address resolution uses ICMPv6 Neighbor Solicitation and Neighbor Advertisement messages. IPv6-to-MAC address mapping is kept in a table similar to the ARP cache, called the neighbor cache.

**IEEE 802.1Q header**   Ethernet header designed to include VLAN-related information for the IEEE 802.1Q standard.

**IEEE 802.1Q standard**   Standard developed to add VLAN information to trunk frames as they traverse trunk links.

**implicit deny**   A hard-coded ACL statement in all ACLs that denies all traffic from passing through the interface. This statement is called implicit because it is not shown in output when you list ACL statements using **show** commands. It is always the last line of any ACL.

**inbound ACLs**   Incoming packets are filtered using inbound ACLs. Inbound ACLs are best used to filter packets when the network attached to an inbound interface is the only source of packets that need to be examined.

**ingress**   The entrance or the way in.

**ingress port**   The port through which a frame enters a switch.

**input errors**   Errors including runts, giants, no buffer, CRC, frame, overrun, and ignored counts reported in the output of the **show interfaces** command.

**inside address**   NAT term to describe the address of the device that NAT is translating.

**inside global address**   Used with NAT for IPv4, a valid public IPv4 address that is given to the packet sourced from an inside host. Normally, the IPv4 public address is assigned as the packet exits the NAT router.

**inside local address**   Used with NAT for IPv4, this address is usually an RFC 1918 private address, which is a type of address that is not usually assigned by a regional Internet registry (RIR) or a service provider. The private IP address is assigned to a device inside a home or corporate environment.

**inside network**   NAT term to describe the internal network.

**interface ID (IID)**   Host portion of an IPv6 global unicast address.

**Interior Gateway Routing Protocol (IGRP)**   Original routing protocol developed by Cisco Systems. It has been replaced by EIGRP.

**Intermediate System-to-Intermediate System (IS-IS)**   A routing protocol that the ISO developed.

**Internet Architecture Board (IAB)**   Committee of the Internet Engineering Task Force (IETF) that oversees the activities of the IETF, the Internet standards process, and the appointment of the RFC Editor.

**Internet Assigned Numbers Authority (IANA)**   An organization that assigns the numbers important to the proper operation of the TCP/IP protocol and the Internet, including assigning globally unique IP addresses.

**Internet Control Message Protocol version 6 (ICMPv6)**   ICMPv6 performs the similar function to ICMP for IPv4. It performs error reporting and diagnostic functions but is also used for neighbor discovery and SLAAC.

**inter-VLAN routing**   The process of routing data between VLANs so that communication can occur between the different networks.

**inverse mask**   Sometimes used as another name for a wildcard mask.

**IOS**   Operating system for Cisco devices.

**IPsec**   A framework of open standards that spells out the rules for secure communications.

IPsec works at the network layer, protecting and authenticating IP packets between participating IPsec peers.

IPv4 addressing space   The total number of IPv4 addresses available.

IPv6 global unicast address   Globally unique IPv6 addresses routable on the IPv6 Internet.

IPv6 link-local address   Locally unique IPv6 addresses that are used to communicate with other IPv6-enabled devices on the same link and only on that link (subnet). Link-local addresses cannot be routed beyond the local network and are commonly used by IPv6 routing protocols. Every IPv6-enabled interface must have a link-local address. However, a global unicast address is not a requirement.

# J–K–L

late collisions   A collision that occurs after 512 bytes of an Ethernet frame (the preamble) have been transmitted.

lease   A DHCP option identifying the amount of time that an IP address is provided to a host.

legacy inter-VLAN routing   Performs inter-VLAN routing by connecting different physical router interfaces to different physical switch ports. The switch ports connected to the router are placed in access mode, and each physical interface is assigned to a different VLAN. Each router interface can then accept traffic from the VLAN associated with the switch interface that it is connected to, and traffic can be routed to the other VLANs connected to the other interfaces.

level 1 parent routes   A level 1 route that has been subnetted. A parent route can never be an ultimate route.

level 1 route   A route with a subnet mask equal to or less than the classful mask of the network address.

level 2 child route   A route that is a subnet of a classful network address. Level 1 parent routes contain level 2 child routes. The source of a level 2 route can be a directly connected network, a static route, or a dynamically learned route. Level 2 child routes are also ultimate routes.

line cards   Switch cards that fit into the switch chassis the way that expansion cards fit into a PC. The larger the chassis, the more modules it can support.

Link Layer Discovery Protocol (LLDP)   A vendor-neutral neighbor discovery protocol similar to CDP. LLDP works with network devices, such as routers, switches, and wireless LAN access points. Like CDP, LLDP advertises its identity and capabilities to other devices and receives the information from a physically connected Layer 2 device.

link-local address   Link-local addresses are only unique on a given link or network. Refer to *IPv6 link-local address*.

local address   NAT term describing any address that appears on the inside portion of the network.

local host route   When an active interface on a router is configured with an IP address, a local host route is automatically added to the routing table. The local routes are marked with "L" in the output of the routing table.

local route interfaces   An entry in the routing table for a local host route. It is added when an interface is configured and active.

logical topology   The path over which the data is transferred in a network.

loopback interface   A software-only interface that emulates a physical interface. A loopback interface is always up and never goes down.

# M

MAC address table   On a switch, a table that lists all known MAC addresses and the bridge/switch port that the bridge/switch should use to forward frames sent to each MAC address. Also known as a CAM table.

Managed Address Configuration flag (M flag)   Flag used in DHCPv6 to indicate whether or not to use stateful DHCPv6. For stateful DHCP, it sets the flag to 1.

management VLAN   A VLAN defined by the network administrator as a means of accessing the management capabilities of a switch. The management VLAN SVI is assigned an IP address and subnet mask. It is a security best practice to define the management VLAN to be a VLAN distinct from all other VLANs defined in the switched LAN.

mean time between failures (MTBF)   The amount of time that elapses between a failure and the next failure such as in the total time required for a device to fail and that failure to be repaired.

metric   The quantitative value used to measure the distance to a given network.

Mode button   A button on the front of Cisco Catalyst 2960 switches that is used to toggle through the port status, port duplex, port speed, and PoE (if supported) status of the port LEDs.

modular configuration switches   A type of switch commonly used in the distribution and core layers of the hierarchical network design model that allows flexibility and customization by adding various line cards. Contrast with a fixed configuration switch.

# N

named ACLs   An ACL that uses a text string to describe the ACL, rather than a number.

NAT overloading   See *Port Address Translation (PAT)*.

NAT64   Implementing NAT to translate IPv6 to IPv4 addresses.

native VLAN   A native VLAN is assigned to an IEEE 802.1Q trunk port. An IEEE 802.1Q trunk port supports tagged and untagged traffic coming from VLANs. The 802.1Q trunk port places untagged traffic on the native VLAN. It is a security best practice to define a native VLAN to be a dummy VLAN distinct from all other VLANs defined in the switched LAN. The native VLAN is not used for traffic in the switched network.

native VLAN mismatches   When trunk ports are configured with different native VLANs. This configuration error generates console notifications and can cause inter-VLAN routing issues, among other problems. This poses a security risk.

Neighbor Advertisement (NA) message   Similar to an ARP reply for IPv4, ICMPv6 messages are sent by devices in response to an ICMPv6 Neighbor Solicitation message containing the IPv6 address and the corresponding MAC address.

neighbor cache    Similar to an ARP cache, IPv6-to-MAC address mapping is kept in a neighbor cache. IPv6 uses ICMPv6 Neighbor Solicitation and Neighbor Advertisement messages to populate the neighbor cache.

Neighbor Solicitation (NS) message    Similar to an ARP request for IPv4, ICMPv6 messages are sent by devices when they know the IPv6 address but need the corresponding MAC address.

network address translation (NAT)    Translation of IP addresses to different addresses. This is commonly used to translate RFC 1918 addresses that are not routed on the Internet to public domain addresses that can be routed on the Internet.

Network Address Translation-Protocol Translation (NAT-PT)    A mechanism employed when using both IPv4 and IPv6 addresses. This method has been deprecated by IETF in favor of NAT64.

network route    A route that has a subnet mask equal to that of the classful mask.

Network Time Protocol (NTP)    NTP synchronizes the time of day among a set of distributed time servers and clients so that you can correlate events when you receive system logs and other time-specific events from multiple network devices. NTP uses the User Datagram Protocol (UDP) as its transport protocol. All NTP communications use coordinated universal time (UTC).

next-hop IP address    The next gateway to which a Layer 3 packet is delivered, used to reach its destination.

next-hop static route    A static route in which only the next-hop IP address is specified.

nonvolatile    Referring to memory, nonvolatile memory does not lose its content when the power is turned off. In contrast, *volatile memory* loses its content when the power is turned off.

normal range VLANs    VLANs with VLAN IDs 1 to 1005. VLAN IDs 1 and 1002 to 1005 are automatically created and cannot be removed.

NTP client    Device that obtains time and date information from a single source using NTP.

NTP server    Device providing NTP services to clients.

NVRAM    RAM that does not lose its contents when the device is powered off.

# O

Open Shortest Path First (OSPF)    A popular scalable, link-state routing protocol. It is based on link-state technology and introduced new concepts such as authentication of routing updates, variable-length subnet masks (VLSM), and route summarization.

Other Configuration flag (O flag)    Flag used in DHCPv6 to indicate to use stateless DHCPv6. The O flag value of 1 is used to inform the client that additional configuration information is available from a stateless DHCPv6 server.

out of the box    Term used to describe the unpacking of a new device/component.

outbound ACLs    Incoming packets are routed to the outbound interface, and then they are processed through the outbound ACL. Outbound

ACLs are best used when the same filter will be applied to packets coming from multiple inbound interfaces before exiting the same outbound interface.

output errors   Errors that prevented the final transmission of datagrams out of the interface that is being examined with the **show interfaces** command.

outside address   NAT term to describe the address of the destination device.

outside global address   A reachable IP address used in NAT for IPv4 and assigned to hosts located on the Internet.

outside local address   NAT term to describe the address of the destination as seen from the inside network. Although uncommon, this address could be different from the globally routable address of the destination.

outside network   NAT term to describe noninternal networks.

# P

packet filtering   Controls access to a network by analyzing the incoming and outgoing packets and passing or dropping them based on given criteria, such as the source IP address, destination IP addresses, and protocol carried within the packet.

PC softphone   A software program that is used to make telephone calls over the Internet using a general use computer.

permanent licenses   An IOS license that never expires. After a permanent license is installed on a router, it is good for that particular feature set for the life of the router, even across IOS versions.

physical topology   The arrangement of the nodes in a network and the physical connections between them. This is the representation of how the media is used to connect the devices.

port address translation (PAT)   Sometimes called NAT overloading. Maps multiple private IP addresses to a single public IP address or a few addresses.

port density   The number of interfaces supported on a switch. Network switches must support the appropriate number of devices on the network.

port forwarding   Sometimes called tunneling. The act of forwarding a network port from one network node to another. This technique can allow an external user to reach a port on a private IP address (inside a LAN) from the outside through a NAT-enabled router.

port security   Switch security feature that limits the number of valid MAC addresses allowed on a port. The MAC addresses of legitimate devices are allowed access, whereas other MAC addresses are denied.

Power over Ethernet (PoE)   The powering of network devices over Ethernet cable. PoE is defined by two different standards: IEEE 802.3af and Cisco.

power-on self-test (POST)   A series of diagnostic tests performed by a device (such as a router, switch, or computer) when booting a computer.

PPP   A Layer 2 WAN protocol that provides router-to-router and host-to-network connections.

**private IP addresses** Addresses assigned from a special IP address range that cannot be routed over the Internet.

**private IPv4 addresses** See *private IP addresses.*

**process switching** In process switching, the first packet is copied to the system buffer. The router looks up the Layer 3 network address in the routing table and initializes the fast-switch cache. The frame is rewritten with the destination address and sent to the outgoing interface that services that destination. Subsequent packets for that destination are sent by the same switching path.

**Product Activation Key (PAK)** The number assigned by Cisco, during the IOS licensing process, that gives a Cisco customer the right to enable an IOS feature set on one of that customer's routers of a particular model series (chosen at the time the PAK was purchased).

**propagate a default route** General term to describe how a routing protocol advertises a default route to all other routers that use the dynamic routing protocol.

**public IP addresses** An IP address, registered with IANA or one of its member agencies, that guarantees that the address is globally unique. Globally unique public IP addresses can be used for packets sent through the Internet.

**public IPv4 addresses** See *public IP addresses.*

**public switched telephone network (PSTN)** A general term referring to the variety of telephone networks and services in place worldwide. Also called the plain old telephone service (POTS).

# Q–R

**rack units** Refers to the device form factor and specifies the thickness of the device, expressed in number of rack units. Most 24-port fixed configuration switches are all 1 rack unit (1U).

**RAM** Volatile memory used in routers that provides temporary storage for various applications and processes including the running IOS, running configuration file, IP routing and ARP tables, and packet buffers.

**rapid frame forwarding** A switch forwarding characteristic referring to the way the cut-through method makes forwarding decision as soon as it has looked up the destination MAC address of the frame in its MAC address table. The switch does not have to wait for the rest of the frame to enter the ingress port before making its forwarding decision.

**recursive lookup** Occurs when a router has to perform multiple lookups in a routing table before forwarding a packet.

**Redundant Power System (RPS)** Refers to an LED on a Catalyst 2960 switch. An RPS is a device that can provide backup power if the switch power supply fails. The LED displays the status of the RPS.

**regional Internet registry (RIR)** Five organizations responsible for allocating IP addresses within their geographic region.

**reliability** A characteristic of a protocol that uses mechanisms such as handshaking, timers, acknowledgement messages, and dynamic windowing to help ensure that the data received is the same as the data sent. Reliable protocols require additional overhead on the network in terms of much larger segment headers.

remote routes   These are remote networks connected to other routers. Routes to these networks can either be statically configured or dynamically learned through dynamic routing protocols.

RIPv1   An early classful distance vector routing protocol that uses hop count as its metric. Routing Information Protocol version 1 has been replaced by RIPv2.

RIPv2   A replacement to RIPv1 that includes support for VLSM.

ROM   Nonvolatile memory used in routers to provide permanent storage for bootup instructions, basic diagnostic software, and limited IOS in case the router cannot load the full-featured IOS.

ROMMON mode   Basic device command line that supports commands to recover a lost or forgotten password, format the flash file system, and reinstall the IOS.

route lookup process   The process that a router uses to match a destination IP address route when a packet arrives on an interface.

router advertisement (RA) message   ICMPv6 messages sent by routers to provide addressing information to hosts using SLAAC. A message type used by an IPv6 router to provide IPv6 addressing information to clients. The router sends the message using the IPv6 all-nodes multicast address of FF02::1.

router solicitation (RS) message   ICMPv6 messages sent by devices to request an ICMPv6 Router Advertisement message. A message type used by an IPv6 client that sends a multicast to address FF02::2 (all-routers) to obtain an IPv6 address using SLAAC, which does not require the services of a DHCPv6 router.

router-on-a-stick   An inter-VLAN routing solution in which a single physical interface routes traffic between multiple VLANs on a network. The router interface is configured to operate as a trunk link and is connected to a switch port that is configured in trunk mode.

routing algorithm   The process used by a routing protocol to determine the best path routes.

Routing Information Protocol (RIP)   A basic and simple distance vector routing protocol.

routing protocol messages   The message exchange used by different routing protocols. Messages are used to establish neighbor relationships and exchange routing table information.

routing table   A data file in RAM that is used to store route information about directly connected and remote networks.

runt frames   Any frame less than 64 bytes in length. These frames are automatically discarded by receiving stations. Also called collision fragment. Runts are caused by malfunctioning NICs and improperly terminated Ethernet cables.

# S

scalability   Indicates how easily the network can accommodate more users and data transmission requirements. For example, a scalable network can expand quickly to support new users and applications without impacting the performance of the service being delivered to existing users.

Services on Demand   The Cisco IOS process that enables customers to use licenses to enable specific feature set packages on their routers.

**severity level**    Used in syslog message formats to describe the type of message. Expressed in Level 0 to Level 7 with smaller numerical levels indicating more critical syslog alarms.

**single-homed**    An Internet access design in which the organization has only one connection to a service provider.

**software clock**    The software clock on a router or switch that starts when the system boots. It is the primary source of time for the system.

**solicited-node multicast address**    IPv6 multicast address associated with an IPv6 unicast address that is mapped to a special Ethernet multicast address.

**speed**    Referring to a network characteristic, this is a measure of the data rate in bits per second (b/s) of a given link in the network.

**stackable configuration switches**    Switches cabled together through a special port and managed as a single switch to provide fault tolerance and bandwidth in an area where a modular switch is not financially feasible.

**standard ACLs**    Used to filter traffic only from source IPv4 addresses.

**standard static route**    A static route that routes to a destination network. Other types of static routes include a default static, summary static, and floating static routes.

**stateful DHCPv6**    Similar to DHCP for IPv4, provides IPv6 address, prefix length, and other information such as DNS server and domain name. Does not provide a default gateway address.

**stateful DHCPv6 client**    An IPv6 client using this option obtains all addressing and configuration information from a stateful DHCPv6 server.

**stateful DHCPv6 server**    Provides all IPv6 configuration information to an IPv6 client.

**stateless address autoconfiguration (SLAAC)**    A plug-and-play IPv6 addressing option that allows a device to obtain an IPv6 global unicast address without communicating with a DHCPv6 server. The address is obtained using ICMPv6 RS and RA messages.

**stateless DHCPv6 client**    An IPv6 client using this option automatically obtains some addressing information but contacts a DHCPv6 server for an additional addressing configuration to use, such as DNS addresses.

**stateless DHCPv6 server**    Provides information other than the IPv6 address and prefix length, such as DNS server and domain name. Does not provide a default gateway address.

**static network address translation (static NAT)**    Uses a one-to-one mapping of local and global addresses, and these mappings remain constant. Static NAT is particularly useful for web servers or hosts that must have a consistent address that is accessible from the Internet. These internal hosts may be enterprise servers or networking devices.

**static routes**    A remote network in a routing table that a network administrator has manually entered into the table.

**static secure MAC addresses**    A port security method used when MAC addresses are manually configured on a switch port.

sticky secure MAC addresses   A port security feature in which MAC addresses are dynamically learned or manually configured and then stored in the address table and added to the running configuration.

store-and-forward switching   A method used inside a switch where the entire frame is received, and the cyclic redundancy check (CRC) is calculated. If valid, the frame is sent to the appropriate port if the destination MAC address was found in the MAC address table or the frame is broadcasted to all ports except the ingress port.

stratum   Hierarchical system of time sources used by NTP. Each level in this hierarchical system is called a stratum. The stratum level is defined as the number of hop counts from the authoritative time source.

stub network   A network with only one exit point. A hub-and-spoke network would be an example of a stub network.

stub router   A router that has only one exit interface from the routing domain and forwards all traffic to a central or a distribution router.

subinterfaces   Software-based virtual interfaces that are associated with a single physical interface. Each subinterface is independently configured with an IP address and VLAN assignment.

summary static route   A single static route that can represent multiple contiguous networks to reduce the number of entries in a routing table.

supernet   Supernetting occurs when the route summarization mask is a smaller value than the default traditional classful mask.

supernet route   A routing table entry that contains a route with a network address and a mask less than the classful mask. For example, a summary address is a supernet route.

switched virtual interface (SVI)   Virtual interfaces for which there is no physical hardware on the device associated. An SVI is created in software. The virtual interfaces are used as a means to remotely manage a switch over a network. They are also used as a method of routing between VLANs.

syslog   A syslog server is a server that receives and stores syslog messages that can be displayed with a syslog application.

System LED   Shows whether the system is receiving power and is functioning properly on a Catalyst 2960 switch. If the LED is off, the system is not powered on. If the LED is green, the system is operating normally. If the LED is amber, the system is receiving power but is not functioning properly.

# T

tag protocol ID (TPID)   A field in the *VLAN tag field* called the Type field. It consists of a 16-bit (2-byte) value called the tag protocol ID (TPID) value. For Ethernet, it is set to hexadecimal 0x8100. Other fields in the 802.1Q VLAN tag frame are the Priority field, CFI field, and VLAN ID.

technology package licenses   These add features to the IOS universal image. Technology packages include IP Base, Data, Unified Communications, and Security. Technology packages are enabled in the universal image via Cisco IOS Software Activation licensing keys.

**three-layer hierarchical model**   A hierarchical design that maximizes performance, network availability, and the ability to scale the network design. Consists of core, distribution, and access layers.

**topology**   The arrangement of networking components or nodes. Examples include star, extended star, ring, and mesh.

**translation**   An IP4 to IP6 migration technique of using NAT64 to translate IPv4 to IPv6 addresses. Other IPv6 migration techniques include dual stack and tunneling.

**trunk mode mismatches**   Situation in which a trunk port is configured in an incompatible trunking mode with the corresponding peer port. This configuration error causes the trunk link to stop working. Be sure both sides of the trunk are configured with compatible trunking modes such as using the switchport mode trunk command on each peer port.

**tunneling**   An IPv4 to IPv6 transitioning technique that encapsulates an IP packet inside another IP packet. For example, encapsulating an IPv6 packet inside an IPv4 packet allows the IPv6 packet to be transmitted over an IPv4-only network. Other IPv6 migration techniques include dual stack and translation.

# U

**ultimate route**   A routing table entry that contains either a next-hop IPv4 address or an exit interface. Directly connected, dynamically learned, and local routes are all considered to be ultimate routes.

**unequal cost load balancing**   All routing protocols support equal cost load balancing, which enables a router to send packets using multiple routes with the same metric. Only EIGRP supports unequal cost load balancing, which means it can do load balancing across links with different metrics.

**unique device identifier (UDI)**   Required to obtain a Cisco license, the UDI is a combination of the Product ID (PID), the Serial Number (SN), and the hardware version.

**unique local addresses (ULA)**   IPv6 similar to RFC 1918 private addresses for IPv4. Unique local addresses are used for local addressing within a site or between a limited number of sites. These addresses should not be routable in the global IPv6 Internet. Unique local addresses are in the range of FC00::/7 to FDFF::/7. The intent of ULA is to provide IPv6 address space for communications within a local site; it is not meant to provide additional IPv6 address space, nor is it meant to provide a level of security.

**untagged frames**   Frames that do not originate from a VLAN and are crossing a trunk link. For example, frames generated by a switch such as BPDU, CDP, and more cross the trunk link as untagged frames.

**USB Type-A to USB Type-B (mini-B USB)**   A cable to connect to the console port of newer ISRg2 routers. It replaces the flat 8-pin console cable.

**USB-to-RS-232 compatible serial port adapter**   Special cable connector that enables a 9-pin serial console cable to connect to a USB port.

**user priority**   A field in the VLAN tag field consisting of a 3-bit value that supports level or service implementation.

# V

**VLAN**   A network of end devices that behave as if they are connected to the same network segment, even though they might be physically located on different segments of a LAN. VLANs are configured through software on the switch and the router (IOS on Cisco routers and switches).

**vlan.dat**   Cisco switch VLAN configuration information is stored within a VLAN database file called vlan.dat. The vlan.dat file is located in Flash memory of the switch.

**VLAN ID**   A field in the *VLAN tag field* consisting of a 12-bit VLAN identification number that supports up to 4096 VLAN IDs. Other fields in the 802.1Q VLAN tag frame are the Type field, a Priority field, and a CFI field.

**VLAN leaking**   Frames are accepted from a VLAN that is different from the one assigned to a particular switch port.

**VLAN tag field**   The 4-byte field inserted in an Ethernet frame. The VLAN tag field consists of a Type field, a Priority field, a Canonical Format Identifier field, and a VLAN ID field.

**VLAN tagged**   Term to describe an 802.1Q Ethernet frame that has been altered to include a VLAN ID in the packet header. The receiving switch uses the VLAN ID to identify which port to send a broadcast packet to.

**VLAN Trunking Protocol (VTP)**   A Cisco-proprietary Layer 2 protocol that enables a network manager to configure one or more switches so that they propagate VLAN configuration information to other switches in the network, as well as synchronize the VLAN information with the other switches in the VTP domain.

**VLAN trunks**   The links between switches that support the transmission of traffic associated with more than one VLAN. An 802.1Q trunk port supports traffic coming from many VLANs (tagged traffic), as well as traffic that does not come from a VLAN (untagged traffic).

**VoIP**   Technology that enables phones to place and transmit telephone calls over an IP network.

**voice VLAN**   Voice VLANs are designed for and dedicated to the transmission of voice traffic involving IP phones or softphones (voice software used instead of a physical phone). QoS configurations are applied to voice VLANs to prioritize voice traffic.

**volatile**   Referring to memory, volatile memory loses its content when the power is turned off. In contrast, *nonvolatile* memory does not lose its content when the power is turned off. RAM is volatile memory.

# W

**wildcard masks**   A string of 32 binary digits that the router uses to determine which bits of the address to examine for a match.

**wireless access points (WAP)**   Network devices that provide connectivity of wireless clients to connect to a data network.

# Index

## Symbols

## A

# W-X-Y-Z